Film Review
1999-2000

James Cameron-Wilson became a committed film buff when he moved to London at the age of 17. After a stint at the Webber Douglas Academy of Dramatic Art he joined *What's On In London* and took over from F. Maurice Speed as cinema editor. Later, he edited the trade newspaper *Showbiz*, was commissioning editor for *Film Review*, was consultant for *The Movie Show* on BSkyB and a frequent presenter of Radio 2's *Arts Programme*. He is also author of the books *Hollywood: The New Generation*, *Young Hollywood*, *The Cinema of Robert De Niro* and *The Moviegoer's Quiz Book*. His film reviews are currently syndicated in the *What's On* magazines distributed in Birmingham, Manchester and Liverpool, and he has a regular column in *Film Review*, Britain's longest-running film magazine. He has also written frequently for *The Times*, as well as contributing to *The Sunday Times*, *The Guardian*, *Flicks*, *Film Review*, *Film Monthly*, *Xposé*, *Shivers*, etc. More recently he took over as film and video critic for Talk Radio, the world's largest talk radio station, and on television he has made 100 appearances on *The Movie Show* both as critic and quizmaster. He has also regularly popped up on CNN, Channel One and BBC Worldwide Television and was Britain's resident 'dial-a-film critic' for two years. Besides the cinema, James Cameron-Wilson's academic interests include the Bermuda Triangle, the Big Bang theory and body clock experimentation, while his personal interests include his wife and eight-year-old daughter.

Includes video releases and websites

Film Review
1999-2000

JAMES CAMERON-WILSON

Founding father: F. Maurice Speed
1911-1998

Reynolds & Hearn Ltd
London

TO KIM, FOR BEING THERE WHEN
I NEEDED HER THE MOST

Acknowledgements

The author would like to express his undying grati-
tude to the following, without whom this book
would not have been possible: David Aldridge,
Charles Bacon, Ewen Brownrigg, Christopher
Cameron, Ian Crane, Cameron Diaz, Marianne Gray,
Marcus Hearn, Peter Jaques, Tracy Keefe, Karen
Krizanovich, David Miller, Paul Morrissey, my moth-
er, Nigel Mulock, Scot Woodward Myers, Frances
Palmer, Virginia Palmer, David Quinlan, Richard
Reynolds, Jonathan Rigby, Adrian Rigelsford, Simon
Rose, Mansel Stimpson, David Nicholas Wilkinson
and Derek Winnert. Till next year...

Founding father:
F.Maurice Speed, 1911-1998

First published in 1999 by
Reynolds & Hearn Ltd
61a Priory Road
Kew Gardens
Richmond
Surrey TW9 3DH

A CIP catalogue record for this book is available from
the British Library.

ISBN 1 903111 00 5

Designed by Paul Chamberlain

Printed in Great Britain by Butler & Tanner Ltd

Contents

Introduction   6

Top 20 UK Box-Office Hits   8

Top 10 Box-Office Stars   9

Releases of the Year   10

Video Releases   144

Faces of the Year   154

Film World Diary   159

Film Soundtracks   166

Bookshelf   169

Websites   172

Awards and Festivals   174

In Memoriam   179

Index   188

Left: *Tobey Maguire and Reese Witherspoon in* Pleasantville

Right: *Philippe Noiret in* Le Bossu

Introduction

Welcome to the new-look *Film Review* annual. Under exciting new management, the world's longest-running film publication is getting a user-friendly face-lift. And about time, too. The trouble with enduring institutions is that they have a habit of getting stuck in their ways. Now, that may be fine for the Reform Club but not for a manual that celebrates an ever-changing medium. And the cinema is getting continually younger – even if its critics are not. But what good are leather-patched fogies pining for the days of Hitchcock and Capra when all their readers want to know is if *Pleasantville* is funnier than *I Know What You Did Last Summer*?

Too many publications seem to cater either to devotees of the buttock-numbingly profound cinema of, say, Theo Angelopolous, or to the show-me-Keanu-with-his-shirt-off variety. There is very little in-between. But I happen to know that there are an awful lot of film buffs

out there who just enjoy the act of going to the cinema. So, maybe we don't all appreciate the nihilistic minimalism of Takeshi Kitano, but that doesn't mean we can't read subtitles.

This year – 1999 – there has been a fervid debate in cinematic circles about the media's disregard for so-called 'art house' pictures. The concern is that most editors think readers are more likely to buy a magazine or newspaper if it features yet another article on *Star Wars* than if it spotlights an interview with a fascinating director from Kazakhstan. But, in my mind, that's like a supermarket deciding only to display white bread because it sells better than pumpernickel. Variety is the seasoning of life, and it would be a sad day indeed if the cinema were reduced to merely showing films set in high school or outer space (or, as in the case of *Starship Troopers*, both).

For me, cinema is a great education, allowing me into the drawing room of worlds I would otherwise

know nothing about. So, when colleagues complain to me that a film is 'so American', I argue that they wouldn't accuse a Zimbabwean film of being 'so Zimbabwean.' I like American movies because they are American. You know, movies like *The Matrix*, *Cookie's Fortune* and *American History X*. But I also like French films because they are French. That is what is so wonderful about the cinema: its infinite variety. And that is why this publication goes to such great pains to treat each and every film on its own terms. We know the cinema is an organic medium and while we may bestow five stars on *Le Bossu*, we also recognise the charms of Ronny Wu's *Bride of Chucky*. So, in that spirit, I hope you appreciate the film annual that gives every movie an equal opportunity – even in such changing times.

James Cameron-Wilson
July 1999

Right: Francis points out to a couple of onlookers that he is a 'he', in Disney's extraordinarily successful A Bug's Life (from Buena Vista)

Below, clockwise from top left: Hugh Grant, Gina McKee and Tim McInnerny see the funny side in Roger Michell's Notting Hill (from PolyGram)

Gwyneth Paltrow and Joseph Fiennes sway to 'The De Lesseps Dance' in John Madden's Shakespeare in Love (from UIP)

War is hell: Tom Hanks in the thick of it in Steven Spielberg's Saving Private Ryan (from UIP)

Animal magic: Eddie Murphy lectures a rat in Betty Thomas' Dr Dolittle (from Fox)

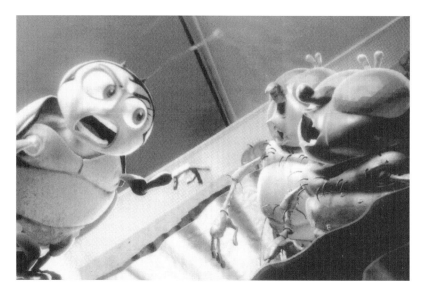

Top 20 UK Box-Office Hits
July 1998 – June 1999

1. A Bug's Life
2. Notting Hill
3. Shakespeare in Love
4. Dr Dolittle
5. Saving Private Ryan
6. Armageddon
7. Godzilla
8. There's Something About Mary
9. The Matrix
10. The Rugrats Movie
11. Sliding Doors
12. Enemy of the State
13. Lost in Space
14. Lock, Stock and Two Smoking Barrels
15. Antz
16. The Truman Show
17. The Mummy
18. The Wedding Singer
19. Mulan
20. The X-Files

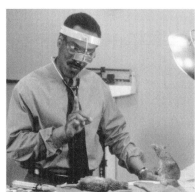

2. Julia Roberts
3. Hugh Grant
4. Tom Hanks
5. Bruce Willis
6. Eddie Murphy
7. Cameron Diaz
8. Will Smith
9. Keanu Reeves
10. Mel Gibson

Top 10 Box-Office Stars
Star of the Year: Gwyneth Paltrow

This was the year that a maverick ant, a giant lizard, a gaggle of rebellious toddlers, another maverick ant, a computer generated mummy and a wise-cracking dragon stormed the box-office. Not Tom Cruise, Arnold Schwarzenegger or even Leonardo DiCaprio, but a deluge of characters manipulated by pen and computer. With the launch of DreamWorks and its offensive on the monopoly of Disney animation, cartoons were suddenly serious business. But not only did DreamWorks' *Antz* do battle with Disney's *A Bug's Life*, but that company's *The Prince of Egypt* hurtled into the fray as well (out-grossing both *Payback* and *You've Got M@il*). In Britain, however, Disney continued to dominate the box-office with the extraordinary success of both *A Bug's Life* and *Mulan*, while a TV spin-off, *The Rugrats Movie*, did unexpectedly good business as well.

But then it was a very good year all round. Take *Sliding Doors*. In last year's chart the Gwyneth Paltrow romance was placed eighth, beating out *Hercules* (1997's most successful cartoon), *Spiceworld The Movie* and *Deep Impact*. This year, even with an additional million in the bank, it didn't make the top ten. Having said that, no one film came close to reaping the box-office rewards of *Titanic*, but at least there was more moolah to go round.

As for the human dimension in this period, it's amazing to see that, with the income generated by *Shakespeare in Love* and *Sliding Doors*, the top spot goes to a woman for the first time in nine years. Furthermore, the last actress to hold that honour, Julia Roberts, nabs second place this year thanks to the popularity of *My Best Friend's Wedding*, *Stepmom* and *Notting Hill*. What a time for actresses to celebrate! Incidentally, runners up this year include Jim Carrey, Brendan Fraser, Adam Sandler, Nicolas Cage and Harrison Ford.

Releases of the Year

This section contains details of all the films released in Great Britain from 1 July 1998 to the end of June 1999 – the period covered by all the reference features in this book.

Leading actors are generally credited with the roles they played, followed by a summary of supporting players. Where an actor further down a cast list is of special interest then his/her role is generally credited as well.

For technical credits the normal abbreviations operate, and are as follows: Dir – for Director; Pro – for Producer; Ex Pro – for Executive Producer; Co-Pro – for Co-Producer; Assoc Pro – for Associate Producer; Line Pro – for Line Producer; Ph – for Cinematographer; Ed – for Editor; Pro Des – for Production Designer; and M – for composer.

Abbreviations for the names of film companies are obvious when used, such as Fox for Twentieth Century Fox, and UIP for Universal International Pictures. The production company (or companies) is given first, the distribution company last.

Information at the foot of each entry is presented in the following order: running time/country of origin/year of production/date of British release/British certification.

All films reviewed by James Cameron-Wilson unless otherwise specified.
Additional contributors: Charles Bacon, Ewen Brownrigg, Marianne Gray, Karen Krizanovich, Scot Wodward Myers, Simon Rose, Mansel Stimpson and Derek Winnert.

Star ratings

★★★★★ Wonderful
★★★★ Very good
★★★ Good
★★ Mediocre
★ Insulting

Left: *Prince of hate: Edward Norton struts his stuff in Tony Kaye's mesmerising, deeply disturbing* American History X *(from Entertainment)*

The Acid House ★★

Three tales from *The Acid House*, a collection of short stories by Irvine Welsh: Recognising a kindred spirit in born loser Boab Cole, God turns the latter into a fly so he can enact an appropriate revenge on his oppressors. Meanwhile, another born loser watches in mounting frustration as his wife takes up with an aggressive, narcissistic skinhead. And, finally, the soul of a repugnant acidhead is accidentally transposed into the body of a new-born baby ... Borrowing its cultural references from Kafka to Bacon and transplanting them into the unutterable squalor of urban Scotland, this potent cocktail of moral decay is a hard film to like. Trading on its power to shock through the sheer repetition of taboo expletives, *The Acid House* is ugly, shameless and thoroughly depressing. It's also rather inventively directed, injecting a warped poetry into the lives of its pathetic, inarticulate and epidermically-challenged characters. FYI: This is probably the first film ever to show a baby masturbating.

● *The Granton Star Cause Boab Cole* Stephen McCole, *God* Maurice Roëves, *Evelyn* Jenny McCrindle, *Boab Cole Snr* Alex Howden, *Doreen Cole*

Ann Louise Ross, Garry Sweeney, Irvine Welsh, John Gardner. *A Soft Touch Johnny* Kevin McKidd, *Catriona* Michelle Gomez, *Larry* Gary McCormack, *Alec Doyle* Tam Dean Burn, Maurice Roëves, William 'Giggs' McGuigan. *The Acid House Coco Bryce* Ewen Bremner, *Rory* Martin Clunes, *Jenny* Jemma Redgrave, *Kirsty* Arlene Cockburn, Jane Stabler, Maurice Roëves. ● *Dir* Paul McGuigan, *Pro* David Muir and Alex Usborne, *Screenplay* Irvine Welsh, *Ph* Alasdair Walker, *Pro Des* Richard Bridgland and Mike Gunn, *Ed* Andrew Hulme *M* songs performed by Primal Scream, Glen Campbell, Nick Cave, Barry Adamson, Jack L, William 'Giggs' McGuigan, Beth Orton, Marc Bolan, Oasis, Death in Vegas, The Chemical Brothers, A Small Good Thing, The Sons of Silence, The Verve, etc, *Costumes* Pam Taitt and Lynn Aitken.

Channel 4/Picture Palace North/Umbrella Prods/ Yorkshire Media Prods/Scottish Arts Council/ National Lottery/Glasgow Film Fund – Film Four. 111 mins. UK. 1998. Rel: 1 January 1999. Cert 18.

Affliction ★★★★

Wade Whitehouse is the sheriff of Lawford, New Hampshire, a small town settling in for an early, snowbound winter. Virtually devoid of crime, the town gives Wade little to do other than serve as a crossing guard, so when an outside hotshot is killed in a hunting accident the cop starts nosing into areas usually beyond his jurisdiction. But the sheriff's gnawing toothache, a burgeoning custody battle for his daughter and some unpleasant childhood memories may be laying the groundwork for something far more volatile … Continuing to draw on his favourite theme of innate human violence, writer-director Paul Schrader (*Blue Collar, Mishima, Light Sleeper*) has found fertile dramatic territory in Russell Banks' 1989 novel *The Sweet Hereafter*. Unfolding like a conventional murder mystery, *Affliction* subtly unearths more complex issues as its damaged protagonist wades blindly into treacherous waters. A convincing character study of a man irredeemably bruised by childhood trauma, the film deftly establishes a mood of imminent violence, bolstered by top-notch acting from a creditable cast.

● *Wade Whitehouse* Nick Nolte, *Margie Fogg* Sissy Spacek, *Glen Whitehouse* James Coburn, *Rolfe Whitehouse* Willem Dafoe, *Lillian* Mary Beth Hurt, *Jack Hewitt* Jim True, *Gordon LaRiviere* Holmes Osborne, *Jill Whitehouse* Brigid Tierney, *Mel Gordon* Steve Adams, Marian Seldes, Sean McCann, Wayne Robson, Eugene Lipinski, Tim Post, Paul Stewart, *young Wade Whitehouse* Brawley Nolte.
● *Dir and Screenplay* Paul Schrader, *Pro* Linda Reisman, *Ex Pro* Nick Nolte and Barr Potter, *Co-Pro* Eric Berg and Frank K. Issac, *Ph* Paul Sarossy, *Pro Des* Anne Pritchard, *Ed* Jay Rabonowitz, *M* Michael Brook; Grieg, *Costumes* Francois Laplante.

Largo Entertainment/Reisman/Kingsgate – Artificial Eye. 114 mins. USA. 1997. Rel: 19 February 1999. Cert 15.

Air Bud ★½

Fernfield, Washington; the present. Mourning the death of his father, photogenic 12-year-old Josh Framm has lost the passion for all that he once held dear, even basketball. Then he befriends a stray golden retriever and his dog days are over. Hell, this pooch can even play basketball – better even than Josh … The remarkable thing about this film is that the canine antics of its star are for real. In fact, the dog came first, then the script – and it shows. While Air Bud – aka Buddy the Wonder Dog – gets to dribble, pass and shoot hoops, his human cohorts smile cheesily, laugh and point (when have you ever seen anybody laugh and point at the same time?) and even get to slip on a banana skin. FYI: Buddy can also play baseball, football, hockey, soccer and catch. No kidding. Watch out for *Air Bud: Golden Receiver*, the inevitable sequel.

● *Norm Snively* Michael Jeter, *Josh Framm* Kevin Zegers, *Jackie Framm* Wendy Makkena, *Arthur Chaney* Bill Cobbs, *Judge Cranfield* Eric Christmas, *Larry Willingham* Brendan Fletcher, *Tom* Shayn Solberg, *Buddy/Air Bud* Buddy, Jay Brazeau, Nicola Cavendish, Norman Browning, Stephen E. Miller, Chris Turner, Christine Kennedy, Frank C. Turner.
● *Dir* Charles Martin Smith, *Pro* William Vince and Robert Vince, *Ex Pro* Michael Strange, Anne Vince, Bob Weinstein and Harvey Weinstein, *Screenplay* Paul Tamasy and Aaron Mendelsohn, *Ph* Mike Southon, *Pro Des* Elizabeth Wilcox, *Ed* Alison Grace, *M* Brahm Wenger; songs performed by Gilbert O'Sullivan and Jimmy Z, *Costumes* Jana Stern.

Walt Disney/Keystone Pictures/CLT-UFA – Warner. 97 mins. USA/Luxembourg/Canada. 1997. Rel: 23 October 1998. Cert U.

American History X ★★★★★

A hundred years after white European settlers colonised America, the New World was a paradise of boundless promise. Now, on the cusp of the Millennium, America is rotting from within, from soaring crime, poverty, drugs, AIDS and illegal immigration – all race-related problems. It is this logic that empowers the virulent hatred of Derek Vinyard, the hypnotic ringleader of a gang of Venice Beach white supremacists. And Vinyard is about to spark a bonfire of rancour that will be nigh impossible to quench …

The power of this eloquent, moving film is that it dares to make its anti-hero a charismatic, rational figure. Then, having made sense of Vinyard's passionate rhetoric, the film sets about dismantling it with even greater effect. Ravishingly shot by first-time feature director Tony Kaye and intelligently argued by neophyte scripter David McKenna, *American History X* is further blessed by an extraordinary turn from Edward Norton in a display that transcends mere performance. Demonic, seductive and potent, Norton wipes away memories of the dewy-eyed boy-next-door he played in Woody Allen's *Everyone Says I Love You* and brings a freshness and conviction that recalls Robert De Niro in *Taxi Driver*. In all, a thought-provoking, emotionally shattering and sublimely crafted film. FYI: Director Kaye attempted to take his name off the credits when Norton made his own changes in the editing suite.

● *Derek Vinyard* Edward Norton, *Danny Vinyard* Edward Furlong, *Stacey* Fairuza Balk, *Cameron Alexander* Stacy Keach, *Davin Vinyard* Jennifer Lien, *Murray* Elliott Gould, *Dennis Vinyard* William Russ, *Seth* Ethan Suplee, *Bob Sweeney* Avery Brooks, *Doris Vinyard* Beverly D'Angelo, *Lamont* Guy Torry, *McMahon* Paul LeMat, Joe Cortese, Jason Bose-Smith, Antonio David Lyons, Alex Sol, Keram Malicki-Sanchez, Giuseppe Andrews, Chris Masterson, Nicholas R. Oleson, Jordan Marder, Anne Lambton, Jim Norton.
● *Dir* and *Ph* Tony Kaye, *Pro* John Morrissey, *Ex Pro* Lawrence Turman, Steve Tisch, Kearie Peak and Bill Carraro, *Co-Ex Pro* Michael De Luca and Brian Witten, *Screenplay* and *Co-Pro* David McKenna, *Pro Des* Jon Gary Steele, *Ed* Jerry Greenberg and Alan Heim, *M* Anne Dudley; original music performed by Bulge, *Costumes* Doug Hall, *Sound* Frederick Howard.

New Line Cinema – Entertainment.
119 mins. USA. 1998. Rel: 26 March 1999. Cert 18.

American Perfekt ★★★

Sandra Thompson is having an exceptionally bad day. On her way from Los Angeles to Pearblossom in Utah, she finds her car trapped in a parking lot by an olive-green station wagon. Later, the same vehicle forces her off the road and a second car knocks her door off. However, the driver of the latter turns out to be a handsome, courteous doctor who fixes her car and drives her to the nearest inn. She calls him her 'white knight', but she's not in Utah yet ... The pleasure of this bizarre road movie is that it never states its intentions. As a palpable sense of menace gathers momentum, Simon Boswell's sweet score tips us off balance. Furthermore, there's a delicious cast of actors who seem arbitrarily plopped together from a number of disparate genres. But the film's true undiluted joy is watching Robert Forster (*Jackie Brown*, TV's *Banyon*) completely disfigure his image as the decent, clean-cut all-American hunk.

● *Alice Thompson* Fairuza Balk, *Jake Gordon Nyman* Robert Forster, *Sandra Thompson* Amanda Plummer, *Sheriff Frank Noonan* Paul Sorvino, *Earnest Santini* David Thewlis, *Sammy Goodall* Chris Sarandon, *Shirley Dutton* Joanna Gleason, Geoffrey Lewis, Jay

Patterson, Michael Kopelow, Belinda Balaski, Rutanya Alda.
● *Dir* and *Screenplay* Paul Chart, *Pro* Irvin Kershner, *Ex Pro* Avi Lerner, Danny Dimbort, Elie Samaha, Boaz Davidson and Trevor Short, *Co-Pro* Dawn Handler and Andrew Schuth, *Ph* William Wages, *Pro Des* Katherine Vallin, *Ed* Michael Ruscio, *M* Simon Boswell; songs performed by The Cowboy Junkies, and The Platters, *Costumes* Florence-Isabelle Megginson, *Sound* Dane Davis.

Mondofin/Nu Image – Blue Dolphin.
96 mins. USA. 1997. Rel: 11 June 1999. Cert 18.

Among Giants ★★½

On the desolate, windswept Yorkshire Moors the landscape is dominated by steep cliffs and an unbroken line of electricity pylons. Nobody would give the latter another thought, but the pylons need maintenance and it takes a certain type of character to risk their neck in painting the things. With 15 miles of pylon to be coated in three months, the ragbag of employees under the supervision of Ray are a rowdy lot – and are none the quieter when an Australian woman joins their ranks ... In spite of its title and general preoccupation with heights, *Among Giants* is a film that achieves its power from its more down-to-earth moments. Whether it be an unscripted look, the strum of a guitar on the soundtrack or an off-the-cuff comment (Frank: 'Don't go enjoying yourself – you'll only brood about it in years to come'), this is a film of incidental pleasure. It's also one of enormous chutzpah, as the very idea of constructing a movie around the painting of electricity pylons is about as far removed from Hollywood formula as one can get. Unfortunately, Simon Beaufoy's script (written prior to *The Full Monty*) does lack a fundamental narrative hook, while the relationship between Ray and Gerry is rather superficially drawn.

● *Ray* Peter Postlethwaite, *Gerry* Rachel Griffiths, *Steve* James Thornton, *Shovel* Lennie James, *Bob* Andy Serkis, *Weasal* Rob Jarvis, *Frank* Alan Williams, *Derek* Steve Huison, *Lyn* Sharon Bower, *barmaid* Emma Cunniffe, David Webber, Alvin Blossom, Sam Wilkinson.
● *Dir* Sam Miller, *Pro* Stephen Garrett, *Ex Pro* Jana Edelbaum, *Co-Ex Pro* David M. Thompson, Jane Barclay and Sharon Harel, *Line Pro* Joy Spink, *Screenplay* Simon Beaufoy, *Ph* Witold Stok, *Pro Des* Luana Hanson, Ed Elen, Pierce Lewis and Paul Green, *M* Tim Atack; songs performed by Big Sky, Alan Williams, Hoyt Axton, etc, *Costumes* Stephanie Collie.

Fox Searchlight/Capitol Films/British Screen/Arts Council of England/BBC/Yorkshire Media/Kudos Prods/National Lottery – Fox.
95 mins. UK. 1998. Rel: 11 June 1999. Cert 15.

Angel Dust ★★

Tokyo is gripped by panic when an unknown assailant starts jabbing young women on the metro with a lethal dose of strychnine: at precisely 6 p.m. on Monday evenings. In a desperate bid to identify the killer, the police hire Dr Setsuko Suma, a female specialist in abnormal criminal personalities. Adopting the mindset of the poisoner, Suma finds that her investigation leads to her very own romantic past … Probing his actors' faces with intrusive close-ups and juxtaposing them in sterile landscapes, director Ishii sets up a promising *mise-en-scène* for this dense psychological thriller. However, once all the psychoanalytical trimmings are stripped away, what remains is both improbable and rather banal. FYI: Angel dust is the nickname for an anaesthetic drug used on elephants.

● *Dr Setsuko* Suma Kaho Minami, *Rei Aku* Takeshi Wakamatsu, *Tomoo* Etsushi Toyokawa, *Yuki Takei* Ryoko Takizawa, Masayuki Shionoya, Yukio Yamato.
● *Dir* Ogo Ishii, *Pro* Taro Maki, Kenzo Horikoshi and Eiji Izumi, *Ex Pro* Satoshi Kanno, *Screenplay* Ishii and Yorozu Ikuta, *Ph* Norimichi Kasamatsu, *Pro Des* Tomoyuki Maruo, *Ed* Ishii and Hiroshi Matsuo, *M* Hiroyuki Agashima.

Twins Japan/Euro Space – ICA
116 mins. Japan. 1994. Rel: 8 January 1999. No cert.

Antz ★★★★★

An hilarious Woody Allen vehicle disguised as a kids' spectacular, *Antz* is an object lesson in how animation can appeal to all ages simultaneously. Part adventure story, part moral fable and part adult comedy, this is the story of a neurotic ant who doesn't fit in. Getting up off his psychiatrist's leaf, Z-4195 (voiced by Woody Allen himself) complains that he feels 'really insignificant.' Flushed with success, Z's shrink (Paul Mazursky) reveals, 'you've made a real breakthrough.' Z: 'I have?' Shrink: 'Yes. You *are* insignificant.' And so Z's break from the crowd reflects the megalomaniacal aspirations of the colony's evil General Mandible (Gene Hackman) who, in order to further his own aims, plots to destroy the very community that supports him. Yet where Z inadvertently introduces a notion of choice to his fellow workers, Mandible is in it for himself. An all-star cast brings real character to some wonderful creations, helping to supplement a terrific story with a myriad of intriguing narrative strands. The fact that the film looks like nothing we've seen before is just icing on the gateau. FYI: It has been alleged that DreamWorks co-founder Jeffrey Katzenberg took the film's idea from Disney, his former employer. Katzenberg, however, accuses Disney of swiping *his* idea for their *A Bug's Life*.

● Voices: *Z-4195* Woody Allen, *Chip* Dan Aykroyd, *The Queen* Anne Bancroft, *Muffy* Jane Curtin, *Barbatus* Danny Glover, *General Mandible* Gene Hackman, *Azteca* Jennifer Lopez, *Weaver* Sylvester Stallone, *Princess Bala* Sharon Stone, *Colonel Cutter* Christopher Walken, John Mahoney, Paul Mazursky, Grant Shaud.
● *Dir* Eric Darnell and Tim Johnson, *Pro* Brad Lewis, Aron Warner and Patty Wooton, *Ex Pro* Penney Finkelman Cox, Sandra Rabins and Carl Rosendahl, *Screenplay* Todd Alcott and Chris Weitz & Paul Weitz, *Pro Des* John Bell, Ed Stan Webb, *M* Harry Gregson-Williams and John Powell; songs performed by Neil Finn, and Doris Day, *Character design/supervising animator* Raman Hui.

DreamWorks/PDI – UIP
83 mins. USA. 1998. Rel: 6 November 1998. Cert PG.

The Apple – Sib ★★★★

Tehran, Iran; 1997. Massoumeh and Zahra Naderi are twin sisters who, in the twelve years of their lives, never had a bath, learned to speak or even ventured outside the front door of their house. When their plight was brought to the attention of the media, director Samira Makhmalbaf immediately sought to record the girls' adjustment to the outside world. Marshalling the cooperation of welfare, neighbours and even the children's 65-year-old father and blind mother, Makhmalbaf has created a remarkable film that blurs the line between documentary and narrative cinema. In fact, so keen was Makhmalbaf to embark on the project that just four days after hearing of the case she was shooting her film on video, before she even had time to secure a 35mm camera. For the most part, the result is spellbinding, almost uncomfortable humanist cinema where, unmindful of the camera, extraordinary acts of intimate drama are acted out. All the more amazing is the fact that Makhmalbaf – the daughter of the filmmaker Mohsen Makhmalbaf (*The Peddler*, *Gabbeh*) – was just 17-years-old when she made the film.

● With Massoumeh Naderi, Zahra Naderi, Ghorbanali Naderi, Zahra Saghrisaz, Azizeh Mohamadi.
● *Dir* Samira Makhmalbaf, *Ex Pro* Iraj Sarbaz, *Screenplay* and *Ed* Mohsen Makhmalbaf, *Ph* Edrahim Ghafori and Mohamad Ahmadi.

MK2 Prods/Makhmalbaf Prods – Artificial Eye.
85 mins. Iran/France. 1997. Rel: 27 December 1998. Cert PG.

Aprile ★★¹/₂

It's hard to know where you are with Nanni Moretti. But that's half the fun. Drawing from his own life to animate his miscellaneous fiction, the director-producer-writer-actor juggles private thoughts, political commentary and immensely personal events to create a quirky, charming and idiosyncratic cinematic journal. Here, he smokes his first joint (in front of his mother, no less), attempts to stage a musical about a Trotskyite pastry chef and comes to terms with imminent fatherhood. Of course, Moretti's personal frustrations and triumphs will not necessarily engage everyone, but they at least display the patina of spontaneity.

● With Nanni Moretti, Silvio Orlando, Silvia Nono, Pietro Moretti, Agata Apicella Moretti, Nuria Schoenberg, Angelo Barbagallo, Silvia Bonucci, Quentin de Fouchecour.
● *Dir* and *Screenplay* Nanni Moretti, Pro Moretti and Angelo Barbagallo, *Ph* Giuseppe Lanci, *Pro Des*

Marta Maffucci, *Ed* Angelo Nicolini, *M* songs performed by Ludovico Einaudi, Yma Sumac, Nusrat Fateh Ali Khan, Perez Prado and his Orchestra, etc, *Costumes* Valentina Taviani.

BAC Films/Sacher Film/RAI/Canal Plus – Metro Tartan.
78 mins. Italy/France. 1998. Rel: 19 March 1999. Cert 15.

Apt Pupil ★★★¹/₂

California; 1984. Intrigued by the horrors of the Holocaust as revealed during a school course, top student Todd Bowden is stunned to recognise a notorious war criminal on his local bus. Following the old man to his house and, to confirm his suspicions, dusting the latter's mail box for fingerprints, Todd confronts the retired Nazi and demands first-hand reports of his atrocities. An uneasy alliance develops between the two men, a power play in which evil will inevitably have the last say ... Following the success of his last film, *The Usual Suspects*, director Bryan Singer again explores the ramifications of extreme evil, this time opening up the psychological avenues of Stephen King's novella of the same name. Aided by a tremendous turn from Ian McKellen as the latent architect of pain, the film builds up some theatrical staying power, even as the leisurely pace ultimately drags the drama down.

● *Arthur Denker* aka *Kurt Dussander* Ian McKellen, *Todd Bowden* Brad Renfro, *Richard Bowden* Bruce Davison, *Archie* Elias Koteas, *Dan Richler* Joe Morton, *Isaac Weiskopf* Jan Triska, *Ben Kramer* Michael Byrne, *Becky Trask* Heather McComb, *Monica Bowden* Ann Dowd, *Joey* Joshua Jackson, *Edward French* David Schwimmer, Mickey Cottrell, James Karen, Marjorie Lovett, David Cooley, Michael Artura, Norbert D. Singer, Mildred Singer, Mary Ottman.
● *Dir* Bryan Singer, *Pro* Singer, Jane Hamsher and Don Murphy, *Ex Pro* Tim Harbert, *Co-Pro* Thomas DeSanto, *Screenplay* Brandon Boyce, *Ph* Newton Thomas Sigel, *Pro Des* Richard Hoover *Ed* and *M* John Ottman, *Costumes* Louise Mingenbach.

Phoenix Pictures/Bad Hat Harry/Canal Plus – Columbia TriStar.
111 mins. USA. 1997. Rel: 21 May 1999. Cert 15.

Arlington Road ★★★★

Arlington, Virginia; today. Michael Faraday teaches mathematics and history and displays an interest in domestic terrorism with a passion that goes beyond the mandate of his job. He has reasons for this: his wife, an FBI agent, was killed in a botched investigation of an innocent terrorist suspect. Fuelled by paranoia, Faraday now thinks his new neighbours may be guilty of covert seditious activity ... Unlike the similarly themed *The Siege*, *Arlington Road* builds its drama

Right: Blindsided: Jeff Bridges looks out for the double-glazing salesman in Mark Pellington's chilling, gripping Arlington Road (from PolyGram)

from the inside out, making the characters – not the action – the driving force of its narrative. Thus, when the action does arrive, it comes armed with our genuine concern for the welfare of the protagonists. As the Everyman trapped in escalating circumstances, Jeff Bridges summons his usual charismatic empathy, while Joan Cusack is inspired casting as the questionable, all-smiling agent of unease. A thoughtful, honest script and clear-headed direction from Pellington (*Going All the Way*) add to the building suspense.

● *Michael Faraday* Jeff Bridges, *Oliver Lang/William Fenimore* Tim Robbins, *Cheryl Lang* Joan Cusack, *Brooke Wolf* Hope Davis, *FBI Agent Whit Carver* Robert Gossett, *Brady Lang* Mason Gamble, *Grant Faraday* Spencer Treat Clark, *Leah Faraday* Laura Poe, Stanley Anderson, Vivianne Vives, Lee Stringer.
● *Dir* Mark Pellington, *Pro* Peter Samuelson, Tom Gorai and Marc Samuelson, *Ex Pro* Tom Rosenberg, Sigurjon Sighvatsson and Ted Tannebaum, *Screenplay* Ehren Kruger, *Ph* Bobby Bukowski, *Pro Des* Therese Deprez, *Ed* Conrad Buff, *M* Angelo Badalamenti and tomandandy; songs performed by Lunatic Calm, and KC & The Sunshine Band, *Costumes* Jennifer Barrett-Pellington, *Sound* Randy Thom.

PolyGram/Lakeshore Entertainment – PolyGram.
117 mins. USA/UK. 1998. Rel: 19 March 1999. Cert 15.

Armageddon ★★★

Sixty-five million years ago an asteroid six miles wide collided with earth and unleashed an explosion equal to the power of 10,000 nuclear warheads. To quote our narrator Charlton Heston, 'it happened before and it will happen again. It's just a question of "when".' Sixty-five million years later an asteroid the size of Texas is headed for earth at 22,000 miles per hour. The only

way to stop it is to plant a nuclear bomb slap bang in the middle of the damn thing. And to do so NASA has to enlist the world's most proficient team of deep core oil drillers – even if they are a bunch of irresponsible, wise-cracking Neanderthals … Budgeted at $140 million and conceived as an intergalactic *Dirty Dozen*, *Armageddon* tries too hard to be all things to all schoolboys. A rollercoaster ride of effects, jokes and testosterone, the film is like a music video stuck on the fast forward button with the sound jacked to the max. To be fair, there are a number of great lines, some mind-boggling effects (see the Empire State building fall! See Paris vaporised!) and a thankful air of self-parody – but the overall effect is of sensorial indigestion.

● *Harry S. Stamper* Bruce Willis, *Dan Truman* Billy Bob Thornton, *Grace Stamper* Liv Tyler, *A.J. Frost* Ben Affleck, *Charles 'Chick' Chapple* Will Patton, *Lev Andropov* Peter Stormare, *General Kimsey* Keith David, *Rockhound* Steve Buscemi, *Jayotis 'Bear' Kurleenbear* Michael Clarke Duncan, *Ronald Quincy* Jason Isaacs, *Max Lennert* Ken Campbell, *Colonel William Sharp* William Fichtner, *Oscar Choi* Owen Wilson, *The President of the United States* Stanley Anderson, Chris Ellis, Jessica Steen, Grayson McCouch, Marshall Teague, J. Patrick McCormack, Grace Zabriskie, Mark Boone Junior, Albert Wong, Udo Kier, John Aylward, Judith Hoag, Lawrence Tierney, Christian Clemenson, Shawnee Smith, Layla Roberts, Googy Gress, Matt Malloy, and *narrator* Charlton Heston.
● *Dir* Michael Bay, *Pro* Bay, Jerry Bruckheimer and Gale Anne Hurd, *Ex Pro* Jonathan Hensleigh, Jim Van Wyck and Chad Oman, *Screenplay* Hensleigh and J.J. Abrams, adapted by Tony Gilroy and Shane Salerno from a story by Hensleigh and Robert Roy Pool, *Ph* John Schwartzman, *Pro Des* Michael White, *Ed* Mark Goldblatt, Chris Lebenzon and Glen Scantlebury, *M* Trevor Rabin; songs performed by

Aerosmith, Shawn Colvin, ZZ Top, Curtis Mayfield, Bob Seger & The Silver Bullet Band, Jon Bon Jovi, Patty Smyth, Journey, Chantal Kreviazuk, etc, *Costumes* Michael Kaplan and Magali Guidasci, *Visual effects* Pat McClung and Richard Hoover.

Touchstone Pictures/Valhalla Motion Pictures – Buena Vista.
151 mins. USA. 1998. Rel: 7 August 1998. Cert 12.

Artemisia ★★¹/₂

Italy; 1610. Agnes Merlet's study of the 17th century Italian painter Artemisia Gentileschi theoretically belongs alongside *Camille Claudel* as a film biography of a notable woman artist. However, modern notes sometimes obtrude and even more problematic is the treatment of sexual matters linking the two sides of the story. We see Artemisia's difficulties as a female artist aggravated by her desire to draw the male genitals, while the personal drama concentrates on her relationship with the painter Tassi to whom she offered up her virginity – unless, as asserted by some but not here, he raped her. Valentina Cervi and Miki Manojlovic are able leads, while Michel Serrault is reliable as ever as Artemisia's father. But the impression left is of a film torn between serious biography and novelettish bodice-ripper, which means that very promising material has been botched. [*Mansel Stimpson*]

● *Artemisia Gentileschi* Valentina Cervi, *Orazio Gentileschi* Michel Serrault, *Agostino Tassi* Miki Manojlovic, *Cosimo* Luca Zingaretti, *Constanza* Emmanuelle Devos, *Roberto* Frederic Pierrot, Maurice Garrel, Brigitte Catillon, Yann Tregouet, Silvia De Santis.
● *Dir* Agnes Merlet, *Pro* Patrice Haddad, *Ex Pro* Lilian Saly, Patricia Allard and Daniel Wuhrmann, *Co-Pro* Christoph Meyer-Wiel and Leo Pescarolo, *Screenplay* Merlet, Christine Miller and Patrick Amos, *Ph* Benoit Delhomme, *Pro Des* Antonello Geleng, *Ed* Guy Lecorne, *M* Krishna Levy, *Costumes* Dominique Borg.

Premiere Heure Long/France 3 Cinema/Schlemmer Film/Canal Plus/Equinoxe, etc – Gala Film.
96 mins. France/Germany/Italy. 1997. Rel: 7 May 1999. Cert 18.

The Assignment ★★

North America/Canada/France/Libya/Israel; early Seventies-late Eighties. After witnessing a cold-blooded terrorist attack on a crowded Paris café, CIA agent Jack Shaw resolves to hunt down the perpetrator at all costs. However, it's not until 15 years later that Shaw hears of an American Naval officer who bears an uncanny resemblance to the terrorist. Can Shaw persuade the latter to help put his audacious assignment into action? Based on the true exploits of Carlos 'The Jackal' Sanchez, Christian Duguay's ambitious film looks fantastic and does contain a number of extremely suspenseful moments. But a shallow, pedestrian script and Sutherland's lethargic performance as Shaw severely undermine the film's pedigree. [*Charles Bacon*]

● *Carlos 'The Jackal' Sanchez/Annibal Ramirez* Aidan Quinn, *Jack Shaw/Henry Fields* Donald Sutherland, *Amos* Ben Kingsley, *Agnieska* Liliana Komorowska, *Carla* Celine Bonnier, *Maura Ramirez* Claudia Ferri, Vlasta Vrana, Von Flores, Al Waxman, Mitchell David Rothpan.
● *Dir* Christian Duguay, *Pro* Tom Berry and Franco Battista, *Ex Pro* David Saunders and Joseph Newton Cohen, *Co-Pro* Stefan Wodoslawsky, *Screenplay* Dan Gordon and Sabi H. Shabtai, *Ph* David Franco, *Pro Des* Michael Joy, *Ed* Yves Langlois, *M* Normand Corbeil; 'The Most Wonderful Time of the Year' sung by Andy Williams, *Costumes* Ada Levin, *Digital effects* Richard Ostiguy.

Triumph Films/Allegro Films – Columbia TriStar.
115 mins. USA. 1997. Rel: 14 August 1998. Cert 18.

At First Sight ★★★

Amy Benic has fallen in love with Virgil Adamson, a smart, funny, blond and blind masseur. And to prove her love Amy is determined to give Virgil the gift of sight. But in order to adjust to a new world of light, contours and perspective (thanks to the latest in ground-breaking technology), Virgil must first leave behind the blind man he once was – the man that Amy fell in love with … If you can overlook the button-pushing premise, the presence of Val ('love me') Kilmer and the manipulative score from Mark Isham, then you will find a sweet, sensitive and handsome date movie bubbling under. Addressing the issues of seeing and being in some depth, *At First Sight* has more in it than at first meets the eye. The film does sag in the middle and is a little too pretty for its own good, but it has some consequential things to say and does so with eloquence. And remember, it's not enough to see, we have to look as well. Loosely based on a true story.

● *Virgil Adamson* Val Kilmer, *Amy Benic* Mira Sorvino, *Jenny Adamson* Kelly McGillis, *Duncan Allanbrook* Steven Weber, *Dr Charles Aaron* Bruce Davison, *Mr Adamson, Virgil's father* Ken Howard, *Phil Webster* Nathan Lane, *Betsy Ernst* Laura Kirk, Margo Winkler, Diana Krall, Brett Robbins, Willie Carpenter, Charles Winkler, Drena De Niro, Gene Kirkwood, Oliver Sacks.
● *Dir* Irwin Winkler, *Pro* Winkler and Rob Cowan, *Line Pro* Roger Paradiso, *Screenplay* Steve Levitt, based on Oliver Sacks' *To See and Not See*, *Ph* John Seale, *Pro Des* Jane Musky, *Ed* Julie Monroe, *M* Mark

Right: A cold affront: Ralph Fiennes and Uma Thurman in Jeremiah Chechik's critically savaged The Avengers (from Warner)

Isham; songs performed by George Shearing, Ella Fitzgerald and Louis Armstrong, The Gap Band, Diana Krall, Village People, etc, *Costumes* John Dunn.

MGM – UIP.
129 mins. USA. 1998. Rel: 30 April 1999. Cert 12.

An Autumn Tale – Conte d'Automne ★★★★

Eric Rohmer sets the last of his four seasonal tales in the Rhone Valley and, unusually, widowed wine-grower Magali is helped twice over to find the new husband she may or may not want: by her son's girl-friend who prompts an older ex-lover of her own, and by her best friend, Isabelle, who inserts a lonely hearts ad on Magali's behalf. The plotting is a bit over-extended and conventional for this to rank with the very best of Rohmer, but it comes close all the same. A wonderful cast (including two unfamiliar but delightful players, Alexia Portal and Alain Libolt) ensures that once again in a Rohmer film the talk and the beguiling characterisations count for more than the action. [*Mansel Stimpson*]

● *Isabelle* Marie Riviere, *Magali* Beatrice Romand, *Gerald* Alain Libolt, *Etienne, the philosophy teacher* Didier Sandre, *Rosine* Alexia Portal, *Leonce* Stephanie Darmon, Aurelia Alcais, Mathieu Davette, Yves Alcais.
● *Dir* and *Screenplay* Eric Rohmer, *Pro* Margaret Menegoz, *Ph* Diane Baratier, Thierry Faure, Franck Bouvat, Bethsabee Dreyfus and Jerome Duc-Mauge, *Ed* Mary Stephen, *M* Claude Marti, Gerard Pansanel, Pierre Peyras and Antonello Salis.

Les Films du Losange/La Sept Cinema/Canal Plus/Sofilmka/Rhone-Alpes Cinema – Artificial Eye.
111 mins. France. 1998. Rel: 26 March 1999. Cert U.

The Avengers ★★

Obsessed with meteorology, a megalomaniac Scottish millionaire devises a method by which to manipulate the world's weather systems. Holding the planet to ransom, he sets out to charge each government for their own weather requirements. So can debonair undercover agent John Steed and his new enigmatic partner – the catsuited, self-assured Emma Peel – trust each other long enough to save Blighty from a prema-ture Arctic winter? Flaunting its Englishness like a banner, this gamely quirky adaptation of the Sixties TV series has much to offer. There is some delicious dialogue, a number of peachy sight gags and a breezy self-parody that is irresistible. Yet, with little basis in reality (James Bond, for all his bad manners, is at least sympathetic), the film loses its footing near the end and descends into arch silliness. Besides, isn't Sean Connery – forty years Uma Thurman's senior – final-ly a bit old for all this flirting and fighting?

● *John Steed* Ralph Fiennes, *Emma Peel* Uma Thurman, *Sir August De Wynter* Sean Connery, *Mother* Jim Broadbent, *Father* Fiona Shaw, *Bailey* Eddie Izzard, *Alice* Eileen Atkins, *Trubshaw* John Wood, *Invisible Jones* Patrick Macnee, *Brenda* Carmen Ejogo, *Tamara* Keeley Hawes, Shaun Ryder, Nicholas Woodeson, Michael Godley, Richard Lumsden, Nadim Sawalha, Christopher Godwin.
● *Dir* Jeremiah Chechik, *Pro* Jerry Weintraub, *Ex Pro* Susan Ekins, *Screenplay* Don MacPherson, *Ph* Roger Pratt, *Pro Des* Stuart Craig, *Ed* Mick Audsley, *M* Joel McNeely; theme by Laurie Johnson; songs performed by Grace Jones and Radio Science Orchestra, Ashtar Command, and Suggs, *Costumes* Anthony Powell.

Jerry Weintraub Productions/Warner Bros Productions – Warner.
89 mins. USA. 1998. Rel: 14 August 1998. Cert 12.

Left: Ghost of a chance: Thandie Newton in the title role of Jonathan Demme's thunderingly mismanaged Beloved (from Buena Vista)

Babe: Pig in the City ★★★¹⁄₂

When Hoggett Hollow farm is threatened with foreclosure by the bank, Mrs Hoggett accepts a lucrative offer to show off her sheep-herding pig – Babe – at a distant fair. However, thanks to the interference of a boastful sniffer dog at the airport, Mrs Hoggett and her pig miss their connecting flight and find themselves stranded in the city … While graced by an eloquent voice-over in the tradition of the first film (which was adapted from the popular novel by Dick King-Smith), this surprising sequel takes a dramatic shift in tone. Set in a phantasmagorically generic city (dominated by a skyline that includes the Hollywood sign, the Eiffel Tower, the Sydney opera house and the Statue of Liberty), the awesome adventure takes a variety of spectacular turns. Yet for all its spellbinding moments and visual inventiveness, there is a deficit of charm that made the first film such a winning classic. Yet for all that, the sequel is a remarkable achievement, even though its dark disposition is likely to scare off younger children. FYI: Christine Cavanaugh, who supplied the voice of the original Babe (and voices Chucky in *The Rugrats Movie*) was replaced by E.G. Daily (Tommy in *The Rugrats Movie*) after she asked for too much moolah for the sequel.

● *Esme Hoggett* Magda Szubanski, *Arthur H. Hoggett* James Cromwell, *Fugly Floom* Mickey Rooney, *The Landlady* Mary Stein. Voices of: *Babe* E.G. Daily, *Ferdinand* Danny Mann, *Zootie* Glenne Headly, *Bob* Steven Wright, *Thelonius* James Cosmo, *Pitbull/Doberman* Stanley Ralph Ross, *Pink Poodle* Russi Taylor, *Flealick* Adam Goldberg, *Fly* Miriam Margolyes, *Rex* Hugo Weaving, Bill Capizzi, Richard Huggett, Jim Cummings, Naomi Watts, and *The Narrator* Roscoe Lee Browne.
● *Dir* George Miller, *Pro* George Miller, Doug Mitchell and Bill Miller, *Ex Pro* Barbara Gibbs, *Screenplay* George Miller, Judy Morris and Mark Lamprell, *Ph* Andrew Lesnie, *Pro Des* Roger Ford, *Ed* Jay Friedkin and Margaret Sixel, *M* Nigel Westlake; Verdi, Rossini; songs performed by Peter Gabriel, Edith Piaf, Glen Miller, Charles Trenet, Louis Jordan, Dean Martin, The Mavericks, The Chieftans, etc, *Costumes* Norma Moriceau, *Animatronics* Neal Scanlan, *Animal Action* Karl Lewis Miller, *Primates* Steve Martin.

Kennedy Miller/Universal – UIP.
98 mins. Australia. 1998. Rel: 4 December 1998. Cert U.

Babymother ★★

Britain's first black musical is, in theory, an occasion for rejoicing, but writer-director Julian Henriques sadly muffs his opportunity. The babymother of the title is a single parent with ambitions in the world of pop music who also has personal issues to confront when a secret in her past is revealed. Stylistically the film, set in Harlesden, north-west London, moves uneasily between songs being performed in a realistic context and those which adopt non-naturalistic modes. In addition, the songs need to be developed more for full impact, and the characters are not sufficiently fleshed out for the drama to be telling. It lasts only 80 minutes and, for once, longer might have been better. [*Mansel Stimpson*]

● *Anita* Anjela Lauren Smith, *Sharon* Caroline Chikezie, *Yvette* Jocelyn Esien, *Byron* Wil Johnson, *Luther* Don Warrington, Tameka Empson, Diane Bailey, Vas Blackwood, Clive Buckley.
● *Dir* Julian Henriques, *Pro* Parminder Vir, *Ex Pro* Margaret Matheson, *Co-Pro* Tracey Seaward, *Line Pro* Yvonne Isimene Ibazebo, *Screenplay* Henriques and Vivienne Howard, *Ph* Ron Fortunato and Peter Middleton, *Pro Des* Choi Ho Man, *Ed* Jason Canovas, *M* John Lunn; songs performed by Superflex, Wil Johnson, Trilla Jenna, etc, *Costumes* Annie Curtis Jones.

Channel Four Films/The Arts Council of England/Formation Films/National Lottery – Film Four. 82 mins. UK. 1998. Rel: 11 September 1998. Cert 15.

Barney's Great Adventure ★¹/₂

As every child knows, Barney is more than just a stuffed purple toy in the shape of a dinosaur. With sufficient amounts of imagination and susceptibility, Barney can become an outsize companion who can talk, sing, dance and, above all, have loads of fun. Down at the farm, Abby and her friend Marcella show Abby's cynical brother Cody what gaiety they can have if they let their fancy run riot. Thus Cody finally gets to meet Barney and they all embark on a riotous adventure chasing a strange egg from outer space … Clearly aimed at a very, very young audience, this inevitable cash-in on the phenomenally successful TV show is as basic and unsophisticated as its concept. We have Barney and the kids singing 'Twinkle, Twinkle, Little Star,' dancing (for want of a better word) to 'Old MacDonald Had a Farm' and reaping all the fun of the fair, circus and what have you. With primitive puns, elementary choreography and surprisingly dodgy 'special' effects, the best that can be said for it is that it is totally innocuous.

● *Grandpa Greenfield* George Hearn, *Grandma Greenfield* Shirley Douglas, *Cody Newton* Trevor Morgan, *Marcella* Kyla Pratt, *Abby Newton* Diana Rice, *Mildred Goldfinch* Renee Madeleine Le Guerrier, Alan Fawcett, Jane Wheeler, *and the voice of Barney* Bob West.
● *Dir* Steve Gomer, *Pro* Sheryl Leach and Dennis DeShazer, *Ex Pro* Ben Myron, *Co-Pro* Jim Rowley, *Co-Ex Pro* Martha Chang, *Screenplay* Stephen White, from a story by White, Leach and DeShazer, *Ph* Sandi Sissel, *Pro Des* Vincent Jefferds, *Ed* Richard Halsey, *M* Jan Rhees; 'Barney – The Song' sung by Bernadette Peters, *Costumes* Francesca Chamberland, *Sound* James LeBrecht.

Good Egg Prods/PolyGram/Lyrick Studios – PolyGram. 76 mins. USA. 1998. Rel: 17 July 1998. Cert U.

Bedrooms & Hallways ★¹/₂

London; today. As he approaches his 30th birthday, Leo is having serious misgivings about his sexuality, doubts not helped by the unorthodox men's support group he attends. For unlike his screaming flatmate, Darren, Leo is not noticeably gay … At times, this gender-hopping farce is so taken with its agenda to shock, that you want to pick it up and spank it. True comedy evolves from true characters and this bunch of stereotypes (albeit played by a splendid cast) are merely cogs in a predictable and calculated wheel of misfortune. Yet, perhaps ironically, it is the film's most obvious caricature – Tom Hollander's sartorially wanting queen – that is its most endearing creation. FYI: Rose Troche previously directed the lesbian comedy *Go Fish*.

● *Leo* Kevin McKidd, *Sally* Jennifer Ehle, *Jeremy Downey* Hugo Weaving, *Darren* Tom Hollander, *Brendan* James Purefoy, *Keith* Simon Callow, *Sybil* Harriet Walter, *Adam* Christopher Fulford, *Angie* Julie Graham, *Terry* Con O'Neill, *John* Paul Higgins, Merelina Kendall, Victoria Williams, Simon Green, Nicola McAuliffe, ·*man at bus stop* Robert Farrar.
● *Dir* Rose Troche, *Pro* Dorothy Berwin and Ceci Dempsey, *Line Pro* Liz Bunton, *Screenplay* Robert Farrar, *Ph* Ashley Rowe, *Pro Des* Richard Bridgland, *Ed* Christopher Blunden, *M* Alfredo D. Troche and Ian MacPherson; 'Love Plus One' performed by Haircut 100, *Costumes* Annie Symons.

Berwin & Dempsey/Pandora Cinema/ARP/Pandora Film/BBC Films – Alliance Releasing. 96 mins. UK/France/Germany 1998. Rel: 9 April 1999. Cert 15.

Beloved ★★

124 Bluestone Road, rural Ohio; 1873. Living alone with her grown-up daughter Denver, former slave Sethe is a proud, determined woman haunted by an unspeakable past. When an old gentleman friend, Paul D, stops by to visit, he decides to stay on to warm Sethe's bed and to help combat the destructive spectral presence that resides in the house … While not without its telling moments, Jonathan Demme's

ambitious adaptation of Toni Morrison's Pulitzer Prize-winning 1987 novel is scuppered by muddy storytelling, abrupt lurches of tone and a general air of incomprehensibility. With its jumble of ghosts, regurgitations (oral and otherwise) and flashbacks, the film refuses to tread a linear path, sowing seeds of confusion and distrust in the viewer. Poor diction from the principals doesn't help, although Fujimoto's photography begs to be hung up and framed. Which leaves the players who, under the circumstances, are rather good, particularly Kimberly Elise and Thandie Newton as the balm and vinegar to Sethe's emotional wounds. Incidentally, 'Thandie' is Zulu for Beloved.

● *Sethe* Oprah Winfrey, *Paul D* Danny Glover, *Beloved* Thandie Newton, *Denver* Kimberly Elise, *Baby Suggs* Beah Richards, *younger Sethe* Lisa Gay Hamilton, *Stamp Paid* Albert Hall, *Ella* Irma P. Hall, *Janey Wagon* Carol Jean Lewis, *young Paul D* Brian Hooks, *Mr Bodwin* Jason Robards, Kessia Kordelle, Jude Ciccolella, Anthony Chisholm, Dorothy Love Coates, Jane White, Yada Beener, Angie Utt, Hill Harper, Harry Northup, Tracey Walter, Robert Castle, Paul Lazar.
● *Dir* Jonathan Demme, *Pro* Demme, Edward Saxon, Gary Goetzman, Oprah Winfrey and Kate Forte, *Ex Pro* Ron Bozman, *Screenplay* Akosua Busia, Richard LaGravenese and Adam Brooks, *Ph* Tak Fujimoto, *Pro Des* Kristi Zea, *Ed* Carol Littleton and Andy Keir, *M* Rachel Portman; songs performed by

Danny Glover, Oprah Winfrey, Kimberly Elise, Thandie Newton, Enoch Brown, Bessie Jones, African Children's Choir, etc, *Costumes* Colleen Atwood.

Touchstone Pictures/Harpo Films/Clinica Estetico – Buena Vista.
171 mins. USA. 1998. Rel: 5 March 1999. Cert 15.

Besieged ★★★¹/₂
Shandurai is a beautiful Kenyan exile studying to be a doctor in Rome. To make ends meet she cleans and maintains the house of a reclusive English composer, Jason Kinsky. Surrounded by exotic bric-a-brac and devoted to his Steinway, Kinsky becomes consumed by Shandurai's beauty and professes his all-consuming love for her, unaware that she has a husband back in Africa ... Working on his most intimate canvas since *La Luna* in 1979, director Bernardo Bertolucci (who co-scripted with his wife Clare Peploe) brings his customary opulence of vision to the cinematic equivalent of a short story. And by accentuating the cultural differences of his protagonists through their love of music – illustrated by some haunting African songs and the piano playing of Stefano Arnaldi – Bertolucci has fashioned a surprisingly vivid and layered love story that touches the heart while preserving a chaste distance from the groin area.

● *Shandurai* Thandie Newton, *Jason Kinsky* David Thewlis, *Agostino* Claudio Santamaria, *singer* John

Above: Black-and-white keyboard: Thandie Newton in Bernardo Bertolucci's intimate and vivid Besieged *(from Alliance Releasing)*

C. Ojwang, *priest* Cyril Nri, Massimo De Rossi, Veronica Lazar, Andrea Quercia.
● *Dir* Bernardo Bertolucci, *Pro* Massimo Cortesi, *Assoc Pro* Clare Peploe, *Screenplay* Bertolucci and Peploe, *Ph* Fabio Cianchetti, *Pro Des* Gianni Silvestri, *Ed* Jacopo Quadri, *M* Alessio Vlad; Mozart, Grieg, J.S. Bach, Beethoven, Chopin; arranged and performed by Stefano Arnaldi, *Costumes* Metka Kosak.

Fiction/Navert/Mediaset – Alliance Releasing.
93 mins. Italy. 1998. Rel: 23 April 1999. Cert PG.

Best Laid Plans ★★★¹/₂

Tropico, Nevada; now. Bryce is a regular guy, a college-educated Yuppie with a promising career ahead of him. Then, one night, fuelled by alcohol, he takes home a sexually enthusiastic young woman and makes love to her. The next thing he knows is that she's accusing him of rape and – worse – she's only 16. With his carefully planned future about to crash, he turns to his old college friend Nick for advice ... The corkscrew thriller is such a well-worn genre that it's hard to grip a fresh thread, yet Theodore Griffin's sly screenplay does manage to engineer a few surprises. Scattering fragments of plot into an escalating prologue, Griffin sets up an intriguing premise, aided here by some stylish direction from Britain's Mike Barker (*The James Gang*) and a compelling turn from Alessandro Nivola as Nick. You don't exactly get inside the characters' heads and the very end is a bit of a disappointment, but otherwise this is an engrossing, tight and extremely atmospheric diversion.

● *Nick* Alessandro Nivola, *Lissa* Reese Witherspoon, *Bryce* Josh Brolin, *badd ass dude* Rocky Carroll, *Charlie* Michael G. Hagerty, *Jimmy* Terrence Howard, *Barry* Jamie Marsh, Gene Wolande, Jonathan McMurty, Terrance Sweeney.
● *Dir* Mike Barker, *Pro* Sean Bailey, Alan Greenspan, Betsey Beers and Chris Moore, *Ex Pro* Mike Newell, *Screenplay* Theodore Griffin, *Ph* Ben Seresin, *Pro Des* Sophie Becher, *Ed* Sloane Klevin, *M* Craig Armstrong; songs performed by Patsy Cline, Eagle Eye Cherry, Massive Attack, Mazzy Star, The Mills Brothers, Gomez, and Neneh Cherry, *Costumes* Susan Matheson.

Fox 2000/Dogstar Films – Fox.
93 mins. USA. 1999. Rel: 14 May 1999. Cert 15.

Beyond Silence – Jenseits der Stille
★★★¹/₂

Martin and Kai Bischoff share an idyllic if unusual existence in a quiet rural town in southern Germany. Profoundly in love, they are also deaf and rely on their eight-year-old daughter, Lara, to guide them through the pitfalls of a hearing world (such as the negotiations for a bank loan). Then Lara is given a clarinet by her aunt and develops a passion for music, a love her parents cannot begin to understand ... Exploring the turbulent love-hate relationship of a daughter and her father and filtering it through his inability to hear and her love of music, *Beyond Silence* is on to a winning formula. From the opening scene in which the camera glides up from the bottom of a lake to the frozen surface, this is a film that is as confidently visual as it is musically commanding. And thus, by juggling the key worlds of its sensorially and emotionally deprived protagonists – dwelling on the beauty of a silent snowfall and the seductive power of a piano recital – the film provides a sensually rich palette on which to play out its psychological paradox. FYI: The deaf American actor Howie Seago and the deaf French actress Emmanuelle Laborit play Lara's parents. The shoot proved problematic as both American and French sign language is different from the German.

● *Lara Bischoff* Sylvie Testud, *Lara as a child* Tatjana Trieb, *Martin Bischoff* Howie Seago, *Kai Bischoff* Emmanuelle Laborit, *Clarissa Bischoff* Sybille Canonica, *Gregor* Matthias Habich, *Marie* Alexandra Bolz, *Tom* Hansa Czypionka, Doris Schade, Horst Sachtleben, Hubert Mulzer, Birge Schade.
● *Dir* Caroline Link, *Pro* Thomas Wobke, Jakob Claussen and Luggi Waldleitner, *Screenplay* Link and Beth Serlin, *Ph* Gernot Roll, *Pro Des* Susann Bieling, *Ed* Patricia Rommel, *M* Niki Reiser; 'I Will Survive' sung by Gloria Gaynor, *Costumes* Katharina von Martius.

Roxy-Film – Arrow Film.
110 mins. Germany/Switzerland. 1996. Rel: 2 April 1999. Cert 12.

The Big Hit ★★

Melvin Smiley is the world's sweetest – and most gullible – hitman. A skilful and resourceful killer, he fits the profile of a typical heel (he's two-timing his Jewish fiancée with a black girlfriend), but all he wants in life is to be liked. Consequently, he's a soft touch to everyone he meets, making him an easy target for his less scrupulous colleagues when a kidnapping scam radically backfires ... A frenetic blend of farce, parody and action-thriller, *The Big Hit* is a broad, vulgar sideshow with many good jokes and a wildly overheated sensibility. With every stereotype in the comic-book canon pulled out and inflated, the film doesn't take itself seriously for a nano-second, nor does it strive for subtlety. Luckily, it has a strong story to hang all this nonsense on – and some career-worst performances from a surprisingly distinguished cast. P.S. With Kirk Wong behind the camera, it's no surprise that Mark Wahlberg eventually ditches both his black-and-white lovers in favour of an Oriental girl, China Cow (who became Wahlberg's off-screen girlfriend as well).

Left: *Life in the fast lane: Bajram Severdzan and Sabri Sulejmani in Emir Kusturica's joyous, life-affirming master-piece,* Black Cat White Cat *(from Artificial Eye)*

● *Melvin Smiley* Mark Wahlberg, *Cisco* Lou Diamond Phillips, *Pam Shulman* Christina Applegate, *Paris* Avery Brooks, *Crunch* Bokeem Woodbine, *Vince* Antonio Sabato Jr, *Jeanne Shulman* Lainee Kazan, *Morton Shulman* Elliott Gould, *Jiro Nishi* Sab Shimono, *Keiko Nishi* China Cow, *Gump* Robin Dunne, *Chantel* Lela Rochon, *Lance* Joshua Peace, Danny Smith, David Usher, Hardee T. Lineham.
● *Dir*: Che-Kirk Wong, *Pro*: Warren Zide and Wesley Snipes, *Ex Pro*: John Woo, Terence Chang and John M. Eckert, *Screenplay*: Ben Ramsey, *Ph*: Danny Nowak*, Pro Des*: Taavo Soodor, *Ed*: Robin Russell and Pietro Scalia, *M*: Graeme Revell; songs performed by Fun Lovin' Criminals, Buck-O-Nine, LaTanya, Molotov, Red Rat, Sugarhill Gang, Save Ferris, E-40, World Party, Mark Wahlberg, etc, *Costumes*: Margaret Mohr.

TriStar Pictures/Amen Ra Films/Lion Rock – Columbia TriStar.
91 mins. USA. 1998. Rel: 25 June 1999. Cert 18.

Black Cat White Cat ★★★★¹/₂

The carefree life of the Balkan gypsy is not what it once was. Yet even the intrusion of the security camera and mobile phone cannot weaken the power and friendship of two 80-year-old men – even if they haven't seen each other in 25 years ... In 1993 Emir Kusturica briefly deserted his native Yugoslavia to direct *Arizona Dream* with Johnny Depp. It was an experience he described as a 'nightmare.' But then every project Kusturica has embarked on – *When Father Was Away on Business, Time of the Gypsies, Underground* (and every one a major award winner,

incidentally) – has, he confesses, 'nearly killed me.' Possessed by a bizarre imagination and an instinctive cinematic style, Kusturica has a way with cinema that recalls the best of Fellini informed by the earthy folk-lore of the Balkans. His *Black Cat White Cat* (award-ed the best director prize at Venice) is yet another robust kaleidoscope of character, plot, music, geese and surreal flourishes, as much a celebration of the director's art as it is of life itself. Yet for all his full-frontal melodramatics, Kusturica is not above the occasional throwaway sight gag, such as a shot of a giant pig consuming a car and the film's ubiquitous orchestra strapped to a tree. Amazingly, the majority of the actors – including the two swaggering octogen-arians – are non-professionals. Filmed on location in Slovenia and on the Danube.

● *Matko Destanov* Bajram Severdzan, *Dadan* Srdan Todorovic, *Ida* Branka Katic, *Zare Destanov, Matko's son* Florijan Ajdini, *Sujka* Ljubica Adzovic, *Zarije Destanov, Matko's father* Zabit Memedov, *Grga Veliki – Big Grga* Jasar Destani, Sabri Sulejmani, Stojan Sotirov, Predrag Pepi Lakovic, Predrag Miki Manojlovic.
● *Dir* Emir Kusturica, *Pro* Karl Baumgartner, *Ex Pro* Maksa Catovic, *Assoc Pro* Marina Girard, *Screenplay* Kusturica and Gordon Mihic, *Ph* Thierry Arbogast, *Pro Des* Milenko Jeremic, *Ed* Svetolik Mica Zajc, *M* Dr Nelle Karajilic, Vojislav Aralica and Dejan Sparavalo; Johann Strauss, *Costumes* Nebojsa Lipanovic.

CiBy 2000/Pandora Film/Komuna/France 2 Cinema/Canal Plus, etc – Artificial Eye.
129 mins. Germany/France/Yugoslavia/Austria/Greece. 1998. Rel: 7 May 1999. Cert 15.

Lee, Avi Arad, Joseph Calamari, and Lynn Harris, *Screenplay* David S. Goyer, *Ph* Theo Van De Sande, *Pro Des* Kirk M. Petruccelli, *Ed* Paul Rubell, *M* Mark Isham; songs performed by New Order, Creedence Clearwater Revival, DJ Krush, Solitaire, Siren, Photek, etc, *Costumes* Sanja Milkovic Hays, *Make-up effects* Greg Cannom.

New Line Cinema/Amen Ra Films/Imaginary Forces – Entertainment.
120 mins. USA. 1998. Rel: 13 November 1998. Cert 18.

Blast From the Past ★★★

At the height of the Cuban missile crisis, 'bona fide genius and borderline nutcase' Calvin Webber constructs a top-secret state-of-the-art fall-out shelter in his back garden. Equipped with ingenious mod cons, deluxe living quarters, fish farm and its own well-stocked supermarket, the shelter is designed to sustain Webber and his pregnant wife in comfort for 35 years. When, at last, Webber feels it is safe to emerge from his cocoon, downtown Los Angeles is a changed place, populated by drunks, vagrants, transvestites and gun-wielding hooligans. It is here that Webber's 35-year-old son, Adam, emerges to superimpose his antiquated charm onto a sick new world … Traversing the same themes as the far more accomplished *Pleasantville*, *Blast From the Past* is not without its own pleasures and, avoiding pretension, manages to establish some neat satire. And Brendan Fraser, introducing a new spin on the likeable innocent he created in *Encino Man* and *George of the Jungle*, makes an agreeably goofy and appealing fish-out-of-water. It won't tax the brain, but it's innocuous fun.

● *Adam Webber* Brendan Fraser, *Calvin Webber* Christopher Walken, *Helen Webber* Sissy Spacek, *Eve Rostokov* Alicia Silverstone, *Troy* Dave Foley, *soda jerk* Joey Slotnick, *Cliff* Nathan Fillion, *Dr Anita Aron* Jenifer Lewis, Rex Linn, Deborah Kellner, Cynthia Mace, Don Yesso, Carmen More, Dale Raoul, Donovan Scott, Hugh Wilson, Danny Zorn, Mary Ann Hermanson, Brian Blondell, *Bogart DJ* Robert Sacchi.
● *Dir* Hugh Wilson, *Pro* Wilson and Renny Harlin, *Ex Pro* Amanda Stern, Sunil Perkash and Claire Rudnick Polstein, *Co-Pro* Mary Kane, *Screenplay* Wilson and Bill Kelly, *Ph* Jose Luis Alcaine, *Pro Des* Robert Ziembicki, *Ed* Don Brochu, *M* Steve Dorff; songs performed by Perry Como, Dean Martin, Louis Prima and Keely Smith, Barry White, B. Real, R.E.M., Everclear, Block, Lisbeth Scott, Squirrel Nut Zippers, Cherry Poppin' Daddies, Village People, Randy Newman, etc, *Costumes* Mark Bridges.

New Line Cinema/Midnight Sun – Entertainment.
109 mins. USA. 1998. Rel: 2 April 1999. Cert 12.

Above: Blades of glory: Wesley Snipes and Stephen Dorff clang it out in Stephen Norrington's bloody stylish Blade *(from Entertainment)*

Blade ★★★½

Labelled The Daywalker by his blood-sucking enemies, Blade – half-man, half-vampire – has retained the integrity of his human side while possessing the strength and immortality of his nocturnal brethren. Committed to wiping out the entire vampire community (which has now infiltrated the government, police force, big business, etc), Blade is aided in his mission by a humble haematologist … By fine-tuning the vampiric creed and plugging it straight into the bloodstream of state-of-the-art CGI, *Blade* proves to be a heady fix for sci-fi horror addicts. Excessively violent and extravagantly stylish (and, in spite of an absence of flesh, persuasively erotic), the film confirms the potential of the English film-maker Stephen Norrington, who made an impressive directorial debut with the low-budget *Death Machine* (1995). As the eponymous hunter, Wesley Snipes – himself a dab hand at capoeria, a form of unarmed combat – brings a command and power to the role of the superhero (introduced by Marvel Comics in 1973) that brooks no argument. In fact, Snipes was so enthused with the project that he took on the mantle of producer as well. FYI: The first black superhero of the cinema was Shaquille O'Neal's *Steel*, beating Blade to the record books by one year.

● *Blade* Wesley Snipes, *Deacon Frost* Stephen Dorff, *Abraham Whistler* Kris Kristofferson, *Karen Jenson* N'Bushe Wright, *Quinn* Donal Logue, *Dragonetti* Udo Kier, *Racquel* Traci Lords, *Mercury* Arly Jover, *Krieger* Kevin Patrick Walls, *Curtis Webb* Tim Guinee, Sanaa Lathan, Eric Edwards, Donna Wong, Kenneth Johnson, Erl.
● *Dir* Stephen Norrington, *Pro* Peter Frankfurt, Wesley Snipes and Robert Engelman, *Ex Pro* Stan

Le Bossu ★★★★★

France; 1699-1716. At an informal fencing class, the low-born Lagardere challenges the Duke of Nevers – the pre-eminent swordsman of France – to a friendly duel. Taking up Lagardere's challenge with some impatience, the duke swiftly puts the upstart in his place. But in the not-too-distant future their paths are to cross more than once, leading to a 20-year saga of betrayal, friendship, revenge and eternal love … Nobody does costume drama better than the French and this robust, colourful and sublimely diverting epic is the *creme de la creme*. Based on the 1858 novel by Paul Henri Feval (1817-87), the film is invested with extraordinary flair by 65-year-old director De Broca and is served in all quarters by the highest standards of excellence. The acting, locations, photography, production design, choreography, costumes, music and editing all bring Feval's terrific story to resounding life, creating a poignant, earthy and rip-roaring entertainment. And the sword fights are some of the most thrilling ever depicted on screen. FYI: Amazingly, this is the seventh screen incarnation of Feval's story.

● *Lagardere* Daniel Auteuil, *Count Gonzague* Fabrice Luchini, *Duc Philippe de Nevers* Vincent Perez, *Aurore* Marie Gillain, *Peyrolles* Yann Collette, *Cocardasse* Jean-Francois Stevenin, *Passepoil* Didier Pain, *Blanche de Caylus* Claire Nebout*, The Regent, Philippe II d'Orleans* Philippe Noiret, *Caylus* Jacques Sereys, Renato Scarpa, Ludovica Tinghi, James Thierree.
● *Dir* Philippe De Broca, *Pro* Patrick Godeau, *Ex Pro* Francoise Galfre, *Screenplay* De Broca, Jean Cosmos and Jerome Tonnerre, *Ph* Jean-Francois Robin, *Pro Des* Bernard Vezat, *Ed* Henri Lanoe, *M* Philippe Sarde; 'Intermezzo' from Pietro Mascagni's 'Cavalleria rusticana', *Costumes* Christian Gasc, *Swordmaster* Michel Carliez.

Aliceleo/TF1 Films/DA Films/Cecchi Gori Group Tiger/Gemini Film/Canal Plus, etc – Pathe. 128 mins. France/Italy/Germany. 1997. Rel: 21 August 1998. Cert 15.

The Boys ★★

The Sydney suburbs; today. Fresh out of prison, Brett Sprague returns to the bosom of his family and immediately shows his mother, two brothers and girlfriend that he is just as despicable a piece of human vermin as he ever was … A film of undeniable menace, *The Boys* flaunts first-time director Rowan Woods' skill at eliciting atmosphere but also forces one to question the validity of the material. Featuring a leading character with no redeeming qualities whatsoever (he can't even rise to the occasion for his horny girlfriend), Stephen Sewell's adaptation of Gordon Graham's award-winning 1991 play merely accentuates the stasis of the piece. So what's the point? Why should we care? Do we have to go to Australia?

● *Brett Sprague* David Wenham, *Michelle* Toni Collette, *Sandra Sprague* Lynette Curran, *Glenn Sprague* John Polson, *Jackie* Jeanette Cronin, *Stevie Sprague* Anthony Hayes, *Nola* Anna Lise, *George 'Abo'* Pete Smith.
● *Dir* Rowan Woods, *Pro* Robert Connolly and John Maynard, *Ex Pro* Douglas Cummins, *Assoc Pro* David Wenham, *Screenplay* Stephen Sewell, *Ph* Tristan Milani, *Pro Des* Luigi Pittorino, *Ed* Nick Meyers, *M* The Necks, *Costumes* Annie Marshall, *Sound* Sam Petty.

Arenafilm/Axiom Films/Australian Film Commission, etc – Film Four. 85 mins. Australia/UK. 1998. Rel: 11 December 1998. Cert 18.

Bride of Chucky ★★★½

For seven years the remains of the killer doll Chucky have been under lock and key. Then his human girlfriend, Tiffany, locates them, steals them from the police and re-assembles them with heavy-duty thread. Working from a manual of *Voodoo for Dummies*, she then brings back Chuck's soul, only to be turned into a doll herself shortly afterwards ... Wickedly self-irreverent and refreshingly inventive, this short and sweet follow-up to the *Child's Play* trio pays homage to James Whales' *Bride of Frankenstein*. And, like its model, it's actually better than the original. Making a virtue of its limitations, the film pulls off that rare feat of being very nasty and yet genuinely funny. Classic line, courtesy of Jennifer Tilly: 'You know me, I'll kill anybody. But I'll only sleep with someone I love.' And Chucky, pre-intercourse with Tiffany: 'Have I got a rubber? Tiff, I'm *all* rubber.'

● *Tiffany* Jennifer Tilly, *Jade* Katherine Heigl, *Jesse* Nick Stabile, *Chief Warren Kincaid* John Ritter, *Damien* Alexis Arquette, *David* Gordon Michael Woolvett, *the voice of Chucky* Brad Dourif, Lawrence Dane, Michael Johnson, James Gallanders, Kathy Najimy, Park Bench.
● *Dir* Ronny Wu, *Pro* David Kirschner and Grace Gilroy, *Ex Pro* Don Mancini and Corey Sienega, *Co-Pro* Laura Moskowitz, *Screenplay* Mancini, *Ph* Peter Pau, *Pro Des* Alicia Keywan, *Ed* David Wu and Randolph K. Bricker. *M* Graeme Revell; songs performed by Rob Zombie, Kidney Thieves, Blondie, Stabbing Westward, The Assholes, White Zombie, Judas Priest, Slayer, etc, *Costumes* Lynne MacKay, *Chucky and Tiffany Dolls* Kirschner, *Chucky and Tiffany Effects* Kevin Yagher.

Universal – Metrodome.
89 mins. USA. 1998. Rel: 18 June 1999. Cert 18.

The Brylcreem Boys ★★

Kildare County, the Republic of Ireland; September-January, 1941-42. When squadron leader Miles Keogh is shot down during a dog-fight with a Messerschmitt, he assumes that he has bailed out over occupied France. But he is in fact in Ireland and soon finds himself incarcerated in a prisoner-of-war camp with the very man who downed his plane ... You can look at *The Brylcreem Boys* two ways. One, as an endearingly old-fashioned attempt to resurrect the P.O.W. yarn, armed with a novel twist. Two, as a hopelessly clunky dodo sabotaged by the worst acting seen in a British film since *Mad Dogs and Englishmen* (1994). The truth lies somewhere in between. The concept is, indeed, a promising one (inspired by real events) in which arch-enemies find themselves trapped in a relatively benign environment in a neutral and beautiful country. But, as soon as the twist is out of the gate, the cliches start to pile up, complete with sneering, bulging-eyed Nazis (shame on you Peter Woodward!). Filmed entirely on the Isle of Man.

● *Miles Keogh* Bill Campbell, *Sam Gunn* William McNamara, *Count Rudolph 'Rudi' Von Stegenbeck* Angus MacFadyen, *Richard Lewis* John Gordon Sinclair, *Hans Jorg Wolff* Oliver Tobias, *Sean O'Brien*

Gabriel Byrne, *Mattie Guerin* Jean Butler, *Captain Deegan* Joe McGann, *Stossel* Peter Woodward, *Colin Parker, the corpse with a teddy bear* Christopher Ryan, Hal Fowler, Tim Hayes, Alistair McLeod, Anders Jillybo, Marc Sinden, Marek Vasut, Rupert Wickham, Aine Ni Mhuiri, Alan Barry, James Tiernan Ryan.
● *Dir* Terence Ryan, *Pro* Ryan, Alan Latham, Paul Madigan and Bernie Stampfer, *Ex Pro* Mohammed Yusef and Kristi Prenn, *Screenplay* Ryan, Jamie Brown and Susan Morrall, *Ph* Gerry Lively, *Pro Des* Steve Hardie, *Ed* Emma Hickox, *M* Richard Hartley; songs performed by Al Bowlly, and Jenny Howe, *Costumes* David Murphy, *Choreography* Jean Butler.

Rough Magic/Freewheel Prods/Ealing Studios – Cromgold/Guerilla Films.
107 mins. UK. 1996. Rel: 23 April 1999. Cert 12.

Buffalo 66 ★★★

Buffalo, New York; the present. Psychotic scuzzball Billy Brown leaves prison with a mission and a full bladder. Determined to avenge himself on the man who inadvertently put him behind bars for five years, Billy must first pay a visit to his parents, who think he has been out of the country on government business. To back up his lies, the ex-con kidnaps a random tap dancer to stand in for his wife and warns her, 'If you make me look bad I'll never talk to you again.' But first he must find a bathroom ... The directorial debut of artist and actor Vincent Gallo (*Palookaville, The Funeral*), *Buffalo 66* is a quirky, mesmerising slice of white trash chic that commands the attention as it peels away the layers of Gallo's fascinating character. An abrasive, anal loser, Billy is shown by turns to be repugnant, comic and affecting as his terrible past is gradually pieced together via a series of innovative narrative techniques. Gallo, who shows much more promise as a director than as an actor, also co-wrote the script, composed the music and even persuaded his father to dub Ben Gazzara's rendition of 'Where Fools Rush In.'

● *Billy Brown* Vincent Gallo, *Layla,* aka *Wendy Balsam* Christina Ricci, *Jimmy Brown* Ben Gazzara, *bookie* Mickey Rourke, *Wendy Balsam* Rosanna Arquette, *Sonny* Jan-Michael Vincent, *Janet Brown* Anjelica Huston, *Goon,* aka *Rocky* Kevin Corrigan, Kevin Pollak, Alex Karras, John Rummel.
● *Dir* Vincent Gallo, *Pro* Chris Hanley, *Ex Pro* Michael Paseornek, Jeff Sackman, John Dunning and Andre Link, *Screenplay* Gallo and Alison Bagnall, *Ph* Lance Acord, *Pro Des* Gideon Ponte, *Ed* Curtiss Clayton, *M* Gallo; songs performed by Vincent Gallo Snr., Nelson Riddle, King Crimson, Stan Getz, and Yes, *Costumes* Alexis Scott.

Cinepix Film Properties/Muse Prods – Metrodome.
110 mins. Canada/USA. 1997. Rel: 2 October 1998. Cert 15.

A Bug's Life ★★

Flik is an inventive ant with a mission: he is determined to reduce the workload of his hard-working brethren. However, when he accidentally spills his colony's entire harvest into an adjacent lake, he has to answer to the extortionate grasshoppers, for whom most of the food was intended … The second computer-animated film from the lucrative partnership of Disney and Pixar (following the enormously successful *Toy Story*), *A Bug's Life* is a brash, chaotic confusion of gags and crude animation. The insects themselves look like shiny Tupperware toys, the knockabout humour is excruciatingly unfunny and the hero a dull stooge. And, unlike the thematically similar, far-superior *Antz*, there's no single scene that takes the breath away. Furthermore, Kevin Spacey – an actor who can display immeasurable evil without batting a sigh – is totally wasted as the voice of the nefarious, all-shouting Hopper. Notwithstanding, the fabricated 'out-takes' played during the closing credits are an inspiration.

● Voices: *Flik* Dave Foley, *Hopper* Kevin Spacey, *Princess Atta* Julia Louis-Dreyfus, *Princess Dot* Hayden Panettiere, *Queen* Phyllis Diller, *Molt* Richard Kind, *Slim* David Hyde Pierce, *Heimlich* Joe Ranft, *Francis* Denis Leary, *Manny* Jonathan Harris, *Gypsy* Madeline Kahn, *Rosie* Bonnie Hunt, Michael McShane, John Ratzenberger, Brad Garrett, *Mr Soil* Roddy McDowall, Edie McClurg, Alex Rocco, David Ossman, John Lasseter, Phil Proctor, Andrew Stanton, Lee Unkrich.
● *Dir* John Lasseter and Andrew Stanton, *Pro* Darla K. Anderson and Kevin Reher, *Screenplay* Stanton, Donald McEnery and Bob Shaw, from an original story by Lasseter, Stanton and Joe Ranft, loosely based on Aesop's fable *The Ant and the Grasshopper*, *Ph* Sharon Calahan, *Pro Des* William Cone, *Ed* Lee Unkrich, *M* Randy Newman, *Sound* Gary Rydstrom, *Supervising animation* Glenn McQueen and Rich Quade.

Walt Disney/Pixar Animation – Buena Vista.
95 mins. USA. 1998. Rel: 5 February 1999. Cert U.

Bulworth ★★★★

Los Angeles; March 1996. Having hired a clandestine operative to pull off his own assassination, incumbent US senator Jay Billington Bulworth discovers a new lease of life. No longer afraid to speak the truth, the candidate sees his popularity soar and his own destiny shift into sharp focus. Meanwhile, falling for a beautiful black woman (less than half his age) and embracing the cause of the cultural underclass doesn't exactly simplify matters … A slyly plotted political satire, *Bulworth* is nothing if not ambitious. A bold combination of *Sullivan's Travels*, *The Candidate*, *Dead Presidents* and *Liar Liar*, the film trains its sights on a number of American social targets and smartly hits them all. Darkly comic, slick, observant, unexpected and even rather touching, *Bulworth* blunts no blows as it rounds up a herd of sacred cows into its political corral. And, as the rejuvenated senator sermonising in profane rhyme, Beatty is a revelation, at times recalling a bizarre blend of Jack Nicholson and Michael Keaton. Formerly known as *Tribulations*.

● *Jay Billington Bulworth* Warren Beatty, *Nina* Halle Berry, *L.D.* Don Cheadle, *Dennis Murphy* Oliver Platt, *Graham Crockett* Paul Sorvino, *Eddie Davers* Jack Warden, *Darnell* Isaiah Washington, *Rastaman* Amiri Baraka, *Constance Bulworth* Christine Baranski, *himself* Larry King, *Bill Feldman* Joshua Malina, *Vinnie* Richard Sarafian, Sean Astin, Ernie Banks, Graham Beckel, Thomas Jefferson Byrd, J. Kenneth Campbell, Christopher Curry, Stanley DeSantis, Nora Dunn, George Furth, Robin Gammell, Jackie Gayle, Jim Haynie, Randee Heller, Brian Hooks, Ariyan Johnson, Deborah Lacey, Helen Martin, Laurie Metcalf, Michael Milhoan, Debra Monk, Deborah Moore, Michele Morgan, Chris Mulkey, Lou Myers, James Pickens Jr., Wendell Pierce, Adrian Ricard, Bee-Be Smith, Florence Stanley, John Witherspoon, and (uncredited) William Baldwin, George Hamilton, Paul Mazursky, Josef Sommer.
● *Dir* Warren Beatty, *Pro* Beatty and Pieter Jan Brugge, *Ex Pro* Lauren Shuler Donner, *Co-Pro* Victoria Thomas and Frank Capra III, *Screenplay* Beatty and Jeremy Pikser and (*uncredited*) James Toback and Aaron Sorkin, *Ph* Vittorio Storaro, *Pro Des* Dean Tavoularis, *Ed* Robert C. Jones and Billy Weber, *M* Ennio Morricone; Hayden, Beethoven; songs performed by Warren Beatty, God's Property, Dr Dre & LL Cool J, Pras Michel, Eve, Black Eyed Peas, B REAL, Public Enemy, NWA, Cypress Hill, Crucial Conflict, Ice Cube, KRS-One, etc, *Costumes* Milena Canonero.

Fox – Fox.
108 mins. USA. 1998. Rel: 22 January 1999. Cert 18.

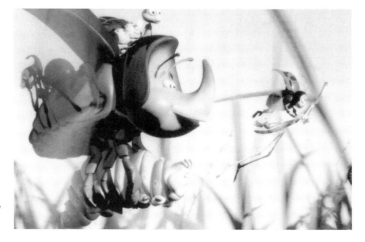

Below: All the fun of the flea circus: a scene from John Lasseter and Andrew Stanton's brash and feverish A Bug's Life (from Buena Vista)

C

Right: Bob Hoskins (third from right) leads the cast of traditional yarn Captain Jack (from Feature Film Co)

Captain Jack ★¹/₂

Pixie-like Whitby captain Bob Hoskins sails his rusty schooner to the Arctic Circle, helped by a motley crew of hastily-gathered misfits: hen-pecked husband David Troughton; Aussie dropout Peter McDonald; lovesick stowaway Sadie Frost; and sisters Gemma Jones and Anna Massey. Although 'loosely' based on a true story, everything is unbelievable, from the smooth-as-a-studio-pond surface of the Arctic to the dreadful Yorkshire accents. As a result, we feel no sense of real achievement. This is yet another example of a British film suffering from a sorely underdeveloped script. Only kids highly susceptible to old-fashioned tales of derring-do might stick with it. [*Simon Rose*]

● *Captain Jack* Bob Hoskins, *Tessa* Sadie Frost, *Eunice* Gemma Jones, *Phoebe* Anna Massey, *Andy* Peter McDonald, *Emmett* David Troughton, *Barbara* Maureen Lipman, *Inspector Lancing* Patrick Malahide, *Deidre* Michele Dotrice, Keith Clifford, Sam Townend, Jimmy Logan, Molly Weir, Andy De La Tour, Nick Stringer, Kathryn Pogson, Ian Liston, Robert Addie, Trevor Bannister, Paul Butterworth.
● *Dir* Robert Young, *Pro* John Goldschmidt, *Ex Pro* Pippa Cross, Chris Craib and William Sarjent, *Screenplay* Jack Rosenthal, suggested by an article by Nick Davies, *Ph* John McGlashan, *Pro Des* Simon Holland, *Ed* Edward Mansell, *M* Richard Harvey, *Costumes* Alyson Ritchie.

Granada Film/Baltic Media/Arts Council of England/National Lottery/Viva Films – Feature Film Co. 100 mins. UK. 1998. Rel: 28 May 1999. Cert PG.

The Castle ★★★★

A man's home is his castle and Darryl Kerrigan's castle is a model of its kind, complete with dummy chimney (for charm), overhead power lines (as a reminder of man's progress) and a garden backing onto the runway of an international airport (very useful should the Kerrigans ever decide to fly anywhere). Despite the fact that the eldest son is in prison for armed robbery, the Kerrigans – Dad, Mum, Wayne, Steve, Tracey and Dale – are a blissfully happy family noted for their ability to look on the bright side of life. So when their home is 'compulsorily acquired' by the airport authority, Darryl refuses to take the matter lying down ... A collaborative effort 'conceived' by the director and three other writers, *The Castle* is a genuine original, an unfashionable portrait of a beatifically functional family that is almost consistently hilarious. Eccentric to a virtue, the Kerrigans suffer their own annoying peccadilloes without judgement, allowing the audience the last laugh. The story itself is old hat but is reworked in such a fresh way that one can only sit back and applaud.

● *Darryl Kerrigan* Michael Caton, *Sal Kerrigan* Anne Tenney, *Dale Kerrigan* Stephen Curry, *Steve Kerrigan* Anthony Simcoe, *Tracey Kerrigan* Sophie Lee, *Wayne Kerrigan* Wayne Hope, *Dennis Denuto* Tiriel Mora, *Con Petropoulous* Eric Bana, *Lawrence Hammill* Charles (Bud) Tingwell, *Farouk* Costas Kilias, Robyn Nevin, Bryan Dawe, Monty Maizels, Lynda Gibson, John Benton, Laurie Dobson, John Flaus.
● *Dir* Rob Sitch, *Pro* Debra Choate, *Ex Pro* Michael Hirsh, Written and conceived by: Sitch, Santo Cilauro, Tom Gleisner and Jane Kennedy, *Ph* Miriana Marusic,

Left: Media circus: Kenneth Branagh, Charlize Theron and Anthony Mason in Woody Allen's tired and tested Celebrity *(from Buena Vista)*

Pro Des Carrie Kennedy, *Ed* Wayne Hyett, *M* Craig Harnath; songs performed by Alison Krauss, Paul Kelly, and Kate Ceberano, *Costumes* Kitty Stuckey.

Frontline Television Prods/Village Roadshow/Working Dog – UIP.
85 mins. Australia. 1997. Rel: 24 July 1998. Cert 15.

Celebrity ★★½

Manhattan; today. 'You can learn a lot about a society by whom it chooses to celebrate,' observes Robin Simon in this whirligig of showbiz writers, movie stars and assorted hangers-on. Kenneth Branagh stars as Woody Allen's alter ego and, armed with the director's mandatory arsenal of neuroses, tics and mannerisms, he makes a fitting replacement. He is Lee Simon, a showbiz-cum-travel hack plagued by writer's block and predatory women, a pathetic figure whose Great American Novel is going nowhere fast. More interesting is the company he keeps, from a sublimely lubricious model (Theron) to a neurotic ex-wife (Davis) he cannot seem to escape. Sadly, the jokes – with their built-in 'laugh here' labels – are more miss than hit. When Davis reassures Branagh that she 'won't get angry' during a marital confessional, we are not surprised when she goes ballistic. And the inclusion of a nun strumming a guitar to 'Kumbaya' is a cheap shot. As for Woody's analysis of the science of celebrity, he offers little new in a crowded satirical field. The best gag is at his own expense, when a director is referred to as pretentious for making his films in black-and-white. Filmed in black-and-white.

● *David* Hank Azaria, *Lee Simon* Kenneth Branagh, *Robin Simon* Judy Davis, *Brandon Darrow* Leonardo DiCaprio, *Nicole Oliver* Melanie Griffith, *Bonnie* Famke Janssen, *Dr Lupus* Michael Lerner, *Tony Gardella* Joe Mantegna, *hooker* Bebe Neuwirth, *Nola* Winona Ryder, *supermodel* Charlize Theron, *Vicky* Gretchen Mol, Greg Mottola, Douglas McGrath, Jodi Long, Dylan Baker, Isaac Mizrahi, Polly Adams, Dayle Haddon, Kate Burton, Debra Messing, Andre Gregory, Larry Pine, David Margulies, William Addy, Tony Sirico, Patti D'Arbanville, Frank Pellegrino, Jim Moody, Mary Jo Buttafuoco, Joey Buttafuoco, Sam Rockwell, Bruce Jay Friedman, Erica Jong, Ned Eisenberg, Tony Darrow, Allison Janney, Howard Erskine, Celia Weston, Donald Trump, Aida Turturro, Jeffrey Wright, Karen Duffy.
● *Dir* and *Screenplay* Woody Allen. *Pro* Jean Doumanian. *Ex Pro* J.E. Beaucaire. *Co-Ex Pro* Jack Rollins, Charles H. Joffe and Letty Aronson. Co-*Pro* Richard Brick. *Ph* Sven Nykvist. *Pro Des* Santo Loquasto. *Ed* Susan E. Morse. *M* Beethoven, Wagner; songs performed by Little Jack Little, The Dave Brubeck Quartet, Janet Marlow, Billie Holiday, Liberace, Teddy Wilson, Stan Getz and Sammy Fain, Erroll Garner, Jackie Gleason and His Orchestra, Ray Cohen, etc. *Costumes* Suzy Benzinger.

Magnolia Prods/Sweetland Films – Buena Vista.
114 mins. USA. 1998. Rel: 18 June 1999. Cert 18.

Central Station – Central do Brasil ★★★★

On the bustling, crowded concourse of Rio de Janeiro's central railway station, the elderly Dora ekes out a living writing letters for the illiterate. Then, in the evening, she takes the letters home, laughs over them with her neighbour and discards them. However, when the author of one correspondence is killed by a bus,

Dora finds herself taking pity on the woman's nine-year-old son, Josue. Through the letter of the deceased, Dora has become the only person who knows the whereabouts of the child's father and for once in her life decides to embark on a selfless act ... An uncompromising yet poetic fable, this award-winning Brazilian film makes no concessions to sentimentality and repeatedly defies expectation. Furthermore, it offers a fascinating and vibrant portrait of contemporary Brazil, a country depicted as turbulent, callous and cynical, yet strangely life-enhancing. These downtrodden people may grumble about their lot, but they do so with passion and gusto. Yet *Central Station* is also melancholy in the extreme, as a touching, grown-up and ultimately haunting contemplation of loss and hope.

● *Dora* Fernanda Montenegro, *Irene* Marilla Pera, *Josue* Vinicius de Olivewira, *Ana* Soia Lira, *Cesar* Othon Bastos, *Pedrao* Otavio Augusto, Stela Freitas, Matheus Nachtergaele, Caio Junqueira.
● *Dir* Walter Salles, *Pro* Martine De Clermont-Tonnerre and Arthur Cohn, *Ex Pro* Elisa Tolomelli, Lillian Birnbaum, Don Ranvaud and Thomas Garvin, *Assoc Pro* Paulo Brito and Jack Gajos, *Screenplay* Joao Emanuel Carneiro and Marcos Bernstein, *Ph* Walter Carvalho, *Pro Des* Cassio Amarante and Carla Caffe, *Ed* Isabelle Rathery and Felipe Lacerda, *M* Antonio Pinto and Jaques Morelembaum, *Costumes* Cristina Camargo.

Videofilmes/Mact Prods/Canal Plus/French Ministry of Culture/Sundance Institute, etc – Buena Vista.
110 mins. Brazil/France/Spain/Japan. 1998. Rel: 12 March 1999. Cert 15.

Character – Karakter ★★½

Rotterdam; the 1920s. Having just passed his bar exam, young Jacob Willem Katadreuffe visits his father – the ruthless bailiff Dreverhaven – for the last time. Later that night, covered in blood, Jacob is arrested for Dreverhaven's murder. Methodically, under the patient gaze of a police interrogator, Jacob recounts the extraordinary story of the battle of wills that formed his relationship with his father … An interminable, unremittingly austere adaptation of the revered Dutch novel by Ferdinand Bordewijk, *Character* is yet another inexplicable winner of the Oscar for Best Foreign Film. While the production's first half is compelling enough with its Kafka-esque vision of dark times, the pay-off is a long time a-coming – and a bit of a let-down at that.

● *Jacob Willem Katadreuffe* Fedja van Huet, *Dreverhaven* Jan Decleir, *Joba* Betty Schuurman, *De Gankelaar* Victor Low, *Lorna Te George* Tamar van den Dop, *Jan Maan* Hans Kesting, Lou Landre, Bernhard Droog, Jack Hedley.
● *Dir* Mike van Diem, *Pro* Laurens Geels, *Line Pro* Volkert Struycken, *Screenplay* Van Diem, Geels and Ruud van Megen, *Ph* Rogier Stoffers, *Pro Des* Jelier & Schaaf, *Ed* Jessica de Koning, *M* Het Paleis van Boem, *Sound* Peter Warnier.

Almerica Film/NPS Made – Gala Film.
125 mins. Netherlands. 1997. Rel: 11 September 1998. Cert PG.

A Civil Action ★★★

Boston, Massachusetts; 1981-89. Jan Schlichtmann is an extremely successful personal-injury attorney and one of Boston's ten most eligible bachelors. But, while affecting an air of humanitarianism, he is really a ruthless materialist, a man who will stop at nothing to wring the most money out of his corporate victims. Then, when he takes on a case of illegally dumped toxic solvents, he pushes himself to the limit in order to see justice done … Marking the second directorial outing of Steven Zaillian (following his outstanding *Searching for Bobby Fischer* in 1993), *A Civil Action* starts superbly but fails to live up to its early promise. In a market glutted with thrilling courtroom dramas, this meticulously crafted docudrama is just not special enough to fire the emotions. Part of the problem is the script which, for all its canny insights and quotable dialogue ('a lawyer who shares his client's pain is as unhelpful as a doctor who recoils from the sight of blood'), just runs out of steam near the end. Nonetheless, this is a thoughtful and intelligent, if occasionally languorous, entertainment. In addition, there is a barn-storming performance from Robert Duvall as Schlichtman's wily, rumpled opponent, a man who knows the law so well that he's no longer bothered by outward appearances.

● *Jan Schlichtmann* John Travolta, *Jerome Facher* Robert Duvall, *Al Love* James Gandolfini, *John Riley* Dan Hedaya, *Judge Skinner* John Lithgow, *James Gordon* William H. Macy, *Anne Anderson* Kathleen

Below: A prince of the action: John Travolta considers his future in Steven Zaillian's meditative and insightful A Civil Action *(from UIP)*

Quinlan, *Kevin Conway* Tony Shalhoub, *Bill Crowley* Zeljko Ivanek, *William Cheeseman* Bruce Norris, *Richard Aufiero* David Thornton, *Al Eustis* Sydney Pollack, *Uncle Pete* Ned Eisenberg, *Mr Granger* Daniel Von Bargen, Peter Jacobson, Mary Mara, Stephen Fry, Margot Rose, Paul Ben-Victor, Sam Travolta, Byron Jennings, Jay Patterson, and (uncredited) Kathy Bates, Edward Herrmann.
● *Dir* and *Screenplay* Steven Zaillian, from the book by Jonathan Harr, *Pro* Scott Rudin, Robert Redford and Rachel Pfeffer, *Ex Pro* Zaillian and David Wisnievitz, *Ph* Conrad L. Hall, *Pro Des* David Gropman, *Ed* Wayne Wahrman, *M* Danny Elfman; songs performed by Captain Beefheart, and U2, *Costumes* Shay Cunliffe.

Paramount Pictures/Touchstone Pictures/Wildwood Enterprises – UIP.
115 mins. USA. 1998. Rel: 9 April 1999. Cert 15.

Class Trip – La Classe de neige ★★★¹/₂

The product of over-protective parents, Nicolas is driven by his father to join his classmates at a mountain lodge for the school's annual ski trip. Already an outsider, Nicolas finds his belated arrival just adds a greater distance between him and his peers. And when his father drives off with his luggage, he is left at the mercy of the charity of his hosts. But there is sound reason for the boy's alienation, a condition Nicolas cloaks in bizarre fantasies … A chilling journey into the disturbed mind of a young boy, Claude Miller's *Class Trip* displays a masterly control of its subject as fantasy blends with reality – and vice versa. Subtly transposing the boy's confused p.o.v. onto the audience, Miller – ably assisted by scenarist Emmanuel Carrere – plumbs the tortured psychology of his pubescent protagonist so that we, like the boy, are unable to distinguish between what is imagined and what is real. But then, in a mindscape like this, is fantasy an escape or a channel for something much darker? The assured camerawork of Schiffman is a major bonus.

● *Nicolas* Clement Van Den Bergh, *Hodkann* Lokman Nalcakan, *Patrick* Yves Verhoeven, *Miss Grimm* Emmanuelle Bercot, *the father* Francois Roy, *the mother* Tina Sportolaro, Chantal Banlier, Anthea Sogno, Cecile Simeone.
● *Dir* Claude Miller, *Pro* Annie Miller, *Screenplay* Claude Miller and Emmanuel Carrere, form the latter's novel, *Ph* Guillaume Schiffman, *Pro Des* Jean-Pierre Kohut-Svelko, *Ed* Anne Lafarge, *M* Henri Texier, Nathan Miller, *Costumes* Jacqueline Bouchard.

Les Films de la Boissiere/PECF/France 3 Cinema/Canal Plus, etc – Blue Light.
97 mins. France. 1998. Rel: 22 January 1999. Cert 15.

Clockwatchers ★★¹/₂

Initially unnerved by the Draconian rules of office life, Iris Chapman, an inefficient temp – or 'transient' – gradually warms to her place in the stifled corridors of the Global Credit Association. Buttressed by the collusion of fellow temps Margaret (the rebel), Paula (the aspiring actress) and Jane (the imminent bride), Iris gains a confidence in her position that brings a new sense of self-worth … As an antidote to the dinosaurs, meteors and car crashes routinely doled out by Hollywood, there is a certain novelty value in a film that builds high drama around a world governed by staples, paper clips and rubber bands. And, indeed, it is the details of office life that gains this slight exercise some comic mileage: Lisa Kudrow painting her fingernails with Tipp-Ex, Jamie Kennedy getting high from sniffing marker pens and Toni Collette stapling the hem of her dress to meet office guidelines. Yet, for all its winning observations, this contemplative comedy of office politics is little more than a 30-minute sketch stretched to breaking point.

● *Iris Chapman* Toni Collette, *Margaret J. Burrell* Parker Posey, *Paula* Lisa Kudrow, *Jane* Alanna Ubach, *Cleo* Helen Fitzgerald, *Art* Stanley DeSantis, *Eddie Poe* Jamie Kennedy, *MacNamee* David James Elliott, *Barbara* Debra Jo Rupp, Kevin Cooney, Bob Balaban, *Bud Chapman* Paul Dooley, Athena Ulbach, O-Lan Jones.
● *Dir* Jill Sprecher, *Pro* Gina Resnick, *Ex Pro* John Flock, *Co-Pro* Karen Sprecher, *Co-Ex Pro* John Quested and Guy Collins, *Screenplay* Jill Sprecher and Karen Sprecher, *Ph* Jim Denault, *Pro Des* Pamela Marcotte, *Ed* Stephen Mirrione, *M* Mader, *Costumes* Edi Giguere.

Goldcrest – Feature Film Co.
91 mins. 1997. USA. Rel: 12 March 1999. Cert 16 [sic].

The Corruptor ★¹/₂

The first Chinese-born cop in New York's 15th precinct, Nick Chen is charged with defusing an escalating turf war in Chinatown. However, he hadn't bargained on the hindrance of his callow new partner, Danny Wallace, a Cantonese-speaking Irish-American. But then there might be more to Danny than meets the eye … Nobly, director James Foley (*At Close Range, Fear*) attempts to introduce a note of sober reality into what is basically a standard cop thriller. But by solemnising the image of an icon more readily associated with the slam-bang, fabulously kitsch pyrotechnics of John Woo, Foley does his star an injustice. For while *The Los Angeles Times* dubbed Chow Yun-Fat 'the coolest actor in the world', Chow's limited emotional range and melon-faced features hardly lend themselves to naturalistic drama. The result, then, is rather like extracting the curry powder from a meat madras. So, for all the geysers of blood, car wrecks and detonations, *The Corruptor* comes off as surprisingly mechanical and uninspiring.

Right: Sarah Michelle Gellar *(top right) takes time off from vampire slaying in* Cruel Intentions *(from Columbia TriStar)*

● *Nick Chen* Chow Yun-Fat, *Danny Wallace* Mark Wahlberg, *Henry Lee* Ric Young, *Schabacker* Paul-Ben Victor, *Sean Wallace* Brian Cox, *Benny Wong* Kim Chan, *Jack* Jon Kit Lee, *May* Marie Matiko, Andrew Pang, Byron Mann, Elizabeth Lindsey, Tovah Feldshuh, Beau Starr, *himself* Chuck Scarborough.
● *Dir* James Foley, *Pro* Dan Halsted, *Ex Pro* Oliver Stone, Terence Chang, Bill Carraro and Jay Stern, *Screenplay* Robert Pucci, *Ph* Juan Ruiz-Anchia, *Pro Des* David Brisbin, *Ed* Howard E. Smith, *M* Carter Burwell; songs performed by Madonna, Third Eye Blind, Frank Sinatra and Count Basie, John Coltrane and Johnny Hartman, DMX, KRS-One and Prodigy, Britney Spears, Marc Dorsey, etc, *Costumes* Doug Hall.

New Line/Illusion Entertainment – Entertainment.
110 mins. USA. 1999. Rel: 21 May 1999. Cert 18.

Cousin Bette ★★★

Paris; 1846-48. On her death bed, the aristocratic Adeline Hulot begs her cousin Bette to look after her family. With barely a hint of menace, Bette promises, 'I'll take care of them all.' And so the embittered spinster sets about laying lethal traps for her financially reckless and morally wanton kin ... Lively direction, exquisite production design and an intriguing mix of actors (cast largely against type) go some way in bringing Honore de Balzac's 1847 novel to life. Jessica Lange in particular is a revelation as the conniving and manipulative Cousin Bette (at one stage described 'as an ugly old hag') who, by resisting the temptation to play to the gods, brings a surprising complexity and empathy to her 'villainess'. Hugh Laurie, too, is sheer pleasure, transforming even the dullest dialogue into priceless wit.

● *Bette Fisher* Jessica Lange, *Jenny Cadine* Elisabeth Shue, *Cesar Crevel* Bob Hoskins, *Baron Hector Hulot* Hugh Laurie, *Hortense Hulot* Kelly Macdonald, *Count Wenceslas Steinbach* Aden Young, *Adeline Hulot* Geraldine Chaplin, *Victorin Hulot* Toby Stephens, *Mariette* Laura Fraser, John Benfield, Janie Hargreaves, Gillian Martell, John Sessions, John Quentin, Heathcote Williams, Philip Jackson.
● *Dir* Des McAnuff, *Pro* Sarah Radclyffe, *Ex Pro* Susan Tarr, Lynn Siefert and Rob Scheidlinger, *Co-Pro* Philippe Guez, *Assoc Pro* Neris Thomas, *Screenplay* Siefert and Tarr, *Ph* Andrzej Sekula, *Pro Des* Hugo Luczyc-Wyhowski, *Ed* Tariq Anwar and Barry Alexander Brown, *M* Simon Boswell; Offenbach, Bellini, Mozart, Mendelssohn; songs performed by Elisabeth Shue, *Costumes* Gabriella Pescucci.

Fox – Fox.
108 mins. USA/UK. 1997. Rel: 11 September 1998. Cert 15.

Croupier ★★★

London; the present. While struggling with his first novel, Jack Manfred lands a job as a croupier at an exclusive casino. And, while initially observing the rigid rules of the club, he gradually succumbs to the odd lapse of propriety, ostensibly to feed his book ... Recalling the sparse, moody thrillers of the Sixties, *Croupier* is a lean, mean thriller with a neat line in intrigue. Dominated by a tightly coiled performance from Clive Owen (resembling a latter-day Laurence Harvey), the film may not engage the gut but it certainly captures the brain.

● *Jack Manfred* Clive Owen, *Bella* Kate Hardie, *Jani de Villiers* Alex Kingston, *Marion Neil* Gina McKee, *David Reynolds* Alexander Morton, *Matt* Paul Reynolds, *Jack Manfred Snr* Nicholas Ball, Nick Reding, Ozzi Yue, Tom Mannion, James Clyde, Emma Lewis, Kate Fenwick, Ciro de Chiara, Barnaby Kay, David Hamilton, Andros Epaminondas, Rhona Mitra, Rosemarie Dunham, Simon Fisher Turner, Sven Morche, Loretta Parnell.
● *Dir* Mike Hodges, *Pro* Jonathan Cavendish, *Ex Pro* James Mitchell, *Co-Pro* Christine Ruppert, *Line Pro* Jake Lloyd, *Screenplay* Paul Mayersberg, *Ph* Mike Garfath, *Pro Des* Jon Bunker, *Ed* Les Healey, *M* Simon Fisher Turner, *Costumes* Caroline Harris.

BFI/Channel Four/Filmstiftung/NRW/WDR/La Sept Cinema/Arte/Little Bird/Tatfilm – BFI.
89 mins. UK. 1997. Rel: 18 June 1999. Cert 15.

Cruel Intentions ★★★

Cursed with too much money and precocious good looks, Kathryn and Sebastian are a pair of Manhattan step-siblings who have seen and had it all. So, to amuse themselves, they set about destroying the lives of the less sexually sophisticated. Then, to up the stakes, Kathryn promises her own body to Sebastian if he can deflower the resolutely virginal daughter of their new headmaster ... *Dangerous Liaisons*-lite for an all-new sexually savvy generation, *Cruel Intentions* is slick, audacious and cold-blooded fun. Of course, what seemed tenable to the bored aristocracy of pre-Revolutionary France doesn't entirely sit comfortably with these American teens (particularly in the age of AIDS), but it's a change from *Sleepless in Seattle*. The only problem is that the young leads here – perhaps because of their own lack of sexual maturity – give the impression that they are just 'playing' adult games when they should be actually living them.

● *Kathryn Merteuil* Sarah Michelle Gellar, *Sebastian Valmont* Ryan Phillippe, *Annette Hargrove* Reese Witherspoon, *Cecile Caldwell* Selma Blair, *Helen Rosemond* Louise Fletcher, *Blaine Tuttle* Joshua Jackson, *Greg McConnell* Eric Mabius, *Ronald Clifford* Sean Patrick Thomas, *Dr Greenbaum* Swoosie Kurtz, *Bunny Caldwell* Christine Baranski, *Marci Greenbaum* Tara Reid, Alaina Reed Hall, Deborah Offner, Herta Ware, Hiep Thi Le, Charlie O'Connell, Drew Snyder.
● *Dir* and *Screenplay* Roger Kumble, *Pro* Neal H. Moritz, *Ex Pro* Michael Fottrell, *Co-Pro* Heather Zeegen, *Ph* Theo Van de Sande, *Pro Des* Jon Gary Steele, *Ed* Jeff Freeman, *M* Edward Shearmur; Beethoven, J.S. Bach; songs performed by Placebo, Bare Jr., Blur, The Cardigans, Kristen Barry, Marcy Playground, Faithless, Abra Moore, Fatboy Slim, Day One, Counting Crows, Craig Armstrong and Elizabeth Fraser, Aimee Mann, The Verve, Skunk Anansie, etc, *Costumes* Denise Wingate.

Columbia/Original Film/Newmarket Capital – Columbia TriStar.
97 mins. USA. 1999. Rel: 11 June 1999. Cert 15.

Crush Proof ★★★¹/₂

Dublin, Ireland; today. Just released from prison, 18-year-old Neal attempts to see his infant son but is promptly chased off by police. Reunited with his friends from the more squalid quarter of Dublin's inner city, Neal sets about avenging himself on the boy who shopped him to the cops. But, following a fatal prank, Neal is on the run again, taking to the hills on horseback ... Utilising edgy, hand-held camerawork, time-jumping cuts and an omnipresent rock soundtrack, Paul Tickell builds a powerful climate of unease and immediacy in what is an extremely impressive directorial debut. Like its primal, bitter hero, the film gives the impression it could go off in any direction at any given moment – to devastating results. And with the deployment of real teenagers in the main roles – as opposed to young twentysomethings playing 'down' – the film gains a potent credibility extremely rare in young cinema. One may find the Irish accents on the impenetrable side, but it's a

small sacrifice for such raw, passionate drama. FYI: The film's associate producer, Sophie Fiennes, is the sister of actors Ralph and Joseph.

● *Neal* Darren Healy, *Nuala* Viviana Verveen, *Liam* Jeff O'Toole, *Sean* Mark Dunne, *Det. Sgt. Hogan* Michael McElhatton, *Suki* Lisa Fleming, *Red Andi* Mary Murray, *Aisling* Fiona Glascott, *Neal's mother* Charlotte Bradley, *Neal's father* Stuart Dunne, Gavin Kelty, John Conroy, Gerard Kearney, Anton Stafford, Gerard Byrne.
● *Dir* Paul Tickell, *Pro* Kees Kasender, *Ex Pro* Terry Glinwood, Bob Hubar and Denis Wigman, *Assoc Pro* Sophie Fiennes, *Screenplay* James Mathers, *Ph* Reiner van Brummelen, *Pro Des* Tom Controy, *Ed* Catherine Reed and Chris Wyatt, *M* Attie Bauw; songs performed by Triple A & Juliet Carion, Speedy J, Eric Burdon & The Animals, Lunatic Calm, and The Youngbloods, *Costumes* Marie Tierney.

WoodLine Prods/Movie Masters/Liquid Films/Continent Film/Irish Film Board, etc – Clarence Pictures.
91 mins. UK/Netherlands/Ireland/Germany. 1998. Rel: 4 June 1999. Cert 18.

Cube ★★★¹/₂

Six disparate characters – a cop, doctor, schoolgirl, autistic savant, escape artist and graphic designer – wake up to find themselves incarcerated in a network of cubical chambers. Interconnected by trap doors, the 14 foot by 14 foot cubes form an interminable maze of escape routes and dead ends armed with vicious and ingenious death traps. If the prisoners could stop panicking for an instant and pool their human resources then maybe they could find a way out ... Following the unsubtle excess of such geometrically-bent sci-fi thrillers as *Event Horizon* and *Sphere*, it's a relief to encounter something a little more intellectually challenging. Relying heavily on claustrophobia and paranoia, director and co-writer Vincenzo Natali builds up an intriguing and suspenseful *mise en scene* in which anything might – and does – happen. It helps, too, that the capable members of the cast are complete unknowns, as there's no foreseeable logic to their characters' termination.

● *Leaven* Nicole deBoer, *Helen Holloway* Nicky Guadagni, *David Worth* David Hewlett, *Kazan* Andrew Miller, *Rennes* Wayne Robson, *Quentin* Maurice Dean Wint.
● *Dir* Vincenzo Natali, *Pro* Mehra Meh and Betty Orr, *Ex Pro* Colin Brunton, *Screenplay* Natali, Andre Bijelic and Graeme Manson, *Ph* Derek Rogers, *Pro Des* Jasna Stefanovic, *Ed* John Sanders, *M* Mark Korven.

Cuba Libre/Canadian Film Centre/Feature Film Projects/Telefilm Canada/Ontario Film Development Corp/Viacom Canada – First Independent.
92 mins. Canada. 1997. Rel: 25 September 1998. Cert 15

Above: Shall We Salsa? Anne Noell, Vanessa L. Williams and Alyra Lennox shimmy to a Latin beat in Randa Haines' vigorous if predictable Dance With Me *(from Entertainment)*

Dance of the Wind – Wara Mandel
★★★¹/₂

New Delhi; today. Under the unflagging tutelage of her mother and guru, Pallavi Sehgel is learning the ancient art of classical Hindustani song. A performer of some renown in her own right, Pallavi is nonetheless devastated when her mother dies, as she feels she has not yet fully mastered her craft, a skill which can only be passed from guru to pupil through oral instruction. Losing her voice completely, Pallavi embarks on a mystical quest to find the missing component of her calling ... Blending parable, allegory and contemporary realism, *Dance of the Wind* is a poetic, deceptively simple and visually bewitching fable that heralds a major new Indian talent in first-time director Rajan Khosa. Sensually lit and richly designed, the film evokes a vivid sense of time and place that is as mesmerising as it is revealing of an ancient culture on the verge of extinction.

● *Pallavi Sehgel, aka Deedi* Kitu Gidwani, *Ranmal* Bhaveen Gosain, *Tara* Roshan Bano, *Karuna Devi* Kapila Vatsyayan, *Shabda* Punarnava Mehta, *Janaki* Ami Arora, *Munir Babar* B.C. Sanyal, *Mr Thakkar* Vinod Hagpal.

● *Dir* Rajan Khosa, *Pro* Karl Baumgartner, Co-*Pro* Keith Griffiths, Jacques Bidou and Phil Van Der Linden, *Line Pro* Nalin Pandya and Raimond Goebel, *Screenplay* Robin Mukherjee, *Ph* Piyush Shah, *Pro Des* Amardeep Behl, *Ed* Emma Matthews, *M* Shubha Medgal, *Costumes* Namrata Joshipura, *Sound* Vikram Joglekar.

Pandora Film/Elephant Eye/Illuminations Films/ JBA Prods/Filmcompany/NFDC – Artificial Eye. 85 mins. Germany/UK/France/The Netherlands/India/ Switzerland. 1997. Rel: 24 July 1998. Cert U.

Dance With Me ★★¹/₂

When John Burnett, the disillusioned owner of a run-down Houston dance studio, hires a new Cuban handyman, little does he anticipate the influence that the Latino will have on his – and his employees' – life. Burnett's star instructor, the beautiful Ruby St. Clair, thinks the newcomer is a cocky upstart, but boy can the boy shimmy ... With a title like *Dance With Me*, you'd expect a little bit of tripping the light fantastic. And there's plenty here to go round: ballroom, cha cha, foxtrot, paso doble, quickstep, rhumba, salsa,

samba, tango – and even ballet. But don't expect too much else in the way of cinematic nourishment. The story's signposts are laid out so blatantly, it's a wonder nobody cracks their head on them. Still, the music's great, the dancing is well choreographed and vigorous and Joan Plowright (of all people) is a scream as a spirited, matronly flirt. It's just a shame that the multi-talented Vanessa L. Williams (nude model, Miss America, singer, dancer, actress, pianist, charity worker, you name it) is made up to look like a drag queen in the grand finale (and, at that, indecently too mature for young Chayanne).

● *Ruby St. Clair* Vanessa L. Williams, *Rafael Infante* Chayanne, *John Burnett* Kris Kristofferson, *Bea Johnson* Joan Plowright, *Patricia Black* Jane Krakowski, *Jewel Lovejoy* Beth Grant, *Stefano* William Marquez, *Julian* Rick Valenzuela, Harry Groener, Scott Paetty, Chaz Oswill, Liz Curtis, Mike Gomez.
● *Dir* Randa Haines, *Pro* Haines, Lauren C. Weissman and Shinya Egawa, *Ex Pro* Ted Zachary, *Assoc Pro* Aldric La'auli Porter and Allan Wertheim, *Screenplay* Daryl Matthews, *Ph* Fred Murphy, *Pro Des* Waldemar Kalinowski, *Ed* Lisa Fruchtman, *M* Michael Convertino; songs performed by Septeto Nacional, Diana Krall, Electra, Roy Orbison, Chet Baker, Jackie Wilson, DLG, Gloria Estefan, Ruben Blades, Cachao, The Manhattan Transfer, Dean Martin, Sinead O'Connor, Gipsy Kings, Aretha Franklin, Vanessa L. Williams and Chayanne, etc, *Costumes* Joe I. Tompkins, *Choreography* Matthews and Liz Curtis.

Mandalay Entertainment – Entertainment.
126 mins. USA. 1998. Rel: 23 April 1999. Cert PG.

Dancing at Lughnasa ★¹/₂

Rose Mundy is a bit potty, Jack Mundy is completely off his rocker and Kate Mundy is only now beginning to realise that she is 'a damned righteous bitch.' It is 1936 in the rolling countryside of Donegal, Ireland, and the five unmarried Mundy sisters are facing a domestic crisis in the midst of their austere, secluded lives ... A wonderful array of actresses and some outstanding production values cannot salvage what is desperately inert cinema. And, as fine a performer as Meryl Streep is, it was inadvisable to cast her in such a fragile ensemble piece, as, inevitably, her star presence upsets the balance of the film. Still, she rustles up a better Irish accent than does Michael Gambon, whose strange English vowels seem markedly out of place. Based on the award-winning play by Brian Friel.

● *Kate Mundy* Meryl Streep, *Father Jack Mundy* Michael Gambon, *Christina Mundy* Catherine McCormack, *Maggie Mundy* Kathy Burke, *Rose Mundy* Sophie Thompson, *Agnes Mundy* Brid Brennan, *Gerry Evans* Rhys Ifans, *Michael Mundy* Darrell Johnston, Lorcan Cranitch, Peter Gowen, Dawn Bradfield, Marie Mullen, John Kavanagh, Kate O'Toole, and *narrator, Michael as an adult* Gerald McSorley.
● *Dir* Pat O'Connor, *Pro* Noel Pearson, *Ex Pro* Jane Barclay, Sharon Harel and Rod Stoneman, *Screenplay* Frank McGuinness, *Ph* Kenneth MacMillan, *Pro Des* Mark Geraghty, *Ed* Humphrey Dixon, *M* Bill Whelan, *Costumes* Joan Bergin.

Ferndale Films/Capitol Films/Sony Pictures Classics/ Channel Four/Irish Film Board, etc – Film Four.
95 mins. Ireland/UK/USA. 1998. Rel: 4 December 1998. Cert PG.

Above: Family outing: Hope Davis, Liev Schreiber and Parker Posey enjoy the view in Greg Mottola's endearing and episodic The Daytrippers *(from Metrodome)*

Dangerous Beauty
See *The Honest Courtesan*.

The Daytrippers ★★½
Long Island/Manhattan; the present. Under the impression that she is perfectly happily married, Eliza D'Amico is somewhat taken aback when she discovers what seems to be a love note written to her husband, Louis. Popping in to confer with her mother and father, she is abruptly caught up in a outing to the city in an attempt to track Louis down. Accompanied not only by her argumentative parents, but by her sister Jo and Jo's new boyfriend, Eliza is made only too aware that she is not the only one with romantic problems ... Inspired by the claim that 97 per cent of all families are dysfunctional, writer-director Greg Mottola has fashioned an endearing and quirky first feature blessed with a top-drawer cast. A tad episodic and rather rough round the edges, *The Daytrippers* is not as funny as it could have been, but it certainly has its moments. Choice episodes: the world's shortest car chase and Carl's inappropriate presence during an acceptance speech.

● *Eliza D'Amico* Hope Davis, *Jim Malone* Pat McNamara, *Rita Malone* Anne Meara, *Jo Malone, Eliza's sister* Parker Posey, *Carl* Liev Schreiber, *Eddie* Campbell Scott, *Louis D'Amico* Stanley Tucci, *Libby* Marcia Gay Harden, Andy Brown, Paul Herman, Marc Grapey, Marcia Haufrecht, Douglas McGrath, Amy Stiller, Stephanie Venditto, Ford Evanson.
● *Dir* and *Screenplay* Greg Mottola, *Pro* Nancy Tenenbaum and Steven Soderbergh, *Ex Pro* Lawrence S. Kamerman, David Heyman and Campbell Scott, *Ph* John Inwood, *Pro Des* Bonnie J. Brinkley, *Ed* Anne McCabe, *M* Richard Martinez; songs performed by Los Islenos, Stan Getz, Freddie McKay, Blair, etc, *Costumes* Barbara Presar.

Fiasco Photoplays/Trick Films – Metrodome.
87 mins. USA. 1996. Rel: 24 July 1998. Cert 15.

Dead Man's Curve ★★½
After stumbling onto a little-known college clause that permits a student a straight-A average should their room-mate take his own life, Tim and Chris hit on a plan. Planting depression-friendly evidence on their room-mate (a copy of *The Bell Jar*, CDs of The Cure, Suzanne Vega, etc), the sick duo unwittingly kick-start a chain reaction of suicides ... A novel and frequently inventive spin on the campus murder genre, *Dead Man's Curve* displays some visual style, above average performances (for this sort of thing) and a smattering of good in-jokes (a psychiatrist confides that she finds films by first-time directors a cause of suicidal depression). However, once the intriguing set-up has been played out and the barrel of suicide gags drained dry (*everybody* smokes in this movie), things descend into

a downward curve of foreseeable plot twists. Sadly, the film is not as clever as it thinks it is, nor is it as funny, scary or tenable. FYI: First-time director Dan Rosen previously wrote the screenplay for *The Last Supper*.

● *Tim* Matthew Lillard, *Chris Mason* Michael Vartan, *Rand* Randall Batinkoff, *Emma* Keri Russell, *Natalie Broder* Tamara Craig Thomas, *Detective Mike Schipper* Anthony Griffin, *Detective Theo Amato* Bo Dietle, *Officer Ruff* Kevin Ruff, *Chancellor C. Alexander* Henry Strozier, *Dr Ashley* Dana Delany, Ben Livingston, Kris McGaha, Nora Pierce, Amy Raymond, Bernard Rosen.
● *Dir* and *Screenplay* Dan Rosen, *Pro* Michael Amato, Theodore Schipper and Jeremy Lew, *Ex Pro* Alain Siritzky, Pierre Kalfon, Michael Chambat and Ian Jessel, *Co-Pro* William Mercer, *Ph* Joey Forsyte, *Pro Des* Robert Harbour, *Ed* Glenn Garland, *M* Shark; JS Bach; songs performed by Closer, Sarah McLachlan, Mad Season, Bauhaus, Wild Colonials, The Cure, Wench, The The, Joy Division, Aimee Mann, The Smiths, Suzanne Vega, Nick Lowe, Semisonic, etc, *Costumes* Shanna Gold.

Alain Siritzky and Hope Street Entertainment/Mount Royal – Metro Tartan.
90 mins. USA. 1997. Rel: 20 November 1998. Cert 15.

The Debt Collector ★★★★
The past is healing over for Nickie Dryden (Billy Connolly), former loan-shark and convicted murderer, now a socially reformed character, sculptor and writer. Just as it seems to be falling into place the policeman responsible for his conviction, Gary Keltie, crashes in to make sure nothing will be forgotten. This is an original and dark Scottish drama, tightly paced and ringing with the sound of good dialogue written by director Neilson. Francesca Annis plays Dryden's classy wife and Annette Crosbie Keltie's old mother. [*Marianne Gray*]

● *Nickie Dryden* Billy Connolly, *Gary Keltie* Ken Stott, *Val Dryden* Francesca Annis, *Flipper* Iain Robertson, *Lana* Annette Crosbie, *Colquhoun* Alistair Galbraith, *Catriona* Shauna MacDonald, *Jobbie* James Thomson, Gordon Orr, Sandy Neilson, Steven Duguid, Jimmy Logan, Andrew Neil, Julie Wilson Nimmo, Dawn Steele.
● *Dir* and *Screenplay* Anthony Neilson, *Pro* Graham Broadbent and Damian Jones, *Line Pro* Liz Bunton, *Ph* Dick Pope, *Pro Des* Mark Geraghty, *Ed* John Wilson, *M* Adrian Johnston; Beethoven; songs performed by Thin Lizzy, Mono, Wide Receiver, The Bobby Harvey Band, etc, *Costumes* Trisha Biggar.

Film Four/Glasgow Film Fund/Dragon Pictures – Film Four.
110 mins. UK. 1999. Rel: 25 June 1999. Cert 18.

The Deep End of the Ocean ★★★

Madison, Wisconsin/Chicago, Illinois; 1988-1997. While attending her 15th high school reunion, wife, mother and photographer Beth Cappadora loses her three-year-old son, Ben, in the crowd. And as the minutes turn into hours and the hours into days, with no sign of Ben turning up, Beth faces a crisis of conscience that threatens her marriage and her sanity ... Ulu Grosbard, who's directed such contemplative, star-driven dramas as *True Confessions* and *Falling in Love*, here takes his time unfolding the emotionally excoriating events of Jacqueline Mitchard's number one best-seller. Yet, while he has coaxed a strong performance from Michelle Pfeiffer, he has failed to pinpoint the real pain – and complexity – of such an unbearable situation. And so it's the events themselves – the disappearance, self-recrimination, vacuum of loss – that ply the hard emotional work of the film, not the Cappadoras' reality. So, while the film prompts a lump in the throat, it's still a TV movie or two away from opening any ocular sluice gates.

● *Beth Cappadora* Michelle Pfeiffer, *Det. Candy Bliss* Whoopi Goldberg, *Pat Cappadora* Treat Williams, *Vincent Cappadora* Jonathan Jackson, *George Karras* John Kapelos, *Sam Karras* Ryan Merriman, *Kerry Cappadora* Alexa Vega, Tony Musante, Rose Gregorio, Lucinda Jenney, Cory Buck, John Roselius, Brenda Strong, K.K. Dodds, Michael McGrady, Michael McElroy.
● *Dir* Ulu Grosbard, *Pro* Kate Guinzburg and Steve Nicolaides, *Ex Pro* Frank Capra III, *Screenplay* Stephen Schiff, *Ph* Stephen Goldblatt, *Pro Des* Dan Davis, *Ed* John Bloom, *M* Elmer Bernstein, *Costumes* Susie DeSanto.

Mandalay Entertainment/Via Rosa – Entertainment. 105 mins. USA. 1999. Rel: 4 June 1999. Cert 12.

Deep Rising ★★

There are areas of the South China Sea that are so deep that no one knows for sure what life inhabits the lower depths. It is here that the world's most expensive and luxurious pleasure palace – *The Argonautica* – makes its maiden voyage. But when a band of highly unpleasant, trigger-happy mercenaries board the liner, the ship is deserted. And then all hell breaks loose ... A by-the-numbers B-movie with a budget and an attitude, *Deep Rising* juggles corn and gore with adolescent relish. Yet while the dialogue is as daft as a navel brush ('this is turning out to be one helluva day'), the colourful cross-cultural cast and rapid pace take up some of the slack. The sets are also very impressive, which is more than can be said for the computer-generated monsters and a soundtrack so melodramatic that it provoked laughter from the critics 30 seconds into the film (a record, surely?).

● *John J. Finnegan* Treat Williams, *Trillian* Famke Janssen, *Simon Canton* Anthony Heald, *Joey Pantucci* Kevin J. O'Connor, *Hanover* Wes Studi, *Captain Atherton* Derrick O'Connor, *Mulligan* Jason Flemyng, *Mamooli* Cliff Curtis, *Mason* Clifton Powell, *T. Ray* Trevor Goddard, *Vivo* Djimon Hounsou, *Leila* Una Damon, Clint Curtis, Jana Sommers, Marti Baldecchi.
● *Dir* and *Screenplay* Stephen Sommers, *Pro* Laurence Mark and John Baldecchi, *Ex Pro* Barry Bernardi, *Ph* Howard Atherton, *Pro Des* Holger Gross, *Ed* Bob Ducsay and John Wright, *M* Jerry Goldsmith; songs performed by Yakudo, *Costumes* Joseph Porro, *Sound* Leslie Shatz, Creature design: Rob Bottin, *Mechanical effects* Darrell Pritchett, *Visual effects* Dream Quest/Industrial Light & Magic/Banned From the Ranch.

Hollywood Pictures – Entertainment. 106 mins. USA. 1998. Rel: 18 September 1998. Cert 15.

Deja Vu ★★★¹/₂

Jerusalem/Paris/Dover/London/Los Angeles; the present. Meeting a mysterious French woman on a business trip to Jerusalem, Dana Howard finds herself magically transformed by the stranger's tale of lost love. Stopping off in Paris to return the woman's irreplaceable ruby brooch, Dana is swept into a rip tide of coincidence that threatens to capsize her impending marriage ... Expanding his scope ever wider, Henry Jaglom out-does Woody Allen yet again by setting his most romantic film in *five* different locations, sowing the seeds for a great tale spun from a series of improvisations. Even if one fails to find the theme of coincidence to one's taste, the film offers many ancillary delights: Vanessa Redgrave and her mother Rachel Kempson acting together for the first time (as mother and daughter), and Noel Harrison, the son of Rex, discussing the arcane pleasures of old-fashioned sweets in bed with Anna Massey. Only Victoria Foyt doesn't seem quite right as the impulsive romantic whisked off her feet, even if she did co-write the thing with her husband, the director.

Above: Without a trace: Treat Williams and Michelle Pfeiffer in Ulu Grosbard's almost emotionally excoriating The Deep End of the Ocean *(from Entertainment)*

Right: *Family business: Vanessa Redgrave with her real-life mother Rachel Kempson in Henry Jaglom's romantic and articulate* Déjà Vu *(from UIP)*

● *Sean Elias* Stephen Dillane, *Dana Howard* Victoria Foyt, *Skelly* Vanessa Redgrave, *Claire Stoner* Glynis Barber, *Alex* Michael Brandon, *John Stoner* Noel Harrison, *woman in cafe* Aviva Marks, *Fern Stoner* Anna Massey, *Skelly's mother* Rachel Kempson, *Konstantine* Vernon Dobtcheff, Graydon Gould, Sabrina Jaglom, Simon Orson Jaglom, Carl Duering, Barbara Hicks, *Noel's sister* Cathryn Harrison, Earl Cameron.
● *Dir* and *Ed* Henry Jaglom, *Pro* John Goldstone, *Co-Pro* Judith Wolinsky, *Screenplay* Jaglom and Victoria Foyt, *Ph* Hanania Baer, *Pro Des* Helen Scott, *M* Gaili Schoen; Schubert; songs performed by Vera Lynn, Lena Horne, and Frank Sinatra, *Costumes* Rhona Russell.

Jagtoria/Rainbow Film Company/Revere Entertainment – UIP.
117 mins. USA/UK. 1997. Rel: 16 October 1998. Cert 15.

The Disappearance of Finbar ★¹/₂

A once-promising footballer, Finbar Flynn has become disillusioned by the squalor of his life on a dilapidated housing estate on the outskirts of Dublin. Then, one fateful day, Finbar climbs to the edge of an unfinished flyover and disappears – plunging the community into a crisis of recrimination and establishing the missing youth as something of an unexpected icon ... Starting out as a dreary, pedestrian – even amateurish – Irish drama, this bizarre international co-production revs up into a quirky road movie of some promise, recalling the work of the Icelandic director Fridrik Thor Fridriksson. Packed with flavoursome songs and some splendid Scandinavian locations, the film strives for a kind of mystical realism but ultimately fails to charm or captivate.

● *Finbar Flynn* Jonathan Rhys Meyers, *Danny Quinn* Luke Griffin, *Detective Roche* Sean McGinley, *Katie Dunnigan* Lorraine Pilkington, *Ellen Quinn* Marie Mullen, *Grandpa Quinn* Don Foley, *Abbi* Fanny Risberg, *Johanna* Sif Ruud, Sean Lawlor, Eleanor Methven, Laura Brennan, Tina Kellegher, Barry McGovern, Ciara Wong, Joe Savino, Rob Brown, Per Mattsson, Mikael Toyra, Sten Ljunggren, Antti Reini, Thomas Hedengran, Lennart Johansson, Thomas Laustiola.
● *Dir* Sue Clayton, *Pro* Bertil Ohlsson and Martin Bruce-Clayton, *Ex Pro* Jonathan Olsberg and Ole Sondberg, *Co-Pro* David Collins and Soren Staermose, *Screenplay* Clayton and Dermot Bolger, from the novel *The Disappearance of Rory Brophy* by Carl Lombard, *Ph* Eduardo Serra, *Pro Des* Ned McLoughlin and Conor Devlin (*Ireland*), and Bengt Froderberg (*Sweden*), *Ed* J. Patrick Duffner and Alan Strachan, *M* Davy Spillane; 'The Ballad of Finbar Flynn' performed by Gets/z Loose, *Costumes* Marie Tierney (*Ireland*) and Kersti Vitali (*Sweden*).

First City Features/Samson Films/Victoria Film/Film Four International/Channel Four/Pandora Cinema/The Irish Film Board/European Script Fund, etc – Ian Rattray.
104 mins. UK/Ireland/Sweden/France. 1996. Rel: 23 October 1998. Cert 15.

Divorcing Jack ★★★★

Belfast, Northern Ireland; 1999. Less willing to tow the editorial line than his colleagues, satirical columnist Dan Starkey has won as many enemies as he has admirers. A new adversary is his wife, who storms off to her parents after catching him sharing a peppermint with a young art student. Yet, for all his alcoholic binges, Dan has been a faithful husband – but with the IRA, Ulster Volunteer Force, Royal Ulster Constabulary and British army about to descend on him, all that could change ... Recalling the dark social commentary of Lindsay Anderson's best work, *Divorcing Jack* succeeds on multiple levels: as satire, farce, thriller and – well, almost – romance. Yet, for the film to have made the leap from entertaining black comedy to something entirely more credible, an actor with more charisma than David Thewlis would have helped. While the latter supplies the requisite sarcasm and alcoholic miasma, it's hard to imagine complete strangers as comely as Rachel Griffiths and Laura Fraser falling so quickly for his charms. Still, it's certainly the best thing Thewlis has done since *Naked*.

● *Dan Starkey* David Thewlis, *Lee Cooper* Rachel Griffiths, *'Cow Pat' Keegan* Jason Isaacs, *Michael Brinn* Robert Lindsay, *Patricia Starkey* Laine Megaw, *Margaret McGarry* Laura Fraser, *Mouse* Alan McKee, *taxi driver* Bronagh Gallagher, *Charles Parker* Richard Gant, George Shane, Brian Devlin, Sean Caffrey, Birdy Sweeney, Ian McElhinney, Kitty Aldridge, Paddy Rocks, Derek Halligan, John Keegan, Brendan McNally.
● *Dir* David Caffrey, *Pro* Robert Cooper, *Ex Pro* Nik Powell, Stephen Woolley and David M. Thompson, *Co-Pro* Frank Mannion and Georges Benayoun, *Line Pro* Jane Robertson, *Screenplay* Colin Bateman, from his novel, *Ph* James Welland, *Pro Des* Claire Kenny, *Ed* Nick Moore, *M* Adrian Johnston; Dvorak, Vivaldi; songs performed by Mike Flowers, The Clash, 3 Colours Red, Linoleum, Stella Parton, Jim Reeves, Country Punk, The Nolans, etc, *Costumes* Pam Tait.

Winchester Films/BBC Films/Scala/Arts Council of England/Arts Council of Northern Ireland/IMA Films/ Canal Plus/Foundry Film – Mosaic Movies. 110 mins. UK/France. 1998. Rel: 2 October 1998. Cert 15.

Dobermann ★★★

Paris; today. For all its high energy, wacky camera angles and visual braggadocio, *Dobermann* is not terribly innovative. The story of an unscrupulous, psychotic cop chasing a gang of unhinged and eccentric bank robbers recalls a huge number of other movies, both in style and content, from the Paris-set *Nikita*, also with Tcheky Karyo, to the Paris-set *Killing Zoe*. But what *Dobermann* does offer is an exaggeration of comic-book chic and violence, which the opening shot of a Doberman urinating on the credits swiftly establishes. The film is also unapologetically sick, its use of a baby for 'catch' and its disposing of the most sympathetic characters a cheap way to drum up hatred for Karyo's sadistic chief inspector (an uncanny impersonation of Steven Berkoff, by the way). Yet, for all that, it is a remarkable piece of film-making, making the most of its limited budget and shooting schedule. Writer-director Jan Kounen will obviously go far.

Above: The fear of God: Paddy Rocks lends an ear to Rachel Griffiths in David Caffrey's darkly entertaining Divorcing Jack (from Mosaic Movies)

Above: Policing the underclass: Tcheky Karyo puts on his mean act in Jan Kounen's sick and outrageous Dobermann (from Metro Tartan)

● *Yann Lepentrec aka Le Dobermann* Vincent Cassel, *Chief Inspector Sauveur Christini* Tcheky Karyo, *Nathalie* Monica Bellucci, *Jean-Claude Ayache aka Moustique* Antoine Basler, *The Priest* Dominique Bettenfeld, *Manu* Romain Duris, *Leo* Francois Levantal, *Olivier Brachet aka Sonia* Stephane Metzger, *Pitbull* Chick Ortega, *Inspector Lefevre* Pascal Demelon, Marc Duret, Ivan Merat-Barboff, Patrick Rocca, Roland Amstutz, Jean Lescot, Florence Thomassin, Laura Mana, Virginie Arnaud, Marc Caro, Elle Chocho, Frederique Dumas, *Roquette* Jan Kounen, Eric Neve.
● *Dir* and *Screenplay* Jan Kounen, *Pro* Frederique Dumas and Eric Neve, *Ex Pro* Marc Baschet, *Assoc Pro* Ken Nakagawa, *Ph* Michel Amathieu, *Pro Des* Michel Barthelemy, *Ed* Benedicte Shorr, *M* Schyzomaniac; 'Voodoo People' performed by Prodigy, *Costumes* Chattoune et Fab, *Sound* Richard Shorr, *Digital effects* Mac Guff Ligne.

Noe Prods/Canal Plus/PolyGram Audiovisuel/France 3 Cinema/La Chauve Souris/Tawak Pictures/Comstock – Metro Tartan.
103 mins. France. 1997. Rel: 15 January 1999. Cert 18.

Below: Freudian shtick: Tom Conti steals the show in Willi Patterson's ill-contrived Don't Go Breaking My Heart (from PolyGram)

Don't Go Breaking My Heart ★★

All over London; the present. Suzanne's beloved husband has been dead for 18 months now, but she's determined to bring up her son and daughter on her own terms. Her friends, though, are resolved to pair her off and smarmy dentist Frank thinks he's the man for the job. So does Tony, an American 'therapeutic psychological sports trainer' who immediately clicks with Suzanne's troubled 14-year-old son ... For all its good intentions, this unashamedly contrived comedy just doesn't work. In spite of some good moments, the film buckles under the weight of its coincidence-loaded scenario and some appallingly slapdash structure. Worse, the film allows its romantic protagonists little screen time to generate any audience empathy, a fatal flaw for a love story. Both Jenny Seagrove and executive producer Anthony Edwards are extremely likeable, it's just that they seem to be in two different movies. Cherish, then, the scene in which Tom Conti hams it up sublimely as an anal psychiatrist more concerned with the alignment of his possessions than with the state of his bewildered patient.

● *Tony* Anthony Edwards, *Suzanne* Jenny Seagrove, *Frank* Charles Dance, *Juliette* Jane Leeves, *Dr Fiedler* Tom Conti, *Maxine* Lynda Bellingham, *Max* George Layton, *Douglas* Philip McGough, *Sharon* Trevyn McDowell, *Richard* Richard Platt, *Diane* Susannah Doyle, *Ben* Ben Reynolds, *Rex* Suggs, *himself* Linford Christie, Ace Ryan, Amanda Holden, Sam Stockman, Pip Miller, Jeremy Child.
● *Dir* Will Patterson, *Pro* Bill Kenwright, *Ex Pro* Anthony Edwards and Dante di Loreto, *Line Pro* Selwyn Roberts, *Screenplay* Geoff Morrow, *Ph* Vernon Layton, *Pro Des* Tony Noble, *Ed* Peter Beston, *M* Rolfe Kent; songs performed by Elton John and Kiki Dee, The Meteors, Five, Julie London, Gerry and the Pacemakers, Leo Sayer, etc, *Costumes* Elizabeth Waller, *Third assistant director* Jim Threapleton.

Bill Kenwright Films/PolyGram – PolyGram.
95 mins. UK. 1998. Rel: 12 February 1999. Cert PG.

The Doom Generation ★¹/₂

In the course of trying to lose her virginity in her car, Amy Blue becomes the reluctant getaway driver for a mysterious, provocative stranger running from violent thugs. Then, before the night is done, the stranger implicates Amy and her boyfriend in the murder of a Korean supermart clerk. But that is just the beginning of the stranger's wild agenda for his new accomplices ... Billed as Gregg Araki's first ... 'heterosexual' feature, *The Doom Generation* is a road movie without direction or signposts. Composed of endless head-and-shoulder couplings, visits to fast food establishments (where every meal costs $6.66) and short outbursts of extreme violence, Araki's satirical safari is sick and thin. With its carnal excess, inventively foul language and alternative rock music, this is artless, confrontational and clinically weird cinema preaching to the perverted.

● *Jordan White* James Duval, *Amy Blue* Rose McGowan, *Xavier Red* Johnathon Schaech, *Brandi* Parker Posey, *George* Dewey Weber, *mangled dog* Bullet, Cress Williams, Dustin Nguyen, Margaret Cho, Lauren Tewes, Christopher Knight, Nicky Katt, Amanda Bearse, Salvator Xuereb, *liquor store clerk* Heidi Fleiss, Don Galloway.
● *Dir, Screenplay* and *Ed* Gregg Araki, *Pro* Araki and Andrea Sperling, *Ex Pro* Nicole Arbib, Pascal Caucheteux and Gregoire Sorlat, *Assoc Pro* Jim Stark and Shelley Surpin, *Ph* Jim Fealy, *Pro Des* Therese Deprez, *M* songs performed by Jesus and Mary Chain, Nine Inch Nails, Porno for Pyros, Belly, Curve, Meat Beat Manifesto, Cocteau Twins, Coil, My Bloody Valentine, Lush, God Lives Underwater, The Verve, etc, *Costumes* Catherine Cooper-Thoman.

Why Not Productions – Metro Tartan.
84 mins. USA/France. 1995. Rel: 18 September 1998. Cert 18.

Dr Dolittle ★★

San Francisco; the present. 'The great thing about being a kid is that it's so easy to pretend,' we are told. But then we grow up and put away childish things. John Dolittle had a perfectly reasonable relationship with his dog when the animal was carted off for teaching him to sniff butt – and young John never talked to a critter again. Now Dolittle is a reputable, work-obsessed physician and his talent for understanding animals has suddenly returned ... The conceit that a cynical grown-up finds himself able to communicate with animals is inherently amusing. So to play it for laughs is not only redundant but bound to reap diminishing returns. While it's fine for the animals themselves to shoot the breeze with 'witty' repartee, Eddie Murphy's frantic mugging merely detracts from the humour. Had someone as humanly credible as Denzel Washington played the distraught family man haunted by voices, *Dr Dolittle* could've been a riot. As it is, it is up to the one-joke premise (inspired by the stories of Hugh Lofting) and the impressive animatronics to save this from being a total turkey. FYI: *Doctor Dolittle* was previously filmed in 1967 with Rex Harrison.

● *Dr John Dolittle* Eddie Murphy, *Archer Dolittle* Ossie Davis, *Dr Mark Weller* Oliver Platt, *Calloway* Peter Boyle, *Dr Gene Reiss* Richard Schiff, *Lisa Dolittle* Kristen Wilson, *Dr Fish* Jeffrey Tambor, *Maya* Kyla Pratt, Raven-Symone, Steven Gilborn, Erik Todd Dellums, Cherie Franklin, Don Calfa.

Voices: Lucky Norm MacDonald, *tiger* Albert Brooks, *Rodney* Chris Rock, Reni Santoni, John Leguizamo, Julie Kavner, Garry Shandling, Ellen DeGeneres, Brian Doyle-Murray, Phil Proctor, Jenna Elfman, Gilbert Gottfried, Tom Towles, Paul Reubens, Jonathan Lipnicki, Hamilton Camp.
● *Dir* Betty Thomas, *Pro* John Davis, Joseph M. Singer and David T. Friendly, *Ex Pro* Sue Baden-Powell and Jenno Topping, *Screenplay* Nat Mauldin and Larry Levin, *Ph* Russell Boyd, *Pro Des* William Elliott, *Ed* Peter Teschner, *M* Richard Gibbs; songs performed by Eddie Kane & DeVille, All Saints, 69 Boyz, Jody Watley, Louis Armstrong, Changing Faces and Ivan Matias, etc, *Costumes* Sharen Davis, *Visual effects* Jon Farhat, *Animatronic creatures* Jim Henson's Creature Shop.

Fox/Davis Entertainment – Fox.
85 mins. USA. 1998. Rel: 31 July 1998. Cert PG.

The Dream Life of Angels – La Vie Revee des Anges ★★

Lille, Nord, France; today. Isabelle Tostin, a 21-year-old backpacker, arrives in town to visit a friend, only to find that he has moved to Belgium. Finding work in a sewing factory, Isabelle befriends Marie, a pot-smoking colleague who reluctantly lets her move in with her. Both rebels at heart, Isabelle and Marie form a tenuous relationship, but beneath their insubordinate skin the young women could not be more dissimilar ... This is one of those stark, humourless 'slice-of-life' French films that you forget almost as soon as you leave the cinema. The two leads, who won the joint best actress award at the 1998 Cannes film festival, are very good and the atmosphere of provincial city life is well caught by Agnes Godard's fluid camera-work. There's even a modicum of charm and an arresting sense of *cinema verite*, but the disconnected lives of these largely unlikeable characters (and a serious lack of plot) do the film no favours.

● *Isabelle Tostin* Elodie Bouchez, *Marie Thomas* Natacha Regnier, *Chris* Gregoire Colin, *Fredo* Joe Prestia, *Charly* Patrick Mercado, *Sandrine* Louise Motte, *Solene* Juliette Richevaux, Frederique Hazard, Stephanie Delerue, Christian Cailleret.
● *Dir* Erick Zonca, *Pro* Francois Marquis, *Screenplay* Zonca, Roger Bohbot, Virginie Wagon and Pierre Schoeller, *Ph* Agnes Godard, *Pro Des* Jimmy Vansteenkiste, *Ed* Yannick Kergoat, *M* songs performed by Kickback, Massive Attack, Les Flying Bumbkins, Rocco and the Rays, and Claire Pichel, *Costumes* Francoise Clavel.

Les Productions Bagheera/France 3 Cinema/Diaphana/Canal Plus, etc – Gala.
113 mins. France. 1998. Rel: 16 October 1998. Cert 18.

Right: *Eel people: Misa Shimizu (on bridge) offers Koji Yakusho (sitting) food for thought in Shohei Imamura's gently haunting The Eel·(from Artificial Eye)*

East Side Story ★★★¹/₂

A Socialist musical comedy may sound like a contradiction in terms, but Dana Ranga's sly, eye-opening documentary begs to differ. Focusing on the 40 or so musicals made behind the Iron Curtain between 1934 and 1973 and charting their perilous survival (in spite of an eager, grateful audience), *East Side Story* turns out to be one of the most amusing and original documentaries of the decade. Punctuated by clips from such cheesy extravaganzas as *Tractor Drivers*, *Vacation on the Black Sea* and *Volga-Volga* (Stalin's favourite) and well-informed commentary from various experts, the film builds up a fascinating picture of a regime struggling with its self-image. P.S. The film-maker Grigorii Aleksandrov was decorated by the military for directing the 1934 musical *The Jolly Fellows*!

● *Dir* Dana Ranga, *Pro* Andrew Horn, *Screenplay* Ranga and Horn, *Ph* Mark Daniels, *Ed* Guido Krajewski.

Anda Films/DocStar/Canal Plus, etc – Downtown Pictures. 80 mins. Germany/USA/France. 1997. Rel: 30 October 1998. Cert U.

The Eel – Unagi ★★★¹/₂

Sentenced to eight years in prison for stabbing his adulterous wife to death, Takuro Yamashita takes a vow of silence, electing only to talk to a detained eel (because it listens to what he says). Finally released on parole, Yamashita opens up his own barber's shop on a remote stretch of river. There, he rescues Keiko, a young woman who has taken an overdose of sleeping pills and who comes to work for him ... A bittersweet fable from the 70-year-old director of *The Ballad of Narayama* (1983) and *Black Rain* (1989), *The Eel* is an extraordinary piece of surreal humanist film-making. Leisurely paced and painterly lit, the film exercises a gentle power that is strangely affecting. Koji Yakusho, who played the secret dancer in the Japanese hit *Shall We Dance?*, beautifully underplays his part of the damaged outsider, while Misa Shimizu, as Keiko, is simply heart-breaking.

● *Takuro Yamashita* Koji Yakusho, *Keiko Hattori* Misa Shimizu, *Jiro Nakajima* Fujio Tsuneta, *Tamotasu Takasaki* Akira Emoto, *Emiko Yamashita* Chiho Terada, *Masaki Saito* Ken Kobayashi, *Seitaro Misato* Sabu Kawahara, Mitsuko Biasho, Makoto Sato, Sho Aihara.
● *Dir* Shohei Imamura, *Pro* Hisa Lino, *Ex Pro* Kazuyoshi Okuyama, *Screenplay* Imamura, Motofumi Tomikawa and Daisuke Tengan, from the story *Glittering in the Dark* by Akira Yoshimura, *Ph* Shigeru Komatsubara, *Pro Des* Hisao Inagaki, *Ed* Hajime Okayasu, *M* Shinichiro Ikebe.

KSS Films/Satellite Cinema/Groove Corp/Imamura Prods – Artificial Eye.
117 mins. Japan. 1996. Rel: 20 November 1998. Cert 18.

8MM ★★★

Tom Welles is a respected surveillance specialist who leads a quiet suburban life with his loving wife and infant daughter. He's then offered a lucrative case by wealthy widow Mrs Christian, who has discovered a disturbing reel of 8mm film in her late husband's safe. It shows the abuse and murder of a girl, and Mrs Christian wants Welles to establish the authenticity of the film ... If lacking the sheer visceral excitement and credibility of *Se7en* – the previous credit from scenarist Andrew Kevin Walker – this dark journey into the underbelly of American exploitation certainly keeps a firm grip on the attention. A compulsive and atmospheric if rather gloomy thriller, *8 MM* strains hard not to get excited over its subject matter and veers away from any naturalistic depiction of a snuff movie. However, it's in the seamy *milieu* of a world that can create such abominations that makes the flesh creep and director Schumacher has gone to considerable lengths to scrub any gloss from his theme. It's just unfortunate that the villains themselves are portrayed as such cartoonish types. Mychael Danna's music, employing an eclectic mix of exotic instruments (including a combo of drums and bagpipes during Welles' escape from a warehouse) is a major plus. An interesting companion piece to *The Lost Son* (qv).

● *Tom Welles* Nicolas Cage, *Max California* Joaquin Phoenix, *Eddie Poole* James Gandolfini, *Dino Velvet* Peter Stormare, *Longdale* Anthony Heald, *Machine* Chris Bauer, *Amy Welles* Catherine Keenner, *Mrs*

Christian Myra Carter, *Janet Matthews* Amy Morton, *Mary Anne Mathews* Jenny Powell, Anne Gee Byrd, Don Creech, Norman Reedus.
● *Dir* Joel Schumacher, *Pro* Schumacher, Gavin Polone and Judy Hofflund, *Ex Pro* Joseph M. Caracciolo, *Screenplay* Andrew Kevin Walker, *Ph* Robert Elswit, *Pro Des* Gary Wissner, *Ed* Mark Stevens, *M* Mychael Danna, *Costumes* Mona May.

Global Entertainment/Columbia Pictures – Columbia TriStar.
123 mins. USA/Germany. 1999. Rel: 23 April 1999. Cert 18.

Elizabeth ★★★★½

England/Scotland; 1554-1570. In one of the most barbaric periods of English history, hundreds of devout Protestants are routinely accused of heresy and burned alive at the stake. An unhappy Mary is queen and is struggling to lay the foundations for a safe Catholic future. But consumed by cancer and plagued by a number of false pregnancies, Mary sees her throne slipping into the hands of her despised half-sister, the Protestant Elizabeth. The latter, refusing to relinquish her beliefs in the face of inhumane intimidation, waits for the day when she will lose her head – or succeed to the throne ... Crowned by a steely and luminous performance from Cate Blanchett in the title role, *Elizabeth* is a vivid, moving and gripping drama that tears history screaming from the page. From the grim detail of everyday life to some unexpected flourishes (Henri Duc d'Anjou, the future king of France, is caught in his chamber in drag), from the high standard of the acting, the costumes, the locations and a magnificent score, the film is a model of cinema excellence. Historians may carp at some dramatic licence (such as Elizabeth's physical dalliance with Robert Dudley) but the overall tone is commandingly authentic.

● *Elizabeth* Cate Blanchett, *Sir Francis Walsingham* Geoffrey Rush, *Duke of Norfolk* Christopher Eccleston, *Robert Dudley, the Earl of Leicester* Joseph

Below: 'Snuff said: Nicolas Cage takes in a beer and movie in Joel Schumacher's atmospheric if gloomy 8MM (from Columbia TriStar)

Above: Before she was a virgin: Cate Blanchett as Elizabeth plays with the affections of Joseph Fiennes' Robert Dudley (from PolyGram)

Fiennes, *Sir William Cecil* Richard Attenborough, *Mary of Guise* Fanny Ardent, *Queen Mary of Tudor* Kathy Burke, *Monsieur de Foix* Eric Cantona, *Alvaro de la Quadra* James Frain, *Henri Duc d'Anjou* Vincent Cassel, *John Ballard* Daniel Craig, *Earl of Arundel* Edward Hardwicke, *Bishop Gardiner* Terence Rigby, *Isabel Knollys* Kelly Macdonald, *Kat Ashley* Emily Mortimer, *The Pope* John Gielgud, *Earl of Sussex* Jamie Foreman, Angus Deayton, Amanda Ryan, Wayne Sleep, Kenny Doughty, Liz Giles, Ben Frain, Joseph O'Connor, Jeremy Hawk, Tim Bevan, Daisy Bevan.
● *Dir* Shekhar Kapur, *Pro* Alison Owen, Eric Fellner and Tim Bevan, *Co-Pro* Debra Hayward and Liza Chasin, *Screenplay* Michael Hirst, *Ph* Remi Adefarasin, *Pro Des* John Myhre, *Ed* Jill Bilcock, *M* David Hirschfelder, *Costumes* Alexandra Byrne.

PolyGram/Channel Four Films/Working Title – PolyGram. 121 mins. UK. 1998. Rel: 2 October 1998. Cert 15.

Enemy of the State ★★★★★

Determined to greenlight a new government surveillance bill, an unscrupulous administrator from the National Security Agency decides to remove opposing US congressman Phil Hamersly from the picture – permanently. However, unbeknownst to the NSA, Hamersly's covert execution is recorded by a motion-activated wildlife camera. The incriminating tape swiftly becomes a hot potato and circuitously ends up in the possession of one Robert Clayton Dean, a slick, streetwise lawyer whose identity is about to vanish off the national grid ... A damning indictment of the US government's increasing invasion of its citizens' priva-

cy, *Enemy of the State* raises a number of alarming questions as it raises the blood pressure. A satisfying mix of conspiracy theory, political argument and flat-out escapism, the film plays like a high-tech variation of *The Fugitive* with a thinking cap. Muscular direction, breath-snatching chase sequences and an array of colourful performances keep up the momentum. P.S. As a retired NSA computer analyst, Gene Hackman virtually updates the role of the surveillance expert he played in Coppola's *The Conversation*.

● *Robert Clayton Dean* Will Smith, *Edward Lyle aka Brill* Gene Hackman, *Thomas Brian Reynolds* Jon Voight, *Rachel Banks* Lisa Bonet, *Carla Dean* Regina King, *Agent Hicks* Loren Dean, *Danny Leon Zavitz* Jason Lee, *'Brill'* Gabriel Byrne, *Emily Reynolds* Anna Gunn, *Eric Dean* Jascha Washington, *Lenny Bloom* Grant Heslov, Stuart Wilson, Laura Cayouette, Barry Pepper, Ian Hart, Jake Busey, Scott Caan, James Le Gros, Dan Butler, Jack Black, Jamie Kennedy, Bodhi Pine Elfman, Rebecca Silva, Carl Mergenthaler, Lillo Brancato, John Capodice, Vic Manni, Ivana Milavich, Elizabeth Berman, Frank Medrano, Albert Wong, Carlos Gomez, Arnie Alpert, *himself* Larry King, Chris Holt, and *uncredited*: *US congressman Philip Hamersly* Jason Robards, *Pintero* Tom Sizemore, *Brian Silverberg* Philip Baker Hall, Brian Markinson, Seth Green, Betsy Brantley, Paul Herman.
● *Dir* Tony Scott, *Pro* Jerry Bruckheimer, *Ex Pro* Chad Oman, James W. Skotchdopole and Andrew Z. Davis, *Screenplay* David Marconi, *Ph* Dan Mindel, *Pro Des* Benjamin Fernandez, *Ed* Chris Lebenzon, *M* Trevor Rabin and Harry Gregson-

Left: State of paranoia? Will Smith runs off with his hotel dressing gown in Tony Scott's muscular, breath-snatching Enemy of the State (from Buena Vista)

Williams, *Costumes* Marlene Stewart, *Sound* Christopher Boyes, Shannon Mills and Tom Myers.

Touchstone Pictures/Scott Free Prods – Buena Vista. 132 mins. USA. 1998. Rel: 26 December 1998. Cert 15.

Eternity and a Day – Mia Eoniotita Ke Mia Mera ★¹/₂

Greece; the present. The day before he is to go into hospital, perhaps never to come out again, the celebrated poet Alexander sifts through his memories. Having denied himself the joy of living while in the pursuit of his art, Alexander has just 24 hours to redress the balance. Unexpectedly, he finds his redemption in the company of a six-year-old Albanian refugee ... Talk about a prophetic title. The surprise winner of the 1998 Palme d'Or at Cannes, *Eternity and Day* is a work of staggering self-indulgence. With each shot extended beyond human endurance, the film creeps from one obscure revelation to the next with the urgency of a whelk. It's like watching molten lead cool. However, a clutch of film historians happen to think that Theo Angelopoulos, whose eleventh film this is, is a cinematic genius.

● *Alexander* Bruno Ganz, *Anna, Alexander's wife* Isabelle Renauld, *the child* Archileas Skevis, *Alexander's mother* Despina Bebedeli, *Alexander's daughter* Iris Chatziantoniou, Helene Gerasimidiou, Fabrizio Bentivoglio.
● *Dir* Theo Angelopoulos, *Pro* Angelopoulos, Eric Heumann, Giorgio Silvagni and Amedeo Pagani, *Screenplay* Angelopoulos, Tonino Guerra, Petros Markaris and Giorgio Silvagni, *Ph* Giorgios Arvanitis and Andreas Sinani, *Pro Des* Giorgos Patsos and Giorgos Ziakas, *Ed* Yannis Tsitsopoulos, *M* Eleni Karaindrou.

Paradis Films/Intermedias/La Sept Cinema/Canal Plus/Euroimages, etc – Artificial Eye. 132 mins. Greece/France/Italy. 1998. Rel: 14 May 1999. Cert PG.

Ever After ★★★★

Summoned to the castle of the formidable Grande Dame, the brothers Grimm are complimented on their fairy tales. However, the dowager is not so sure of their interpretation of the 'cinder story.' So she begins to set a few facts straight ... Drew Barrymore may not be everybody's idea of a model Cinderella: Los Angeles-born and well-upholstered, she hardly summons up the image of a deprived French waif. Still, this reinvention of the classic fairy tale introduces a human face that is quite affecting. Lush production values, bewitching locations and a sweeping score immediately puts one in the mood for magic, and yet the magic, as the director points out, 'comes from within, not from some fairy godmother.' Thus, with transmogrified mice and pumpkins put to one side, the strength of the story itself – with its recipe of terrible injustice, unrequited love and the indomitability of the human spirit – is left to cast its spell. There's also some sparkling dialogue and a genuinely charming Prince (full of self-doubt and boyish ardour), all of which adds up to a wonderful entertainment for all the family. So why *Ever After* was branded with a PG-13 rating in the States is one of the great mysteries of the late 20th century. Filmed in the eye-catching region of Dordogne, in France.

● *Danielle* Drew Barrymore, *Rodmilla* Anjelica Huston, *Prince Henry* Dougray Scott, *Grande Dame* Jeanne Moreau, *Leonardo Da Vinci* Patrick Godfrey, *Marguerite* Megan Dodds, *Jacqueline* Melanie Lynskey, *King Francis* Timothy West, *Queen Marie* Judy Parfitt, *Auguste* Jeroen Krabbe, *young Danielle*

Anna Maguire, *Pierre Le Pieu* Richard O'Brien, Lee Ingleby, Kate Lansbury, Matyelok Gibbs, Walter Sparrow, Peter Gunn, Joerg Stadler, Andrew Henderson, Mark Lewis, Janet Henfrey, Ursula Jones, Amanda Walker, Tony Doyle, Susan Field.
● *Dir* Andy Tennant, *Pro* Mireille Soria and Tracey Trench, *Co-Pro* Kevin Reidy and Timothy M. Bourne, *Screenplay* Tennant & Rick Parks, and Susannah Grant, *Ph* Andrew Dunn, *Pro Des* Michael Howells, *Ed* Roger Bondelli, *M* George Fenton, *Costumes* Jenny Beavan, *Sword master* Graeme Crowther.

Fox – Fox.
121 mins. USA. 1998. Rel: 9 October 1998. Cert PG.

Eve's Bayou ★★★★

Louisiana; 1962. Opening with the words, 'the summer I killed my father, I was just ten years old ...', *Eve's Bayou* settles confidently into its dream-like world of dark secrets, voodoo and childhood apprehension. Yet for all that, the story – as relayed through the eyes of young Eve (luminously portrayed by Jurnee Smollett) – is as much one of adventure, humour and love as it is of tragedy. Marking the directorial debut of actress Kasi Lemmons (*Candyman*, *Fear of a Black Hat*), *Eve's Bayou* is remarkable in that, unlike most projects from Afro-American film-makers, race is not an issue, badge or style. This is a keenly observed tale about people and Lemmons reveals a talent for drawing exceptional performances from her cast and for placing them in effective and inventive tableaux. She also exhibits a keen sense of pace and visual poetry that infuses her film with a redolence one can almost taste. FYI: Vondie Curtis Hall, the actor who recently made his own directorial debut with *Gridlock'd*, is Lemmons' husband.

Below: Mother of prevention: Lynn Whitfield cradles her children Meagan Good, Jake Smollett and Jurnee Smollett in Kasi Lemmons' poetic, keenly observed Eve's Bayou (from Alliance Releasing)

● *Louis Batiste* Samuel L. Jackson, *Roz Batiste* Lynn Whitfield, *Mozelle Batiste Delacroix* Debbi Morgan, *Julian Grayraven* Vondie Curtis Hall, *Uncle Harry* Branford Marsalis, *Matty Mereaux* Lisa Nicole Carson, *Lenny Mereaux* Roger Guenveur Smith, *Eve Batiste* Jurnee Smollett, *Elzora* Diahann Carroll,

Cisely Batiste Meagan Good, Ethel Ayler, Jake Smollett, Afonda Colbert, Victoria Rowell, Leonard Thomas, *narrator* Tamara Tunie.
● *Dir* and *Screenplay* Kasi Lemmons, *Pro* Caldecot Chubb and Samuel L. Jackson, *Ex Pro* Mark Amin, Eli Selden, Nick Wechsler and Julie Silverman Yorn, *Co-Ex Pro* Michael Bennett and Margaret Matheson, *Ph* Amy Vincent, *Pro Des* Jeff Howard, *Ed* Terilyn A. Shropshire, *M* Terence Blanchard; songs performed by Gena Delafose, Ray Charles, Louis Armstrong, Etta James, Bobby 'Blue' Bland, Erykah Badu, etc, *Costumes* Karyn Wagner.

Trimark Pictures/Chubbco/Addis – Wechsler-Alliance Releasing.
108 mins. USA. 1997. Rel: 14 August 1998. Cert 15.

eXistenZ ★★★¹/₂

'eXistenZ' is a futuristic game that plugs straight into the spinal chord and then adapts its basic plot points to the player's own character. In fact, it feels so real that it is often hard to separate fantasy from reality. While testing her magnum opus, games designer Allegra Geller invites a group of enthusiasts to join her in a secret unveiling ceremony. Then, mid-game, Allegra is attacked by an anti-eXistenZialist protester, and the prototype is exposed to potentially irreversible damage. So, in order to check for contamination, Allegra persuades her mild-mannered minder to enter her bizarre game with her ... Taking his twin fascinations with biotechnology and virtual reality and plugging them into a futuristic morality tale, David Cronenberg has created a playful, imaginative and fantastically obscene confection that will delight his fans and probably win him a few new ones. I mean, who else could dream up a gun constructed from bone and gristle or an all-new body orifice acquired on the black market? A fascinating entry in a cinematic field that, to some degree or other, has already been explored in *Tron*, *The Lawnmower Man*, *Virtuosity* and *The Game*.

● *Allegra Geller* Jennifer Jason Leigh, *Ted Pikul* Jude Law, *Kiri Vinokur* Ian Holm, *Yevgeny Nourish* Don McKellar, *Hugo Carlaw* Callum Keith Rennie, *Merle* Sarah Polley, *Wittold Levi* Christopher Eccleston, *Gas* Willem Dafoe, *Nader* Robert A. Silverman, Oscar Hsu, Kris Lemche, Kirsten Johnson, Gerry Quigley.
● *Dir* and *Screenplay* David Cronenberg, *Pro* Cronenberg, Robert Lantos and Andras Hamori, *Co-Pro* Michael MacDonald, Damon Bryant and Bradley Adams, *Assoc Pro* Sandra Tucker, *Ph* Peter Suschitzky, *Pro Des* Carol Spier, *Ed* Ronald Sanders, *M* Howard Shore, *Costumes* Denise Cronenberg, *Visual effects* Jim Isaac.

Alliance Atlantis/Serendipity Point/Natural Nylon/Telefilm Canada, etc – Alliance Releasing.
97 mins. Canada/UK. 1999. Rel: 30 April 1999. Cert 15.

Ellen Albertini Dow, *Grace O'Shea* Heather Matarazzo, *Truman Capote* Louis Negin, *Andy Warhol* Sean Sullivan, Cameron Mathison, Noam Jenkins, Jay Goede, Skipp Sudduth, Daniel Lapaine, Erika Alexander, Thelma Houston, Mary Griffin, Lauren Hutton, Michael York, Elio Fiorucci, Cindy Crawford, Sheryl Crow, Donald Trump, Georgina Grenville, Art Garfunkel, Peter Bogdanovich, Lorna Luft, Valerie Perrine, Beverly Johnson, Bruce Jay Friedman, Ultra Nate, Amber, Jocelyn Enriquez.
● *Dir and Screenplay* Mark Christopher, *Pro* Richard N. Gladstein, Dolly Hall and Ira Deutchman, *Ex Pro* Bob Weinstein, Harvey Weinstein, Bobby Cohen and Don Carmody, *Ph* Alexander Gruszynski, *Pro Des* Kevin Thompson, *Ed* Lee Percy, *M* songs performed by Gary's Gang, Chic, Edwin Starr, Mary Griffin, Candi Staton, Diana Ross, Dan Hartman, Sylvester, The Miracles, Instant Funk, Odyssey, Rose Royce, Ashford & Simpson, S.O.S. Band, Bonnie Pointer, Thelma Houston, Grace Jones, Bachman-Turner Overdrive, Salma Hayek, Blondie, Silver Convention, Sylvia, etc, *Costumes* Ellen Rutter, *Choreography* Lori Eastside.

Miramax/Redeemable Features/Dollface/Filmcolony – Buena Vista.
93 mins. USA. 1998. Rel: 22 January 1999. Cert 15.

Finding North ★★¹/₂

Travis Furlong is a homosexual in a suicidal mood. His lover has just died and he is not sure that he wants to go it alone. Rhonda Portelli is a Jewish bank clerk with a big mouth who spots Travis, naked, perched on the edge of Brooklyn Bridge. Later, Travis walks into her bank and she decides that they are destined to be soul mates. So she joins him on a journey of self-discovery as they travel to a small town in Texas to fulfil the last, bizarre wish of Travis's dead boyfriend ... As amiable, compassionate and well-acted as *Finding North* is, it cannot disguise a somewhat dated feel and condescending manner. Furthermore, Travis is such a dour, snotty individual that he's not a travelling companion many would want to spend time with. On the other hand, Rhonda is a scintillating voice in an AIDS-suffocated wilderness, but her very likability throws off the balance of this unusual two-hander. [*Ewen Brownrigg*]

● *Rhonda Portelli* Wendy Makkena, *Travis Furlong* John Benjamin Hickey, *Mrs Portelli* Angela Pietropinto, *Mr Portelli* Freddie Roman, *Aunt Bonnie* Molly McClure, Spiro Malas, Jonathan Walker, Anne Bobby, Gareth Moran, Steven Jones, Mary Sheldon, Sara Proctor.
● *Dir* Tanya Wexler, *Pro* Steven A. Jones and Stephen Dyer, *Ex Pro* Hal 'Corky' Kessler, *Co-Pro* Mike Dempsey, *Screenplay* Kim Powers, *Ph* Michael Barrett, *Pro Des* James B. Smythe, *Ed* Thom Zimny, *M* Cafe Noir; songs performed by Johnny Cash, Johnny Gimble, Merle Travis, Don Walser, etc, *Costumes* Katelyn Burton, *Sound* Marshall Grupp.

SoNo Pictures – Millivres Multimedia.
95 mins. USA. 1997. Rel: 11 June 1999. Cert 15.

Above: Eye of the storm: Steve Hytner, Ben Affleck and Sandra Bullock experience some emotional turbulence in Bronwen Hughes' tepid Forces of Nature *(from UIP)*

Fire ★★★¹⁄₂

New Delhi; the present. Sita, the beautiful young bride of the wayward Jatin, moves in with her husband's extended family at the premises of a thriving takeaway restaurant. Immediately ignored by her new husband, Sita finds some solace in her friendship with Radha, her patient and long-suffering sister-in-law. In fact, the women form such a strong bond that their liaison begins to undermine the male superiority of the household ... It is interesting that the few Indian films that have reached the United Kingdom of late have been decidedly un-Indian in tone. And when one considers that even the depiction of a kiss was prohibited in Indian cinema as recently as 1978, films such as *Bandit Queen, Kama Sutra* and now *Fire* seem particularly shocking. Here, the sight of a servant masturbating to a porn video in front of the mute, bed-ridden mother of his employer wields a shock value far greater than a similar scene would within a western context. Yet Deepa Mehta's *Fire* – whose story stands as a metaphor for the cultural turbulence of contemporary India – is anything but contentious, but is a thoughtful, moving and even amusing contemplation of the changing face of women in a male-dominated, spiritual and suppressed society.

● *Radha* Shabana Azmi, *Sita* Nandita Das, *Ashok* Kulbushan Kharbanda, *Jatin* Jaaved Jaaferi, *Mundu* Ranjit Chowdhry, *Biji* Kushal Rekhi, *Julie* Alice Poon, Vinay Pathak, Avijit Dutt.
● *Dir* and *Screenplay* Deepa Mehta, *Pro* Mehta and Bobby Bedi, *Ex Pro* Suresh Bhalla and David Hamilton, *Line Pro* Anne Masson, *Ph* Giles Nuttgens, *Pro Des* Aradhana Seth, *Ed* Barry Farrell, *M* A.R. Rahman, *Costumes* Neelam Mansingh.

Trial by Fire Films – Pathe.
108 mins. Canada. 1996. Rel: 13 November 1998. Cert 15.

Firelight ★★★¹⁄₂

1837-1846; Houlgate, Normandy/Selcombe Place, East Sussex. In order to pay off her father's debts, Elisabeth Laurier, a young Swiss woman, agrees to secretly bear a stranger's baby for the sum of £500. Eight years later, unable to keep away from her child any longer, Elisabeth takes on the job of governess to her daughter, Louisa. Despised by her own child, Elisabeth must pretend that she is not Louisa's mother; Louisa pretends that she has a mother who lives in a secluded lake house; and Louisa's father pretends that he doesn't desperately love the new governess ... William Nicholson, the scenarist of *Shadowlands* and *Nell*, has concocted a seething period romance mercifully free of any loyalty to an established text. Borrowing the recipe of suppressed passion employed so well by the likes of Jane Austen and Thomas Hardy, Nicholson has rustled up a terrific story that serves his mandate to great effect. Adopting the painterly style of the Dutch masters of the 17th century, he also reveals a beguiling visual mastery.

● *Elisabeth Laurier* Sophie Marceau, *Charles Godwin* Stephen Dillane, *John Taylor* Kevin Anderson, *Constance* Lia Williams, *Louisa Godwin* Dominique Belcourt, *Lord Clare,* aka *Jimmy* Joss Ackland, *Molly Holland* Sally Dexter, *Amelia 'Amy' Godwin* Annabel Giles, Emma Amos, Maggie McCarthy, Wolf Kahler, Valerie Minifie, Hugh Walters, Peter Needham.
● *Dir* and *Screenplay* William Nicholson, *Pro* Brian Eastman, *Ex Pro* Susan Cartsonis, Rick Leed, Matt Williams, David McFadzean and Carmen Finestra, *Ph* Nic Morris, *Pro Des* Rob Harris, *Ed* Chris Wimble, *M* Christopher Gunning, *Costumes* Andrea Galer.

Hollywood Pictures/Wind Dancer/Carnival Films – Buena Vista.
103 mins. USA/UK. 1997. Rel: 14 August 1998. Cert 15.

Forces of Nature ★¹⁄₂

Ben Holmes is a straight-laced copywriter about to take the biggest step of his life. However, before he can get from New York to Georgia for his wedding, he must shake off his accidental travelling companion, the free-spirited, tempestuous and extremely attractive Sarah Lewis ... Following in the wake of *Speed 2, Hope Floats* and *Practical Magic*, this tepid romantic road movie continues the downward spiral of America's current sweetheart. But that is not to denigrate the value of Sandra Bullock herself, who is about the sole reason for seeing this misguided star vehicle. For any road movie to work, it needs at least credibility or momentum – if not both – and *Forces of Nature* falls down on both counts. Lazily contrived and blandly executed, the film offers little emotional or moral focus, providing a quandary for the audience, who doesn't know which romantic permutation to root for.

● *Sarah Lewis* Sandra Bullock, *Ben Holmes* Ben Affleck, *Bridget Cahill* Maura Tierney, *Alan* Steve Zahn, *Virginia Cahill* Blythe Danner, *Hadley Cahill* Ronny Cox, *Richard* Michael Fairman, *Steve* David Strickland, *Debbie* Meredith Scott Lynn, Janet Carroll, Richard Schiff, George D. Wallace, Steve Hytner, John Doe, Jack Kehler, Anne Haney, Bert Remsen, Bill Erwin.
● *Dir* Bronwen Hughes, *Pro* Susan Arnold, Donna Arkoff Roth and Ian Bryce, *Screenplay* Marc Lawrence, *Ph* Elliot Davis, *Pro Des* Lester Cohen, *Ed* Craig Wood, *M* John Powell; songs performed by Propellerheads, Gomez, David Strickland, Faithless, Swervedriver, Sandra Bullock, Stephen Stills, Peggy Lee, Tricky and Carmen Ejogo, Sarah McLachlan, U2, Chris Tart, etc, *Costumes* Donna Zakowska.

DreamWorks – UIP.
106 mins. USA. 1999. Rel: 7 May 1999. Cert 12.

For Richer or Poorer ★★

With their marriage on the rocks and their finances down the drain, high-flying Manhattan couple Brad and Caroline Sexton skip town in a stolen taxi. With the IRS on their trail, they hide out in an Amish community and discover what hard work is really like. But, with all the meaningless trappings of their former lives gone, Brad and Caroline find time for themselves again ... For a modestly proportioned sect, the Amish get an extraordinary amount of cinematic attention. Here, they represent all the cosy values of suburban Americana, which is really not the point. Still, this frequently very silly, sentimental comedy is considerably better than the 1994 *Holy Matrimony* which ploughed similar ground. [*Ewen Brownrigg*]

● *Brad Sexton* Tim Allen, *Caroline Sexton* Kirstie Alley, *Samuel Yoder* Jay O. Sanders, *Phil Kleinman* Michael Lerner, *Bob Lachman* Wayne Knight, *Derek Lester* Larry Miller, Miguel A. Nunez Jr, Megan Cavanagh, John Pyper-Ferguson, Carrie Preston, Ethan Phillips, John Caponera, Marla Maples.
● *Dir* Bryan Spicer, *Pro* Sid, Bill and Jon Sheinberg, *Ex Pro* Richard Baker, Rick Messina and Gayle Fraser Baigelman, *Screenplay* Jana Howington and Steve Lukanic, *Ph* Buzz Feitshans IV, *Pro Des* Stephen Hendrickson, *Ed* Russell Denove, *M* Randy Edelman; songs performed by Sarah Vaughan, Yello, The O'Jays, etc, *Costumes* Abigail Murray.

Universal/Bubble Factory/Yorktown Prods – UIP.
115 mins. USA. 1997. Rel: 27 November 1998. Cert 12.

Funny Games ★★★★

Austria; today. Georg and Anna and their young son Georgie have just arrived at their lakeside retreat for the summer holidays. While father and son are working down on the new boat, Anna prepares for supper. Then a guest of their neighbours pops in asking to borrow four eggs. When he drops them and asks for four more, Anna begins to sense that something is not right. Shortly afterwards the visitor is joined by a friend and they propose a bizarre wager: they bet that Georg, Anna and Georgie will not be alive in 12 hours' time ... By rights, Michael Haneke's unflinching contemplation of contemporary suburban violence should be one of the most terrifying thrillers you will ever see. Yet by inverting the conventions of the genre and taking away the traditional signposts (there is no scary music, little on-screen violence, averted nudity), Haneke reaches a different emotional plateau in our psyche. Repugnance, shock and horror are all present and accounted for, but our fear is somewhat neutralised by Frank Giering's direct collusion with the camera, forcing us into the uncomfortable position of voyeur at a sick parlour game. The effect is unsettling, disorientating even, but whatever one's thoughts on the director's motives, one cannot deny that *Funny Games* is riveting, provocative cinema.

● *Anna* Susanne Lothar, *Georg* Ulrich Muhe, *Paul* Arno Frisch, *Peter* Frank Giering, *Georgie* Stefan Clapczynski, Doris Kunstmann, Christoph Bantzer.
● *Dir* and *Screenplay* Michael Haneke, *Pro* Veit Heiduschka, *Ph* Jurgen Jurges, *Pro Des* Christoph Kanter, *Ed* Andreas Prochaska, *Costumes* Lisy Christl.

Wega-Film – Metro Tartan.
103 mins. Austria. 1997. Rel: 30 October 1998. Cert 18.

Left: *No laughing matter: Arno Frisch prevents young Stefan Clapczynski from seeing his mother's humiliation in Michael Haneke's unsettling and provocative* Funny Games *(from Metro Tartan)*

Above: Gypsy Moth: Romain Duris stars as the Frenchman inexplicably drawn to the world of the Boyash gypsy (seen here with Rona Hartner), in Tony Gatlif's vibrant, richly atmospheric Gadjo Dilo (from Alliance Releasing)

Gadjo Dilo ★★★★

On a singular quest to locate a mysterious gypsy singer, Stephane, a young Frenchman, treks to the heart of Romania with little more than the clothes on his back. Befriended by an old man in a drunken haze, Stephane accepts an offer of bed and board. As it happens, the old man is the elder of a local gypsy settlement and has a hard time convincing his clan that this stranger, or 'gadjo', is not a bandit nor a chicken thief. Gradually, Stephane wins the trust of these excitable, defensive people and, in turn, is seduced by their passionate, care-free lifestyle ... This authentic, richly atmospheric film paints a vibrant and powerful picture of gypsy life, from the routine profanity, drinking and spitting to the love of colour, dance and music. It also features perhaps the most erotic sequence of pre-foreplay ever captured on celluloid. FYI: Filming real Boyash gypsies in their own setting, writer-director Tony Gatlif (*Les Princes*, *Latcho Drom*, *Mondo*) felt compelled to change the last 40 minutes of his script when the French actor Romain Duris fell in love with one of the gypsy women. For Gatlif, the honesty of his picture was everything.

● *Stephane* Romain Duris, *Sabina* Rona Hartner, *Izidor* Izidor Serban, Ovidiu Balan, Dan Astileanu, Florin Moldovan.
● *Dir*, *Screenplay* and *M* Tony Gatlif, *Pro* Guy Marignane, *Ph* Eric Guichard, *Pro Des* Brigitte Brassart, *Ed* Monique Dartonne.

Princes Films/Canal Plus-Alliance Releasing. 101 mins. France. 1997. Rel: 21 August 1998. Cert 15.

Gang Related ★¹/₂

Divinci and Rodriguez are about as dirty as two cops can get. Posing as drug dealers, they hand over confiscated dope to buyers, take the money, kill the buyer and then disguise the homicide as some 'gang-related' job. However, when they inadvertently murder an undercover agent, they attract the full scrutiny of the DEA. So they manufacture evidence and pin it on an anonymous down-and-out. At least, they thought he was anonymous ... Affecting a wry, sardonic humour, *Gang Related* pushes its way onto well-worn turf with some style, but is neither funny enough nor gripping enough to elevate the material. In fact, the film's only real surprise is why somebody of Dennis Quaid's stature should end up in a supporting role in such drivel. FYI: Tupac Shakur, who plays Rodriguez, was murdered in a drive-by shooting shortly after completing his role in the film. His last words on celluloid: 'I hate my fucking life.'

● *Frank K. Divinci* James Belushi, *Rodriguez* Tupac Shakur, *Cynthia Webb* Lela Rochon, *Arthur Baylor* James Earl Jones, *'Joe Doe'/William Dane McCall* Dennis Quaid, *Elliot Goff* David Paymer, *Helen Eden* Wendy Crewson, *Richard Simms* Gary Cole, *Manny Ladrew* T.C Carson, *Captain Henderson* James Handy, *Richard Stein* Brad Greenquist, Kool Moe Dee, Victor Love, Tiny Lister Jr., Chris Hendrie, Deborah Rennard.
● *Dir* and *Screenplay* Jim Kouf, *Pro* Brad Krevoy, Steve Sabler and John Bertolli, *Ex Pro* Lynn Bigelow-Kouf, *Ph* Brian J. Reynolds, *Pro Des* Charles Breen, *Ed* Todd Ramsay, *M* Mickey Hart; songs performed

by 2PAC, Phil Collins, Marcus Barone, etc, *Costumes* Shari Feldman.

Orion Pictures – Feature Film Co.
111 mins. USA. 1997. Rel: 14 August 1998. Cert 15.

Get Real ★★★★★

Basingstoke, Hampshire; today. Steven Carter discovered sex late in life. Until he was ten, he thought conception had something to do with ice cream, but a year later he already knew that he was gay. The anxieties of adolescence are bad enough, but when you know your sexuality is 'dodgy' and that you are the personification of what the school bullies call 'queer' and a 'faggot', life can be unbearable. Then Steven, now 16, discovers that the school's dashing star athlete, John Dixon, is starting to question his own sexual identity ... Films this touching, funny, painful, credible and illuminating are hard to find. The fact that this is a British feature from a first-time director shot on a skimpy budget makes it closer to a miracle. Distinguished by a number of first-rate performances (Ben Silverstone, Charlotte Brittain and Jacquetta May are all exceptional), an easy, economic style and an insightful and witty script (John: 'Guess what.' Steven: 'You're pregnant?'), *Get Real* proves as engaging as it is poignant. Based on Patrick Wilde's play *What's Wrong With Angry?*

● *Steven Carter* Ben Silverstone, *John Dixon* Brad Gorton, *Linda* Charlotte Brittain, *Jessica* Stacy A. Hart, *Kevin* Tim Harris, *Mrs Carter* Jacquetta May, *Graham Carter* David Lumsden, Kate McEnery, Patrick Nielsen, James D. White, David Elliot, Morgan Jones, Richard Hawley, Steven Mason, Steven Elder, Ian Brimble, Judy Buxton, Martin Milman.
● *Dir* Simon Shore, *Pro* Steven Taylor, *Ex Pro* Anant Singh and Helena Spring, *Screenplay* Patrick Wilde, *Ph* Alan Almond, *Pro Des* and *Costumes* Bernd Lepel, *Ed* Barrie Vince, *M* John Lunn; songs performed by Aretha Franklin, Dodgy, The Troggs, Cameo, Drug Free America, The Backstreet Boys, Charlotte Brittain, The Milk and Honey Band, etc.

Graphite Films/Distant Horizon/British Screen/Arts Council of England/National Lottery – UIP.
110 mins. UK/South Africa. 1998. Rel: 14 May 1999. Cert 15.

The Gingerbread Man ★★½

As the first wave of Hurricane Geraldo makes itself felt on the streets of Savannah, Georgia, top lawyer Rick Magruder is celebrating yet another victory. Shortly afterwards, he offers Mallory Doss, a caterer, a ride home after her car has been stolen. Back at her house, the attorney learns that the young woman is being stalked by her own father, a frightening figure 'several beers short of a six pack.' The case – and Mallory herself – proves too alluring to resist ... Abandoning the high-powered conspiracy plotting of his novels, John Grisham delivers a rather pedestrian tale of deception and intrigue in this, his first original story for the screen. Drenched in atmosphere by director Robert Altman, *The Gingerbread Man* affects a Southern Gothic feel that goes some way in distracting the attention away from the predictable curve of the story. However, it's hard to root for Kenneth Branagh's hero, who is portrayed as a smug, irresponsible and somewhat foolish man. Furthermore, few of the characters ring true (in spite of generally fine accents from a cosmopolitan cast), while the lovely, fine-boned Embeth Davidtz is miscast as a piece of white trash.

● *Rick Magruder* Kenneth Branagh, *Mallory Doss* Embeth Davidtz, *Clyde Pell* Robert Downey Jr, *Lois Harlan* Daryl Hannah, *Pete Randle* Tom Berenger, *Duvall Dixon Doss* Robert, *Leeanne* Famke Janssen, *Konnie Dugan* Troy Beyer, Clyde Hayes, Mae Whitman, Jesse James, Julia R. Perce, Sonny Seiler, Walter Hartridge, Wilbur T. Fitzgerald, Paul Carden, Natalie Hendrix.
● *Dir* Robert Altman, *Pro* Jeremy Tannenbaum, *Ex Pro* Mark Burg, Glen A. Tobias and Todd Baker, *Screenplay* Al Hayes, *Ph* Changwei Gu, *Pro Des* Stephen Altman, *Ed* Geraldine Peroni, *M* Mark Isham, *Costumes* Dona Granata, *Sound* Randle Akerson and Richard King.

Island/Enchanter Entertainment – PolyGram.
114 mins. USA. 1997. Rel: 24 July 1998. Cert 15.

Girls Town ★½

Following the suicide of a close friend, three sartorially challenged high school seniors channel their frustration into some nasty anti-social behaviour ... Influenced by the cinema of John Cassavetes and Mike Leigh, *Girls Town* is a technically crude, ultra low-budget drama with more attitude than entertainment value. Largely a collaborative effort between first-time director Jim McKay and his three stars, the film offers *cinema verite* in spades culminating in some bum-numbing social commentary.

● *Patti Lucci* Lili Taylor, *Angela* Bruklin Harris, *Emma* Anna Grace, *Nikki* Aunjanue Ellis, *Dylan* Guillermo Diaz, *Anthony* Michael Imperioli, *Richard Helms* Tom Gilroy, Ramya Pratt, Asia Minor, Ernestine Jackson, John Ventimiglia, Mary Joy, Tara Carnes, Yassira.
● *Dir* Jim McKay, *Pro* Lauren Zalaznick, *Co-Pro* Sarah Vogel and Kelley Forsyth, *Screenplay* McKay, Denise Casano, Anna Grace, Bruklin Harris and Lili Taylor, *Ph* Russell Lee Fine, *Pro Des* David Doernberg, *Ed* McKay and Alex Hall, *M* Guru; songs performed by Vic Chestnut, Isley Brothers, Yo Yo, Neneh Cherry, P.J. Harvey, Luscious Jackson, Salt-n-Pepa, Queen Latifah, etc, *Costumes* Carolyn Grifel.

A C-Hundred Film Corp/Boomer Pictures – Metrodome. 89 mins. USA. 1996. Rel: 6 November 1998. Cert 15.

Gloria ★★

New York City; the present. Having served a three-year jail term on behalf of her hoodlum boyfriend, Gloria is none too pleased to find that he has got rid of her cats. And when she overhears that he is planning to knock off the seven-year-old witness to a mob killing, she takes the boy and makes a run for it. But what Gloria doesn't realise is that the kid possesses a floppy disc loaded with Mafia names and addresses ... A remake of John Cassavetes' gritty 1980 comic thriller starring Gena Rowlands, *Gloria* is mildly entertaining some of the time and downright irritating a lot of the time. The main flaw is the ineffectual rapport between Gloria and her whining ward (which displays none of the resonance of the bad-woman-takes-up-with-orphan-boy scenario in the similarly themed *Central Station*). Still, George C. Scott is on terrific form as an oily gentleman mobster dripping charm and menace in equal volume.

● *Gloria Greenly* Sharon Stone, *Kevin* Jeremy Northam, *Diane* Cathy Moriarty, *Nicky* Jean-Luke Figueroa, *Sean* Mike Starr, *Angela* Sarita Choudhury, *Jack* Bobby Cannavale, *Ruby* George C. Scott, *Terry* Barry McEvoy, *Raymond* Don Billett, *Zach* Tony DiBenedetto, *Brenda* Bonnie Bedelia, Jerry Dean, Teddy Atlas, Miriam Colon, Desiree F. Casado, Ray Garvey, Donald J. Lee Jr.
● *Dir* Sidney Lumet, *Pro* Gary Foster and Lee Rich, *Ex Pro* G. Mac Brown and Chuck Binder, *Screenplay* Steven Antin, *Ph* David Watkin, *Pro Des* Mel Bourne, *Ed* Tom Swartwout, *M* Howard Shore; songs performed by The Latin Brothers, La Makina, Enrico Caruso, etc, *Costumes* Dona Granata.

Mandalay Entertainment/Eagle Point – Entertainment. 110 mins. USA. 1998. Rel: 18 June 1999. Cert 15.

Gods and Monsters ★★★¹/₂

In the autumn of his life, James Whale, the celebrated director of *Frankenstein*, *Bride of Frankenstein* and *The Invisible Man*, embarks on an unlikely friendship with his gardener, Clayton Boone. Now resigned to a strict medical regimen and to sketching in his studio, the director offers to pay his new friend to sit for him as an artist's model. At first intrigued by the old man's former glory, Clayton quickly tires of Whale's homosexual banter, creating an uneasy alliance of attracted opposites ... An articulate, tender and frequently sparkling fictionalisation of the last days of a largely forgotten icon, *Gods and Monsters* – based on Christopher Bram's novel *Father of Frankenstein* – is a rare delight. Ian McKellen is magnificent in a compatible part, masterfully blending wit, pathos and affected airs, while Bill Condon's direction deftly navigates the subject's subtle complexities. Only Lynn Redgrave, in an extraordinary caricature as Whale's 'European' housekeeper, seems to belong in another movie. FYI: Intriguingly, Condon's previous feature was the mediocre horror film *Candyman: Farewell to the Flesh*.

● *James Whale* Ian McKellen, *Clayton Boone* Brendan Fraser, *Hanna* Lynn Redgrave, *Betty* Lolita Davidovich, *Harry* Kevin J. O'Connor, *David Lewis* David Dukes, *Sarah Whale* Pamela Salem, *Edmund Kay* Jack Plotnick, *Elsa Lanchester* Rosalind Ayres, *Colin Clive* Matt McKenzie, *George Cukor* Martin Ferrero,

Left: Creating myths: Ian McKellen and Brendan Fraser go party in Bill Condon's articulate and tender Gods and Monsters (from Downtown Pictures)

Princess Margaret Cornelia Hayes O'Herlihy, *elder Boris Karloff* Jack Betts, *Michael Boone* Jesse James, Sarah Ann Morris, Mark Kiely, Lisa Darr.

● *Dir* and *Screenplay* Bill Condon, *Pro* Paul Colichman, Gregg Fienberg and Mark R. Harris, *Ex Pro* Clive Barker and Stephen P. Jarchow, *Ph* Stephen M. Katz, *Pro Des* Richard Sherman, *Ed* Virginia Katz, *M* Carter Burwell; and Franz Waxman, *Costumes* Bruce Finlayson.

Regent Entertainment/Flashpoint/BBC Films – Downtown Pictures.
105 mins. USA/UK. 1998. Rel: 26 March 1999. Cert 15.

Godzilla ★★★¹/₂

Panama/Tahiti/Jamaica/New York; now. When, in 1995, the French government unleashed its nuclear resources in the South Pacific, the radiation fallout had an unusual effect on a native lizard. The creature has now grown to an inordinate size and is headed for Manhattan ... While failing to generate the gut-tugging excitement of such event movies as *Jurassic Park* and *Independence Day*, TriStar Pictures' summer behemoth of 1998 is not without its pleasures. The special effects, if not entirely realistic, are certainly awesome (see the Chrysler building trashed!); there's plenty of humour (hear Jean Reno take off Elvis Presley!); there's plenty of cutting commentary on environmental, political and media issues; and the pace is never allowed to lag. On the downside, the film is *terribly* derivative (*King Kong* meets *Jurassic Park* via *Alien*), unnecessarily noisy and at times so confusing that Hank Azaria appears to have his broken camera serviced while on the run from a heard of T-rexes. But, heh, the lizard delivers. FYI: Godzilla, a Tyrannosaurus rex woken from its ancient slumber by atomic testing, was first introduced in 1954 in the tacky Japanese film *Gojira*.

● *Dr Niko Tatopoulos* Matthew Broderick, *Philippe Roache* Jean Reno, *Audrey Timmonds* Maria Pitillo, *Victor 'Animal' Palotti* Hank Azaria, *Col. Hicks* Kevin Dunn, *Mayor Ebert* Michael Lerner, *Charles Caiman* Harry Shearer, *Lucy Palotti* Arabella Field, *Dr Elsie Chapman* Vicki Lewis, *Sgt. O'Neal* Doug Savant, Malcolm Danare *Dr Mendel Craven, Admiral Phelps* Richard Gant, Lorry Goldman, Christian Aubert, Francois Giroday, Robert Lesser, Ralph Manza, Chris Ellis, Jack Moore, Clyde Kusatsu, Glenn Morshower, Leonard Termo, Barney; *Creature voices* Gary Hecker, Frank Welker.
● *Dir* Roland Emmerich, *Pro* Dean Devlin, *Ex Pro* Roland Emmerich, Ute Emmerich and William Fay, *Screenplay* Devlin and Roland Emmerich, from a story by Devlin, Emmerich, Ted Elliott and Terry Rossio, based on the character created by Toho Co. Ltd, *Ph* Ueli Steiger, *Pro Des* Oliver Scholl, *Ed* Peter Amundson and David J. Siegel, *M* David Arnold; songs performed by The Wallflowers, Puff Daddy and Jimmy Page, Jamiroquai, Ben Folds Five, Foo Fighters, Rage Against the Machine, Fantastic Strings, etc, *Costumes* Joseph Porro, *Visual effects* Volker Engel, *Godzilla design* Patrick Tatopoulos.

Centropolis Entertainment/Fried Films/Independent Pictures – Columbia TriStar.
139 mins. USA. 1998. Rel: 17 July 1998. Cert PG.

The Governess ★★★¹⁄₂

London/the Isle of Skye; the 1840s. Refusing to comply with an arranged marriage, the spirited and independent Rosina da Silva decides to support her family through work. But in order to find suitable employment, Rosina, a Sephardic Jewess, is forced to change her name and take on the identity of a Protestant governess. Thus transformed, she enters the privileged, gentile household of the Cavendish family on the Isle of Skye where she is captivated by her employer's experiments with capturing real-life images on paper ... Exploring a number of intriguing themes – anti-Semitism, class, sexism, sexual ignorance and the birth of photography – writer-director

Below: Make mine a size 22,349B: Hank Azaria and lizard in Roland Emmerich's awesome and noisy Godzilla (from Columbia TriStar)

Sandra Goldbacher has pulled off a remarkable first feature. Not only has she caught the atmosphere of an obscure, bygone world, but she has brought it vividly to life. And despite a limited budget the film looks wonderful.

● *Rosina da Silva/Mary Blackchurch* Minnie Driver, *Charles Cavendish* Tom Wilkinson, *Henry Cavendish* Jonathan Rhys Meyers, *Mrs Cavendish* Harriet Walter, *Cavendish* Florence Hoath, *Rebecca* Emma Bird, Arlene Cockburn, Adam Levy, Countess Koulinskyi, Bruce Myers, Diana Brooks, Cyril Shaps.
● *Dir* and *Screenplay* Sandra Goldbacher, *Pro* Sarah Curtis, *Ex Pro* Sally Hibbin, *Ph* Ashley Rowe, *Pro Des* Sarah Greenwood, *Ed* Isabel Lorente, *M* Edward Shearmur, *Costumes* Caroline Harris.

Parallax/Pandora Cinema/British Screen/Arts Council of England/BBC Films/Miramax/National Lottery – Alliance Releasing.
114 mins. UK/France. 1997. Rel: 23 October 1998. Cert 15.

Guru in 7 ★¹⁄₂

London; the present. When his girlfriend leaves him for Los Angeles, Indian artist Sanjay takes on an audacious bet: that he will have sexual intercourse with a different woman every day for the next week. If he succeeds, he will become The Guru, 'the one and only' ... While writer-director Shani Grewal brings a vibrant freshness to his story-telling and Nitin Chandra Ganatra, as Sanjay, supplies a certain cocky charm, this low-rent Asian *Alfie* gets exhausting after a while. Furthermore, a preponderance towards the gutter and frenzied camera moves creates the uneasy sensation of having your cake and throwing it up. It's also interesting that in such a bonk-friendly scenario the word AIDS isn't mentioned once. FYI: Grewal previously directed the Norman Wisdom turkey *Double X*.

● *Mr Walia* Saeed Jaffrey, *Joan, 'the oyster lady'* Jacqueline Pearce, *Sanjay* Nitin Chandra Ganatra, *Ram* Antony Zaki, *Jill Thomas* Ernestina Quarcoo, *Amrit* Dhirendra, *Gaynor* Amanda Pointer, *Holly* Elle Lewis, *Tina* Suchitra Malik, *Nora* Lea Rochelle, *Rani, Sanjay's mother* Adlyn Ross, *Sujjan, Sanjay's father* Gurdial Sira, Harvey Virdi, Lynne Michelle, Guy Ransom, Ravi Kapoor, Lalita Ahmed, Philippa Thomas, Philip Davies, Robert Ashe, Balwant Grewal, Harjeet Grewal, *wooden actor* Shani Grewal.
● *Dir, Pro, Screenplay* and *Ed* Shani Grewal, *Ex Pro* Arthur G. Lawrence, *Assoc Pro* Rosemary Sadler, *Ph* James Bishop, *M* Matthew Best, Neil Hourigan, Sean Maher and Sunny Sehgal, *Costumes* June Hudson, *Sound* Mike Crowley.

Balhar Film – Ratpack Films.
107 mins. UK. 1997. Rel: 10 July 1998. Cert 18.

Left: And let the screaming commence: Jamie Lee Curtis faces her worst nightmare in Steve Miner's nasty Halloween: H20 (from Buena Vista)

Halloween: H20 ★★¹/₂

Summer Glen, northern California; 31 October 1998. Twenty years after she was hunted down by her seriously deranged brother Michael Myers, Laurie Strode has changed her name to Keri Tate and is headmistress of the exclusive Hillcrest Academy. But even after group therapy, meditation, psychoanalysis and various forms of self-help, Laurie cannot control her drinking, nightmares and constant hallucinations. Today it's Halloween again and she really does have an axe to grind ... Utilising all the old standbys of the genre – creaking doors, underlit interiors and endless sudden bangs – this seventh edition of the *Halloween* franchise still manages to scare up some tension. However, the accent is more on nastiness than humour, although for horror fans there are a few good in-jokes. Janet Leigh, real-life mother of Jamie Lee Curtis and the shower victim of Hitchcock's *Psycho*: 'Miss Tate, I know it's not my place, but if I could be maternal for a moment. We've all had bad things happen to us...' FYI: The film is dedicated to the late Donald Pleasence (star of five of the previous *Halloween* films), but his name is misspelt!

● *Laurie Strode/Keri Tate* Jamie Lee Curtis, *Will Brennan* Adam Arkin, *Molly Cartwright* Michelle Williams, *Charlie* Adam Hann-Byrd, *Sarah* Jodi Lyn O'Keefe, *Norma* Janet Leigh, *John Tate* Josh Hartnett, *Ronny* LL Cool J, *Jimmy Howell* Joseph Gordon-Levitt, *Marion* Nancy Stephens, Branden Williams, Larisa Miller, Lisa Gay Hamilton, *Michael* Chris Durand.
● *Dir* Steve Miner, *Pro* Paul Freeman, *Ex Pro* Moustapha Akkad, *Co-Ex Pro* Bob Weinstein, Harvey Weinstein and Kevin Williamson, *Screenplay* Robert Zappia and Matt Greenberg, *Ph* Daryn Okada, *Pro Des* John Willet, *Ed* Patrick Lussier, *M* John Ottman; theme by John Carpenter, *Costumes* Deborah Everton, *Sound* Steve Boeddeker.

Miramax/Dimension Films/Nightfall Prods – Buena Vista. 87 mins. USA. 1998. Rel: 23 October 1998. Cert 18.

Hana-Bi ★★★¹/₂

Detective Nishi leaves his partner in a stakeout so as to visit his wife in a nearby hospital. At the time he is informed that his wife's cancer is terminal, Nishi's partner is shot and paralysed. Consumed with grief and guilt, Nishi abruptly rearranges the moral goal posts of his life ... With his emotionless features, faint twitch and stocky, Harvey Keitel-esque stature, 'Beat' Takeshi Kitano exudes the hypnotic presence of a cobra. As a director, his singular style proves equally mesmeric. Defying the expected grammar of the medium, he takes huge leaps through narrative time, luxuriates in a poetic passage and then cuts in with a comic interlude – all punctuated with sudden bursts of terrible violence. The effect is unsettling, beguiling and persuasively arresting. But who says you can make films this way? Winner of the Golden Lion at the 54th Venice Film Festival. FYI: Not only does Kitano direct, write and star in *Hana-Bi*, but he painted the pictures that appear throughout the film. P.S. Translated literally, 'hana-bi' means 'flower-fire', a deconstruction of *hannabi*, the Japanese word for fireworks.

● *Yoshitaka Nishi* Beat Takeshi, *Miyuki, Nishi's wife* Kayoko Kishimoto, *Horibe* Ren Osugi, *Nakamura* Susumu Terajima, *Tesuka, owner of junkyard* Tetsu Watanabe, Hakuryu, Yasuel Yakushiji, Makoto Ashikawa, Yuko Daike.
● *Dir* and *Screenplay* Takeshi Kitano, *Pro* Masayuki Mori, Yasushi Tsuge and Takio Yoshida, *Co-Pro* Hiroshi Ishikawa and Kazuhiro Furukawa, *Ph* Hideo Yamamoto, *Pro Des* Norihiro Isoda, *Ed* Kitano and Yoshinori Ota, *M* Joe Hisaishi.

Bandai Visual/Television Tokyo/Tokyo FM/Office Kitano – Alliance Releasing.
103 mins. Japan. 1997. Rel: 24 July 1998. Cert 18.

Happiness ★★★★★

With his award-winning *Welcome to the Dollhouse* (1996), writer-director Todd Solondz exhibited a ruthless tenderness tempered by an unblinking cruelty all in

Right: The gentle gunman: 'Beat' Takeshi in his own poetic, violent Hana-Bi (from Alliance Releasing)

the name of human comedy. Here, with his second (award-winning) feature, he expands his canvas to embrace a cross-section of society's dejected, a group of interconnected souls cocooned in their separate cubicles of anxiety, frustration and hopes for happiness. Broaching such taboo subjects as paedophilia, a yearning for rape and the problems of masturbation, Solondz holds up an uncomfortable mirror to the hopelessness of contemporary society, sweetening his bitter pill with unexpected doses of po-faced comedy. With its carefully measured tone, ironic use of music and outstanding cast, *Happiness* is the year's most poignant, confrontational, funny, shocking, uncomfortable and moving film. A masterpiece of embarrassment.

● *Joy Jordan* Jane Adams, *Diane Freed* Elizabeth Ashley, *Bill Maplewood* Dylan Baker, *Helen Jordan* Lara Flynn Boyle, *Lenny Jordan* Ben Gazzara, *Vlad* Jared Harris, *Allen* Philip Seymour Hoffman, *Mona Maplewood* Louise Lasser, *Andy Kornbluth* Jon Lovitz, *Kristina* Camryn Manheim, *Ann Chambeau* Marla Maples, *Billy Maplewood* Rufus Read, *Trish Maplewood* Cynthia Stevenson, *Johnny Grasso* Evan Silverberg, Justin Elvin, Gerry Becker, Arthur Nascarella, Molly Shannon, Doug McGrath, Anne Bobby, Dan Moran, Matt Malloy, Joe Lisi, Jose Rabelo.
● *Dir* and *Screenplay* Todd Solondz, *Pro* Ted Hope and Christine Vachon, *Ex Pro* David Linde and James Schamus, *Line Pro* Pamela Koffler, *Ph* Maryse Alberti, *Pro Des* Therese Deprez, *Ed* Alan Oxman, *M* Robbie Kondor; Vivaldi, Mozart, Samuel Barber; songs performed by Barry Manilow, Anatoly Aleshin, Air Supply; 'Happiness' sung by Jane Adams, and by Michael Stipe and Rain Phoenix, *Costumes* Kathryn Nixon.

October Films/Good Machine/Killer Films – Entertainment.
139 mins. USA. 1998. Rel: 16 April 1999. Cert 18.

Heart ★★★★★

Maria Ann McCardle has just lost her son, Sean, in a senseless motoring accident. Following a fit of jealous rage, Gary Ellis has just had a heart attack. Gary inherits Sean's heart and feels like a new man. Maria feels that by being close to Gary will keep her closer to her son. Gary, meanwhile, suspects that his wife, Tess, is having an affair with a heartless novelist ... Jimmy McGovern knows his drama. Having written the award-winning television productions *Cracker*, *Hearts and Minds* and *Hillsborough* and the theatrical release *Priest*, McGovern has established himself as one of the most potent forces in British drama. Here he has dreamed up a cracking good story that grabs you by the throat as it kicks you in the guts. First-time theatrical director Charles McDougal (who worked with McGovern on *Cracker* and *Hillsborough*) deftly and economically twists the strands of McGovern's narrative together, spurring the story on in short, sharp edits. Indeed, the film's longest scene lasts no longer than two minutes. Gripping, darkly humorous and utterly brilliant, *Heart* is a splenetic entertainment not for the faint-hearted.

● *Gary Ellis* Christopher Eccleston, *Maria Ann McCardle* Saskia Reeves, *Tess Ellis* Kate Hardie, *Alex Madden* Rhys Ifans, *Nicola Farmer* Anna Chancellor, *Mr Kreitman* Bill Paterson, Matthew Rhys, Kate Rutter, Alan Eccleston, Alison Swannon, Simon Molloy, John McGuirk.
● *Dir* Charles McDougall, *Pro* Nicola Shindler, *Ex Pro* Pippa Cross and Gub Neal, *Co-Ex Pro* Janette Day, *Screenplay* Jimmy McGovern, *Ph* Julian Court, *Pro Des* Stuart Walker and Chris Roope, *Ed* Edward Mansell, *M* Stephen Warbeck; songs performed by Ann Peebles, Sneaker Pimps, Space Monkeys, Dionne Warwick, Sam & Dave, Al Green, Echo and the Bunnymen, John McGuirk, Jim Reeves, Mazzy Star, Detroit Emeralds, etc, *Costumes* James Keast, *Christopher Eccleston's ears* Salford Prosthetics.

Granada Film/Merseyside Film Production Fund – Feature Film Co.
85 mins. UK. 1997. Rel: 11 June 1999. Cert 18.

He Got Game ★★¹/₂

Coney Island, Brooklyn, New York; the present. Jesus Shuttlesworth, the most feted high school basketball player in North America, has a week to decide whether to accept one of countless tempting college scholarships or to join the National Basketball Association. Everybody, it seems, wants a piece of his future, whether it be his coach, girlfriend or uncle. Then, at this most crucial point in his life, his estranged father turns up with yet another offer ... There are so many good things about *He Got Game*. Denzel Washington, as Jesus' penitent father, delivers yet another powerful, credible performance; Spike Lee's story addresses a number of complex issues with intelligence and complexity; and the technical artistry is second to none. Yet, equally, there are some pretty naff things: clumsy exposition ('your mother, Martha, my sister' elaborates Michele Shay), an overdose of sentimentality and an overpowering sense of self importance that weighs the film down. Furthermore, Spike Lee spends so much time reminding us that he's behind the camera that he constantly distracts us from his central drama.

● *Jake Shuttlesworth* Denzel Washington, *Jesus Shuttlesworth* Ray Allen, *Dakota Burns* Milla Jovovich, *Lala Bonilla* Rosario Dawson, *Coleman 'Booger' Sykes* Hill Harper, *Mary Shuttlesworth* Zelda Harris, *Uncle Bubba* Bill Nunn, *Aunt Sally* Michele Shay, *Sweetness* Thomas Jefferson Byrd, *Big Time Willie* Roger Guenveur Smith, *Billy Sunday* John Turturro *Coach, Martha Shuttlesworth* Lonette McKee, *Coach Cincotta* Arthur J. Nascarella, Ned Beatty, Jim Brown,

Joseph Lyle Taylor, Travis Best, Walter McCarty, John Wallace, Rick Fox, Al Palagonia, Avery Glymph, Jennifer Esposito, Shaquille O'Neal.
● *Dir* and *Screenplay* Spike Lee, *Pro* Lee and Jon Kilik, *Ph* Malik Hassan Sayeed, *Pro Des* Wynn Thomas, *Ed* Barry Alexander Brown, *M* Aaron Copland; songs by Public Enemy; songs performed by Public Enemy, Stephen Stills, KRS-One, and The Aleems, *Costumes* Sandra Hernandez.

Touchstone Pictures/40 Acres and A Mule Filmworks – Buena Vista.
134 mins. USA. 1998. Rel: 4 September 1998. Cert 18.

Henry Fool ★★★

New Jersey; today. Is Henry Fool a prophet, poet, vagabond, fugitive, charlatan or saviour? Whatever he may be, he acts as a catalyst in the dead-end lives of the Grim family, unleashing a cultural and sexual potential that his white trash benefactors didn't know they had. Turning up unannounced one day to rent the Grims' squalid basement, the enigmatic stranger takes Simon Grim – a nerdy, subdued refuse worker – under his wing and liberates his creative juices ... A twisted study of 'ambition, talent and influence', Hal Hartley's *Henry Fool* actually embraces a number of disparate themes – genius, sex, social dysfunction, poetry, publishing, the media and paedophilia – with the director's characteristic offbeat power. At best provocative and unpredictable, the film suffers from an air of contrivance and pretension, but is confidently composed and splendidly photographed. FYI: The appropriately moody soundtrack is scored by Hartley himself.

● *Henry Fool* Thomas Jay Ryan, *Simon Grim* James Urbaniak, *Fay Grim* Parker Posey, *Mary Grim* Maria Porter, *Mr Deng* James Saito, *Warren* Kevin Corrigan, *Father Hawkes* Nicholas Hope, *Vicky* Jan Leslie Harding, *Pearl, aged 14* Christy Romano, *Angus James* Chuck Montgomery, Liam Aiken, Miho Nikaido, Gene Ruffini, Diana Ruppe, Veanne Cox, Marissa Chibas, Don Creech, Camille Paglia, Dave Simonds, Paul Greco, Katreen Hardt.
● *Dir, Pro, Screenplay* and *M* Hal Hartley, *Ex Pro* Larry Meistrich, Daniel J. Victor and Keith Abell, *Assoc Pro* Jerome Brownstein and Thierry Cagianut, *Ph* Mike Spiller, *Pro Des* Steve Rosenzweig, *Ed* Steve Hamilton, *Costumes* Jocelyn Joson.

True Fiction Pictures/The Shooting Gallery/Zenith Prods – Columbia TriStar.
137 mins. USA. 1997. Rel: 13 November 1998. Cert 18.

Hideous Kinky ★★¹/₂

Morocco; 1972. Estranged from the father of her two daughters – Beau, eight, and Lucy, six – Julia heads for Morocco to escape 'cold and sad' London. Yet

Above: Road to Morocco: Kate Winslet, Bella Riza and Carrie Mullan get Hideous Kinky (from UIP)

while embracing the spiritual culture of this exotic new land, Julia is not immune to the ingrained problems of such an alien world ... An atmospheric and lovingly photographed evocation of Esther Freud's semi-autobiographical novel, *Hideous Kinky*, if nothing else, paints a colourful and vivid portrait of Morocco. Less successful, though, is the film's narrative structure, as director Gillies MacKinnon (*Small Faces*, *Regeneration*) insists on presenting his drama as a mosaic of abruptly truncated sequences. In addition, a 22-year-old Kate Winslet seems entirely wrong for the role of the headstrong 25-year-old mother of two, thus relinquishing the acting honours to the young Bella Riza and Carrie Mullan who, as her daughters, both dominate and steal the show.

● *Julia* Kate Winslet, *Bilal* Said Taghmaoui, *Bea* Bella Riza, *Lucy* Carrie Mullan, *Santoni* Pierre Clementi, *Charlotte* Abigail Cruttenden, *Ben Said* Ahmed Boulane, *Patricia* Michelle Fairley, Sira Stampe, Amidou, Kevin McKidd, Peter Youngblood Hills, Mohcine Barmouni.
● *Dir* Gillies MacKinnon, *Pro* Ann Scott, *Ex Pro* Mark Shivas and Simon Relph, *Co-Pro* Emmanuel Schlumberger, Annabel Karouby and Marina Gefter, *Line Pro* Paul Sarony, *Screenplay* Billy MacKinnon, *Ph* John de Borman, *Pro Des* Louise Marzaroli and Pierre Gompertz, *Ed* Pia Di Ciaula, *M* John Keane; songs performed by Canned Heat, Richie Havens, Love, America, Jefferson Airplane, Crosby, Stills & Nash, etc, *Costumes* Kate Carin, *Make-up/hair design* Mel Gibson, *Third assistant director* Jim Threapleton.

The Film Consortium/BBC Films/Arts Council of England/Greenpoint Films/European Script Fund/National Lottery – UIP.
99 mins. UK/France. 1998. Rel: 5 February 1999. Cert 15.

High Art ★★★¹/₂

New York City; today. Determined to make her mark in the world of publishing, Syd, 24, is more than just another pretty face. Recently promoted to assistant editor at the trendy photography magazine *Frame*, she works all hours, but is still relegated to fetching tea and sandwiches for her editor. Then she discovers that her neighbour, a lesbian heroin addict called Lucy Berliner, used to be a feted, cutting-edge photographer ... Lisa Cholodenko's debut feature is to be commended for managing the near impossible: for creating credible characters and situations without sacrificing its visual allure. A smart, sexy and atmospheric film, *High Art* is also a gift to its cast, its three female leads in particular making powerful impressions. But it is Ally Sheedy, the bright-eyed ingenue of such Eighties hits as *WarGames*, *St Elmo's Fire* and *Short Circuit*, who is the true revelation. All her puppy fat gone and the bloom in her cheeks long faded, she resembles an even scrawnier Sigourney Weaver. What a transformation. FYI: The Australian Radha Mitchell previously played the lesbian Danni in *Love and Other Catastrophes*.

● *Lucy Berliner* Ally Sheedy, *Syd* Radha Mitchell, *James* Gabriel Mann, *Greta Krauus* Patricia Clarkson, *Arnie* Bill Sage, *Dominique Pujot, editor of*

Left: Sisters without mercy: Emily Watson and Rachel Griffiths in Anand Tucker's emotionally gruelling Hilary and Jackie *(from Film Four)*

'Frame' Anh Duong, *Harry, Syd's boss* Davis Thornton, *Vera, Lucy's mother* Tammy Grimes, Helen Mendes, Cindra Feuer, Anthony Ruivivar, and *uncredited: Joan* Sarita Choudhury.
● *Dir* and *Screenplay* Lisa Cholodenko, *Pro* Dolly Hall, Jeff Levy-Hinte and Susan A. Stover, Assoc *Pro* Lori E. Seid, *Ph* Tami Reiker, *Pro Des* Bernhard Blythe, *Ed* Amy E. Duddleston, *M* Shudder To Think, *Costumes* Victoria Farrell, *Sound* Jonah Lawrence.

October Films/391 – Blue Light.
101 mins. USA. 1998. Rel: 9 April 1999. Cert 18.

Hilary and Jackie ★★★¹/₂

United by their love of music, Hilary and Jackie Du Pré are as close as two sisters can be. Something of a child prodigy on the flute, Hilary encourages her younger sibling to develop her own identity by mastering the cello. In fact, Hilary is prepared to give Jackie anything she wants, but then takes a back seat, as the latter's flamboyant mastery of her music brings her international acclaim ... If one is to believe *A Genius in the Family*, the warts'n'all biography penned by Jackie's siblings Hilary and Piers Du Pré, then Britain's greatest cellist of the 20th century was a pretty troubled and impossible soul. Thus, this emotionally gruelling adaptation of their exposé is not an easy film to spend time with. Nevertheless, its parts are to be admired: a sly, committed performance from Emily Watson as Jackie, a controlled, reactive one from Australia's limitlessly versatile Rachel Griffiths (adopting an impeccable English accent), some virtuoso cello from Caroline Dale (who, incidentally, also trained Ms Watson to play) and a number of choice incidental moments plucked from a remarkable life.

All told, a moving and haunting experience. FYI: Director Anand Tucker, who was born in Bangkok and brought up in Hong Kong, is the child of an Indian father and German mother.

● *Jackie Du Pré* Emily Watson, *Hilary Du Pré* Rachel Griffiths, *Daniel Barenboim* James Frain, *Kiffer* David Morrisey, *Derek Du Pré* Charles Dance, *Iris Du Pré* Celia Imrie, *Piers Du Pré* Rupert Penry-Jones, *cello teacher* Bill Paterson, *Dame Margot Fonteyn* Nyree Dawn Porter, Auriol Evans, Keeley Flanders, Grace Chatto, Maggie McCarthy, Vernon Dobtcheff, Anthony Smee, Heather Weeks, Ralph De Souza, Kate Hetherington, Ariana Daykin, George Kennaway, John Gough.
● *Dir* Anand Tucker, *Pro* Andy Paterson and Nicolas Kent, *Ex Pro* Guy East, Nigel Sinclair and Ruth Jackson, *Screenplay* Frank Cottrell Boyce, *Ph* David Johnson, *Pro Des* Alice Normington, *Ed* Martin Walsh, *M* Barrington Pheloung; Elgar, Haydn, J.S. Bach, Brahms, Franck, Matthias Georg Monn, Handel, Schumann, Beethoven, and Dvorak, *Costumes* Sandy Powell.

Oxford Film/Intermedia Films/Film Four/British Screen/Arts Council of England – Film Four.
121 mins. UK. 1998. Rel: 22 January 1999. Cert 15.

Holy Man ★★

Miami; today. Slick TV executive Ricky Hayman is suffering from a case of '27 months of flatness.' And if he fails to immediately turn around the figures of the Good Buy Shopping Network he is out of a job. With his flash lifestyle spiralling out of control, Ricky needs a miracle fast. However, he never expected the miracle to be in the shape of a self-styled guru advocating the demise of consumerism ... While it's always fun to ridicule the ludicrous excesses of the media and advertising, it's a rather old joke. Of course, the shopping channel itself has been largely spared the mockery of the cinema, and it's here that *Holy Man* comes into its own. And with a number of real-life celebrities selling themselves out in the cause of a good chuckle, the film gains some comic mileage. But it's still Jeff Goldblum who gets the real laughs. He's the sort of actor who can turn a throwaway line like, 'Oh, you're new on this planet, aren't you?' into something very funny. Bless him.

● *'G'* Eddie Murphy, *Ricky Hayman* Jeff Goldblum, *Kate Newell* Kelly Preston, *McBainbridge* Robert Loggia, *Barry* Jon Cryer, *Scott Hawkes* Eric McCormack, Sam Kitchin, Robert Small, Marc Macaulay, Mary Stout, Edie McClurg, Kim Staunton, Lori Viveros Herek, Whitney Dupree, Mark Brown, and, as themselves: Morgan Fairchild, Betty White, Florence Henderson, James Brown, Soupy Sales, Dan Marino, Willard Scott, Nino Cerruti.
● *Dir* Stephen Herek, *Pro* Herek and Roger Birnbaum, *Ex Pro* Jeffrey Chernov and Jonathan Glickman, *Co-Pro* Ray Murphy and Rebekah Rudd, *Screenplay* Tom Schulman, *Ph* Adrian Biddle, *Pro Des* Andrew McAlpine, *Ed* Trudy Ship, *M* Alan Silvestri; songs performed by Underworld, Malcolm Lockyer, Gloria Estefan, Stevie Wonder, etc, *Costumes* Aggie Guerard Rodgers.

Touchstone Pictures – Buena Vista.
114 mins. USA. 1998. Rel: 19 February 1999. Cert PG.

The Honest Courtesan ★★

Venice; the 1500s. Prohibited from academic study and marrying the aristocrat she loves – because of her poor social standing – Veronica Franco takes her mother's advice to become a courtesan. Thus she is able to exploit both her lust for books and bonking ... In spite of its basis in truth, *The Honest Courtesan* seldom rings a credible note, with the motivations of its characters seemingly built on intellectual quicksand (the strangest conceit of all being that Veronica should enjoy such carnal activity will *all* her clients). This absurdity aside, the film is sumptuously shot and Bisset and McCormack make a thrilling mother-daughter double-act. Previously known as *A Destiny of Her Own*. US title: *Dangerous Beauty*. [Charles Bacon]

● *Veronica Franco* Catherine McCormack, *Marco Venier* Rufus Sewell, *Maffio* Oliver Platt, *Beatrice* Moira Kelly, *Domenico Venier* Fred Ward, *Paola Franco* Jacqueline Bisset, *The Doge* Peter Eyre, *Giulia De Lezze* Naomi Watts, *Pietro Venier* Jeroen Krabbe, *Laura Venier* Joanna Cassidy, Melina Kanakaredes, Daniel Lapaine, Justine Miceli, Jake Weber, Simon Dutton, Grant Russell, Michael Culkin, Richard O'Callaghan, David Gant.
● *Dir* Marshall Herskovitz, *Pro* Herskovitz, Edward Zwick, Arnon Milchan and Sarah Caplan, *Ex Pro* Michael Nathanson and Stephen Randall, *Assoc Pro* Debra Michael Petro, *Screenplay* Jeannine Dominy, from the biography of Veronica Franco by Margaret Rosenthal, *Ph* Bojan Bazelli, *Pro Des* Norman Garwood, *Ed* Steven Rosenblum and Arthur Corburn, *M* George Fenton, *Costumes* Gabriella Pescucci. Fights: William Hobbs.

Monarchy EnterprisesRegency Enterprises/Bedford Falls – Fox.
112 mins. USA. 1997. Rel: 30 April 1999. Cert 15.

Hope Floats ★★¹/₂

When happy housewife and mother Birdee Pruitt agrees to a TV show 'makeover', she finds herself the subject of national humiliation when her best friend Connie announces that she's sleeping with Birdee's husband. Fleeing back to mother in the sleepy town of Smithville, Texas – with her nine-year-old daughter in tow – Birdee is forced to face up to her old mistakes and to 'give life a chance for hope to float up' ... After this and *Waiting to Exhale*, director Forest Whitaker is in danger of ordaining himself the chaplain of chick flicks, with all the gloss, sentiment and slow motion that that entails. Notwithstanding, he has a talent for directing actors and the three generations of women here all give him their best work (particularly Mae Whitman who, at nine, is already a veteran of six major films). There are also a number of wonderfully canny observations and poignant moments that manage to escape the contrivances of a wantonly commercial package (that, oddly, loses its way in the last five minutes). Great soundtrack – and don't they let us know it.

● *Birdee Pruitt nee Calvert* Sandra Bullock, *Justin Matisse* Harry Connick Jr, *Ramona Calvert* Gena Rowlands, *Bernice Pruitt* Mae Whitman, *Bill Pruitt* Michael Pare, *Travis* Cameron Finley, *Toni Post* Kathy Najimy, Bill Cobbs, Connie Ray, Mona Lee Fultz, Sydney Berry, Rachel Lena Snow, Christina Stojanovich, Allisa Alban, Dee Hennigan, and *uncredited*: *Connie Phillips* Rosanna Arquette.
● *Dir* Forest Whitaker, *Pro* Lynda Obst, *Ex Pro* Mary McLaglen and Sandra Bullock, *Screenplay* Steven Rogers, *Ph* Caleb Deschanel, *Pro Des* Larry Fulton, *Ed* Richard Chew, *M* Dave Grusin; songs performed by Jonelle Mosser, Sheryl Crow, The Rolling Stones, Barry Manilow, Lyle Lovett, Bob Seger and Martina McBride, Whiskeytown, The Mavericks, Gillian Welch, The Temptations, Jack Ingram, Garth Brooks, Deana Carter, Trisha Yearwood, Bryan Adams, etc, *Costumes* Susie DeSanto, *Choreography* Patsy Swayze.

Fox/Fortis Films – Fox.
114 mins. USA. 1998. Rel: 13 November 1998. Cert PG.

The Horse Whisperer ★★★

When their only daughter is crippled in a terrible riding accident in upstate New York, Robert and Annie MacLean face even greater pressure on their work-obsessed lives than before. On a whim, Annie decides to drive her daughter (against her will) and the badly wounded steed to Montana to seek out a legendary 'horse whisperer', a man known for his gift for rehabilitating horses ... This is the one that Robert Redford optioned for $3 million from the unfinished novel by first-time English writer Nicholas Evans. Since then the book has met widespread acclaim and become a universal best-seller, proving that Redford knows a good thing when he sniffs it. His movie – the first in which he has directed himself – certainly looks wonderful, boasts many powerful moments and is masterfully directed. But at almost three hours long there are as many wide open spaces in the narrative as there are in Montana, resulting in a work of languid self-importance. Patient viewers may find themselves rewarded, but many will be bored by Redford's Evian school of film-making.

● *Tom Booker* Robert Redford, *Annie MacLean* Kristin Scott Thomas, *Robert MacLean* Sam Neill, *Diane Booker* Dianne Wiest, *Grace MacLean* Scarlett Johansson, *Frank Booker* Chris Cooper, *Liz Hammond* Cherry Jones, *Joe Booker* Ty Hillman, *Ellen Booker* Jeanette Nolan, Catherine Bosworth, Steve Frye, Don Edwards, Jessalyn Gilsig, William 'Buddy' Byrd.
● *Dir* Robert Redford, *Pro* Redford and Patrick Markey, *Ex Pro* Rachel Pfeffer, *Screenplay* Richard LaGravenese and Eric Roth, *Ph* Robert Richardson, *Pro Des* Jon Hutman, *Ed* Tom Rolf, Freeman Davies Jr and Hank Corwin, *M* Thomas Newman; Beethoven, *Costumes* Judy L. Ruskin, *Sound* Gary Rydstrom and Steve Boeddeker.

Touchstone Pictures/Wildwood Enterprises – Buena Vista. 169 mins. USA. 1998. Rel: 28 August 1998. Cert PG.

How Stella Got Her Groove Back ★

Stella, a high-flying money broker for a top San Francisco firm, has forgotten how to groove. Materially well-appointed and physically in peak condition, Stella, now 40, is missing the one thing every woman should have: a man. Then, a spontaneous week's vacation in Jamaica with her best friend, Delilah, delivers the goods. It's unfortunate, then, that the man in question is half Stella's age ... Drowning some weighty black female issues in an avalanche of gloss, this commercial for Angela Bassett's biceps is about as devastatingly insightful as a ditty by Whitney Houston. Bereft of laughs, tears and drama, this is one film desperately in search of a groove. Can you believe that scenarist Ron Bass (*Rain Man*, *The Joy Luck Club*) had a hand in this?

● *Stella Payne* Angela Bassett, *Winston Shakespeare* Taye Diggs, *Delilah* Whoopi Goldberg, *Vanessa* Regina King, *Angela* Suzanne Douglas, *Quincy* Michael J. Pagan, *Dr Shakespeare* Glynn Turman, *Mrs Shakespeare* Phyllis Yvonne Stickney, Sicily, Richard Lawson, Barry 'Shabaka' Henley, James Pickens Jr., Lou Myers, Art Metrano, Carl Lumbly.
● *Dir* Kevin Rodney Sullivan, *Pro* Deborah Schindler, *Ex Pro* Terry McMillan, Ron Bass and Jennifer Ogden, *Screenplay* McMillan and Bass, from McMillan's semi-autobiographical novel of the same name, *Ph* Jeffrey Jur, *Pro Des* Chester Kaczenski, *Ed* George Bowers, *M* Michel Colombier; songs performed by Soul II Soul, Jr Walker & The Allstars, Bob Marley and the Wailers, James Brown, Diana King, Maxi Priest, Mary J. Blige, Shaggy with Janet, Maze, Parliament, Stevie Wonder, Me'Shell N'degeocello, Boyz II Men, etc, *Costumes* Ruth E. Carter.

Fox – Fox.
124 mins. USA. 1998. Rel: 5 February 1999. Cert 15.

Human Traffic ★★★¹/₂

Cardiff, Wales; today. Jip, Lulu, Koop, Moff and Nina are close, close friends who know how to party. And as the interminable drudgery of their working week comes to a close, they determine to have the weekend of their lives: drinking, clubbing and popping Es until the cows come home... In a bumper year of fresh and innovative films adding their voice to the chorus of British cinema (cf. *Crush Proof*, *Virtual Sexuality*), *Human Traffic* adds its own distinctive cry. Charting the decadent leisure time of five friends wired to party, *Human Traffic* eschews the moral fall-out of *Trainspotting* to glow in the twilight of its own dubious revelry. An ensemble of wonderful new actors fill their parts with gusto, while the soundtrack throbs, the camera dances and the bonhomie rocks. Vital, relevant and pulsating cinema that dares to shout for its own generation.

● *Jip* John Simm, *Lulu* Lorraine Pilkington, *Koop* Shaun Parkes, *Nina* Nicola Reynolds, *Moff* Danny Dyer, *Lee* Dean Davies, *Felix* Andrew Lincoln, *Pablo Hassan* Carl Cox, Howard Marks, Jo Brand, Nicola Heywood-Thomas.
● *Dir* and *Screenplay* Justin Kerrigan, *Pro* Allan Niblo and Emer McCourt, *Ex Pro* Renata S. Aly, Nigel Warren-Green, Michael Wearing and Kevin Menton, *Ph* David Bennett, *Pro Des* Dave Buckingham, *Ed* Patrick Moore, *M* Rob Mello and Matthew Herbert; songs performed by Fatboy Slim, Grim, Universal, Brainbug, Aphrodite, Public Enemy, Lucid, Quake, System F, Death in Vegas, Liquid Child, Orbital, Echoboy, Durango, Primal Scream, Position Normal, Mad Doctor X, etc, *Costumes* Claire Anderson.

Fruit Salad Films/Metrodome/Irish Screen – Metrodome. 95 mins. UK/Ireland. 1999. Rel: 4 June 1999. Cert 18.

Above: Love and other vulgarities: Cate Blanchett and Jeremy Northam practice some mouth music in Oliver Parker's sparkling An Ideal Husband (from Pathe)

I Stand Alone
See *Seul contre tous*.

An Ideal Husband ★★★¹/₂
Sir Robert Chiltern is a politician whose intellectual and emotional resources are seemingly separated 'through some violence of will-power'. He is also a man of rare character and a generous husband to the beautiful and doting Lady Chiltern. But with the arrival from Vienna of Mrs Cheveley, Sir Robert's standing in the community is suddenly threatened. Now, only Sir Robert's frivolous and arrogant friend Lord Goring would seem to offer salvation ... If you're going to film a play by Oscar Wilde, it helps to have an actor of the calibre of Rupert Everett around. Having re-invented himself in *My Best Friend's Wedding*, Everett eases himself into the pivotal role of the vain but decent Lord Goring with consummate aplomb. Indeed, this is an actors' film and it flaunts a wonderful cast, with Minnie Driver a perky comic foil as the cheerfully scheming Mabel Chiltern and Julianne Moore a revelation as the malevolently machiavellian Mrs Cheveley. Happily, director Parker opens out the play just enough to let the cinema in without disturbing its theatrical juices. Great dialogue, too (Lord Goring: 'I love talking about nothing, father. It is the only thing I know anything about'). Previously filmed in 1948 by Alexander Korda, with Paulette Goddard and Michael Wilding, and in 1998 (!) by Bill Cartlidge, with Sadie Frost and James Wilby.

● *Lady Gertrude Chiltern* Cate Blanchett, *Mabel Chiltern* Minnie Driver, *Lord Arthur Goring* Rupert Everett, *Mrs Cheveley* Julianne Moore, *Sir Robert Chiltern* Jeremy Northam, *Lord Caversham* John Wood, *Lady Markby* Lindsay Duncan, *Phipps* Peter Vaughan, *Tommy Trafford* Ben Pullen, *Sir Edward* Simon Russell Beale, *Lady Olivia Basildon* Delia Lindsay, *Oscar Wilde* Michael Culkin, Jeroen Krabbe, Marsha Fitzalan, Neville Phillips, Nickolas Grace, Jill Balcon, Janet Henfrey, Toby Robertson, *Bunbury* Oliver Parker, Peter Parker, Oliver Ford Davies.
● *Dir* and *Screenplay* Oliver Parker, *Pro* Barnaby Thompson, Uri Fruchtmann and Bruce Davey, *Ex Pro* Susan Landau, Ralph Kamp and Andrea Calderwood, *Co-Pro* Nicky Kentish Barnes and Paul Tucker, *Ph* David Johnson, *Pro Des* Michael Howells, *Ed* Guy Bensley, *M* Charlie Mole, *Costumes* Caroline Harris.

Icon Entertainment/Pathe Pictures/ Arts Council of England/Fragile/Miramax – Pathe.
100 mins. UK. 1999. Rel: 16 April 1999. Cert PG.

The Idiots – Idioterne ★★★¹/₂

In order to subvert the middle-class values that they abhor, a circle of educated, professional young friends attempt to find their 'inner idiot' by posing as 'retards'. Whether causing disorder in public or 'spassing out' in the privacy of their own commune, the 'idiots' find a solidarity and sense of family previously denied them ... It's hard to warm to Lars von Trier's latest courtship with controversy, even if it is pretty unforgettable and occasionally quite moving. It is also disturbing and challenging, credible and funny, all of which is news that should thrill the director. The second in the 'Dogme 95 manifesto' series (cf. *Festen*), *The Idiots* was inspired by Rudolf Steiner's unorthodox theory that (in the words of von Trier) 'mongoloids were like angels, a kind of gift to mankind.' Here, the film confronts our own queasiness towards and acceptance of the mentally handicapped, while challenging those very sensibilities with generous helpings of comedy. Are we meant to laugh, cry or fume? Precisely. It's a shame, though, that the by-now-notorious orgy scene (featuring authentic intercourse) has overtaken the film's more serious themes. FYI: Von Trier wrote his script in exactly four days.

● *Karen* Bodil Jorgensen, *Stoffer* Jens Albinus, *Susanne* Louise Hassing, *Henrik* Troels Lyby, *Jeppe* Nikolaj Lie Kaas, *Ped* Henrik Prip, *Josephine* Louise Mieritz, *Axel* Knud Romer Jorgensen, *Katrine* Anne-Grethe Bjarup Riis, Luis Mesonero, Trine Michelsen, Erik Wedersoe, Anders Hove, Louise B. Clausen, Ditlev Weddelsberg.
● *Dir, Screenplay* and *Ph* Lars von Trier, *Pro* Vibeke Windelov, *Ex Pro* Peter Aalbaek Jensen, *Ed* Molly Malene Stensgaard, *Sound* Per Streit.

Zentropa Entertainment/DR TV/La Sept Cinema/Canal Plus, etc – Metro Tartan.
114 mins. Denmark/France/Italy/The Netherlands/ Germany/Sweden. 1998. Rel: 14 May 1999. Cert 18.

If Only ★¹/₂

West London; the present. Pretty psychologist Sylvia Ward is due to marry self-assured agricultural engineer Dave Summers tomorrow, but her ex-boyfriend, out-of-work actor Victor Bukowski, is having none of it. Petitioning her with flowers and contrition – and terrorising her fiance – Victor sees his world about to collapse. Then, with the wave of a magic wand, he is transported back in time for a second chance. If only he doesn't make the same mistakes again ... Borrowing its concept from *Groundhog Day* and blowing it, *If Only* is yet another British romantic comedy that hangs its premise on a gimmick. Celestial dustbin men are all very well, but Douglas Henshall's hero is such an unappealing, unredeemable character that it's hard to know where to

anchor one's sympathies. Worse, many of the film's comic moments are glaringly unfunny and the dialogue bloated with platitudes. Previously known as *The Man With Rain In His Shoes*.

● *Sylvia Weld* Lena Headey, *Victor Bukowski* Douglas Henshall, *Louise* Penelope Cruz, *Rafael* Gustavo Salmeron, *Don Migel* Eusebio Lazaro, *Dave Summers* Mark Strong, *Alison Hayes* Charlotte Coleman, *Freddy Smith* Neil Stuke, *Diane* Elizabeth McGovern, *Carol* Heather Weeks, *pianist* Dave Fishley, Antonio Gil Martinez, Inday Ba, Paul Popplewell, Emma Freud, Caprice Bourett.
● *Dir* Maria Ripoll, *Pro* Juan Gordon, *Ex Pro* Jon Slan and Gareth Jones, *Line Pro* Sheila Fraser Milne, *Screenplay* Rafa Russo, *Ph* Javier Salmones, *Pro Des* Grant Hicks, *Ed* Nacho Ruiz-Capillas, *M* Luis Mendo, Bernardo Fuster and Angel Illarramendi, *Costumes* John Krausa.

HandMade Films/Paragon Entertainment/Wild Rose Prods/Parallel Pictures, etc – Pathe.
94 mins. Spain/France/Canada/UK/Luxembourg. 1998. Rel: 27 November 1998. Cert 15

The Impostors ★¹/₂

The North Atlantic; the 1930s. When two out-of-work actors ridicule a drunken, self-opinionated ham, the latter sends the police after them. Hiding out in a crate on board an ocean liner, the unfortunate fugitives fall asleep and wake up to find that they have inadvertently become stowaways ... Having displayed a masterful command of human comedy with the

Above: Naked lies: Knud Romer Jorgensen, Louise Hassing, Luis Mesonero and Jens Albinus indulge themselves in Lars von Triers' disturbing and moving The Idiots (from Metro Tartan)

critically revered *Big Night*, Stanley Tucci bravely takes on an entirely different form of humour with this, his second outing as director. An affectionate homage of the golden era of slapstick, *The Impostors* parades an impressive array of comic stereotypes brought resoundingly to life by a splendid cast. But such farce can all too easily preclude audience empathy and here the film deteriorates into a succession of over-the-top skits that become increasingly tiresome. Still, one has to applaud some of the performances, not least Billy Connolly's athletic homosexual, Campbell Scott's bottled-up Nazi and Steve Buscemi's terminally morose crooner. Previously known as *Ship of Fools*.

● *Maurice* Oliver Platt, *Arthur* Stanley Tucci, *Sheik* Teagle F. Bougere, *Pancetta Leaky* Elizabeth Bracco, *Happy Franks* Steve Buscemi, *Sparks* Billy Connolly, *Captain* Allan Corduner, *Emily* Hope Davis, *Mrs Essendine* Dana Ivey, *Maxine* Allison Janney, *Johnny the Frenchman* Richard Jenkins, *Marco* Matt McGrath, *Jeremy Burtom* Alfred Molina, *Queen* Isabella Rossellini, *Meistrich* Campbell Scott, *First Mate* Tony Shalhoub, *Lily* Lily Taylor, David Lipman, E. Katherine Kerr, Michael Emerson, Matt Malloy, Lewis J. Stadlen, Michael Higgins, Ken Costigan, and *uncredited*: Woody Allen.
● *Dir* and *Screenplay* Stanley Tucci, *Pro* Tucci and Beth Alexander, *Ex Pro* Jonathan Filley, *Ph* Ken Kelsch, *Pro Des* Andrew Jackness, *Ed* Suzy Elmiger, *M* Gary DeMichele; songs performed by The Forever Tango Orchestra, Eddie Condon, Sidney Bechet, Louis Armstrong, Steve Buscemi, Hope Davis, Lucienne Boyer, Artie Shaw, Elizabeth Bracco and Lewis J. Stadlen, Isham Jones, etc, *Costumes* Juliet Polcsa.

Fox Searchlight/First Cold Press – Fox.
100 mins. USA. 1998. Rel: 21 May 1999. Cert 15.

In Dreams ★¹/₂

Massachusetts; today. Children's illustrator Claire Cooper is having increasingly disturbing psychic visions in which she 'witnesses' murders before they happen. When her own daughter is abducted by a serial killer, she goes off the edge and enters into a treacherous game of cat-and-mouse with the psychopath's own intuitive powers ... By desaturating the colour and incessantly shuffling Claire's visions with reality and flashbacks, director Jordan has created a dream movie. That is, *In Dreams* exercises all the soporific powers of a real dream complete with its accompanying illogicality. From the (promising) opening shots of a town underwater to Claire's first nightmare, the film beds down into its own stylistic trance and stays there until the bitter end. The same premise was used to much better effect in the 1990 low-budget thriller *Fear* starring Ally Sheedy.

● *Claire Cooper* Annette Bening, *Paul Cooper* Aidan Quinn, *Dr Silverman* Stephen Rea, *Vivian Thompson*

Robert Downey Jr, *Detective Jack Kay* Paul Guilfoyle, *Rebecca Cooper* Katie Sagona, *Dr Stevens* Dennis Boutsikaris, *Ruby* Krystal Benn, Ken Cheeseman, Devon Cole Borisoff, Lonnie Farmer, Margo Martindale, Geoff Wigdor, Wally Dunn, Dossy Peabody, *Dobie* Pete.
● *Dir* Neil Jordan, *Pro* Stephen Woolley, *Co-Pro* Redmond Morris, *Screenplay* Jordan and Bruce Robinson, from the novel *Doll's Eyes* by Bari Wood, *Ph* Darius Khondji, *Pro Des* Nigel Phelps, *Ed* Tony Lawson, *M* Elliot Goldenthal; songs performed by The Andrews Sisters, Bread, The Righteous Brothers, and Roy Orbison, *Costumes* Jeffrey Kurland.

DreamWorks/Amblin – UIP.
99 mins. USA. 1998. Rel: 30 April 1999. Cert 18.

The Inheritors – Die Siebtelbauern
★★¹/₂

Austria; the early 1930s. Following the mysterious murder of a farmer, the deceased's seven employees are left his valuable property in his will. Resisting offers to sell up for chicken feed, the farmhands resolve to manage the estate themselves, much to the indignation of their foreman. That mere peasants will hold such an enviable position in the local community will not to be taken lightly by rival landowners ... A genuine curiosity, *The Inheritors* borrows elements of the traditional Western – homesteaders fighting for their land, an outlaw stalking the bad guys – and overlays a strong flavour of European pastoral Gothic. The result is decidedly unnerving as the film meanders blindly into unpredictable territory, piquing the interest even as it plays on one's patience. Yet, regardless of its uneven tone, it's a startling original, is evocatively crafted and makes the most of its haunting Alpine setting. Original English title: *The One-Seventh Farmers*.

● *Emmy* Sophie Rois, *Lukas Candelmas* Simon Schwarz, *Severin* Lars Rudolph, *Old Nane* Julia Gschnitzer, *Danninger* Ulrich Wildgruber, *Rosalind* Elisabeth Orth, *Grossknecht* Tilo Pruckner, *Lisbeth* Susanne Silverio, *Liesl* Kirsten Schwab, Christoph Gusenbauer, Werner Prinz, Dietmar Nigsch, Gertraud Maybock.
● *Dir* and *Screenplay* Stefan Ruzowitzky, *Pro* Danny Krausz and Kurt Stocker, *Ex Pro* Manfred Fritsch, *Ph* Peter von Haller, *Pro Des* Isi Wimmer, *Ed* Britta Burkert-Nahler, *M* Erik Satie; Verdi, *Costumes* Nicole Fischnaller.

Dor Film – Metrodome.
95 mins. Austria. 1997. Rel: 28 May 1999. Cert 15.

Insomnia ★★★

A connoisseur of the covert clue, Swedish homicide detective Jonas Engstrom is called to the northern reaches of Norway to help puncture an air-tight murder mystery. Unsettled by the constant sunshine and unable to sleep at night (thanks to a recalcitrant hotel blind), Engstrom finds that his traditional powers of perception are drastically undermined. And when he starts making fatal mistakes, he becomes embroiled in a situation possibly beyond his control ... Leisurely paced and dotted with eccentric detail, *Insomnia* benefits from its unusual setting in which light, rather than dark, casts a troubling shadow. As with most Scandinavian films that reach these shores, the humour is as rarefied as dry ice, while Stellan Skarsgard, giving another performance of subtly loaded disquiet, is constantly watchable.

● *Jonas Engstrom* Stellan Skarsgard, *Erik Vik* Sverre Anker Ousdal, *Hilde Hagen* Gisken Armand, *Jon Holt* Bjorn Floberg, *Eilert* Bjorn Moan, *Froya Selmer* Marianne O. Ulrichsen, *Tanja Lorentzen* Maria Mathiesen, Maria Bonnevie, Kristian Figenschow, Thor Michael Aamodt, Frode Rasmussen.
● *Dir* Erik Skjoldbjaerg, *Pro* Arne Frilseth, *Ex Pro* Petter Borgli, Tomas Backstrom and Tom Remlov, *Screenplay* Skjoldbjaerg and Nikolaj Frobenius, *Ph* Erling Thurmann-Andersen, *Pro Des* Eli Bo, *Ed* Hakon Overas, *M* Biosphere, *Costumes* Runa Fonne.

Norsk Film/Nordic Screen – United Media.
97 mins. Norway. 1997. Rel: 13 November 1998. Cert 15.

I Still Know What You Did Last Summer ★★

A year after her school chums were gutted by the mysterious bloke in the sou'wester, Julie James is struggling with her sanity at a Boston college. But when her ebullient room-mate Karla wins a holiday for four in the Caribbean – for guessing that Rio de Janeiro is the capital of Brazil – Julie hopes to put her nightmares behind her. How silly can a girl get? Marginally better produced than its predecessor, this surprisingly humourless sequel to the inexplicable horror hit of 1997 is still hamstrung by the tired conventions of the genre. There's also an unforgivable lack of suspense, one too many false alarms and a hyperactive score that is determined to do all the work. Having said that, there are also a few reasonable performances (from Brandy, Mekhi Phifer and a deliciously hammy Jeffrey Combs), one nice twist and some fluid, attractive camerawork. But it's still not good enough.

● *Julie James* Jennifer Love Hewitt, *Ray Bronson* Freddie Prinze Jr, *Karla Wilson* Brandy, *Tyrell* Mekhi Phifer, *Ben/Fisherman* Muse Watson, *Estes* Bill Cobbs, *Will Benson* Matthew Settle, *Mr Brooks* Jeffrey Combs, *Nancy* Jennifer Esposito, John Hawkes, Ellerine!, Benjamin Brown, Mark Boone Jr.
● *Dir* Danny Cannon, *Pro* Neal H. Moritz, Erik Feig, Stokely Chaffin and William S. Beasley,

Screenplay Trey Callaway, *Ph* Vernon Layton, *Pro Des* Doug Kraner, *Ed* Peck Prior, *M* John Frizzell; songs performed by Imogen Heap, Orgy, Jennifer Love Hewitt, Whitesnake, Dire Straits, Born Jamericans, Bijou Phillips, Lamb, etc, *Costumes* Dan Lester.

Columbia/Mandalay Entertainment/Global Ent./Medien KG – Columbia TriStar.
100 mins. USA/Germany. 1998. Rel: 6 May 1999. Cert 18.

I Think I Do ★★½

Washington DC; the 1990s. When Bob makes a pass at his college roommate Brendan, Brendan socks him in the jaw. Years later, at the wedding of mutual friends, Bob and Brendan meet up again. Bob is now a successful TV writer and is engaged to his leading man. But Brendan now has other plans ... An ensemble romantic comedy with a gay twist, this first feature from gay director Brian Sloan apes the confusion of 1930s/1940s screwball comedies with some skill and a smattering of good lines (groom snapping at his bride: 'Oh darling, sarcasm is *so* romantic'). Yet while these are fun characters to spend time with, we cannot entirely believe in nor connect with them. Consequently, the film's seemingly arbitrary ending leaves a nagging question mark knotted on the brow.

● Alexis Arquette (*Bob*), Christian Maelen (*Brendan*), Marianne Hagan (*Sarah*), Jamie Harrold (*Matt Lynch*), Lauren Velez (*Carol Anita Gonzalez*), Guillermo Diaz (*Eric*), Tuc Watkins (*Sterling Scott*), Maddie Corman (*Beth*), Elizabeth Rodriguez (*Celia*), Marni Nixon (*Aunt Alice*), Patricia Mauceri (*Mrs Gonzalez*), Dechen Thurman.
● *Dir* and *Screenplay* Brian Sloan, *Pro* Lane Janger, *Ex Pro* Jon Gerrans, Marcus Hu, Robert Miller and

Below: Killing time: Jennifer Love Hewitt, Brandy and Jennifer Esposito get the holiday blues in Danny Cannon's by-the-numbers I Still Know What You Did Last Summer (from Columbia TriStar)

Above: Through a glass darkly: Labina Mitevska smoulders in Michael Winterbottom's intriguing, surreal I Want You (from PolyGram)

Daryl Roth, *Line Pro* Scott Hornbacher, *Ph* Milton Kam, *Pro Des* Debbie Devilla, *Ed* Francois Keraudren, *M* Wagner, Mendelssohn, Mozart; songs performed by Voice of the Beehive, David Cassidy & The Partridge Family, Lisa Frazier, etc, *Costumes* Kevin Donaldson and Victoria Farell.

Danger Filmworks/House of Pain Prods/Source Entertainment/Daryl Roth Prods – Millivres Multimedia. 93 mins. USA. 1997. Rel: 12 February 1999. Cert 15.

I Want You ★★★

Farhaven, the English seaside; today. A dial-a-stripper disrobes to the sound of Elvis Costello singing 'I Want You' on a tinny tape recorder. A convicted killer on parole, Martin stares at the gyrating woman, his thoughts elsewhere. He has some unfinished business with Helen, who runs a local hairdressing salon. Helen, meanwhile, is having trouble with her boyfriend, a disc jockey, and has been befriended by a strange 14-year-old boy. The boy is mute but he sees everything, bugs it, records it ... Photographed through a yellow filter by Kieslowski's regular camera-man, this intriguing, psychological mosaic holds the interest through the sheer force of its imagery and fragmented narrative. Yet as the pieces slowly come together, the triteness of the story becomes all too apparent. There's much to ruminate on and Sussex has never looked more surreal, but this tale of obsession, loss and voyeurism lacks the emotional sting its agenda might suggest.

● *Helen* Rachel Weisz, *Martin* Alessandro Nivola, *Smokey* Labina Mitevska, *Honda* Luka Petrusic, *Bob* Ben Daniels, *Sonja* Geraldine O'Rawe, *Sam* Steve John Shepherd, Carmen Ejogo, Graham Crowden, Phyllida Law, Mary Macleod, Des McAleer, Julian Rivett, Julie Smith, Berwick Kaler, Dee Dee Menta.
● *Dir* Michael Winterbottom, *Pro* Andrew Eaton, *Ex Pro* Stewart Till, *Assoc Pro* Gina Carter, *Screenplay* Eoin McNamee, *Ph* Slawomir Idziak, *Pro Des* Mark Tildesley, *Ed* Trevor Waite, *M* Adrian Johnston; songs performed by Elvis Costello & The Attractions, Rare, The Troggs, Julian Cope, Chakra, Kirsty MacColl, One Dove, Travis, and Violet, *Costumes* Rachael Fleming.

PolyGram/Revolution Films – PolyGram. 87 mins. UK. 1998. Rel: 30 October 1998. Cert 18.

Jack Frost ★¹/₂

Medford, Colorado; the present. When Jack Frost is at home he is the perfect husband and father. But he's so bent on becoming a successful rock musician that he's seldom around when he's needed. So, when he's turned into a snowman, does he have a snowball's chance in hell of making up for lost time? After a promising start, this latest attempt by Hollywood to breath life into an inanimate myth completely falls apart. Part of the problem is the relative seriousness of the film's first third (which attempts to address such issues as the struggle between family and career and absentee fatherhood) before abruptly lurching into cartoonish fantasy. And the snowman himself, surrounded by patently fake snow, looks like a fat dwarf in a white suit. It just won't do. FYI: In his last movie, *Desperate Measures*, Michael Keaton played a homicidal maniac who takes Joseph Cross hostage. Here, he plays his father.

● *Jack Frost* Michael Keaton, *Gabby Frost* Kelly Preston, *Mac MacArther* Mark Addy, *Charlie Frost* Joseph Cross, *Tuck Gronic* Andy Lawrence, *Sid Gronic* Henry Rollins, Eli Marienthal, Will Rothhaar, Mika Boorem, Dweezil Zappa, Googy Gress, Scott Kraft, *Chester* Mr Chips, Trevor Rabin.
● *Dir* Troy Miller, *Pro* Mark Canton and Irving Azoff, *Ex Pro* Matthew Baer, Jeff Barry, Richard Goldsmith and Michael Tadross, *Screenplay* Mark Steven Johnson and Steve Bloom & Jonathan Roberts and Jeff Cesario, *Ph* Laszlo Kovacs, *Pro Des* Mayne Berke, *Ed* Lawrence Jordan, *M* Trevor Rabin; songs performed by Michael Keaton and The Jack Frost Band, REO Speedwagon, Hanson, Gary Glitter, Lucinda Williams, Stevie Ray Vaughn, Fleetwood Mac, Edgar Winter Group, Billy Idol, Spice Girls, Foghat, Lisa Loeb, etc, *Costumes* Sarah Edwards.

Azoff Entertainment/Canton Company – Warner. 102 mins. USA. 1998. Rel: 12 February 1999. Cert PG.

Jackie Chan's Who Am I? – Ngo Hai Sui ★¹/₂

Who indeed? Following a plane crash in the African bush (engineered by a deviant branch of the CIA), the sole survivor loses his memory and is christened 'Whoami' by the natives. As it happens, the Chinese amnesiac is actually a commando working for the US government, the latter proving determined that Whoami doesn't remember his part in the abduction of a team of scientific specialists ... For a minute there it looks as if Jackie Chan is branching out into something more interesting. However, once the first hour runs out of ideas the plot swings to Rotterdam and the old martial arts routines are wheeled on. While Chan has some fun with wooden clogs and canal bridges, the choreography is not as inspired as usual

and the story fizzles out into a tired and irrational finale. [*Ewen Brownrigg*]

● *Jackie* aka *Whoami* Jackie Chan, *Christine* Michelle Ferre, *Yuki* Mirai Yamamoto, *Morgan* Ron Smerczak, *General Sherman* Ed Nelson, Tom Pompert, Yannick Mbali, Washington Sixolo.
● *Dir* Jackie Chan and Benny Chan, *Pro* Barbie Tung, *Ex Pro* Leonard Ho, *Screenplay* Lee Reynolds, Susan Chan and Jackie Chan, *Ph* Poon Hang Sang, *Pro Des* Oliver Wong, *Ed* Peter Cheung and Yau Chi Wai, *M* Nathan Wang, *Costumes* Thomas Chong.

Raymond Chow/Golden Harvest – Columbia TriStar. 107 mins. Hong Kong. 1998. Rel: 11 June 1999. Cert 12.

Just the Ticket ★¹/₂

Andy Garcia is a fine actor but he should let others produce his movies. The last time he was creatively involved on a project yielded the dull and dumber *Steal Big, Steal Little*. Garcia is good at dangerous and good at haunted, but he can't do goofy. Here, he plays a 'loveable and charming' ticket tout who rules the streets of Manhattan with a dash of risk, a soupcon of intuition and a whole lotta balls. He then meets his match in a slick mover and shaker who steals his patch and outbids him for his tickets. And, with his dream in tatters, he's losing his grip on his lady friend, too ... Lacking any discernible plot or fleshed-out characters, *Just the Ticket* is anything but. Previously known as *The Scalper* and *Piece a Cake*. FYI: Garcia also wrote the theme tune for Andie MacDowell, his co-star and executive producer.

● *Gary Starke* Andy Garcia, *Linda Paliski* Andie MacDowell, *Benny Moran* Richard Bradford, *Mrs Paliski* Elizabeth Ashley, *Zeus* Fred Asparagus, *Casino* Andre Blake, *San Diego Vinnie* Patrick Breen, *Cyclops* Laura Harris, *Ray Charles* Bill Irwin, *Barry the Book* Ron Leibman, *Mrs Haywood* Irene Worth, Ronald Guttman, Donna Hanover, Chris Lemmon, Louis Mustillo, Paunita Nichols, Don Novello, Abe Vigoda, *himself* Joe Frazier, Sullivan Cooke, Alice Drummond, Molly Wenk, Michael P. Moran, *'Good Call Johnny' DJ* Richard Wenk, Robert Castle, Sully Boyar.
● *Dir* and *Screenplay* Richard Wenk, *Pro* Andy Garcia and Gary Lucchesi, *Ex Pro* Andie MacDowell, Yoram Pelman and Marivi Lorido Garcia, *Co-Pro* John H. Starke, *Ph* Ellen Kuras, *Pro Des* Franckie Diago, *Ed* Christopher Cibelli, *M* Rick Marotta, Andy Garcia; songs performed by Israel Lopez 'Cachao' and his Orchestra, Louis Prima, Bobby Darin, Dr John, Stevie Wonder, etc, *Costumes* Susan Lyall.

CineSon Prods/United Artists – First Independent. 115 mins. USA. 1998. Rel: 18 June 1999. Cert 15.

K

THE KING AND I

The all new Animated Family Spectacular Adapted from the musical by Rodgers and Hammerstein

JAMES G. ROBINSON presents
A MORGAN CREEK PRODUCTION IN ASSOCIATION WITH RANKIN/BASS PRODUCTIONS "THE KING AND I" RICHARD RODGERS AND OSCAR HAMMERSTEIN II
WILLIAM KIDD ROBERT MANDELL ARTHUR RANKIN PETER BAKALIAN AND JACQUELINE FEATHER & DAVID SEIDLER
JAMES G. ROBINSON, ARTHUR RANKIN AND PETER BAKALIAN RICHARD RICH

www.thekingandi.com

The King and I ★¹/₂

An English schoolteacher is summoned to Siam to tutor the children of the king. And so an uneasy alliance develops between the arrogant monarch and his outspoken guest ... The first animated film to be based on a Broadway musical, *The King and I* collapses inelegantly between two stools. Neither a stirring, emotional musical in the traditional sense (unlike Disney's *Beauty and the Beast* which *became* a Broadway musical), nor an enchanting, gripping children's film, this is a misfire guaranteed to keep Warner Bros at the bottom of the animation market (following the company's first effort, the mediocre *The Magic Sword: Quest For Camelot*). Featuring flat backdrops and an array of charmless characters, the film is dull, bland and irritatingly banal. Of course, there are the wonderful songs in its favour and a couple of effective scenes (the children's first foray into Bangkok, the sortie of the king's statues) and the voice talents are top-notch. But in an increasingly competitive genre, this is one pretender that shouldn't bother waiting to be king.

● Voices: *Anna* Miranda Richardson, *singing voice of Anna* Christiane Noll, *King of Siam* Martin Vidnovic, *The Kralahome* Ian Richardson, *Crown Prince* Allen Hong, *singing voice of Crown Prince* David Burnham, *Tuptim* Armi Arabe, *singing voice of Tuptim* Tracy Venner Warren, *Master Little* Darrell Hammond, *Louis* Adam Wylie.

● *Dir* Richard Rich, *Pro* James G. Robinson, Peter Bakalian and Arthur Rankin, *Ex Pro* Robert Mandell, *Co-Pro* Terry L. Noss and Thomas J. Tobin, *Screenplay* Bakalian, Jacqueline Feather and David Seidler, *M* Richard Rodgers; lyrics: Oscar Hammerstein II, *Arranger* William Kidd.

Morgan Creek/Rankin/Bass/Nest Entertainment – Warner. 89 mins. USA. 1998. Rel: 28 May 1999. Cert U.

Kissing a Fool ★★

Chicago; today. In spite of their wildly divergent interests, sports broadcaster Max Abbitt and novelist Jay Murphy have been best friends since toddlerhood. Now Jay has introduced Max to his alluring book editor Samantha Andrews and the two are engaged within a fortnight. But, being the schmuck that he is, Max forces Jay to test Samantha's fidelity ... Talk about contrived. This is the sort of low-concept sitcom that challenges its viewers to guess who its cute, wise-cracking protagonists will end up with. The trouble is that the plotting is so thin and uninteresting that one is always one reel ahead of the

movie. But all is not lost: Bonnie Hunt is in fine fettle (isn't she always?) and Mili Avital, as Sam, delivers a star-making performance.

● *Max Abbitt* David Schwimmer, *Jay Murphy* Jason Lee, *Samantha Andrews* Mili Avital, *Linda* Bonnie Hunt, *Natasha* Vanessa Angel, *Dara* Kari Wuhrer, *Andrea* Judy Greer, Frank Medrano, Bitty Schram, Sammy Sosa, Jerry Springer, Philip R. Smith.
● *Dir* Doug Ellin, *Pro* Tag Mendillo, Andrew Form and Rick Lashbrook, *Ex Pro* David Schwimmer and Stephen Levinson, *Screenplay* Ellin and James Frey, *Ph* Thomas Del Ruth, *Pro Des* Charles Breen, *Ed* David Finfer, *M* Joseph Vitarelli; songs performed by Harry Connick Jr., Bad Company, Air Supply, The Mighty Blue Kings, Gravity Kills, Cordrazine, Etta James, and Rebekah, *Costumes* Sue Kaufman.

Universal – UIP.
93 mins. USA. 1998. Rel: 18 September 1998. Cert 15.

Kiss or Kill ★★★

Nikki and Al are lovers and small-time con artists. Nikki lures married businessmen back to their hotel rooms, drugs them and steals their valuables. However, when one patsy dies on her, Nikki discovers an incriminating video in his briefcase showing a famous footballer in bed with a young boy. Now, not only are the police hot on the couple's trail, but so is the vengeful sportsman ... This is a typically quirky road movie from Bill Bennett (*Backlash*, *Spider and Rose*), bathed in a supernatural light and studded with eccentric turns from a cast of familiar Australian faces. However, Bennett's technique of erratic jump-cutting serves more to irritate and distract than to unnerve, spoiling the flow of what could have been an even more gripping ride.

● *Nicole Ann 'Nikki' Davis* Frances O'Connor, *Alan James 'Al' Fletcher* Matt Day, *Det. Hummer* Chris Haywood, *Adler Jones* Barry Otto, *Det. Crean* Andrew S. Gilbert, *Zipper Doyle* Barry Langrishe, *Stan* Max Cullen, *Paul Nathan* Geoff Revell, *Possum Harry* John Clarke, *Bel Jones* Jennifer Cluffe, Tiffany Peters, Eliza Lovell, Michael Hill.
● *Dir* and *Screenplay* Bill Bennett, *Pro* Bill Bennett and Jennifer Bennett, *Ex Pro* Mikael Borglund and Gary Hamilton, *Co-Pro* Corrie Soeterboek, *Ph* Malcolm McCulloch, *Pro Des* Andrew Plumer, *Ed* Henry Dangar, *Sound* Wayne Pashley.

Australian Film Finance Corp/Movie Network/South Australian Film Corp/Australian Film Commission – Alliance Releasing.
96 mins. Australia. 1997. Rel: 10 July 1998. Cert 18.

Above: Jason Lee and David Schwimmer in the contrived comedy Kissing a Fool (from UIP)

Knock Off ★★

Tsui Hark's second American feature once again teams him with Jean-Claude Van Damme and, once again, breaks no new ground. *Knock-Off* is just that, a knock-off of the generic, Hong Kong action flicks that define Tsui's 20-year career. The movie does have its humorous moments and, to some degree, pokes fun at its entire genre. They are a welcome relief from the meandering plot of counterfeit clothing impregnated with micro explosives. Van Damme's wooden acting is always fun to watch and Rob Schneider displays some genuine range as his undercover CIA agent partner. Starting with a rickshaw race straight out of *Ben Hur*, the film is loaded with dynamic action-sequences and incredible stunt work. This alone merits a viewing. [*Scot Woodward Myers*]

● *Marcus Ray* Jean-Claude Van Damme, *Tommy Hendricks* Rob Schneider, *Karen Leigh* Lela Rochon, *Lt. Han* Michael Fitzgerald Wong, *Harry Johansson* Paul Sorvino, Carmen Lee, Glen Chin, Jeff Joseph Wolfe, Moses Chan, Michael Miller, Peter Nelson, Leslie Cheung.
● *Dir* Tsui Hark, *Pro* Nansun Shi, *Assoc Pro* Peter Nelson and Richard G. Murphy, *Co-Pro* Raymond Fung, *Screenplay* Steven E. de Souza, *Ph* Arthur Wong, *Pro Des* James Leung and Bill Lui, *Ed* Mak Chi Sin, *M* Ron Mael and Russell Mael, *Costumes* Ben Luk and William Fung.

Knock Films/MDP Worldwide/Film Workshop/Val d'Oro Entertainment – Columbia TriStar.
91 mins. USA. 1998. Rel: 30 April 1999. Cert 18.

Below: On the road again: Chris Haywood and Andrew S. Gilbert follow their noses in Bill Bennett's quirky and erratic Kiss or Kill (from Alliance Releasing)

The Knowledge of Healing ★★★

The prospect of a 90-minute documentary about Tibetan medicine can hardly inspire unbridled excitement, yet this modest, clear-sighted film is fascinating in its own right. Carefully unwrapping the enormous volumes of the Gyushi – the bible of Tibetan medicine – Dr Tenzin Choedrak, the Dalai Lama's personal physician, explains that the doctrine addresses 1,600 different ailments and comprises 2,993 ingredients made up of various herbs, fruits and roots. A number of treatments are observed in action, while a variety of advocates talk about the remarkable healing power of the doctrine. One robust heart patient tells how, ten years earlier, conventional doctors had given him a maximum of five months to live; another, a young nun, matter-of-factly reveals how she was stripped and tortured by Chinese soldiers with electric cattle-prods. While the somewhat prosaic presentation of the film may lull some viewers into a contented trance, a more vibrant approach would hardly have been in keeping with the subject matter.

● With The XIV Dalai Lama of Tibet, Dr Tenzin Choedrak, Dr Chimit-Dorzhi Dugarov, Alfred Hassig, etc.
● *Dir* Franz Reichle, *Pro* Marcel Hoehn, *Ph* Pio Corradi, *Ed* Reichle and Myriam Flury.

Artificial Eye.
89 mins. Switzerland. 1996. Rel: 13 November 1998. Cert U.

Kurt and Courtney ★★★★

Documentaries are often perceived as dull, but this one is anything but. Nick Broomfield's latest feature is bizarre, amusing, controversial and thought-provoking. This is so whether or not the viewer is already familiar with the rock singer Kurt Cobain found dead in 1994 aged 27. His widow, Courtney Love, punk star turned actress, refused her co-operation but, as we see, others were forthcoming when Broomfield chose to investigate Cobain's life and death on film. Courtney's eccentric father embraced the theory that his son-in-law, an apparent suicide, was actually murdered, and even casts his daughter in the role of murderess. Broomfield, espousing no extreme theories, keeps his head while revealing a world peopled by extraordinary figures. Furthermore, his film chillingly illustrates the powerful influence of major corporations. Totally fascinating. [*Mansel Stimpson*]

● With: Nick Broomfield, Mari Earle, Tracy Marander, Tom Grant, Dylan Carson, El Duce, Chelsea, Larry Flynt, Vincent Schiavelli, Courtney Love, etc.
● *Dir* and *Pro* Nick Broomfield, *Ex Pro* Nick Fraser, *Ph* Joan Churchill and Alex Vendler, *Ed* Mark Atkins and Harley Escudier, *M* songs performed by Theatre of Sheep, Napalm Beach, Earth, The Mentors, etc.

Strength Ltd – Downtown Pictures/Mainline Pictures.
95 mins. UK. 1997. Rel: 3 July 1998. Cert 15.

The Land Girls ★★★

Landford, Dorset; 1941. With Britain's food supply and agricultural inheritance threatened by the exodus of young farm hands to the front line, volunteers of The Women's Land Army were encouraged to take their place. Rallying to the cause, three young women from very different backgrounds sign up to muck in at a remote farm in South-West England. There, they learn the intricacies of milking cows, ploughing pasture and fitting in with the arduous ways of rural life. But, girls being girls, there's still time for a little extracurricular activity ... Exploring a little-known chapter of World War II life, *The Land Girls* is a spirited, exquisitely photographed drama distinguished by top-drawer acting. In fact, it's hard to single out any one performance as everybody is so *right*, from Anna Friel's perky flirt to Maureen O'Brien's noble, long-suffering farmer's wife. The film may lack some plausibility and dramatic grit, but it's never less than completely involving.

● *Stella* Catherine McCormack, *Ag* Rachel Weisz, *Prue* Anna Friel, *Joe Lawrence* Steven Mackintosh, *Mr Lawrence* Tom Georgeson, *Mrs Lawrence* Maureen O'Brien, *Philip* Paul Bettany, Lucy Akhurst, Gerald Down, Nick Mollo, Michael Mantas, Nicholas Le Prevost, Celia Bannerman, Ann Bell, Nigel Planer, Russell Barr, John Gill, Grace Leland, Martha Mackintosh, Jacob Leland.
● *Dir* David Leland, *Pro* Simon Relph, *Ex Pro* Ruth Jackson, *Co-Pro* Andrew Warren, *Screenplay* Leland and Keith Dewhurst, adapted from the novel by Angela Huth, *Ph* Henry Braham, *Pro Des* Caroline Amies, *Ed* Nick Moore, *M* Brian Lock, *Costumes* Shuna Harwood.

InterMedia/Greenlight Fund/Channel Four/Greenpoint/ West Eleven Films/National Lottery/Arts Council of England – Film Four.
111 mins. UK/France. 1997. Rel: 4 September 1998. Cert 12.

The Last Days of Disco ★★

The very early 1980s; Manhattan. Alice and Charlotte are throwing a dinner party as an incentive to find an apartment, Tom and Jennifer are seeing each other on the sly during their trial separation, Des discovered that he was gay on Wednesday and Evelyn 'Champagne' King is in the charts ... Completing his wry trilogy of ensemble romantic comedies (following *Metropolitan* and *Barcelona*), Whit Stillman treads old ground with his customary wit. Yet while the mannered delivery of his actors is spot-on and much of the dialogue they deliver is priceless, the ins and outs of the 'story' are both repetitive and dramatically static. Still, there are revelatory performances from Kate Beckinsale and Matt Keeslar and plenty of indelible songs from the disco period – if you like that sort of thing.

Above: Hormones and agriculture: Anna Friel and Steven Mackintosh get to know each other in David Leland's spirited, exquisitely photographed The Land Girls (from Film Four)

● *Alice Kinnon* Chloe Sevigny, *Charlotte Pingress* Kate Beckinsale, *Des McGrath* Chris Eigeman, *Jimmy Steinway* Mackenzie Astin, *Josh Neff* Matt Keeslar, *Nina* Jennifer Beals, *Tom Platt* Robert Sean Leonard, *The Tiger Lady* Jaid Barrymore, *Holly* Tara Subkoff, *Bernie* David Thornton, *Dan* Matthew Ross, *Van* Burr Steers, Sonsee Ahray, Carolyn Farina, Taylor Nichols, George Plimpton, Anthony Haden-Guest.
● *Dir, Pro* and *Screenplay* Whit Stillman, *Ex Pro* John Sloss, *Ph* John Thomas, *Pro Des* Ginger Tougas, *Ed* Andrew Hafitz and Jay Pires, *M* Mark Suozzo; songs performed by Carol Douglas, Chic, Cheryl Lynn, Evelyn 'Champagne' King, Diana Ross, The O'Jays, Dean Martin, Blondie, Amii Stewart, Sister Sledge, Harold Melvin and the Blue Notes, The Chi-Lites, Norma Jean, etc, *Costumes* Sarah Edwards.

Westerly Disco/Gramercy/Castle Rock – Warner.
113 mins. USA. 1998. Rel: 4 September 1998. Cert 15.

Left Luggage ★★

Antwerp; 1972. Twenty-seven years after the end of the War, Herr Silberschmidt is still searching for the two suitcases of family silver and photographs he buried somewhere in the city. While this 'left luggage' serves as a neat metaphor for the enduring residue of the war, it is something that Silberschmidt's spirited daughter has little time for. Then, unable to meet her rent, she agrees to work as a nanny for a family of strict Hasidic Jews ... It's hard to knock a film when it's down, but this earnest, gauche adaptation of Carl Friedman's 1993 novel *The Shovel and the Loom* just hasn't got what it takes. An authentic European pudding, the film expects us to believe that the film's heroine, Chaja Silberschmidt – all jolly hockey sticks and peaches 'n' cream – is the Jewish daughter of Holocaust survivors. Slow motion, affectionate stereotypes and much dramatic hand-wringing all add to the embarrassment. Of course, it might have worked better with subtitles.

Below: Old boys' club: Danny Glover and Mel Gibson cut up in Richard Donner's entertaining, violent Lethal Weapon 4 *(from Warner)*

● *Mrs Kalman* Isabella Rossellini, *Mr Silberschmidt* Maximilian Schell, *Mr Kalman* Jeroen Krabbe, *Mrs Silberschmidt* Marianne Sagebrecht, *Mr Apfelschnitt* Chaim Topol, *Chaja Silberschmidt* Laura Fraser, *concierge* David Bradley, *Simcha Kalman* Adam Monty, *Sofie* Heather Weeks, *Mrs Goldblum* Miriam Margolyes, *Mr Goldblum* Lex Goudsmit, Alex de Jong.
● *Dir* Jeroen Krabbe, *Pro* Ate de Jong, Hans Pos and Dave Schram, *Ex Pro* Craig Haffner and Brad Wilson, *Co-Pro* Dirk Impens and Rudy Verzyck, *Assoc Pro* Krabbe, Maria Peters and Edwin de Vries, *Screenplay* de Vries, *Ph* Walter Vanden Ende, *Pro Des* Hemmo Sportel, *Ed* Edgar Burcksen, *M* Hennie Vrienten, *Costumes* Yan Tax and Bernadette Corstens.

Shooting Star/Flying Dutchman/Favourite Films, etc – Downtown Pictures.
100 mins. The Netherlands/Belgium/USA. 1997. Rel: 13 November 1998. Cert PG.

Lethal Weapon 4 ★★★

With age creeping up on him, undercover cop Martin Riggs is no longer the 'lethal weapon' he once was. That distinction now belongs to Wah Sing Ku, a human killing machine working for the Los Angeles Triad – a man who will stop at nothing to expedite the illegal entry into the US of his family. Meanwhile, Riggs and partner Roger Murtaugh have been promoted to captains and are expecting some new additions to their own respective families ... This 11-year-old franchise from Warner Bros is still hard to beat for entertainment value – but falls down on a number of other counts. The violence, punctuating cheerful, wise-cracking interludes, really is objectionable (Mel Gibson pushing his thumb into a man's eye socket, a pregnant Rene Russo punched to the ground, etc). Notwithstanding, the stunts really are amazing and the obligatory car chase – with Riggs dragged behind a speeding truck on a coffee table – stands as the best of the year. FYI: *Lethal Weapon 4* started production on 8 January 1998 with an incomplete script and was showing on over 3,000 screens six months later, which must be something of a record in Hollywood turnaround.

● *Martin Riggs* Mel Gibson, *Roger Murtaugh* Danny Glover, *Leo Getz* Joe Pesci, *Lorna Cole* Rene Russo, *Lee Butters* Chris Rock, *Wah Sing Ku* Jet Li, *Captain Ed Murphy* Steve Kahan, *Uncle Benny* Kim Chan, *Trish Murtaugh* Darlene Love, *Rianne Murtaugh* Traci Wolfe, *Hong* Eddy Ko, *Stephanie Woods* Mary Ellen Trainor, Jack Kehler, Calvin Jung, Damon Hines, Ebonie Smith, Steven Lam, Michael Chow, Tony Keyes, Richard Riehle, Phil Chong, Roger Yuan, Philip Tan.
● *Dir* Richard Donner, *Pro* Donner and Joel Silver, *Ex Pro* Steve Perry and Jim Van Wyck, *Co-Pro* J. Mills Goodloe and Dan Cracchiolo, *Screenplay* Channing Gibson, from a story by Jonathan Lemkin, Alfred Gough and Miles Millar,

Ph Andrzej Bartkowiak, *Pro Des* J. Michael Riva, *Ed* Frank J. Urioste and Dallas Puett, *M* Michael Kamen, Eric Clapton and David Sanborn; songs performed by Van Halen, Eric Clapton, WAR, and John Fogerty, *Costumes* Ha Nguyen, *Sound* John Pospisil.

Warner/Silver Pictures/Doshudo – Warner.
128 mins. USA. 1998. Rel: 18 September 1998. Cert 15.

Life Is All You Get – Das Leben ist eine Baustelle ★★★¹/₂

Berlin; today. On his way to work at the local slaughterhouse, Jan Nebel is swept up in a violent demonstration, inadvertently knocks down two policeman and flees the scene with a beautiful and enigmatic woman called Vera. Shortly afterwards, he is arrested, heavily fined and loses his job. Fortunately, he meets up with Vera again, but not before he discovers that a former girlfriend has been diagnosed HIV-positive ... Even as this funny, poignant and absurd film cultivates a genuine 'what-on-earth-is-going-to-happen-next?' feeling, it doesn't monitor what has passed. Loose ends are left dangling, characters vanish and the plot seems to possess a life of its own, darting where it chooses like an unchecked garden hose. Furthermore, Jurgen Vogel's hero is a most unsympathetic character, his lank, unwashed hair, bad teeth and morose demeanour inexplicably acting as a turn-on for highly desirable women. Yet co-writer-director Wolfgang Becker's jaundiced eye for the more run-down corners of Berlin (punctuated by glamorous billboards for sexy lingerie), inventive narrative turns and plentiful comic background incident constantly beguiles the attention.

● *Jan Nevel* Jurgen Vogel, *Vera* Christiane Paul, *Buddy* Ricky Tomlinson, *Harri* Armin Rohde, *Lilo* Martina Gedeck, *Kristina* Christina Papamichou, *Jenni* Rebecca Hessing, *slaughterhouse boss* Wolfgang Becker, Meret Becker, Andrea Sawatzki, Peter Gavajda, Richy Muller, Andreja Schneider.
● *Dir* Wolfgang Becker, *Pro* Stefan Arndt, *Ex Pro* Gebhard Henke and Andreas Schreitmuller, *Line Pro* Mathias Schwerbrock, *Screenplay* Becker and Tom Tykwer, *Ph* Martin Kukula, *Pro Des* Claus-Jurgen Pfeiffer, *Ed* Patricia Rommel, *M* Jurgen Knieper and Christian Steyer, *Costumes* Heidi Platz.

X Filme creative pool GmbH/Filmstiftung Nordrhein Westfalen – City Screen.
118 mins. Germany. 1997. Rel: 17 July 1998. Cert 18.

Life is Beautiful – La Vita e Bella ★★★¹/₂

Italy; 1939-1945. When a fun-loving Jewish man is shipped off to a concentration camp with his young son, he pretends it is an elaborate game in order to

Above: Ich bin ein Berliner: Jurgen Vogel in Wolfgang Becker's funny and touching Life is All You Get *(from City Screen)*

shield the latter from the horrors around them ... This is a strange one. Yet, for all its faults Roberto Benigni's surprising brew of parody and tragedy still exercises an enormous power. Beautifully shot by Pasolini's regular cameraman and melodically scored by Nicola Piovani (*Dear Diary*, *Fiorile*), it is everything a sentimental Italian fable should be. And while much of the slapstick of the first half really doesn't work, it does supply the emotional ballast for what is to come. As an exploration of the Holocaust, then, *Life is Beautiful* is no *Schindler's List*, but it is a brave, heartfelt and above all touching chapter.

● *Guido Orefice* Roberto Benigni, *Dora Orefice* Nicoletta Braschi, *Joshua Orefice* Giorgio Cantarini, *Ferruccio* Sergio Bustric, *Dora's mother* Marisa Paredes, *Dr Lessing* Horst Buchholz, Giustino Durano, Lydia Alfonsi, Giuliana Lojodice, Pietro De Silva.
● *Dir* Roberto Benigni, *Pro* Elda Ferri and Gianluigi Braschi, *Line Pro* Mario Cotone, *Screenplay* Benigni and Vincenzo Cerami, *Ph* Tonino Delli Colli, *Ed* Simona Paggi, *Pro Des* and *Costumes* Danilo Donati, *M* Nicola Piovani; Offenbach.

Mario e Vittorio Cecchi Gori/Roberto Benigni/Melampo Cinematografica – Buena Vista.
116 mins. Italy. 1997. Rel: 12 February 1999. Cert PG.

Little Voice ★★★¹/₂

Scarborough, Yorkshire; the present. Virtually mute since the death of her father, LV – or 'Little Voice' – only really comes alive when she sings along to the albums of Judy Garland, Marilyn Monroe, Shirley Bassey & co, recordings left by her father. Meanwhile, her loud, promiscuous mother struggles to find love in a string of meaningless one-night stands. Then, one evening, seedy entrepreneur Ray Say overhears LV's magic voice and resolves to turn her into a star ... Originally conceived as a theatrical vehicle for the impersonating skills of Jane Horrocks, *Little Voice* is a performer's dream. Encouraged to act to the gods,

Right: In search of happiness: Roberto Benigni, the ultimate optimist, entertains his son (Giorgio Cantarini) in the actor's triumphant Life is Beautiful (from Buena Vista)

Michael Caine, Brenda Blethyn and Ms Horrocks sink their collective teeth into some wonderful parts, recalling such actor-friendly stage-to-film successes as *Educating Rita* and *Shirley Valentine*. However, as Little Voice's tentative suitor and emotional counterpart, the media-exposed Ewan McGregor seems an odd choice – an unknown actor would have been far more effective. But this is Horrocks' show and she is a wonder to behold (thankfully retaining the part even after Gwyneth Paltrow had expressed an interest in doing the film version).

● *Ray Say* Michael Caine, *Mari Hoff* Brenda Blethyn, *Mr Boo* Jim Broadbent, *Billy* Ewan McGregor, *Laura Hoff* aka *LV/Little Voice* Jane Horrocks, *Sadie* Annette Badland, *George* Philip Jackson, *LV's dad* Graham Turner, *Bunnie Morris* Alex Norton, Fred Feast, Karen Gregory, Melodie Scales, Kitty Roberts.
● *Dir* and *Screenplay* Mark Herman, from the play *The Rise and Fall of Little Voice* by Jim Cartwright, *Pro* Elizabeth Karlsen, *Ex Pro* Nik Powell and Stephen Woolley, *Co-Pro* Laurie Borg, *Co-Ex Pro* Bob Weinstein, Harvey Weinstein and Paul Webster,

Ph Andy Collins, *Pro Des* Don Taylor, *Ed* Mike Ellis, *M* John Altman; songs performed by Michael Caine, Jane Horrocks, Ethel Merman, Shirley Bassey, Chumbawamba, Frankie Laine, Roger Whittaker, Frank Sinatra, Elvis Presley, Judy Garland, Tom Jones, Marilyn Monroe, Procol Harum, The Trammps, and Gracie Fields, *Costumes* Lindy Hemming.

Miramax/Scala – Buena Vista.
96 mins. UK/USA. 1998. Rel: 8 January 1999. Cert 15.

Living Out Loud ★★★¹/₂

In the throes of divorce from her philandering cardiologist husband of 16 years, nurse Judith Nelson isn't taking spinsterhood well. Consumed by loneliness – 'all our friends were his friends' – she takes to imagining bizarre encounters with strangers and even weirder acts of suicide. Up to his eyeballs in debt, elevator operator Pat Francato is finding that divorce is taking the fun out of his marriage. 'This *can't* be my life!', he wails to his brother. And then Pat notices Judith, a tenant in the building he tends. Judith and Pat are two lonely, scarred souls flat out of luck. It's just that, at 40, Judith is still a very attractive woman and Pat, short, bald and 54, isn't ... Marking the directorial debut of leading scriptwriter Richard LaGravenese (*The Fisher King*, *The Bridges of Madison County*, *The Horse Whisperer*), *Living Out Loud* is a gently observed human comedy that frequently rings surprisingly true. Holly Hunter glows in the best part she's had in aeons and is backed up by a solid turn from Queen Latifah as the torch singer who inspires and supports her. However, as Judith's romantic foil, Danny DeVito is maybe a little *too* improbable (in spite of the concessions of the script), while the *Ally McBeal*esque fantasy sequences smudge the line between what is imagined and what isn't.

● *Judith Nelson* Holly Hunter, *Pat Francato* Danny DeVito, *Liz Bailey* Queen Latifah, *Bob Nelson* Martin Donovan, *The Kisser* Elias Koteas, *Philly Francato* Richard Schiff, *Mary* Suzanne Shepherd, *The Masseur* Eddie Cibrian, *Gary* Clark Anderson, Mariangela Pino, Ellen McElduff, Fil Formicola, Jenette Goldstein, Lin Shaye, John F. Donohue, Kate McGregor-Stewart, Tamlyn Tomita, Rachel Leigh Cook, Christian Hill, Willie Garson, Carole Ruggier.
● *Dir* and *Screenplay* Richard LaGravanese, *Pro* Danny DeVito, Michael Shamberg and Stacey Sher, *Co-Pro* Eric McLeod, *Ph* John Bailey, *Pro Des* Nelson Coates, *Ed* Jon Gregory and Lynzee Klingman, *M* George Fenton; songs performed by Queen Latifah, Dean Martin, Mel Torme, Clark Anderson, Etta James, Brownstone, Danny DeVito, Sly and the Family Stone, etc, *Costumes* Jeffrey Kurland.

New Line Cinema/Jersey Films – Entertainment.
100 mins. USA. 1998. Rel: 5 February 1998. Cert 15.

Lock, Stock and Two Smoking Barrels ★★★★¹/₂

London; today. Eddy, Tom, Bacon and Soap are four best mates who find themselves in debt to Harry ''ack You Up With a 'atchett' Lonsdale, self-proclaimed 'porn king' and London's toughest gangster. They're given one week to cough up £500,000 or lose a finger for every day the debt remains unpaid. With crime their only option, the lads make the mistake of stealing a stash of cash and marijuana from arguably the most brutal gang in England ... Displaying the visual panache of *Trainspotting* and the cheeky charm of *The Italian Job*, this ingenious comic thriller heralds the arrival of the most exciting new British director since Danny Boyle. Bursting with energy and originality, the film turns the crime caper on its head, resuscitating a genre which all but stopped with *Mona Lisa*. A formidable roster of colourful characters are animated by a terrific cast that makes the most of Guy Ritchie's cracking dialogue ('assumption is the brother of all fuck-ups'). Besides, any thriller which shows its main men preferring their hot caffeine over anything harder deserves a big, warm hug.

● *Tom* Jason Flemyng, *Soap* Dexter Fletcher, *Eddy* Nick Moran, *Bacon* Jason Statham, *Winston* Steven Mackintosh, *Big Chris* Vinnie Jones, *JD* Sting, *Lenny the Baptist* Lenny McLean, *Plank* Steve Sweeney, *Dog* Frank Harper, *Nick the Greek* Stephen Marcus, *Rory Breaker* Vas Blackwood, *Tanya* Vera Day, *Harry ''ack You Up With a 'atchett'* Lonsdale P.H. Moriarty, Jake Abraham, Stephen Callender-Ferrier, Elwin David, Charlie Forbes, Peter McNicholl, Suzy Ratner, Nicholas Rowe, Matthew Vaughn.
● *Dir* Guy Ritchie, *Pro* Matthew Vaughn, *Ex Pro* Steve Tisch, Peter Morton, Angad Paul, Stephen Marks, Trudie Styler, Jon Slan and Gareth Jones, *Co-Pro* Georgia Masters, *Line Pro* Ronaldo Vasconcellos, *Assoc Pro* Sebastian Pearson and Jan Roldanus, *Ph* Tim Maurice-Jones, *Pro Des* Iain Andrews and Eve Mavrakis, *Ed* Niven Howie, *M* David A. Hughes & John Murphy; songs performed by Ocean Colour

Below: Will Ray Say get the canary to sing? Jane Horrocks and Michael Caine shoot the breeze in Mark Herman's relentlessly entertaining Little Voice *(from Buena Vista)*

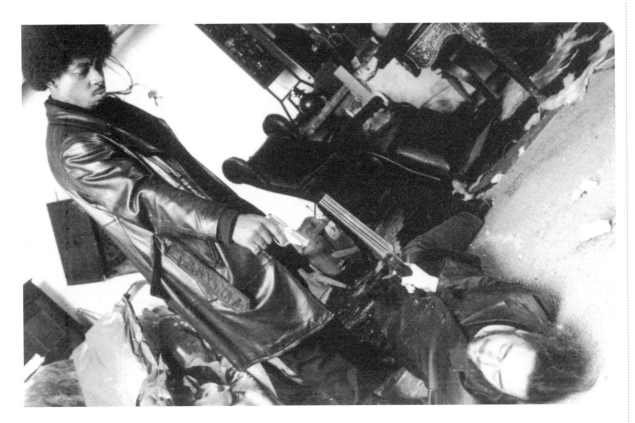

Above: Gun play: Vas Blackwood and Steve Sweeney face-off in Guy Ritchie's chic and audacious Lock, Stock and Two Smoking Barrels *(from PolyGram)*

Scene, James Brown, Dusty Springfield, The Stooges, Robbie Williams, The Stone Roses, Pete Wingfield, Evil Superstars, etc, *Costumes* Stephanie Collie.

Ska Films – PolyGram.
106 mins. UK. 1998. Rel: 28 August 1998. Cert 18.

Lost in Space ★½

Outer space; 2058. With two decades left of usable resources, planet earth is in dire straits. So brainy Dr John Robinson and his far-from-happy family set off in search of atmospherically complimentary planets. Unfortunately, a seditious stowaway upsets their plans and they are thrown into the deepest recesses of the galaxy ... A $90 million adaptation of the campy 1965-68 television series (itself a sci-fi modification of Johan Wyss' *Swiss Family Robinson*), *Lost in Space* lives up to its name. Incoherent to the point of being incomprehensible, the film is beleaguered by muffled dialogue, a somnambulant turn from William Hurt and yet another by-the-numbers villain from Gary ('where's my cheque?') Oldman. There's also an extremely silly alien monkey (a Muppet reject?) and some rickety giant spiders which look like they've crawled out of a McDonald's happy meal. Which is a shame as much of Akiva Goldsman's screenplay is actually quite witty and intriguing.

● *Dr Zachary Smith* Gary Oldman, *John Robinson* William Hurt, *Don West* Matt LeBlanc, *Maureen Robinson* Mimi Rogers, *Judy Robinson* Heather Graham, *Penny Robinson* Lacey Chabert, *Will Robinson*

Jack Johnson, *older Will* Jared Harris, *General* Mark Goddard, *first reporter* Marta Kristen, *Principal* June Lockhart, *second reporter* Angela Cartwright, Lennie James, Edward Fox, and *voice of the Robot* Dick Tufeld.
● *Dir* Stephen Hopkins, *Pro* Hopkins, Mark W. Koch, Akiva Goldsman and Carla Fry, *Ex Pro* Mace Neufeld, Bob Rehme, Richard Saperstein and Michael De Luca, *Co-Ex Pro* Michael Ilitch Jr, *Screenplay* Goldsman, *Ph* Peter Levy, *Pro Des* Norman Garwood, *Ed* Ray Lovejoy, *M* Bruce Broughton; songs performed by Apollo Four Forty, Juno Reactor & The Creatures, Propellerheads, Death in Vegas, Fatboy Slim, Space, and The Crystal Method, *Costumes* Vin Burnham (*outer space*), and Robert Bell and Gilly Hebden (*earthbound*), *Visual effects* Angus Bickerton, *Animatronic creatures* Jim Henson's Creature Shop.

New Line Cinema/Prelude Pictures/Irwin Allen Prods – Entertainment.
130 mins. USA. 1998. Rel: 31 July 1998. Cert PG.

The Lost Son ★★★

Xavier Lombard is a French private detective working in London, a solitary figure with a past he cannot shut out of his dreams. Then, when he's hired by a wealthy Austrian to locate the latter's son, he finds his past catching up with him – and sees a chance for final redemption ... A dark, contemplative and chilling *film noir* thriller, *The Lost Son* approaches its taboo subject (organised child abuse) with intelligence and restraint. Far from appropriating such opprobrious activity for

shock value, the film positions the disaffected lives of its characters to draw the viewer in, letting the facts themselves – £10,000 for a 24-hour session in a sound-proofed room – speak volumes. And while the film may be noticeably lacking in warmth and humour, the disparate backgrounds of its cosmopolitan *dramatis personae* add considerable colour. Making the most of its unusual locations (London appears both familiar and exotic), the film provides a seductive visual palette permeated by atmospheric detail. It's a pity, then, that the plot eventually descends into banality.

● *Xavier Lombard* Daniel Auteuil, *Deborah* Nastassja Kinski, *Emily* Katrin Cartlidge, *Carlos* Ciaran Hinds, *Nathalie* Marianne Denicourt, *Friedman* Bruce Greenwood, *Mrs Spitz* Billie Whitelaw, *Mr Spitz* Cyril Shaps, Jamie Harris, Hemal Pandya, Billy Smyth, Michael Liebmann, Mark Benton, David Heyman.
● *Dir* Chris Menges, *Pro* Finola Dwyer, *Ex Pro* Nik Powell, Stephen Woolley, Georges Benayoun and Sarah Radclyffe, *Line Pro* Paul Cowan, *Assoc Pro* Judy Menges, *Co-Pro* Marina Gefter, *Ph* Barry Ackroyd, *Pro Des* John Beard, *Ed* Pamela Power and Luc Barnier, *M* Goran Bregovic; Faure, *Costumes* Rosie Hackett.

Scala/Ima Films/Film Consortium/Canal Plus/Arts Council of England/Film Four/France 2 and France 3/National Lottery – UIP.
102 mins. UK/France. 1998. Rel: 25 June 1999. Cert 18.

Love and Death On Long Island
★★★★¹/₂

London, England/Long Island, New York; the present. Happily isolated from the second half of the twentieth century, widowed writer and eccentric Charles De'Ath (pronounced 'day-arth') is a stranger to television, e-mail and UHT milk. Then, having locked himself out of his house, he spends an afternoon at 'the pictures' – ostensibly to see a new E.M. Forster adaptation. Instead, he's subjected to 'a puerile romp' called *Hotpants College II*, but is transfixed by a young actor in the cast. In fact, De'Ath is so moved by the actor's beauty that he finds himself reluctantly succumbing to adolescent obsession ... Taking a relatively simple idea – updated from the novella by Gilbert Adair – first-time feature director Richard Kwietniowski has fashioned an exquisite character study that adroitly juxtaposes the incongruous worlds of musty Edwardian England with brash contemporary America. This is the best thing John Hurt has done in many years and he invests his part with a comic subtlety that is both hilarious and painfully touching.

● *Giles De'Ath* John Hurt, *Ronnie Bostock* Jason Priestley, *Audrey* Fiona Loewi, *Mrs Barker* Sheila Hancock, *Henry* Gawn Grainger, *Irving Buckmuller* Maury Chaykin, Elizabeth Quinn, Linda Busby, Bill Leadbitter, Ann Reid, Danny Webb, Tusse Silberg, Magnus Magnusson, Harvey Atkin.
● *Dir* and *Screenplay* Richard Kwietniowski, *Pro* Steve Clark-Hall and Christopher Zimmer,

Above: Past caring: Daniel Auteuil finds his past catching up with him in Chris Menges' contemplative and chilling The Lost Son *(from UIP)*

Ph Oliver Curtis, *Pro Des* David McHenry, *Ed* Susan Shipton, *M* The Insects and Richard Grassby-Lewis, *Costumes* Andrea Galer.

British Screen/National Lottery/Sales Company/Telefilm Canada/Nova Scotia Film Development Corp – Pathe. 93 mins. UK/Canada. 1996. Rel: 3 July 1998. Cert 15.

Loved ★★★

Returning to her family's California home after an absence of four years, Hedda Amerson is immediately served with a subpoena to testify against a man accused of victimising women. It transpires that she was the first of three women to have hurled themselves into the path of oncoming traffic as an escape from the abusive relationship with the unnamed defendant. But Hedda insists that only she was responsible for her actions and that her intimacy with the man was beyond reproach ... A contemplation on the various ramifications of what it means to be loved, Erin Dignam's second feature is a thoughtful, multi-layered piece that is part mystery, part courtroom drama, part love story and part allegory. Intelligently paced and cannily developed, the film is graced by a startlingly naked and luminescent performance from Robin Wright Penn (who was voted best actress at the Seattle Film Festival) and is extremely well served by Villalobos's painterly photography and Baerwald's intuitive score. Yet in spite of some interesting observations of male domination – and the female facilitation of it – *Loved* fails to cultivate any satisfactory conclusion. FYI: The part of Hedda was written especially for Ms Wright Penn who developed the project closely with the film-maker for three years.

● *K.D. Deitrickson* William Hurt, *Hedda Amerson* Robin Wright Penn, *Brett Amerson* Amy Madigan, *Elenore Amerson* Joanna Cassidy, *Debra Gill* Jennifer Rubin, *the unnamed defendant* Anthony Lucero, *Michael* Sean Penn, *Leo Amerson* Paul Dooley, *Kate Amerson* Lucinda Jenney, *Judge Gibson Strickland* Michael Tomlinson, LaTanya Richardson, Evelyn Dignam, Richard Schiff.
● *Dir* and *Screenplay* Erin Dignam, *Pro* Philippe

Below: Culture clash: John Hurt and Jason Priestley in Richard Kwietniowski's exquisite Love and Death On Long Island *(from Pathe)*

Caland and Sean Penn, *Ex Pro* Mark Damon and Pierre Caland, *Co-Pro* Patricia Morrison, *Ph* Reynaldo Villalobos, *Pro Des* Barry Robison, *Ed* Gillian Hutshing and David Rogow, *M* David Baerwald; 'Miller's Angels' performed by Counting Crows, *Costumes* Amy State.

Crosslight/MDP Worldwide/Clyde is Hungry Films/Palisades Pictures – Downtown. 103 mins. USA. 1996. Rel: 26 February 1999. Cert 15.

Love is the Devil ★★★¹/₂

London/New York/Paris; 1964-1971. Frequently cited as 'Britain's greatest painter since Turner', Francis Bacon led a private life every bit as degenerate as his disturbing public canvases. Burgled in 1964, he bedded the intruder – George Dyer – and made him his artistic muse. The relationship lasted seven years, built on Bacon's attraction to George's 'amorality and innocence' and Dyer's desire for material comfort. It was a volatile, destructive liaison, an attraction of opposites that was bound to lead to tears ... Refused permission to use any of the painter's work, director (and artist) John Maybury has filmed his chilling portrait of Bacon in the manner of the artist's oeuvre. Thus the actor's faces are often distorted in mirrors and obscured behind bottles, while the squalid interiors are rendered dark and claustrophobic. Maybury certainly captures the spirit and power of Bacon's paintings and is served by a magnificent performance from Sir Derek Jacobi who, at times, uncannily resembles his subject. A daring, visceral and eloquent film, *Love is the Devil* achieves its objective with a boldness and insight that recalls the work of Derek Jarman and early Ken Russell.

● *Francis Bacon* Derek Jacobi, *George Dyer* Daniel Craig, *Muriel Belcher* Tilda Swinton, *Isabel Rawsthorne* Anne Lambton, *Daniel Farson* Adrian Scarborough, *John Deakin* Karl Johnson, *Henrietta Moraes* Annabel Brooks, *David Hockney* Hamish Bowles, Richard Newbold, Tallulah, Andy Linden, Gary Hume; *with cameos by*: Natalie Gibson, Chiara Menage, Daniel Farson, Sandy Fawkes, Norman Rosenthal, Sue Tilley, Amanda Menage, Ben Gibson, Suzie Bick, Lucy Ferry, Rifat Ozbek, Anita Pallenberg, Sarah Lucas, Tracey Emin, Gillian Wearing.
● *Dir* John Maybury, *Pro* Chiara Menage, *Ex Pro* Frances-Anne Solomon and Ben Gibson, *Prod Ex* Christopher Cameron and Christopher Collins, *Screenplay* Maybury, James Cohen and Don Jordan, *Ph* John Mathieson, *Pro Des* Alan MacDonald, *Ed* Daniel Goddard, *M* Ryuichi Sakamoto, *Costumes* Annie Symons, *Sound* Paul Davies, *Caterers* Bad Catering.

BBC Films/BFI/Arts Council of England/Premiere Heure/ Uplink/National Lottery – Artificial Eye. 90 mins. UK/France/Japan. 1998. Rel: 18 September 1998. Cert 18.

Mad City ★★¹⁄₂

The Museum of Natural History, Madeline, California; the present. When museum security guard Sam Baily is made redundant, he demands his job back at the point of a Remington shotgun. However, he hadn't anticipated the presence of a group of school children, nor that of Max Brackett, a local TV news reporter. Then, when he accidentally shoots a fellow guard, Sam sets off a siege situation which Brackett intends to make the most of. The longer the siege endures, the greater Brackett's national exposure ... While spotlighting a number of intriguing issues relating to the ethics of the media, *Mad City* lacks the gritty immediacy of, say, *Welcome To Sarajevo*, and fails to be more than just a glossy, sentimental Hollywood melodrama. This is a shame as director Costa-Gavras is the man who brought us *Z, State of Siege, Missing* and *Music Box*, all powerful and credible films dealing with important questions. Here, Dustin Hoffman and John Travolta play some very obvious notes in a schematic conceit that has all the piquancy of a plate of bubble gum. Inspired by the media frenzy that surrounded the siege at Waco, Texas.

● *Max Brackett* Dustin Hoffman, *Sam Baily* John Travolta, *Kevin Hollander* Alan Alda, *Laurie Callahan* Mia Kirshner, *Sheriff Alvin Lemke* Ted Levine, *Lou Potts* Robert Prosky, *Mrs Banks* Blythe Danner, *Dohlen* William Atherton, *Miss Rose* Tammy Lauren, *Jenny* Lucinda Jenney, Akosua Busia *Diane, himself*

Jay Leno, William O'Leary, Raymond J. Barry, Ebbe Roe Smith, Bingwa, Sylvia Short, Scanlon Gail, Charlie Holliday, John Landis, Jason Cottle, Randall Batinkoff, David Clennon, Stephen E. Kaufman, Richard Portnow, Dirk Blocker, and *uncredited*: *Clifford Williams* Bill Nunn.

● *Dir* Costa-Gavras, *Pro* Arnold Kopelson and Anne Kopelson, *Ex Pro* Wolfgang Glattes, Stephen Brown and Jonathan D. Krane, *Screenplay* Tom Matthews, from a story by Matthews and Eric Williams, *Ph* Patrick Blossier, *Pro Des* Catherine Hardwicke, *Ed* Francoise Bonnot, *M* Thomas Newman; Puccini, *Costumes* Deborah Nadoolman, *Sound* Bertrand Lenclos.

Warner/Punch Prods – Warner.
114 mins. USA. 1997. Rel: 10 July 1998. Cert 15.

Madeline ★★¹⁄₂

'In an old house in Paris, that was covered with vines, lived 12 little girls in two straight lines...' Thus begins the text of the popular picture books penned between 1939 and 1961 by the Austrian-born Ludwig Bemelmans. Here, the plucky orphan Madeline is given an English bloom, the long-suffering (yet patient) Miss Clavel an American accent and the other 11 children of the convent school a sort of politically expedient cultural makeover. Yet, within the context of a bustling city like Paris such international inconsistencies hardly

Above: Has he got news for you: John Travolta retaliates in Costa-Gavras's routine Mad City *(from Warner)*

matter. What *does* matter is that the film-makers have tried to cram in so many of the books' storylines that there's little room for any of the original's effortless charm. Thus, Madeline is rushed to hospital with appendicitis, almost drowns in the Seine (and is subsequently rescued by the faithful dog Genevieve) and the school itself is threatened with closure. FYI: The closing song, 'In Two Straight Lines', is written and sung by Carly Simon who, as a child, had the original paintings from the book hanging on her bedroom wall.

● *Miss Clavel* Frances McDormand, *Lord Covington* Nigel Hawthorne, *Madeline* Hatty Jones, *Leopold, the tutor* Ben Daniels, *Lady Covington* Stephane Audran, *Helene, the cook* Chantal Neuwirth, *Pepito* Kristian De La Osa, *Aggie* Clare Thomas, *Victoria* Bianca Strohman, Arturo Venegas, Katia Caballero, Christina Mangani, Rachel Dennis, George Harris, Marie-Noelle Eusebe, Julien Maurel, *Genevieve* Nani.
● *Dir* Daisy von Scherler Mayer, *Pro* Saul Cooper and Pancho Kohner, *Ex Pro* Stanley R. Jaffe, *Screenplay* Mark Levin and Jennifer Flackett, from a story by Levin, Flackett and Malia Scotch Marmo, *Ph* Pierre Aim, *Pro Des* Hugo Luczyc-Wyhowski, *Ed* Jeffrey Wolf, *M* Michel Legrand, *Costumes* Michael Clancy.

TriStar/Jaffilms – Columbia TriStar.
89 mins. USA. 1998. Rel: 12 February 1999. Cert U.

The Magic Sword: Quest For Camelot ★★

Arthurian England; a thousand years ago. An evil knight called Ruber steals King Arthur's magic sword Excalibur – and promptly loses it in the Forbidden Forest. When Ruber subsequently kidnaps Lady Juliana, the latter's feisty daughter Kayley overhears Ruber's plan to take over Camelot and sets off to warn King Arthur. But first she must outrun Ruber's entourage of mutant sidekicks and recover the missing sword ... As Warner Bros' first foray into the animation

Below: Maids of Paris: Frances McDormand and Hatty Jones confer in Daisy von Scherler Mayer's bustling, cosmopolitan Madeline (from Columbia TriStar)

market, *The Magic Sword* is unlikely to keep any Disney executives awake at night. While the poster's tag line invites us to 'Share the Magic', there's very little enchantment in evidence and the animation is disappointing. Animal movement, depth of field and lip-synching are all well below the standard one has come to expect of contemporary animation. Having said that, the story – adapted from Vera Chapman's manipulation of the Arthurian legend – is strong, and a two-headed dragon voiced by Eric Idle and Don Rickles is a comic conceit that works. Otherwise, the humour is weak (many lines appropriated from other movies) and Gary Oldman's South London accent for Ruber rather distracting (Ron Moody meets Arthur Mullard).

● Voices: *Kayley* Jessalyn Gilsig, *singing voice of Kayley* Andrea Corr, *Garrett* Cary Elwes, *singing voice of Garrett* Bryan White, *Ruber* Gary Oldman, *Devon* Eric Idle, *Cornwall* Don Rickles, *Juliana* Jane Seymour, *singing voice of Juliana* Celine Dion, *King Arthur* Pierce Brosnan, *singing voice of King Arthur* Steve Perry, *Griffin* Bronson Pinchot, *Bladebeak* Jaleel White, *Lionel* Gabriel Byrne, *Merlin* John Gielgud, *Ayden* Frank Welker, *young Kayley* Sarah Rayne.
● *Dir* Frederik Du Chau, *Pro* Dalisa Cooper Cohen, *Assoc Pro* Zahra Dowlatabadi, *Screenplay* Kirk De Micco, William Schifrin, Jacqueline Feather and David Seidler, from the novel *The King's Damosel* by Vera Chapman, *Pro Des* Steve Pilcher, *Ed* Stanford C. Allen, *M* Patrick Doyle; songs: David Foster (music) and Carole Bayer Sager (lyrics).

Warner – Warner.
86 mins. USA. 1998. Rel: 24 July 1998. Cert U.

Marquise ★¹/2

The 1600s; France. Renowned for her 'vertical and horizontal dancing' at dubious market venues, Marquise pines to be a great actress. Spotted by the celebrated playwright Moliere, she is invited to join his troupe and so begins her journey of theatrical and sexual conquests, leading her to the boudoir of the great Jean Racine and on to the court of Louis XIV ... In spite of such fertile dramatic material and an abundance of colourful real-life characters, Vera Belmont's *Marquise* cannot rise above the farcical and melodramatic nature of its own theatrical shenanigans. Furthermore, Sophie Marceau (who more and more is coming to resemble a younger Isabelle Adjani) is hardly up to the demands of the part, reducing the indignation and artistic frustration of Marquise to so many temper tantrums. Notwithstanding, the film is visually intoxicating and there is a wonderful turn from Thierry Lhermitte as a wildly eccentric Louis XIV.

● *Marquise du Parque* Sophie Marceau, *King Louis XIV* Thierry Lhermitte, *Jean Baptiste Racine* Lambert Wilson, *Moliere* Bernard Girardeau, *Rene du Parque*

ANTONIO
BANDERAS

ANTHONY
HOPKINS

CATHERINE
ZETA-JONES

THE MASK OF ZORRO

aka *Gros Rene* Patrick Timsit, *Floridor* Georges Wilson, *Marie* Estelle Skornik, Anemone, Remo Girone, Franck De La Personne, Marianne Basler.
● *Dir* and *Pro* Vera Belmont, *Screenplay* Belmont and Gerard Mordillat, *Ph* Jean Marie Dreujou, *Pro Des* Gianni Quanranta, *Ed* Martine Giordano, *M* Jordi Savall, *Costumes* Olga Berluti.

Stephan Films/Arama Entertainment/Canal Plus/ Eurimage, etc – Downtown Pictures.
122 mins. France/Italy/Spain/Switzerland. 1997. Rel: 9 October 1998. Cert 15.

The Mask of Zorro ★★¹/₂
Alta California, Mexico; 1821-41. A defender of the people against the tyrannical regime of the Spanish government, Zorro – identified by his black mask, sombrero and cloak – is an almost mythical figure with a remarkable athletic agility and spectacular prowess with a sword. When he is eventually bested by the cruel governor Don Rafael Montero, he vows his revenge. Twenty years later, Zorro re-emerges – as brave, acrobatic and determined as ever ... Robust, old-fashioned and rather heavy-handed, *The Mask of Zorro* betrays the feel of a latter-day James Bond film – that is, a cumbersome, self-impressed and overloaded epic with an exhausting finale. Visually imposing and heartily acted (Catherine Zeta-Jones is particularly impressive), the film suffers from protracted exposition and a muddled script, as if too many writers had got in their say. Originally, Robert Rodriguez (*El Mariachi*, *Desperado*) had been hired to

direct, but his concept exceeded TriStar's proposed $44 million budget. So the studio hired Martin Campbell (*No Escape*, *GoldenEye*) instead, who turned in this unwieldy crowd-pleaser at a cost of $65m. Hmmm.

● *Alejandro Murrieta/Zorro* Antonio Banderas, *Don Diego de la Vega/Zorro* Anthony Hopkins, *Elena* Catherine Zeta-Jones, *Don Rafael Montero* Stuart Wilson, *Captain Harrison Love* Matt Letscher, *prison warden* Maury Chaykin, *Don Luiz* Tony Amendola, *Three-Fingered Jack* L.Q. Jones, *Esperanza de la Vega* Julieta Rosen, Pedro Armendariz, Jose Perez, William Marquez, Victor Rivers, Luisa Huertas, Tony Genaro, Diego Sandoval, Erika Carlson.
● *Dir* Martin Campbell, *Pro* Doug Claybourne and David Foster, *Ex Pro* Steven Spielberg, Walter F. Parkes and Laurie MacDonald, *Screenplay* John Eskow, Ted Elliott and Terry Rossio, from a story by Elliott, Rossio and Randall Jahnson, *Ph* Phil Meheux, *Pro Des* Cecilia Montiel, *Ed* Thom Noble, *M* James Horner, *Costumes* Graciela Mazon, *Sound* Hector C. Gika. *Swordmaster* Robert Anderson.

TriStar Pictures/Amblin Entertainment/Zorro Prods – Columbia TriStar.
138 mins. USA. 1998. Rel: 11 December 1998. Cert PG.

The Matrix ★★★★★
Do not believe what you see, hear, smell, taste or even think. It is a trick, a digital scam superimposed on the 'real' world so as to cloak the ugly reality that we are

Right: Laurence Fishburne escapes The Matrix (from Warner)

living in a dystopia ruled by machines. With the sun long gone, the machines need our own electrical fields as an energy source and have brain-washed us to preserve their status quo. But a gaggle of resistance fighters, humans who have broken out of our ersatz 'present', have a new conscript, the Chosen One ... Taking strands of theology, mythology, philosophy and the latest in scientific conjecture, the Wachowski brothers (Andy and Larry) have fashioned an audacious and stylish entertainment that succeeds on almost every level it aspires to. At once satirical, pop-cultural, intellectual and gut-kickingly thrilling, the film achieves a perfect pitch between parody and reality, without overplaying its hand in either direction. It's also visually enthralling, introducing brand-new photographic effects that take the breath away. And, as the Chosen One ('cute, but none too bright'), Keanu is a real sport. Remember, this is the dude who played Buddha.

● *Thomas Anderson/Neo* Keanu Reeves, *Morpheus* Laurence Fishburne, *Trinity* Carrie-Anne Moss, *Agent Smith* Hugo Weaving, *Cypher* Joe Pantoliano, *the Oracle* Gloria Foster, *Tank* Marcus Chong, *Switch* Belinda McClory, Julian Arahanga, Matt Doran, Anthony Ray Parker, Paul Goddard, Robert Taylor.
● *Dir* and *Screenplay* Andy and Larry Wachowski, *Pro* Joel Silver, *Ex Pro* The Wachowskis, Barrie Osborne, Andrew Mason, Erwin Stoff and Bruce Berman, *Co-Pro* Dan Cracchiolo, *Ph* Bill Pope, *Pro Des* Owen Paterson, *Ed* Zach Staenberg, *M* Don Davis; songs performed by Massive Attack, Rob Zombie, Prodigy, Lunatic Calm, Rob D, Meat Beat Manifesto, Django

Reinhardt, Duke Ellington, Propellerheads, Rage Against the Machine, and Marilyn Manson, *Costumes* Kym Barrett, *Fight co-ordinator* Yuen Wo Ping.

Warner/Village Roadshow/Groucho II – Warner. 139 mins. USA. 1999. Rel: 11 June 1999. Cert 15.

Meet Joe Black ★★★

When media tycoon William Parrish is visited by Death in the human form of a handsome stranger, he is granted permission to live up until his 65th birthday celebration. However, he is not allowed to divulge the identity of the young man who shadows his every move. Then, to complicate matters, Death discovers an overwhelming attraction for peanut butter, Parrish's daughter and life itself ... Self-indulgent, over-long and meticulously mounted, *Meet Joe Black* takes way too long to deliver its *coup de theatre*. And yet there is so much to commend this update of Mitchell Leisen's 1934 *Death Takes a Holiday* (itself adapted from Alberto Casella's play). Sure, it all suffers hopelessly from pomposity and grand gestures, but there is an eager audience for this slick, life-enhancing hokum. And with the triple-threat of Brad Pitt (all gooey-eyed confusion), Claire Forlani (a vision of loveliness) and a suitably tortured Anthony Hopkins, Ferretti's eye-caressing production design and a finale that will destroy your tear ducts (if it doesn't make you gag), this romantic allegory is escapism to die for. Favourite line: 'Death and taxes' (but you'll have had to see the film to know why).

● *Joe Black* Brad Pitt, *William Parrish* Anthony Hopkins, *Susan Parrish* Claire Forlani, *Drew* Jake Weber, *Allison* Marcia Gay Harden, *Quince* Jeffrey Tambor, *Eddie Sloane* David S. Howard, *Jamaican woman* Lois Kelly-Miller, *butler* Richard Clarke, Jahnni St John, Marylouise Burke, Diane Kagan.
● *Dir* and *Pro* Martin Brest, *Ex Pro* Ronald L. Schwary, *Assoc Pro* Celia Costas, *Screenplay* Ron Osborn & Jeff Reno, Kevin Wade and Bo Goldman, *Ph* Emmanuel Lubezki, *Pro Des* Dante Ferretti, *Ed* Joe Hutshing and Michael Tronick, *M* Thomas Newman, *Costumes* Aude Bronson-Howard and David C. Robinson, *Visual effects* Industrial Light & Magic.

Universal/City Light Films – UIP.
181 mins. USA. 1998. Rel: 15 January 1998. Cert 12.

Men With Guns ★★★

Latin America; the present. After the death of his wife, prominent doctor Humberto Fuentes decides to take a vacation with a difference. Rather than revisiting the same old beaches, he resolves to make contact with the students he taught in an international health programme that encouraged young medics to work amongst the poor. Recalling his own advice that the worst enemies of medicine are bacteria and ignorance, Fuentes gradually realises that his social and political ignorance has become the greatest stain on his proud legacy ... A bleak, tragic drama of some poetic power, *Men With Guns* was inspired by real events that occurred in Guatemala and marks yet another humanist triumph for writer-director John Sayles (*Matewan*, *Lone Star*). As the noble but hopelessly blinkered doctor, Argentinean actor Federico Luppi (*Cronos*) supplies just the right amount of dignity tinged with despondency, while the eclectic soundtrack of authentic Latin music is another plus.

● *Dr Humberto Fuentes* Federico Luppi, *Domingo, the soldier* Damian Delgado, *Conejo, the boy* Dan Rivera Gonzalez, *Graciela, the mute girl* Tania Cruz, *Padre Portillo, the priest* Damian Alcazar, *Andrew* Mandy Patinkin, *Harriet* Kathryn Grody, Iguandili Lopez, Rafael De Quevedo, Carmen Madrid, Esteban Soberanes, Roberto Sosa, Maggie Renzi, Shari Gray.
● *Dir*, *Screenplay* and *Ed* John Sayles, *Pro* R. Paul Miller and Maggie Renzi, *Ex Pro* Jody Patton, Lou Gonda and John Sloss, *Co-Pro* Bertha Navarro, *Ph* Slawomir Idziak, *Pro Des* Felipe Fernandez Del Paso, *M* Mason Daring; songs performed by El General, Les Miserables Brass Band, Susana Baca, Toto La Momposina, etc, *Costumes* Mayes C. Rubeo.

Lexington Road/Clear Blue Sky/Independent Film Channel/Anarchists' Convention – Columbia TriStar.
128 mins. USA. 1997. Rel: 18 September 1998. Cert 15.

Mercury Rising ★★★

A covert government agency (the NSA) invests millions of dollars into a top-secret code protecting the identities of American agents abroad. A nine-year-old autistic boy 'sees through' the code and unravels its secrets. Only one man, a renegade FBI agent, twigs that there's now a price on the boy's head ... Autism is a subject barely explored in the cinema, and maybe *Mercury Rising* is not the movie to launch a new global understanding of the condition, but it at least provides a novel base on which to propel the action. For the most part this well-paced thriller follows the traditional dotted line of Hollywood formula (maverick cop, ice-blooded assassin, top-secret government agency), but it does hold the interest more than most. Only John Barry's patronising theme for the autistic boy truly grates. Previously known as *Simple Simon*.

● *Art Jeffries* Bruce Willis, *Nicholas Kudrow* Alec Baldwin, *Tommy B. Jordan* Chi McBride, *Stacey* Kim Dickens, *Simon* Miko Hughes, *Dean Crandell* Robert Stanton, *Leo Pedranski* Bodhi Pine Elfman, *Emily Lang* Carrie Preston, *Lomax* Kevin Conway, L.L. Ginter, Peter Stormare, John Carroll Lynch, Kelley Hazen, John Doman, Richard Riehle, Maricela Ochoa, Betsy Brantley, Margaret Travolta, Lisa Summerour.
● *Dir* Harold Becker, *Pro* Brian Grazer and Karen Kehela, *Ex Pro* Joseph M. Singer and Ric Kidney, *Co-Pro* Maureen Peyrot and Paul Neesan, *Screenplay* Lawrence Konner and Mark Rosenthal, based on the novel *Simple Simon* by Ryne Douglas Peardon, *Ph* Michael Seresin, *Pro Des* Patrizia Von Brandenstein, *Ed* Peter Honess, *M* John Barry, *Costumes* Betsy Heimann.

Universal/Imagine – UIP.
111 mins. USA. 1998. Rel: 2 October 1998. Cert 15.

Above: Drop dead gorgeous: Brad Pitt invites you to Meet Joe Black *(from UIP)*

Right: Rain boy: Bruce Willis teams up with an autistic nine-year-old (Miko Hughes) in Harold Becker's novel, efficiently paced Mercury Rising (from UIP)

Message in a Bottle ★★

Consumed by the death of his wife, boat restorer Garret Blake types heartfelt, achingly honest letters to her that he seals in beautiful blue bottles and then sets on the ocean wave. One day, out jogging on the beach, divorcee and single mother Theresa Osborne stumbles upon a bottle and is profoundly touched by its contents. Sharing her enchantment with her colleges at the *Chicago Tribune*, Theresa becomes inadvertently responsible for the letter's publication and the subsequent hunt for its mysterious author. Soon, Theresa herself sets off for North Carolina's Outer Banks to unmask the love-lorn scribe ... Adapted from Nicholas Sparks' best-selling novel, *Message in a Bottle* emerges as a picturesque romance with its emotions as hermetically sealed as the letters of its troubled protagonist. In spite of classy turns from Robin Wright Penn and Paul Newman (the latter in delightfully salty mood) and some handsome photography, the film is as lifeless as last night's takeaway. A number of intriguing narrative strands are poorly resolved, while two key sequences – a love scene and a pivotal storm – are rendered anaemic by a sedative score.

● *Garret Blake* Kevin Costner, *Theresa Osborne* Robin Wright Penn, *Dodge Blake* Paul Newman, *Johnny Land* John Savage, *Lina Paul* Illeana Douglas, *Charlie Toschi* Robbie Coltrane, *Jason Osborne* Jesse James, *Alva* Viveka Davis, *Helen* Rosemary Murphy, Bethel Leslie, Tom Aldredge, Richard Hamilton, Caleb Deschanel, Anthony Genovese.
● *Dir* Luis Mandoki, *Pro* Denise Di Novi, Jim Wilson and Kevin Costner, *Screenplay* Gerald DiPego, *Ph* Caleb Deschanel, *Pro Des* Jeffrey Beecroft, *Ed* Steven Weisberg, *M* Gabriel Yared; songs performed by Beth Nielsen Chapman, Sinead Lohan, Faith Hill, Hootie & The Blowfish, Sarah McLachlan, Sheryl Crow, etc, *Costumes* Bernie Pollack.

Warner/Bel – Air Entertainment/Tig – Warner.
131 mins. USA. 1999. Rel: 23 April 1999. Cert 12.

Metroland ★★¹/₂

Greater London/Paris; 1963-1977. Chris Lloyd is content with his cosy lot in Metroland, happy with his wife, daughter, mortgage and vegetable patch. Then his best friend, Toni, turns up from his travels in America and Chris sees his life in a new light. Has he sold out to the *bourgeoisie*? And, if so, what is he going to do about it? The problem with any film that spans a number of years is that it's hard to hold its emotional focus. As it is, scenarist Adrian Hodges has shifted the action from Julian Barnes' 1980 novel into the later phases of the story and opened these scenes out. Philip Saville guides things along at a lively clip but, even so, he lacks the visual daring to make the piece work as a temporal homage. However, the cutting insights of Barnes' novel do occasionally show through and Emily Watson (reminiscent of a young Sarah Miles) is excellent as Chris' shrewd, down-to-earth wife.

● *Chris Lloyd* Christian Bale, *Toni* Lee Ross, *Marion Lloyd* Emily Watson, *Annick* Elsa Zylberstein, *Henri* Rufus, *Joanna* Amanda Ryan, *retired commuter* John Wood, Jonathan Aris, Ifan Meredith, Brian Protheroe.
● *Dir* Philip Saville, *Pro* Andrew Bendel, *Ex Pro* John Wyn-Evans and Martine de Clermont-Tonnerre, *Line Pro* Joy Spink, *Screenplay* Adrian Hodges, *Ph* Jean-Francois Robin, *Pro Des* Don Taylor, *Ed* Greg Miller, *M* Mark Knopfler; songs performed by The Stranglers, Hot Chocolate, Dire Straits, The Subverts, Django Reinhardt, Francoise Hardy, and Elvis Costello, *Costumes* Jenny Beavan.

Blue Horizon/Mact/Filmania/Pandora Cinema/The Arts Council of England/BBC Films/Canal Plus – Metrodome. 101 mins. UK/France/Spain. 1997. Rel: 21 August 1998. Cert 18.

The Mighty ★★★★¹/₂

Cincinnati, Ohio; today. Maxwell Cullen is an overweight simpleton who has become the laughing stock of his peers. Forced to spend another year in seventh grade, he shuts himself off from the outside world and lives in a vacuum of self-pity. Then he meets Kevin, a hunchback his own age who is forced to hobble around on crutches but who celebrates the limitless scope of his imagination. With Kevin's mind and Max's brawn, the ill-matched duo could just about conquer the world ... Based on the children's novel *Freak the Mighty* by Rodman Philbrick, this has all the makings of a self-indulgent, unremittingly sentimental wallow. Yet under the magical direction of Peter Chelsom – he who brought us the warm, funny and offbeat *Hear My Song* and *Funny Bones* – *The Mighty* is a kids' film that adroitly blends fantasy and realism to heart-breaking effect. From the striking photography to the wonderful music, the film is a triumphant marriage of craftsmanship and compassion. As Kevin, Kieran Culkin – Macaulay's younger brother – is simply inspiring, while

Sharon Stone, as his mother, delivers arguably the most creditable performance of her career. Only the cartoonish characterisation of Max's father and a gross caricature from Gillian Anderson prevents this from being an all-time classic.

● *Gwen Dillon* Sharon Stone, *Gram* Gena Rowlands, *Grim* Harry Dean Stanton, *Loretta Lee* Gillian Anderson, *Kenny Kane* James Gandolfini, *Kevin Dillon* Kieran Culkin, *Maxwell Kane* Elden Henson, *Iggy* Meatloaf, *Mrs Addison* Jenifer Lewis, Joe Perrino, Eve Crawford, John Bourgeois, Rudy Webb, Jordan Hughes.
● *Dir* Peter Chelsom, *Pro* Jane Startz and Simon Fields, *Ex Pro* Bob Weinstein, Harvey Weinstein and Julie Goldstein, *Co-Pro* Don Carmody, *Screenplay* Charles Leavitt, *Ph* John De Borman, *Pro Des* Caroline Hanania, *Ed* Martin Walsh, *M* Trevor Jones; 'The Mighty' performed by Sting, *Costumes* Marie Sylvie Deveau.

Miramax/Scholastic Productions – Buena Vista. 100 mins. USA. 1998. Rel: 26 December 1998. Cert PG.

Mighty Joe ★★★

In the Pangani Mountains of Central Africa there is a legend that tells of a ferocious gorilla 15-feet tall. Fearless American zoologist Gregg O'Hara is determined to see the creature for himself – before poachers get there first. And, when he finally encounters the ape, he discovers that it is a gentle, intelligent giant cared for a by a beautiful 21-year-old woman ... A technologically miraculous update of Ernest B. Schoedsack's 1949 companion piece to *King Kong*, *Mighty Joe* is an engaging slice of politically correct hokum. Mighty Joe himself – a combination of animatronics, computer-generated effects and a chap in a gorilla suit – is a truly amazing creation, while the human stereotypes are suitably appealing and unsavoury where applicable. FYI: Terry

Below: Building mountains: Elden Henson and Sharon Stone in Peter Chelsom's soul-reviving The Mighty *(from Buena Vista)*

Right: *Jaywalking bumper style:* Mighty Joe *forgets his Green Cross Code (from Buena Vista)*

Moore, who starred in the first film, makes a priceless cameo in tandem with the original special effects wizard Ray Harryhausen (in the scene immediately prior to Joe's public inauguration). US title: *Mighty Joe Young.*

● *Gregg O'Hara* Bill Paxton, *Jill Young* Charlize Theron, *Strasser* Rade Sherbedgia, *Garth* Peter Firth, *Harry Ruben* David Paymer, *Cecily Banks* Regina King, *Kweli* Robert Wisdom, *Pindi* Naveen Andrews, *Dr Baker* Lawrence Pressman, *Dr Ruth Young* Linda Purl, *young Jill* Mika Boorem, Geoffrey Blake, Christian Clemenson, Cory Buck, Liz Georges, Richard Riehle, Cynthia Allison, Ray Harryhausen, Terry Moore, Tony Genaro, Tracey Walter, Dina Merrill.
● *Dir* Ron Underwood, *Pro* Ted Hartley and Tom Jacobson, *Ex Pro* Gail Katz, *Screenplay* Mark Rosenthal and Lawrence Konner, and (uncredited) Callie Khouri, based on a screenplay by Ruth Rose and a story by Merian C. Cooper, *Ph* Don Peterman and Oliver Wood, *Pro Des* Michael Corenblith, *Ed* Paul Hirsch, *M* James Horner, *Costumes* Molly Maginnis, *Visual effects* Hoyt Yeatman, *Mighty Joe design* Rick Baker.

Walt Disney/RKO Pictures/The Jacobson Company – Buena Vista.
114 mins. USA. 1998. Rel: 26 March 1999. Cert PG.

The Misadventures of Margaret ★★

Manhattan; the present. Seven years after they fell madly in love in Paris, Margaret and Edward Nathan are beginning to feel the strain in their marriage. Margaret is now a successful novelist researching an erotic project set in 18th century France, Edward an English professor steering an attractive young student through her studies of Walt Whitman. Fuelled by paranoia and a fear of missed opportunities, Margaret is now convinced that she married too young ... Packed with priceless one-liners and colourful performances, this breezy adaptation of Cathleen Schine's novel *Rameau's Niece* never quite finds its footing as a credible examination of sexual angst, thus depriving it of the last laugh. Like weak cappuccino, it is chichi, frothy and ultimately lacking a buzz. Still, the film must set a record for the number of exposed penises seen in a mainstream New York comedy. But then, technically, it is Anglo-French.

● *Margaret Nathan* Parker Posey, *Edward Nathan* Jeremy Northam, *Richard Lanne* Craig Chester, *Till Turner* Elizabeth McGovern, *Lily* Brooke Shields, *Art Turner* Corbin Bernsen, *Martin* Patrick Bruel, *The Philosopher* Stephane Freiss, *Sarah from Brighton* Amy Phillips, Justine Waddell, Alexis Denisof, Sylvie Testud, Al MacKenzie, Kerry Shale.
● *Dir* and *Screenplay* Brian Skeet, *Pro* Ian Benson, *Ex Pro* Andy Harries, Pippa Cross and Dominique Green, *Ph* Romain Winding, *Ed* Clare Douglas and Tariq Anwar, *Pro Des* Martin Childs, *M* James Shearman; songs performed by Francoise Hardy, St Etienne, Chris Montez, Rebecca Pidgeon, Noël Coward, Patti Rothberg, etc, *Costumes* Edi Giguere.

TF1 International/Granada/Lunatics & Lovers/Canal Plus, etc – Feature Film Company.
92 mins. UK/France. 1998. Rel: 23 April 1999. Cert 15.

Les Misérables ★★★

France; 1812-1832. Imprisoned for almost 20 years for stealing a loaf of bread, Jean Valjean has been turned into an animal by an unjust penal code. Then, while on parole, he is subjected to an act of such selfless compassion that he vows to mend his ways and dedicate his life to the advancement of others. But one man's blinkered preoccupation with 'justice' is to haunt Valjean for many more years to come ... It is not for nothing that Victor Hugo's powerful 1862 novel has been filmed at least 15 times before. It is a wonderful story drawing on the timeless themes of inequity, betrayal and obsession and this latest adaptation by Rafael Yglesias (*Fearless*, *Death and the Maiden*) distils the essence of Hugo's narrative with a sure hand. And if Bille August's direction lacks the inspirational touch of a Lean or Spielberg, he does bring an epic sweep to his subject that frequently piques the emotions. Furthermore, he is abetted by two powerful performances from Neeson and Rush, by some sterling camerawork and production design, and by a location manager who deserves an Oscar. Filmed in the Czech Republic and Paris.

● *Jean Valjean* Liam Neeson, *Javert* Geoffrey Rush, *Fantine* Uma Thurman, *Cosette* Claire Danes, *Marius* Hans Matheson, *Captain Beauvais* Reine Brynolfsson, *bishop* Peter Vaughan, *Bertin* Christopher Adamson, Tim Barlow, Timothy Bateson, Veronika Bendova, David Birkin, Patsy Byrne, Kathleen Byron, Edna Dore, Janet Henfrey, Gerard Horan, Kelly Hunter, Lennie James, David McKay, Alex Norton, Ralph Nossek, Edward Tudor Pole, Tony Vogel.
● *Dir* Bille August, *Pro* Sarah Radclyffe and James Gorman, *Co-Pro* Caroline Hewitt, *Screenplay* Rafael Yglesias, *Ph* Jorgen Persson, *Pro Des* Anna Asp, *Ed* Janus Billeskov-Jansen, *M* Basil Poledouris, *Costumes* Gabriella Pescucci.

Mandalay Entertainment – Entertainment. 134 mins. USA. 1998. Rel: 20 November 1998. Cert 12.

Mojo ★

Soho, London; the summer of 1958. In a poky little nightclub called the Atlantic, a young singer called Silver Johnny is making an impression with the girls. The club's owner, Ezra, is grooming Johnny to be a major attraction, but a local gangster is determined to muscle in on the action ... A stagy, claustrophobic look at the beginnings of rock 'n' roll, *Mojo* is a classic case of why film should leave theatre well alone. A huge success at London's Royal Court Theatre, *Mojo* has been adapted for the screen by its author and his brother and directed by the former. The former has done nothing to tone down the broad performances of his actors and has done little to open the play out. The superimposed pop songs of the period merely draw attention to the inertia.

● *Mickey* Ian Hart, *Skinny Luke* Ewen Bremner, *Baby* Aidan Gillen, *Sweets* Martin Gwynn Jones, *Silver Johnny* Hans Matheson, *Sid Potts* Andy Serkis, *Ezra* Ricky Tomlinson, *Sam Ross* Harold Pinter, Kenneth Bryans, Paul Ebsworth, Al Fiorentini.
● *Dir* Jez Butterworth, *Pro* Eric Abraham, *Ex Pro*

George Faber, Steve Butterworth and Nick Marston, *Screenplay* Jez and Tom Butterworth, *Ph* Bruno De Keyzer, *Pro Des* Hugo Luczyc-Wyhowski, *Ed* Richard Milward, *M* Murray Gold; songs performed by Donald Byrd, Nick Cave, Little Lewis, Hans Matheson, Marc Almond, The Stone Cold Strollers, Saint Etienne, Warm Jets, David McAlmont, The Skyliners, Beth Orton, Buddy Holly, etc, *Costumes* Pam Tait.

Portobello Pictures/BBC Films/British Screen – Portobello. 92 mins. UK. 1997. Rel: 10 July 1998. Cert 15.

Monk Dawson ★

Educated by Benedictine monks, Eddie Dawson resolves to make the world a better place. However, on taking up the cloth, he quickly learns to resent the hypocrisy of the Catholic church, where a child born out of wedlock is entitled to less spiritual support than the compliant and well-heeled. But Dawson is not one to accept compromise lightly ... Like a clerical *Forrest Gump*, this episodic adaptation of the 1969 novel by Piers Paul Read encompasses a number of key moments in recent British history, which seem to have little to do with Dawson's spiritual safari. But the real fun is to be had spotting the constant cliches and walking stereotypes, all and every one a welcome relief from the insipid turn from John Michie as Dawson. Trembling with good intentions, this first feature from 23-year-old director Tom Waller is as awkward and embarrassing as a virgin's grope.

● *Eddie Dawson* aka *Father John* John Michie, *Bobby Winterman* Ben Taylor, *Jenny Stanten* Paula

Below: In the mouth of despair: Uma Thurman sheds her glamorous image as Fantine, in Bille August's epic, handsome Les Misérables *(from Entertainment)*

Right: A myth and hit: Mulan (pro-nounced Moo-wun) takes the Huns for a ride in Disney's exciting and moving cartoon (from Buena Vista)

Hamilton, *David Allenby* Martin Kemp, *Fr Timothy* Rupert Vansittart, *Mrs Carter* Frances Tomelty, *Mollie Jolliffe/prostitute* Rhona Mitra, *Theresa Carter* Kate Steavenson-Payne, *Henry Poll* Mark Caven, Michael Cashman, Roger Brierley, Amanda Jenner, Roger Hammond, Richenda Carey, Donald Pickering, Nicola Oliver, Candida Gubbins, Debora Weston, Jeff Nuttall, Geoffrey Beavers, Denys Hawthorne, Patrick Durkin.
● *Dir*, *Pro* and *Ed* Tom Waller, *Assoc Pro* Samantha Keston, *Screenplay* James Magrane and Matthew McIntyre, *Ph* Teoh Gay Hian, *Pro Des* Harold Chapman, *M* Mark Jensen, *Costumes* Julian Day.

De Warrenne Pictures – Winstone.
107 mins. UK. 1997. Rel: 31 July 1998. Cert 18.

Mr Nice Guy – Yige Hao Ren ★★★
Melbourne; today. When a popular TV cook rescues a female reporter from a gang of drug dealers, her incriminating video ends up in his own collection of cuisine tapes. Now the reluctant hero has become the chief target of two rival mobs who will stop at nothing to retrieve the cassette. However, this unassuming chef can chop more than vegetables ... Jackie Chan's first starring vehicle in English, *Mr Nice Guy* lacks the spectacle of his more recent efforts but still provides the requisite stunts and charm. If anything, Chan's ingenuity is even more evident here than usual (you'll be amazed what he can do with a horse and carriage). [*Ewen Brownrigg*]

● *Jackie* Jackie Chan, *Giancarlo* Richard Norton, *Miki* Miki Lee, *Lakeisha* Karen McLymont, *Diana* Gabrielle Fitzpatrick, *Baggio* Barry Otto, Vince Poletto, *cyclist* Sammo Hung, Peter Houghton, Peter Lindsay.
● *Dir* Samo Hung, *Pro* Chua Lam, *Ex Pro* Leonard Ho, *Screenplay* Edward Tang and Fibe Ma, *Ph*

Raymond Lam, *Pro Des* Horace Ma, *Ed* Peter Cheung, *M* Peter Kam, *Costumes* Lui Fung Shan.

New Line/Raymond Chow/Golden Harvest – Entertainment.
86 mins. Hong Kong. 1996/1998. Rel: 28 August 1998. Cert 12.

Mulan ★★★★
When ancient China is invaded by the Huns, the Emperor orders one man from every family to help defend the realm. But seeing how frail her father is, young Fa Mulan steals her father's armour and, disguised as a man, takes his place in the Imperial Army. Yet her act – for all its good intentions – is punishable by death ... It's not until you look at what the other studios have to offer that you begin to appreciate how good Disney's animation really is. And, after the disappointment of its crude and anodyne *Hercules*, the Mouse House is back on top form with this moving, exciting and beautifully drawn epic. Mulan herself is a wonderful creation (inspired by a 1,000-year-old Chinese myth), a spirited, resourceful and stubborn heroine, while the spectacular Chinese scenery is exploited to the full. The scene in which the Hun army spills over the rim of a snow-covered mountain – and is then buried by an avalanche – is one of the most thrilling sequences ever captured by ink. The songs, too, from former rock star Matthew Wilder and lyricist David Zippel, are first-rate.

● Voices: *Fa Mulan aka Ping* Ming Na-Wen, *singing voice of Fa Mulan* Lea Salonga, *Fa Zhou* Soon-Tek Oh, *Shang* B.D. Wong, *singing voice of Shang* Donny Osmond, *Fa Li* Freda Foh Shen, *Mushu* Eddie Murphy, *Yao* Harvey Fierstein, *Chien-Po* Jerry S. Tondo, *Ling* Gedde Watanabe, *singing*

voice of Ling Matthew Wilder, *Shan-Yu* Miguel Ferrer, *Chi Fu* James Hong, *Grandmother Fa* June Foray, *The Emperor* Pat Morita, *the matchmaker* Miriam Margolyes, George Takei, Frank Welker, James Shigeta.
● *Dir* Barry Cook and Tony Bancroft, *Pro* Pam Coats, *Assoc Pro* Kendra Haaland and Robert S. Garber, *Screenplay* Rita Hsiao, Christopher Sanders, Philip Lazebnik, Raymond Singer and Eugenia Bostwick-Singer, from a story by Robert D. San Souci, *Pro Des* Hans Bacher, *Ed* Michael Kelly, *M* Jerry Goldsmith; songs: Matthew Wilder (music) and David Zippel (lyrics); 'True To Your Heart' performed by 98° and Stevie Wonder.

Walt Disney – Buena Vista.
89 mins. USA. 1998. Rel: 9 October 1998. Cert U.

The Mummy ★¹/₂

Egypt; 1290 BC/1923 AD. Condemned to eternal life sealed in a sarcophagus, the high priest Imhotep is released by tomb raiders three thousand years later. Deranged with thoughts of revenge (and bent on finding his girlfriend), the priest sets about renovating his decomposed body. And, as soon as he's whole again, his power will be inconceivable ... One of the more mystifying hits at the US box-office (it smashed records in May 1999), *The Mummy* does employ some magnificent effects set against an inspirational background of ancient curses and heroic greed. However, while attempting to emulate the style of Indiana Jones with a dash of old-fashioned lunacy, the film stumbles blindly between a variety of stools. At times extremely nasty in content (brain-eating scarab beetles, decomposing faces, etc), the film is also excessively infantile, displaying the sort of slapstick that would irritate a 12-year-old. And to deprive John Hannah of his mellifluous Scottish brogue is akin to hiring Pamela Anderson to play the Elephant Woman. Excruciating.

● *Rick O'Connell* Brendan Fraser, *Evelyn* Rachel Weisz, *Jonathan* John Hannah, *Imhotep* Arnold Vosloo, *the Egyptologist* Jonathan Hyde, *Beni* Kevin J. O'Connor, *Pharaoh Seti* Aharon Ipale, *Anck-Su-Namun* Patricia Velasquez, Oded Fehr, Omid Djalili, Erick Avari, Carl Chase, Stephen Dunham, Corey Johnson, Tuc Watkins, Bernard Fox.
● *Dir* Stephen Sommers, *Pro* James Jacks and Sean Daniel, *Ex Pro* Kevin Jarre, *Co-Pro* Patricia Carr, *Screenplay* Sommers, from a story by Sommers, Lloyd Fonvielle and Kevin Jarre, *Ph* Adrian Biddle, *Pro Des* Allan Cameron, *Ed* Bob Ducsay, *M* Jerry Goldsmith, *Costumes* John Bloomfield, *Special effects* Chris Corbould, *Visual effects* John Berton.

Universal/Alphaville – UIP.
125 mins. USA. 1999. Rel: 24 June 1999. Cert 12.

My Favorite Martian ★¹/₂

When Tim O'Hara, an accident-prone TV reporter, witnesses a UFO crash-landing, he thinks his gravy train has arrived. Then the alien ship's pilot, who affects human form, moves in with him and becomes a particularly irritating avuncular figure ... If you like your humour zany, broad and ludicrous, then this is for you. With Christopher Lloyd repeating his mad doc routine from the *Back to the Future* trilogy – and infecting the rest of the cast with a severe bout of over-acting – *My Favorite Martian* is every bit as awful as it looks. Based on the 1963-66 CBS sitcom (which spawned a cartoon series in the early Seventies), the film blunders into timeworn territory with the comic dexterity of an ox. In its 'favor', though, the pace is brisk and the opening sequence a classic, but basically this is a badly assembled hotchpotch of half-formed ideas. FYI: Ray Walston, who played the alien in the original, gets to send his character up rotten in a priceless cameo.

● *Tim O'Hara* Jeff Daniels, *Uncle Martin* Christopher Lloyd, *Brace Channing* Elizabeth Hurley, *Lizzie* Daryl Hannah, *Dr Elliott Coleye* Wallace Shawn, *Mrs Lorelei Brown* Christine Ebersole, *Ben Channing* Michael Lerner, *Armitan* Ray Walston, Shelley Malil, Jeremy Hotz, T.K. Carter, Troy Evans, and *uncredited*: voice of Zoot Wayne Knight.
● *Dir* Donald Petrie, *Pro* Robert Shapiro, Jerry Leider and Marc Toberoff, *Ex Pro* Barry Bernardi, *Co-Pro* Daryl Kass, *Screenplay* Sherri Stoner and Deanna Oliver, *Ph* Thomas Ackerman, *Pro Des* Sandy Veneziano, *Ed* Malcolm Campbell, *M* John Debney; Verdi, Richard Strauss; theme by George Greeley; songs performed by Tab Benoit, James Brown, Louis Armstrong, John Hobbs, etc, *Costumes*

Below: Stargate Night Live: Brendan Fraser, Rachel Weisz and John Hannah curse the day they agreed to appear in Stephen Sommers' moronic The Mummy (from UIP)

Above: Painting the town red: Peter Mullan (right) lets off some steam in Ken Loach's emotionally compelling My Name is Joe (from Film Four)

Hope Hanafin, *Visual effects* Phil Tippett and John T. Van Vliet, *Animatronic effects* Alec Gillis and Tom Woodruff Jr.

Walt Disney Pictures – Buena Vista.
94 mins. USA. 1999. Rel: 28 May 1999. Cert PG.

My Giant ★¹/₂

Romania/Chicago/New York/New Mexico/Las Vegas; today. With his career on the skids, annoying talent scout Sammy Kanin tries turning a 7'7" Romanian monk into a movie star. Only in America ... Some critics were crueller to this than others, but the fact remains that *My Giant* is predictable, derivative and cloying. From the star of *Father's Day* and the director of *Hudson Hawk*. FYI: The 7'7" Gheorghe Muresan is the Romanian-born basketball player with the NBA's Washington Wizards. [*Charles Bacon*]

● *Sammy Kanin* Billy Crystal, *Serena Kanin* Kathleen Quinlan, *Max* Gheorghe Muresan, *Lillianna* Joanna Pacula, Zane Carney, Jere Burns, Harold Gould, Dan Castellaneta, Raymond O'Connor, Doris Roberts, Eric Lloyd, Lorna Luft, Lindsay Crystal, Peter Schindler, Max Goldblatt, *himself* Steven Seagal, Heather Thomas, Walt G. Ludwig.
● *Dir* Michael Lehmann, *Pro* Billy Crystal, *Ex Pro* Peter Schindler, *Screenplay* David Seltzer, from a story by Seltzer and Crystal, *Ph* Michael Coulter, *Pro Des* Jackson DeGovia, *Ed* Stephen Semel, *M* Marc Shaiman, *Costumes* Rita Ryack.

Castle Rock/Face – Warner.
103 mins. USA. 1998. Rel: 12 February 1999. Cert PG.

My Name is Joe ★★★¹/₂

Ruchill, Glasgow; today. 'My name is Joe and thank fuck I am not an alcoholic' announces Joe Kavanagh to camera. After years of alcoholism, Joe, edging towards 38, is off the wagon and determined to salvage the remains of his life. When he meets attractive health visitor Sarah Downie he sees the key to a new beginning, but how many of his old ways has he really shaken off? After the international backdrop of *Land and Freedom* and *Carla's Song*, director Ken Loach returns to the more intimate drama for which he is known. However, even by Loach standards, the Glaswegian accents here are so impenetrable that it's hard to know what's going in for the first 30 minutes or so. Then, when the film does settle into its stride, the characters have become so real to us that the subsequent emotional violence is almost unbearable.

● *Joe Kavanagh* Peter Mullan, *Sarah Downie* Louise Goodall, *Shanks* Gary Lewis, *Maggie* Lorraine McIntosh, *Liam* David McKay, *Sabine* AnneMarie Kennedy, *McGowan* David Hayman, Scott Hannah, Gordon McMurray, David Hough, John Comerford.
● *Dir* Ken Loach, *Pro* Rebecca O'Brien, *Ex Pro* Ulrich Felsberg, *Screenplay* Paul Laverty, *Ph* Barry Ackroyd, *Pro Des* Martin Johnson, *Ed* Jonathan Morris, *M* George Fenton; Beethoven; songs performed by Status Quo, and Norman Greenbaum, *Costumes* Rhona Russell.

Parallax Pictures/Road Movies Vierte/Scottish Arts Council/National Lottery/The Glasgow Film Fund/Channel Four Films/La Sept Cinema/Alta Films, etc – Film Four.
105 mins. UK/Germany/France/Italy/Spain. 1998. Rel: 6 November 1998. Cert 15.

The Negotiator ★★★★

Chicago; the present. Lieutenant Danny Roman is the best hostage negotiator in his department. Then, shortly after he has defused yet another potentially inflammable confrontation, he is framed for the murder of his partner. Not knowing who to trust in a police force riddled with corruption, Roman sets up his own hostage situation, holding the chief of Internal Affairs captive at gunpoint. Enter rival cop Chris Sabian, arguably the best negotiator in his department ... An explosive combination of siege thriller, whodunnit and moral quandary, *The Negotiator* is enriched by breathless direction, handsome production values and some excellent writing. And how nice to see a big-budget action-thriller that derives its power from the acting smarts of its two leading men – two of the best actors in Hollywood – rather than from an assault from the special effects department. FYI: *The Negotiator* is dedicated to J.T. Walsh (here playing yet another shifty figure of authority), who died shortly after the film's completion.

● *Danny Roman* Samuel L. Jackson, *Chris Sabian*

Kevin Spacey, *Commander Adam Beck* David Morse, *Commander Grant Frost* Ron Rifkin, *Chief Al Travis* John Spencer, *Inspector Niebaum* J.T. Walsh, *Karen Roman* Regina Taylor, *Maggie* Siobhan Fallon, *Rudy* Paul Giamatti, *Farley* Stephen Lee, *Linda Roenick* Rhonda Dotson, Bruce Beatty, Michael Cudlitz, Carlos Gomez, Dean Norris, Nestor Serrano, Leonard Thomas, Jack Shearer, Kelsey Mulrooney, and *uncredited: Nate Roenick* Paul Guilfoyle.

● *Dir* F. Gary Gray, *Pro* David Hoberman and Arnon Milchan, *Ex Pro* David Nicksay, Robert Stone and Webster Stone, *Screenplay* James DeMonaco and Kevin Fox, *Ph* Russell Carpenter, *Pro Des* Holger Gross, *Ed* Christian Wagner, *M* Graeme Revell; songs performed by Craig Armstrong, Rednex, Dwight Yoakam, and Marvin Gaye, *Costumes* Francine Jamison-Tanchuck.

Regency Enterprises/Mandeville Films/New Regency – Warner.
139 mins. USA/Germany. 1998. Rel: 27 November 1998. Cert 15.

Above: *Talk to the criminals: Samuel L. Jackson makes a point in F. Gary Gray's explosive* The Negotiator *(from Warner). J.T. Walsh listens*

Neil Simon's The Odd Couple II ★★

Sarasota, Florida/all over California; the present. After 17 years of blissful partition, serial divorcee Felix Unger and terminal divorcee Oscar Madison find their paths about to converge again. Oscar's son, an actor, is getting married to Felix's daughter, an actress. As fate would have it, Felix and Oscar bump into each other at Los Angeles airport and what should have been a straightforward drive to their children's wedding turns into an expedition of mind-boggling bad luck ... Like an old people's reunion, this belated sequel to the 1968 comedy throws up as much melancholy as mirth. Now 73 and 78 respectively, Jack Lemmon and Walter Matthau crack jokes about old age and mug shamelessly as if their very resurrection is some kind of big joke. Neil Simon, who penned the original, has mustered a few good one-liners for Matthau ('we mix like oil and frozen yoghurt'), but the barrel soon runs dry after the first reel. FYI: This is the tenth time Lemmon and Matthau have worked together on a film.

● *Felix Ungar* Jack Lemmon, *Oscar Madison* Walter Matthau, *Thelma* Christine Baranski, *Beaumont* Barnard Hughes, *Brucey Madison* Jonathan Silverman, *Holly* Jean Smart, *Holly* Lisa Waltz, Mary Beth Peil, Doris Belack, Ellen Geer, Jay O. Sanders, Rex Linn, Richard Riehle, Lou Cutell, Mary Fogarty, Alice Ghostley, Rebecca Schull, Joaquin Martinez, Amy Yasbeck, Liz Torres, Cliff Bemis, Michelle Johnston.
● *Dir* Howard Deutch, *Pro* Neil Simon, Robert W. Cort and David Madden, *Assoc Pro* Elena Spiotta, *Screenplay* Simon, *Ph* Jamie Anderson, *Pro Des* Dan Bishop, *Ed* Seth Flaum, *M* Alan Silvestri; songs performed by Bob Seger & The Silver Bullet Band, Crit Harmon, Glenn Miller, Elvis Presley, etc, *Costumes* Lisa Jensen.

Paramount – UIP.
96 mins. USA. 1998. Rel: 13 November 1998. Cert 15.

A Night at the Roxbury ★

Beverly Hills; today. Steve and Doug Butabi are a pair of overgrown, mismatched and socially calamitous brothers under the impression that they are the epitome of cool. Dedicated followers of fashion, they haunt the local disco scene, fall over a lot and scare off any remotely available babes. When, with the help of TV has-been Richard Grieco, they attain access to the glitzy Roxbury nightclub, they are mistaken for genuine movers and shakers ... Yet another full-blown Hollywood extension of a recurring skit from TV's *Saturday Night Live*, this is 'comedy' at its most witless and embarrassing. So let's change the subject...

● *Steve Butabi* Will Ferrell, *Doug Butabi* Chris Kattan, *Kamehl Butabi* Dan Hedaya, *Emily Sanderson* Molly Shannon, *himself* Richard Grieco, *Barbara Butabi* Loni Anderson, *Craig* Lochlyn Munro, *Dooey* Colin Quinn, Jennifer Coolidge, Michael 'Big Mike' Duncan, Meredith Scott Lynn, Gigi Rice, Elisa Donovan, Dwayne Hickman, Roy Jenkins, Mary Anne Kellogg, Kristen Dalton, Twink Caplan, Mark McKinney, and *uncredited*: *Danny Zadir* Chazz Palminteri.
● *Dir* John Fortenberry, *Pro* Lorne Michaels and Amy Heckerling, *Ex Pro* Robert K. Weiss, *Screenplay* Steve Koren, Will Ferrell & Chris Kattan, *Ph* Francis Kenny, *Pro Des* Steven Jordan, *Ed* Jay Kamen, *M* David Kitay; songs performed by Haddaway, 3rd Party, No Mercy, Bamboo, KC & The Sunshine Band, Ace of Base, Bee Gees, N-Trance and Rod Stewart, Cyndi Lauper, Brainbug, The Hollies, Amber, REM, Tamala, Faithless, Bruce Springsteen, etc, *Costumes* Mona May.

Paramount/SNL Studios – UIP.
82 mins. USA. 1998. Rel: 19 March 1999. Cert 15.

No ★★★

The latest film by that intellectual playwright Robert Lepage confirms his cinematic skills. The title of his film, located in Osaka (filmed in colour) and Montreal (mainly seen in black-and-white), refers both to Noh theatre and to the no vote for Quebec's separatism. The settings are linked by a Canadian actress (Cadieux), pregnant by her boyfriend (Martin) left behind in Montreal in 1970 to be caught up with terrorist friends to whom he gives shelter. The film's surface is often engaging, especially in those scenes in Osaka where the actress is playing Feydeau and finds her own life echoing stage farce after she catches the attentions of the Canadian cultural attache whose suspicious wife, an ex-actress, is highly critical. But the political issues are over-complex and, while the film seems to have serious aims (as witness the introduction of a character blinded in 1945 at Hiroshima), its intentions remain obscure. Entertaining, but baffling. [*Mansel Stimpson*]

● *Sophie Maltais* Anne-Marie Cadieux, *Hanako* Marie Brassard, *Michel* Alexis Martin, *Patricia Hebert* Marie Gignac, *Walter Lapointe* Richard Frechette, *Francois-Xavier* Eric Bernier, Patrice Godin, Jean Charest, Lynda Lepage-Beaulieu.
● *Dir* Robert Lepage, *Pro* Bruno Jobin, *Screenplay* Lepage and Andre Morency, *Ph* Pierre Mignot, *Pro Des* Monique Dion, *Ed* Aube Foglia, *M* Michel F. Cote and Bernard Falaise, *Costumes* Marie-Chantale Vaillancourt, *Sound* Raymond Vermette.

In Extremis Images/Alliance Vivafilm/Telefilm Canada, etc – Alliance Releasing.
85 mins. Canada. 1998. Rel: 9 April 1999. Cert 15.

Notting Hill ★★★★¹⁄₂

Thirtysomething divorcee William Thacker runs a faltering bookshop in Notting Hill, London, and shares a house with an unwashed Welshman. Then, one Wednesday, Anna Scott – the world's highest-paid actress and all-round goddess – walks into his shop to buy a book on Egypt. One thing leads to another and William spills an orange juice down the front of her designer outfit ... Saying that *Notting Hill* is better than *Four Weddings and a Funeral* – or vice versa – is like declaring cats are better than dogs. While both films have much in common – same star, writer, producers and effective balance of romance and comedy – *Notting Hill* is powered by a different and marvellous narrative device. What if we, mere mortals, were to come in contact with a world-class celebrity? How would we react? What fools would we make of ourselves? Of course, Hugh Grant has had his share of the spotlight (don't mention Divine Brown), but there is something so effortlessly human and English about him that we can believe his dazzlement in the presence of Julia Roberts. And Ms Roberts who, at times, seems indistinguishable from the part she plays, is a genuine coup for the part of the Hollywood luminary. Not only does her own fame, beauty and celebrity precede her, but she brings the wounded humanity of Anna heart-breakingly to

life. In short, then, *Notting Hill* and *Four Weddings* are two different movies following the same agenda – to amuse, touch and make us feel good about being human.

● *Anna Scott* Julia Roberts, *William Thacker* Hugh Grant, *Bernie* Hugh Bonneville, *Honey Thacker* Emma Chambers, *Martin* James Dreyfus, *Spike* Rhys Ifans, *Max* Tim McInnery, *Bella* Gina McKee, *Tony* Richard McCabe, Dylan Moran, Roger Frost, Julian Rhind-Tutt, Lorelei King, John Shrapnel, Clarke Peters, Mischa Barton, Henry Goodman, Melissa Wilson, Emily Mortimer, Sam West, Patrick Barlow, Andy De La Tour, Ann Beach, and *uncredited*: *Jeff* Alec Baldwin, *Anna's co-star* Matthew Modine.
● *Dir* Roger Michell, *Pro* Duncan Kenworthy, *Ex Pro* Tim Bevan, Richard Curtis and Eric Fellner, *Screenplay* Curtis, *Ph* Michael Coulter, *Pro Des* Stuart Craig, *Ed* Nick Moore, *M* Trevor Jones; songs performed by Elvis Costello, Pulp, Texas, Ronan Keating, Al Green, Bill Withers, Shania Twain, and Bob Marley and Lauryn Hill, *Costumes* Shuna Harwood.

PolyGram/Working Title/Notting Hill Pictures – PolyGram.
124 mins. UK. 1999. Rel: 21 May 1999. Cert 15.

Above: Bedsitcom: Julia Roberts, Rhys Ifans and Hugh Grant deliberate on fame, love and the whole damn thing in Roger Michell's funny and enchanting Notting Hill (from PolyGram)

Right: Guy stuff: Lyle Lovett and Martin Donovan contemplate the female mystique in Don Roos' cheeky The Opposite of Sex (from Columbia TriStar)

The Odd Couple II

See *Neil Simon's The Odd Couple II.*

On Connait La Chanson – The Same Old Song ★★★

Paris; today. Six characters in various walks of life find that their paths converge in a romantic spiral that will engulf, liberate and confuse them. But then Paris is like that ... Alain Resnais' most commercially successful film to date, *On Connait La Chanson* is an affectionate homage to the TV oeuvre of Dennis Potter. But, far from breaking out into full-blown Cole Porter or Irving Berlin production numbers, Resnais' characters mime to snatches of famous Gallic songs that serve as their interior voice. The French, apparently, found this hilarious, but English-speaking audiences will be understandably nonplused by what is little more than a running gimmick. Notwithstanding, there is a wealth of humour in these self-obsessed bourgeoisie, with particularly fine work from Andre Dussollier, Jean-Pierre Bacri and Resnais' wife, Sabine Azema.

● *Claude* Pierre Arditi, *Odile Lalande* Sabine Azema, *Nicolas* Jean-Pierre Bacri, *Simon* Andre Dussollier, *Camille Lalande* Agnes Jaoui, *Marc Duveyrier* Lambert Wilson, *Jane* Jane Birkin, *Father* Jean-Paul Roussillon, Nelly Borgeaud, Jean-Pierre Darroussin, Charlotte Kady, Jacques Mauclair, Francoise Bertin.
● *Dir* Alain Resnais, *Pro* Bruno Pesery, *Screenplay* Agnes Jaoui and Jean-Pierre Bacri, *Ph* Renato Berta, *Pro Des* Jacques Saulnier, *Ed* Herve de Luze, *M* Bruno Fontaine; songs performed by Jacques

Dutronc, Sylvie Vartan, Gilbert Becaud, Alain Souchon, Dalida, Alain Delon, Jane Birkin, Johnny Halliday, Edith Piaf, Eddy Mitchell, Serge Gainsbourg, Maurice Chevalier, Josephine Baker, Arletty, Charles Aznavour, Simone Simon, etc, *Costumes* Jackie Budin.

Arena Films/Camera One/France 2 Cinema/Vega Film/ Greenpoint/Canal Plus, etc – Pathe. 122 mins. France/Switzerland/UK/Italy. 1997. Rel: 4 December 1998. Cert PG.

The One-Seventh Farmers

See *The Inheritors.*

The Opposite of Sex ★★¹/₂

A cynical, opinionated and promiscuous 16-year-old, Dedee Truitt knows about sex. 'Sex always ends in children, disease or relationships,' she observes. 'I want the opposite of that.' After the death of her step-father, Dedee runs away from home and turns up on the doorstep of her half-brother Bill, a gay and con-scientious school teacher. She doesn't mean to screw up his life, it's just that she can't help herself ... A cheeky sex comedy for juvenile adults, *The Opposite of Sex* has wit to spare but constantly squanders it. While the offbeat cast – former child star, leading light of independent cinema, TV comedienne and country & western singer – play their parts with commendable straight faces, director Roos constantly nudges the humour with bouncy music and sitcom editing. Still, any film that plies its two female leads with all the best lines deserves some recognition.

● *Dedee Truitt* Christina Ricci, *Bill Truitt* Martin Donovan, *Lucia Dalury* Lisa Kudrow, *Carl Tippett* Lyle Lovett, *Jason Bock* Johnny Galecki, *Randy* William Lee Scott, *Matt Matteo* Ivan Sergei, Megan Blake, Colin Ferguson, Dan Bucatinsky, Chauncey Leopardi, Rodney Eastman, Heather Fairfield, Susan Leslie.
● *Dir and Screenplay* Don Roos, *Pro* David Kirkpatrick and Michael Besman, *Ex Pro* Jim Lotfi and Steve Danton, *Ph* Hubert Taczanowski, *Pro Des* Michael Clausen, Ed David Codron, *M* Mason Daring; songs performed by Jeanie Stahl, Mason Daring, and Shane Koss and Adrian Hierholzer, Costumes Peter Mitchell.

Rysher Entertainment/Sony Pictures Classics – Columbia TriStar.
101 mins. USA. 1998. Rel: 15 January 1999. Cert 18.

Orgazmo ★

In order to pay for his upcoming marriage, a God-fearing Mormon from Utah is lured into starring in a porn film ... Attempting to do for erotica what *Airplane!* did for crash landings, *Orgazmo* is low-rent parody suffering from a tumescence of the obvious. The experience is like watching a porn film without the sex. From the creator of TV's *South Park*.

● *Joe Young/Joe Hung* Trey Parker, *Ben Chapleski/Choda Boy* Dian Bachar, *Lisa* Robyn Lynne, *Maxxx Orbison* Michael Dean Jacobs, *Dave, the lighting guy* Matt Stone, Ron Jeremy, Andrew W. Kemler, David Dunn, Chasey Lain, Max Hardcore, Kristy Lake, Jacklyn Lick, Serenity, The Brazilian Bombshell, etc.
● *Dir and Screenplay* Trey Parker, *Pro* Fran Rubel Kuzui, Jason McHugh and Matt Stone, *Ex Pro* Kaz Kuzui, Mark Damon and Noriaki Nakagawa, *Ph* Kenny Gioseffi, *Pro Des* Tristan Paris Bourne, *Ed* Parker and Michael R. Miller, *M* Paul Robb, *Costumes* Kristen Anacker, *Stunts* Philip Tan.

Kuzui Enterprises/MDP Worldwide/Avenging Conscience – First Independent.
94 mins. USA. 1997. Rel: 9 April 1999. Cert 18.

Orphans ★★★¹/₂

The night before the funeral of Rose Flynn, the latter's four grown-up children each undergoes a life-threatening catharsis ... Marking the feature directorial debut of the award-winning Scottish actor Peter Mullan (*My Name is Joe*), *Orphans* is a bleak, fiercely Glaswegian comedy of terrors. Contrary to many a comedy-drama that shoots down the laughs half-way through (usually with an easy dose of violence), Mullan takes the more difficult route of introducing an element of humour once he has established his characters and the tragedy that engulfs them. The effect is commanding, personal cinema scattered with memorable moments and shored up by a compassion that keeps the ugliness just about palatable. As a healthy cross between Bill Forsyth and Ken Loach, Mullan could be a godsend to Scottish cinema. P.S. Viewers who found the 'hair gel' sequence in *There's Something About Mary* repugnant are in for a real shock here.

● *Michael Flynn* Douglas Henshall, *Thomas Flynn* Gary Lewis, *John Flynn* Stephen McCole, *Sheila Flynn* Rosemarie Stevenson, *Tanga* Frank Gallagher, *Hanson* Alex Norton, Laura O'Donnell, Dave Anderson, Malcolm Shields, John Comerford, Deirdre Davis, Debbie Walsh, Gilbert Martin, Laurie Ventry, Maureen Carr, Eric Barlow, Frances Carrigan, Sheila Donald, Lenny Mullan, Dorothy Jane Stewart.
● *Dir* and *Screenplay* Peter Mullan, *Pro* Frances Higson, *Ex Pro* Paddy Higson, *Ph* Grant Scott Cameron, *Pro Des* Campbell Gordon, *Ed* Colin Monie, *M* Craig Armstrong; songs performed by Hugh Ferris and Lex Keith, Gary Lewis, and Billy Connolly, *Costumes* Lynn Aitken.

Channel Four/Scottish Arts Council/Glasgow Film Fund/ Antoine Green Bridge/Scottish Film Production Fund – Downtown.
101 mins. UK. 1997. Rel: 7 May 1999. Cert 18.

Other Voices Other Rooms ★★★★

This haunting film version of Truman Capote's first novel gets the book's decadent, nostalgic mood, lyrical tone and claustrophobic atmosphere just right. There are commanding performances, too, from David Speck as an early teenager who comes to a Deep South Gothic mansion to meet the sick father he hasn't seen in years and Lothaire Bluteau as the weird cousin of the house's owner. With gorgeous, glowing cinematography and intense, moody direction by the splendidly named David Rocksavage, it looks like a labour of love. [*Derek Winnert*]

● *Randolph Skully* Lothaire Bluteau, *Amy Skully* Anna Thomson, *Joel Sansom* David Speck, *Missouri Fever aka Zoo* April Turner, *Edward 'Ed' R. Sansom* Frank Taylor, *Jesus Fever* Leonard Watkins, Audrey Dollar, Elizabeth Byler, Moses Gibson, Terri Dollar.
● *Dir* David Rocksavage, *Pro* Rocksavage and Peter Wentworth, *Ex Pro* Robert C. Stigwood and Lili Mahtani, *Screenplay* Rocksavage and Sara Flanigan, *Ph* Paul Ryan, *Pro Des* Amy McGary, *Ed* Cynthia Scheider, *M* Chris Hajian; Debussy, Bizet, *Costumes* Jane Greenwood.

Golden Eye Films – Downtown.
98 mins. USA/UK. 1995. Rel: 11 June 1999. Cert 12.

Above: Stolen moments: Jennifer Lopez and George Clooney in Steven Soderbergh's wry and atmospheric Out of Sight *(from UIP)*

Out of Sight ★★★

Miami/Detroit; the present. Jack Foley has robbed some 200 banks and has never used a gun. But he keeps getting caught, so when he breaks out of Glades Correctional Institution – and kidnaps a beautiful Federal Marshall in the process – he is determined to stay out. However, his abductee, who escapes his clutches soon afterwards, is equally determined to see him behind bars. It's a damned odd way to carry on a romance ... To say that this is the best film that George Clooney has made is not necessarily a compliment. But it's a relief to see the charismatic actor handed decent dialogue and taking intelligent direction. Wryly comic and atmospherically wrought, this shrewd adaptation of the Elmore Leonard novel is fun while it lasts but doesn't leave a lasting impression. There are, however, some wonderful moments which go some way in tempering the awkward flashback structure. FYI: Michael Keaton appears in an uncredited cameo, reprising the police inspector character he played in the 1997 Elmore Leonard adaptation *Jackie Brown*.

● *Jack Foley* George Clooney, *Karen Sisco* Jennifer Lopez, *Buddy Bragg* Ving Rhames, *Maurice Miller* Don Cheadle, *Marshall Sisco* Dennis Farina, *Richard Ripley* Albert Brooks, *Adele* Catherine Keener, *Glenn Michaels* Steve Zahn, *Daniel Burdon/FBI* Wendell B. Harris Jr, *White Boy Bob* Keith Loneker, *Kenneth* Isaiah Washington, *Midge* Nancy Allen, Donna Frenzel, Luis Guzman, Paul Soileau, Susan Hatfield, Brad Martin, Paul Calderon, Viola Davis, and *uncredited*: *Ray Nicolette* Michael Keaton, *Hejira* Samuel L. Jackson.
● *Dir* Steven Soderbergh, *Pro* Danny DeVito, Michael Shamberg and Stacey Sher, *Ex Pro* Barry Sonnenfeld and John Hardy, *Screenplay* Scott Frank, *Ph* Elliot Davis, *Pro Des* Gary Frutkoff, *Ed* Anne V. Coates, *M* Cliff Martinez; songs performed by Willy Bobo, Pancho Sanchez, The Isley Brothers, Esquivel, Walter Wanderly, and Harry Garfield, *Costumes* Betsy Heimann.

Universal/Jersey Films – UIP.
123 mins. USA. 1998. Rel: 27 November 1998. Cert 15.

Painted Angels ★½

The Wild West; the 1870s. Five prostitutes struggle to make a living – and to hang on to some kind of collective purpose – in a rudimentary brothel in a small town in the American prairies ... An earnest attempt to show the utter emotional squalor of frontier life for immigrant women, *Painted Angels* lavishes so much attention on mundane detail that it becomes embalmed in narrative inertia. Worse still, the resources of the production prove so limited that the set is reduced to a modest metropolis of seven buildings, prompting unintentional humour when, for instance, a rival bordello opens 'at the other end of town.' Notwithstanding, there is an eye-opening performance from Kelly McGillis – the female lead of *Top Gun* and *Witness* – as a fleshy, embittered prostitute past her prime. FYI: The screenplay is a collaboration by the husband-and-wife team of actress Anna Mottram and first-time director Jon Sanders.

● *Annie Ryan* Brenda Fricker, *Nettie* Kelly McGillis, *Katya* Meret Becker, *Eileen* Bronagh Gallagher, *Georgie* Lisa Jakub, *Ada* Anna Mottram, *Louie* Josiah Wu, *Dr Belcher* Kent Allen, *Frank* Bruce McFee, Greg Lawson, Elyssa Dombowsky, Kieran Semple.
● *Dir* Jon Sanders, *Pro* Ann Scott, Christina Jennings and Stephen Onda, *Ex Pro* Mark Shivas, *Line Pro* Laurie McLarty, *Screenplay* Sanders and Anna Mottram, *Ph* Gerald Packer, *Pro Des* Hayden Griffin, *Ed* Maysoom Pachachi, *M* Douglas Finch, *Costumes* Madeleine Stewart.

Cinepix Properties/Shaftesbury Films/Greenpoint Films/ Heartland Motion Pictures/British Screen/Telefilm Canada/BBC Films, etc – Artificial Eye. 109 mins. Canada/UK. 1997. Rel: 26 February 1999. Cert 12.

The Parent Trap ★★★

At summer camp in Maine, Annie James from London and Hallie Parker from California develop an intense dislike for each other. However, when they are banished to an 'isolation cabin' to cool off, they realise that they have more in common than just their freckled looks. Discovering that they are identical twins, Annie and Hallie secretly decide to swap places so that they can each spend time with the parent they never knew ... Broad, sentimental and conceptually ludicrous, *The Parent Trap* grows in appeal as its irresistible story takes hold. While the film is set in a fantastical world of material comfort and unconditional love, the comic and dramatic scenes are handled skillfully enough to generate a genuine concern for the plight of this winsomely dysfunctional family. Only the soundtrack, with its heavy-handed, obvious musical cues, is a major irritant. FYI: This is the *seventh* film to chronicle the adventures of the meddlesome twins. The novel by Erich Kastner was first filmed in 1951 as *Das doppelte Lottchen*, then in 1953 as *Twice Upon a Time*, then in 1961 as *The Parent Trap* with Hayley Mills. Hayley then returned in three TV sequels as the twins grown-up.

● *Nick Parker* Dennis Quaid, *Elizabeth James* Natasha Richardson, *Annie James/Hallie Parker* Lindsay Lohan, *Meredith Blake* Elaine Hendrix, *Chessy* Lisa Ann Walter, *Martin* Simon Kunz,

Above: Parrot fashion: Cheech Marin argues about his billing with Paulie *(from UIP)*

Grandfather Ronnie Stevens, Polly Holliday, Maggie Wheeler, Joanna Barnes, Hallie Meyers-Shyer, Vendela K. Thommessen, Alexander Cole, J. Patrick McCormack, Annie Meyers-Shyer, Terry Kerr, Bruce Block, *Sammy, the dog* Bob.
● *Dir* Nancy Meyers, *Pro* Charles Shyer, *Co-Pro* Bruce A. Block, *Assoc Pro* Julie B. Crane, *Screenplay* Meyers, Shyer and David Swift, *Ph* Dean A. Cundey, *Pro Des* Dean Tavoularis, *Ed* Stepehn A. Rotter, *M* Alan Silvestri; songs performed by Nat King Cole, Bob Geldof, George Thorogood & The Destroyers, The Lovin' Spoonful, The La's, DJ Jazzy Jeff & The Fresh Prince, Linda Ronstadt, OMC, Ray Charles and Betty Carter, Natalie Cole, etc, *Costumes* Penny Rose.

Walt Disney Pictures – Buena Vista.
129 mins. USA. 1998. Rel: 11 December 1998. Cert PG.

Parting Shots ★

When photographer Harry Sterndale discovers he has six weeks to live, something snaps – and it isn't his camera! He decides to bump off all those who've annoyed him – and then hires a hitman to dispose of himself ... All set for a black comedy thriller in the tradition of *Kind Hearts and Coronets*? With a much-loved British cast to interpret the fun? Well, so far, so good. But then writer-director Michael Winner (for, lo, this is a Michael Winner film) hires non-actor Chris Rea to play Harry and the trouble with Harry is that he has only one note and one expression. Then Winner encourages his real actors either to be desperately over-earnest and actory (Kendall, Rigg), go through their over-familiar acts in a forced and boring way (Hoskins, Cleese) or mug and send it up outrageously (Lumley). All three courses prove fatal and never gel into a coherent comedy whole. This leaves Oliver Reed's sterling performance (his sixth for Winner) – as the relentless hitman – as the best in the film, a reasonable parting shot for the actor in his last picture. [*Derek Winnert*]

● *Harry Sterndale* Chris Rea, *Jill Saunders* Felicity Kendal, *Gerd Layton* Bob Hoskins, *Renzo Locatelli* Ben Kingsley, *Freda* Joanna Lumley, *Jamie Campbell Stewart* Oliver Reed, *Lisa*, Diana Rigg, *Maurice Walpole* John Cleese, Gareth Hunt, Peter Davison, Patrick Ryecart, Edward Hardwicke, Nicholas Gecks, Ruby Snape, Sheila Steafel, Trevor Baxter, Timothy Carlton, Nicky Henson, Caroline Langrishe, John Tordoff, Andrew Neil, Peter Gale, Jack Galloway, Roland Curram, Jenny Logan.
● *Dir*, *Pro* and *Ed* Michael Winner, *Assoc Pro* Ron Purdie, *Screenplay* Winner and Nick Mead, *Ph* Ousama Rawi, *Pro Des* Crispian Sallis, *M* Les Reed and Chris Rea.

Scimitar Films – UIP.
99 mins. UK. 1998. Rel: 14 May 1999. Cert 12.

Patch Adams ★★★

It wasn't until Hunter 'Patch' Adams admitted himself to a psychiatric ward that he decided to commit his life to helping others. And it was at the Medical College of Virginia that, as a student, he pioneered the belief that it is better to treat the patient – the human being – than the disease. And so, drawing on his innate sense of buffoonery, Patch determines that humour is the best medicine, whatever his superiors may think ... Now, it would be easy to dismiss this as a medical *Dead Poets Society* with an extra layer of icing. It is dreadfully sentimental, with every emotional variation underlined by Marc Shaiman's manipulative score, but the true story of this remarkable man has a lot to say and the film broadcasts the message in an expansive, accessible way. Williams, while really *too* old for the part, is perfect at conveying the rebellious mischief of Adams and is suitably tempered by the coolness of Monica Potter and Philip Seymour Hoffman. But just imagine how this subject would have benefited had it not been processed by the director of *Ace Ventura* and the writer of *Ace Ventura 2*. Still, in an increasingly cynical world we sometimes need a film like *Patch Adams*.

● *Hunter 'Patch' Adams* Robin Williams, *Carin* Monica Potter, *Mitch* Philip Seymour Hoffman, *Dean Walcott* Bob Gunton, *Truman Schiff* Daniel London, *Bill Davis* Peter Coyote, *Dr Eaton* Josef Sommer, *Joletta* Irma P. Hall, *Dean Anderson* Harve Presnell, *Rudy* Michael Jeter, *Arthur Mendelson* Harold Gould, *Larry* Douglas Roberts, Frances Lee McCain, Daniella Kuhn, Jake Bowen, James Greene, Bruce Bohne, Barry 'Shabaka' Henley, Richard Kiley, Ellen Albertini Dow.
● *Dir* Tom Shadyac, *Pro* Barry Kemp, Mike Farrell, Marvin Minoff and Charles Newirth, *Ex Pro* Shadyac and Marsha Garces Williams, *Co-Pro* Steve Oedekerk and Devorah Moos-Hankin, *Screenplay* Steve Oedekerk, based on Hunter Doherty Adams and Maureen Mylander's book *Gesundheit: Good Health Is a Laughing Matter*, *Ph* Phedon Papamichael, *Pro Des* Linda Descenna, *Ed* Don Zimmerman, *M* Marc Shaiman; Beethoven; songs performed by Derek and the Dominoes, Crosby Stills Nash & Young, The Rascals, Van Morrison, Eric Clapton, Dave Mason, Sly & The Family Stone, The Band, and George Harrison, *Costumes* Judy Ruskin-Howell.

Universal/Blue Wolf/Farrell/Minoff/Bungalow 78 – UIP.
116 mins. USA. 1998. Rel: 12 March 1999. Cert 12.

Paulie ★★★★

Paulie – not Polly – is a blue-crown conure parrot who learns to talk at the same time as his speech-impaired, five-year-old owner, Marie Alweather. But unlike other parrots, Paulie understands what he's going on about and is not afraid to talk back. Unfortunately, he and Marie are separated just as he has allowed her to find her own voice. Determined to

Left: Nice night for a killing: an uncredited James Coburn takes Mad Mel's aggression in his stride – in Brian Helgeland's stylish, hard-hitting Payback (from Warner)

be reunited with his young soul mate, the communicative conure embarks on a series of extraordinary adventures ... Contrary to one's expectations, this tale of a precocious parrot is actually a moving, funny and enchanting film that should appeal to viewers of all ages. Indeed, seldom are children's films blessed with such fine human performances, with Gena Rowlands and Tony Shalhoub in particular bringing a depth of humanity to their roles that makes Paulie all the more believable. The only disappointment is the actual tone of the parrot's voice, which sounds like a sanitised Joe Pesci. FYI: Paulie was brought to life through the use of computer generated imagery, animatronics and 14 bona fide conures.

● *Ivy* Gena Rowlands, *Misha* Tony Shalhoub, *Ignacio* Cheech Marin, *Dr Reingold* Bruce Davison, *Benny/the voice of Paulie* Jay Mohr, *adult Marie Alweather* Trini Alvarado, *Artie* Buddy Hackett, *young Marie Alweather* Hallie Kate Eisenbergh, *Warren Alweather* Matt Craven, *Ruby/voice of Lupe* Tia Texada, *Lila Alweather* Laura Harrington, Bill Cobbs, Nicole Chamberlain, Charles Parks, Dig Wayne.
● *Dir* John Roberts, *Pro* Mark Gordon, Gary Levinsohn and Allison Lyon Segan, *Ex Pro* Ginny Nugent, *Screenplay* Laurie Craig, *Ph* Tony Pierce-Roberts, *Pro Des* Dennis Washington, *Ed* Bruce Cannon, *M* John Debney; songs performed by The Box Tops, Tom Jones, WAR, and The Bee Gees, *Costumes* Mary Zophres.

DreamWorks/Mutual Film – UIP.
91 mins. USA. 1998. Rel: 24 July 1998. Cert U.

Payback ★★★★

Chicago; the present. Porter, his wife Lynn and their sadistic accomplice Val Resnick have just taken $130,000 in hot booty from a gang of Chinese hoods. Porter is then shot in the back by his wife and left for dead. When he eventually comes round, Porter wants revenge and his half of the money. And, while Resnick has given all the takings to a vicious organisation known as The Outfit, Porter is not above taking on the syndicate single-handed ... Ditching his image as the tough, crazy and fun-loving hero in favour of the tough, crazy and cold-blooded anti-hero, Mel Gibson proves as watchable as ever. Even when he's purloining a beggar's spoils or pinching a waitress' tip, he does it with such authority and style that he solicits grudging admiration. A gripping, flashy update of Donald E. Westlake's novel *The Hunter* (previously filmed by John Boorman as *Point Blank*), *Payback* works because: a) it's extremely well crafted and b) it refuses to compromise Porter's ruthless disposition. And remember, that's $70,000 Porter is demanding, not $130,000. FYI: When Mel Gibson saw director Helgeland's first cut he was so dissatisfied that he suggested completely changing the last third of the picture. Helgeland refused, Gibson had him replaced and immediately set about making his character more sympathetic (and restoring the life of Rosie's murdered dog!). Previously known as *Payroll*.

● *Porter* Mel Gibson, *Val Resnick* Gregg Henry, *Rosie* Maria Bello, *Stegman* David Paymer, *Detective Hicks* Bill Duke, *Lynn Porter* Deborah Kara Unger, *Mr Carter* William Devane, *Pearl* Lucy Alexis Liu, *Det. Leary* Jack Conley, *Mr Bronson* Kris Kristofferson, *Johnny Bronson* Trevor St John, John

Glover, Justin Ashforth, Ed Pfeifer, and *uncredited*: *Justin Fairfax* James Coburn.
● *Dir* Brian Helgeland and an anonymous contributor, *Pro* Bruce Davey (and Mel Gibson), *Ex Pro* Stephen McEveety, *Screenplay* Helgeland and Terry Hayes, *Ph* Ericson Core, *Pro Des* Richard Hoover, *Ed* Kevin Stitt, *M* Chris Boardman; songs performed by Boardman, James Brown, Dean Martin, Vic Damone, Jimi Hendrix, B.B. King, Lou Rawls, etc, *Costumes* Ha Nguyen.

Warner/Paramount/Icon – Warner.
101 mins. USA. 1998. Rel: 26 March 1999. Cert 18.

Pecker ★

You see, to achieve real art you have to dispel the lie that cloaks the truth. Pecker, an irritatingly cheerful 18-year-old from a blue-collar corner of Baltimore, sees art all around him. But, immortalised by the black-and-white photographs of his thrift shop camera, Pecker's world becomes a romantic ideal to the glitterati of Manhattan ... Director John Waters (*Multiple Maniacs*, *Pink Flamingos*) is no stranger to outrage. However, the homilies he offers up for parody here are so threadbare that the film is an offence to the word satire. Take away the bad taste and all that is left is monotonous banality.

● *Pecker* Edward Furlong, *Shelley* Christina Ricci, *Jimmy, Pecker's father* Mark Joy, *Joyce, Pecker's mother* Mary Kay Place, *Tina* Martha Plimpton, *Matt* Brendan Sexton III, *Rorey Wheeler* Lili Taylor, *Memama* Jean Schertler, *Little Chrissy* Lauren Hulsey, Bess Armstrong, Mink Stole, Patricia Hearst, Cindy Sherman, Greg Gorman.
● *Dir* and *Screenplay* John Waters, *Pro* John Fielder and Mark Tarlov, *Ex Pro* Mark Ordesky, Joe Revitte, Jonathan Weisgal and Joe Caracciolo Jr, *Ph* Robert Stevens, *Pro Des* Vincent Peranio, *Ed* Janice Hampton, *M* Stewart Copeland; songs performed by Paul Evans, The Nutty Squirrels, The Grid, etc, *Costumes* Van Smith.

Fine Line Features/Entertainment – Entertainment.
86 mins. USA. 1998. Rel: 5 February 1999. Cert 15.

Right: Psycho bubble: Mima fears for her life in Satoshi Kon's innovative and imaginative Perfect Blue *(from Manga Entertainment)*

Perdita Durango ★★

Both sides of the Mexican border; today. When ex-bull-fighter, bank robber and total lech Romeo Dolorosa meets up with Perdita Durango, a horny Tex-Mex bitch from hell, the jaunty couple decide to abduct a couple of young virgins for a ritual sacrifice ... When the sight of an old woman dragged out of a burning house by her hair and then dumped in a river elicits no compassion, you know you are suffering from overkill. Earlier scenes – a naked corpse having its heart cut out, the rape of a teenage virgin, a man crushed under the wheels of a giant truck – are just some of the delights dished up by Àlex de la Iglesia, director of the deranged *Accion Mutante* and outrageous *Day of the Beast*. A loose sequel to *Wild at Heart*, *Perdita Durango* – based on Barry Gifford's *59° and Raining: The Story of Perdita Durango* – aims to be an in-yer-face, non-stop action bonanza, but with none of the camp style or alleviating humour of, say, *Desperado*, it comes off as an unpleasant, pointless exercise in excess.

● *Perdita Durango* Rosie Perez, *Romeo Dolorosa* Javier Bardem, *Duane* Harley Cross, *Estelle* Aimee Graham, *Woody Dumas* James Gandolfini, *Adolfo* Screamin' Jay Hawkins, *Catalina* Damian Bichir, *Reggie* Carlos Bardem, *Santos* Don Stroud, *Doyle* Alex Cox, Santiago Segura, Harry Portet, Carlos Arau, Regina Orozco, Erika Carlson, Chely Godinez.
● *Dir* Àlex de la Iglesia, *Pro* Andrés Vicente Gómez, *Ex Pro* Fernando Bovaira, Miguel Necoechea, Pablo Barbachano and Max Rosenberg, *Screenplay* Àlex de la Iglesia, Barry Gifford, Jorge Guerricaechevarrla and David Trueba, *Ph* Flavio Mtnz. Labiano, *Pro Des* Baffra and José Luis Arrizabalaga, *Ed* Teresa Font, *M* Simon Boswell; J.S. Bach; songs performed by Los Tigres del Norte, Southern Culture On the Skids, Herb Alpert & The Tijuana Brass, Electric Playboys, Johnny Cash, Glen Matlock, etc, *Costumes* Maria Estela Fernandez and Glenn Ralston.

Sogetel/Lolafilms/Canal Plus, etc – Metrodome.
124 mins. Spain/Mexico/USA. 1997. Rel: 26 February 1999. Cert 18.

Perfect Blue ★★★

Mima Kirigoe is a 21-year-old singer with the cult trio Cham. However, with the group's greatest glory already behind them, Mima decides to pursue an acting career while her name is still in lights. Accepting a small role in a daytime soap, she quickly finds her transition from pop icon to actress an unsettling one. And as reality, paranoia and the narrative of the series merge, Mima begins to fear for her sanity and her life ... A departure from the more traditional and exploitative strain of Anime, *Perfect Blue* borrows a number of concepts from Western culture (Terry Gilliam and Kurt Vonnegut being major influences) and moulds them for the Japanese market. Adapting such ideas for

Left: To have and have not: Gwyneth Paltrow and Michael Douglas in Andrew Davis' too, too silly A Perfect Murder (from Warner)

animation is a courageous step and certainly pushes the envelope of the genre. With a suitable budget and more artists it could have been really special.

● Voices: *Mima Kirigoe* Junko Iawao, *Rumi* Rika Matsumoto, *Tadokoro* Shinpachi Tsuji, *Uchida* Masaaki Okura.
● *Dir* Satoshi Kon, *Pro* Hitomi Nakagaki, Yoshihisa Ishihara, Yutaka Togo, Masao Maruyama and Hiroaki Inoue, *Screenplay* Sadayuki Murai. Art *L Dir* Nobutaka Ike, *Ed* Harutoshi Ogata, *M* Masahiro Ikumi, *Character design* Hisashi Eguchi, *Director of animation* Hideki Hamazu.

Manga Entertainment.
84 mins. Japan. 1998. Rel: 21 May 1999. No cert.

A Perfect Murder ★★

New York City; today. Steven Taylor is an extremely successful international industrialist. His beautiful young wife Emily Bradford Taylor, a United Nations translator, is heir to a $100m fortune. David Shaw is a 'trashy but potent' artist and is Emily's lover. But for how long can Emily and David keep their affair secret? And what will Taylor do if he finds out? Updating Frederick Knott's play *Dial M for Murder* (previously filmed by Alfred Hitchcock in 1954 and made for TV in 1981), director Davis and scripter Kelly have embalmed their characters in deep gloss. Saddled with lines like 'too much study can pollute the soul,' Michael Douglas trots out yet another variation of his *Wall Street/The Game* persona while Gwyneth Paltrow is completely wasted. Welded to the dotted lines of the plot's corkscrew twists, the characters have little room to reveal human verisimilitude, consequently depriving the viewer of any emotional involvement. Yet for all that, some agile camerawork,

seamless editing and lush production design provide some transitory entertainment value.

● *Steven Taylor* Michael Douglas, *Emily Bradford Taylor* Gwyneth Paltrow, *David Shaw* aka *William Lagrange* Viggo Mortensen, *Mohamed Karaman* David Suchet, *Raquel Martinez* Sarita Choudhury, *Bobby Fain* Michael P. Moran, *Sandra Bradford* Constance Towers, Novella Nelson, Will Lyman, Maeve McGuire, Jean Debaer, Monica Parker, Michael H. Ingram.
● *Dir* Andrew Davis, *Pro* Arnold Kopelson and Anne Kopelson, Christopher Mankiewiz, Peter Macgregor-Scott, *Ex Pro* Stephen Brown, *Co-Pro* Nana Greenwald and Mitchell Dauterive, *Screenplay* Patrick Smith Kelly, *Ph* Dariusz Wolski, *Pro Des* Philip Rosenberg, *Ed* Dennis Virkler, *M* James Newton Howard, *Costumes* Ellen Mirojnick, *Sound* Lance Brown, *Hair design* Alan Dangerio.

Warner/Kopelson Entertainment – Warner.
107 mins. USA. 1998. Rel: 16 October 1998. Cert 15.

Pi ★★¹/₂

New York; the present. When Maximillian Cohen was six-years-old he stared into the sun and suffered temporary blindness and a nervous breakdown. Now a drug-addled, paranoid recluse, he is obsessed with finding a pattern in the transcendental solution to the circumference of a circle divided by its diameter. Should he make this mathematical breakthrough, Max reasons, imagine the effect this would have on predicting the stock market. But at what cost to Max's sanity? Shot in grainy black-and-white and liberally employing a hand-held camera (to emphasise Max's increasing dementia), *Pi* hardly aids its accessibility to a mainstream audience. Yet its multi-layered narrative, abundant metaphor and the writer-director's obvious passion for his subject does engage the senses on a number of levels. And even as it fails both to be a joyride for numerologists and a sound exploration of unstable genius, it does bring mathematics alive – and for that achievement alone it rates as one of the most original films of the decade.

● *Maximillian Cohen* Sean Gullette, *Sol Robeson* Mark Margolis, *Lenny Meyer* Ben Shenkman, *Marcy Dawson* Pamela Hart, Stephen Pearlman, Samia Shoaib, Ajay Naidu, Kristyn Mae-Anne Lao, Lauren Fox, Joanne Gordon, Stanely Herman, Clint Mansell, Abraham Aronofsky.
● *Dir* and *Screenplay* Darren Aronofsky, from a story by Aronofsky, Sean Gullette and Eric Watson, *Pro* Watson, *Ex Pro* Randy Simon, *Co-Pro* Scott Vogel, *Co-Ex Pro* David Godbout, Tyler Brodie and Jonah S. Smith, *Ph* Matthew Libatique, *Pro Des* Matthew Marraffi, *Ed* Oren Sarch, *M* Clint Mansell; songs performed by Stanely Herman, Orbital, Joanne Gordon, etc, *Sound* Brian Emrich.

Protozo Pictures/Harvest Filmworks/Truth & Soul/ Plantain Films – Pathe.
84 mins. USA. 1997. Rel: 8 January 1999. Cert 15.

The Players Club ★

Determined to pay her own way through college and raise her four-year-old son by herself, Diana Armstrong takes a job as a stripper at the notorious Players' Club. At first apprehensive and humiliated, Diana quickly grows a thick skin and learns to keep her head up in a cheap, brutal business ... Strident, garish and ugly, *The Players Club* is described as 'a real story' by first-time writer-director Ice Cube. Yeah, right. Chock full of cliche, stereotypes and over-acting, the film is about as real as Ice Cube's name. Makes Demi Moore's *Striptease* seem rather good.

● *Dollar Bill* Bernie Mac, *Ebony* Monica Calhoun, *L'il Man* A.J. Johnson, *Reggie* Ice Cube, *Clyde* Alex Thomas, *Ronnie* Chrystale Wilson, *Professor Mills* Ronn Riser, *Jimmy Armstrong* Dick Anthony Williams, *Diana Armstrong* aka *'Diamond'* LisaRaye, *Blue* Jamie Foxx, *Freeman* John Amos, Faizon Love, Charles O. Murphy, Adele Givens, Tracy C. Jones, Larry McCoy, Badja Djola, Tiny Lister, Judy Ann Elder, Monte Russell, Oren Williams, Samuel Monroe Jr.
● *Dir, Ex Pro* and *Screenplay* Ice Cube, *Pro* Patricia Charbonnet and Carl Craig, *Ph* Malik Sayeed, *Pro Des* Dina Lipton, *Ed* Suzanne Hines, *M* Hidden Faces; songs performed by K-Ci and JoJo, Brandy, Poison Clan, Mia X, Stan Watson and Donelle McNeil, R. Kelly, Republica, Ice Cube, Brownstone, Master P, Public Announcement, etc, *Costumes* Dahlia Foroutan.

New Line Cinema/Ghetto Bird Prods – Entertainment.
103 mins. USA. 1997. Rel: 6 November 1998. Cert 18.

Playing God ★½

Los Angeles; the present. Disqualified from practising medicine after killing a patient under the influence of amphetamines, top surgeon Eugene Sands has descended into a drug-induced private hell. Then, after saving a man's life in a nightclub shooting, he's put on the payroll of a depraved gangster. Eugene had forgotten how good it feels to save lives, but for how long can he hang on to his own? David Duchovny's first film since his televisual deification as Fox Mulder, *Playing God* throws out some intriguing elements but fails to build on them. Duchovny, who never seems to occupy a human space, looks as dopey and mysterious as usual, while the normally luminous Angelina Jolie is reduced to a pouting zombie. Only Timothy Hutton seems to be having any fun, but even he undermines the picture by failing to invest any real danger into his psychotic nasty. Most memorable line?: 'Why? *Why* Delilah?'

● *Dr Eugene Sands* David Duchovny, *Raymond Blossom* Timothy Hutton, *Claire* Angelina Jolie, *Gage* Michael Massee, *Vladimir* Peter Stormare, *Cyril* Andrew Tiernan, Gary Dourdan, John Hawkes, Will Foster Stewart, Philip Moon, Pavel D. Lynchnikoff, Tracey Walter, Sandra Kinder, Keone Young, Stacey Travis.
● *Dir* Andy Wilson, *Pro* Marc Abraham and Laura Bickford, *Ex Pro* Armyan Bernstein and Thomas A. Bliss, *Co-Pro* Melanie Greene and Nancy Rae Stone, *Screenplay* Mark Haskell Smith, *Ph* Anthony B. Richmond, *Pro Des* Naomi Shohan, *Ed* Louise Rubacky, *M* Richard Hartley; songs performed by LTJ Bukem, Family of God, Willie Dixon & The Big Three Trio, The Propellerheads, The Bee Gees, Morcheeba, etc, *Costumes* Mary Zophres.

Beacon Pictures – Blue Dolphin.
94 mins. USA. 1997. Rel: 11 December 1998. Cert 18.

Pleasantville ★★★★★

For David, the future doesn't look good. Faced with a world of uncertain employment, HIV infection and the depletion of the ozone layer, the reclusive teenager spends his spare hours soaking up the cosy ambience of *Pleasantville*, a 1950s soap opera. Here is a cosmos of wholesome American values, stable family life, safe sex and expressions like 'swell' and 'gee whiz'. However, when David and his rebellious twin sister find themselves inexplicably transported into the fictitious community of Pleasantville, they discover that black-and-white is not the rosy picture it cracks itself up to be ... Starting out as a sly satire of the golden era of American TV, this genuine original subtly shifts gear into a vividly entertaining morality tale. Capitalising on some wonderful computer effects, the film juggles comedy, fantasy and romance with accomplished skill, then shrewdly introduces a political agenda that addresses such issues as racism, sexism

and socialism, stirring up a diverting amalgam of *Father Knows Best*, *The Wizard of Oz* and *Nineteen Eighty-Four*. Yet, while it's easy to draw comparisons to everything from *The Purple Rose of Cairo* to *The Truman Show*, this satirical eye-opener strictly occupies its own universe and will be one reason to mark 1998 as a cinematic year to remember. Favourite scene: when aspiring painter Jeff Daniels is introduced to 'real' art for the first time.

● *David/Bud Parker* Tobey Maguire, *Bill Johnson* Jeff Daniels, *Betty Parker* Joan Allen, *George Parker* William H. Macy, *Big Bob* J.T. Walsh, *Jennifer/Mary Sue Parker* Reese Witherspoon, *TV repairman* Don Knotts, *Margaret* Marley Shelton, *David's mom* Jane Kaczmarek, *Skip* Paul Walker, Giuseppe Andrews, Marissa Ribisi, Jason Behr, Dawn Cody, Maggie Lawson, Andrea Taylor, Jim Patric, Nancy Lenehan, Patrick T. O'Brien, Erik MacArthur, David Tom, Johnny Moran.
● *Dir* and *Screenplay* Gary Ross, *Pro* Ross, Jon Kilik, Robert J. Degus and Steven Soderbergh, *Ex Pro* Michael De Luca and Mary Parent, *Co-Pro* Allen Alsobrook, Allison Thomas and Edward Lynn, *Ph* John Lindley, *Pro Des* Jeannine Oppewall, *Ed* William Goldenberg, *M* Randy Newman; songs performed by Fiona Apple, Esquivel, Diamond Slim, Mister Jones, The Four Aces, Pat Boone, Gene Vincent, Larry Williams, Talkback, Dave Brubeck Quartet, Miles Davis, Elvis Presley, Etta James,

Buddy Holly, etc, *Costumes* Judianna Makovsky, *Visual effects* Chris Watts.

New Line/Larger Than Life – Entertainment. 124 mins. USA. 1998. Rel: 12 March 1999. Cert 12.

Plunkett & Macleane ★★★★

London and its environs; 1748. When dissolute dandy James Macleane ends up in Newgate Prison with the notorious highwayman Will Plunkett, an uneasy alliance is hatched. With Macleane's connections and Plunkett's wiles, some serious money could be made ... If you think about it, the award-winning director of the REM video 'Everybody Hurts' and the U2 music promo 'Staring at the Sun' (who also happens to be the son of Ridley Scott, director of *The Duellists*), is the perfect man to bring a new vision to the highwayman yarn. Grimy, violent and startlingly fresh in its execution, *Plunkett & Macleane* mixes gallows humour with a cocky charm straight out of *Lock, Stock and Two Smoking Barrels*. Add a pinch of Peter Greenaway visuals, an outrageously camp soundtrack and some choice dialogue and you have a unique entertainment that stirs the blood as it tickles the funny bone. As for the actors, Robert Carlyle makes a convincing hard man with a soft centre, Jonny Lee Miller has never been more engaging and Liv Tyler handles her English vowels perfectly. Incidentally, the oft-repeated word 'wanker' was not in common usage

Above: *Stuck in Nerdville: William H. Macy and Joan Allen in Gary Ross' swell* Pleasantville *(from Entertainment)*

until the late 19th century. But then the film-makers probably knew that.

● *Will Plunkett* Robert Carlyle, *Captain James Macleane* Jonny Lee Miller, *Lady Rebecca Gibson* Liv Tyler, *Thief Taker General Chance* Ken Stott, *Lord Sidney Henry Gibson* Michael Gambon, *Lord Rochester* Alan Cumming, *Harrison* Terence Rigby, Tommy Flanagan, Stephen Walters, James Thornton, Christian Camargo, Neve McIntosh, Nicholas Farrell, Claire Rushbrook, Tim McMullan, Jeff Nuttal, Jacob Yentob, Victoria Harrison, Emma Faulkner, Jack Walters, Susan Porrett, Nichola McAuliffe, Anna Keaveney, Jacques Mathou, Michael Culkin, Dave Atkins.

● *Dir* Jake Scott, *Pro* Tim Bevan, Eric Fellner and Rupert Harvey, *Ex Pro* Gary Oldman, Douglas Urbanski and Matthew Stillman, *Co-Pro* Jonathon Finn and Natascha Wharton, *Line Pro* Donna Grey, *Screenplay* Robert Wade, Neil Purvis and Charles McKeown, based on an original screenplay by Selwyn Roberts, *Ph* John Matheson, *Pro Des* Norris Spencer, *Ed* Oral Norrie Ottey, *M* Craig Armstrong; songs performed by Armstrong, The Tiger Lillies, etc, *Costumes* Janty Yates, *Tyburn poetry* Murray Lachlan-Young.

PolyGram/Arts Council of England/Working Title/ National Lottery – PolyGram.
101 mins. UK. 1999. Rel: 2 April 1999. Cert 15.

Practical Magic ★

Below: Men behaving badly: Jonny Lee Miller and Robert Carlyle discuss the crime rate in Jake Scott's impudent and energetic Plunkett and Macleane *(from PolyGram)*

Sally and Gillian Owens are two gorgeous, loving sisters who have acquired their mother's talent for white witchcraft. They have also inherited the family curse which rather cruelly disposes of any man they should fall in love with. Not surprisingly, then, the sisters decide to turn their back on sorcery in favour of romance ... The tragedy of this sappy, misguided adaptation of Alice Hoffman's novel is that the subject was so rife with golden opportunities. Yet the screen-

play is so unfocussed and the playing so woolly and broad, that there's nothing here to hold the interest. Mses Bullock and Kidman do their damndest to be bewitching, but they're cursed with wretched material. You'll find more magic in a Budweiser commercial.

● *Sally Owens* Sandra Bullock, *Gillian Owens* Nicole Kidman, *Aunt Jet* Dianne Wiest, *Aunt Frances* Stockard Channing, *Gary Hallet* Aidan Quinn, *Carla* Chloe Webb, *Jimmy Angelow* Goran Visnjic, *Kylie* Evan Rachel Wood, *Antonia* Alexandra Artrip, *Maria Owens* Caprice Benedetti, *Sally Owens aged 11* Camilla Belle, *Gillian Owens aged 10* Lora Anne Criswell, *Linda Bennett* Margo Martindale, Mark Feuerstein, Annabella Price, Martha Gehman, Lucinda Jenney, Cordelia Richards, Mary Gross, Herta Ware, Ellen Geer, Peter Shaw.

● *Dir* Griffin Dunne, *Pro* Denise Di Novi, *Ex Pro* Mary McLaglen and Bruce Berman, *Co-Pro* Robin Swicord, *Screenplay* Swicord, Akiva Goldsman and Adam Brooks, *Ph* Andrew Dunn, *Pro Des* Robin Standefer, *Ed* Elizabeth Kling, *M* Alan Silvestri; songs performed by Faith Hill, Marvin Gaye, George Jones and Tammy Wynette, Joni Mitchell, Elvis Presley, Harry Nilsson, Stevie Nicks, etc, *Costumes* Judianna Makovsky.

Warner/Village Roadshow/Fortis Films – Warner.
104 mins. USA. 1998. Rel: 22 January 1998. Cert 12.

A Price Above Rubies ★★¹/₂

The wife of an upstanding Hasidic scholar, Sonia Horowitz should be proud of her lot. But her increasing discomfort in what she views as an irrational world – that of the Orthodox Jew in New York – sends her teetering towards insanity. She doesn't understand why she cannot touch her husband during sex, or why her need for a life outside the home is looked down on. Then her brother-in-law makes a startling proposal ... Boaz Yakin's first film since the award-winning *Fresh* is a creditable exploration of a world out of time and of the cracks that threaten to undermine it. Yet, rather like its subject, the film displays a one-note worthiness that doesn't do it any favours. Still, there are fine performances, fine production values and some fine insights. Fine then. An interesting companion piece to the British *The Governess*. Previously known as *A Price Below Rubies* (huh?).

● *Sonia Horowitz* Renee Zellweger, *Sender Horowitz* Christopher Eccleston, *Ramon* Allen Payne, *Mendel Horowitz* Glenn Fitzgerald, *Rachel Horowitz* Julianna Margulies, *Rebbitzn* Kim Hunter, *Rebbe* John Randolph, *the beggar woman* Kathleen Chalfant, Peter Jacobson, Edie Falco, Tim Jerome, Phyllis Newman, Joyce Reehling, Daryl Edwards, Don Wallace, Asia Minor.

Left: Enough already: Christopher Eccleston bends the rules in Boaz Yakin's creditable, one-note A Price Above Rubies *(from Film Four)*

● *Dir* and *Screenplay* Boaz Yakin, *Pro* Lawrence Bender and John Penotti, *Ex Pro* Bob Weinstein and Harvey Weinstein, *Co-Pro* Joann Fregalette Jansen, *Line Pro* Adam Brightman, *Ph* Adam Holender, *Pro Des* Dan Leigh, *Ed* Arthur Coburn, *M* Leslie Barber, *Costumes* Ellen Lutter.

Miramax/Pandora Cinema/Channel Four – Film Four. 116 mins. USA. 1997. Rel: 14 May 1999. Cert 15.

Primary Colors ★★★

Disillusioned by the amoral manipulation of American politics, black congressional aide Henry Burton finds himself swept up in the presidential campaign of one Governor Jack Stanton. A complete outsider, Stanton seduces Burton with his affable charm and assurances that he stands for the honour and the heart of the American people. Burton believes him and is summarily pitched into the eye of the maelstrom of political campaigning ... While presenting some fascinating insights, great speeches, notable performances and a handful of priceless moments (the exposé of a doctored tape recording, Stanton outwitting a rival candidate on a tacky radio show), *Primary Colors* is still a shapeless whale of a movie that doesn't know when to bare its teeth. Still, if this is really a watered down edition of Joe Klein's anonymously written powder keg about the Clintons, then Slick Willie is even more of a loveable rogue than his accomplice Travolta would have us believe. FYI: Emma Thompson, as a thinly disguised Hillary Clinton, refused to have her ankles padded, while her bedroom scene with co-star Adrian Lester was left on the cutting room floor.

● *Governor Jack Stanton* John Travolta , *Susan Stanton* Emma Thompson, *Richard Jemmons* Billy Bob Thornton, *Henry Burton* Adrian Lester, *Daisy* Maura Tierney, *Howard Ferguson* Paul Guilfoyle, *Governor Fred Picker* Larry Hagman, *Libby Holden* Kathy Bates, *Mamma Stanton* Diane Ladd, *March Cunningham* Rebecca Walker, *Lucille Kaufman* Caroline Aaron, *Jennifer Rogers* Stacy Edwards, Tommy Hollis, Rob Reiner, J.C. Quinn, Allison Janney, Robert Klein, Mykelti Williamson, Brian Markinson, Geraldo Rivera, Charlie Rose, Larry King, O'Neal Compton, Bonnie Bartlett, Cynthia O'Neal, Chelcie Ross, John Vargas, Tony Shalhoub, Robert Cicchini, Rolando Molina, Ross Benjamin, Gia Carides, Robert Easton, Bill Maher, *CNN voice-over* James Earl Jones.
● *Dir* and *Pro* Mike Nichols, *Ex Pro* Neil Machlis and Jonathan D. Krane, *Co-Pro* Michele Imperato, *Screenplay* Elaine May, *Ph* Michael Ballhaus, *Pro Des* Bo Welch, *Ed* Arthur Schmidt, *M* Ry Cooder; songs performed by Willie Nelson, Ry Cooder, Ronnie Dawson, Nat King Cole, Olivia Newton-John, Tammy Wynette, etc, *Costumes* Ann Roth.

Universal/Mutual Film Company/Icarus – UIP. 143 mins. USA. 1998. Rel: 30 October 1998. Cert 15.

The Prince of Egypt ★★★★★

A baby boy of Hebrew slaves is floated down the River Nile to escape the infanticide imposed by the all-powerful Pharaoh Seti. Chanced upon by the Queen herself, the boy is raised to be the future prince of Egypt and shares an invincible bond with his megalomaniacal brother, Rameses. But when Moses discovers his true identity, his new ideals clash with everything that he has been brought up to believe ... Breaking fresh ground both technically and thematically, *The Prince of Egypt* is moving and awe-inspiring cinema. Eschewing such staple ingredients of animation as talking animals and contemporary references, the film draws its power from the narrative of the biblical book of Exodus and, with the aid of theological and Egyptological consultants, strives for historical accuracy. But it is the imagery that overwhelms, a ground-breaking combination of traditional methods and computer animation that brings a hieroglyphic flashback, the flight out of Egypt and the parting of the Red Sea all resoundingly to life. And the potential for sequels is endless. FYI: The visual references of the film include the biblical drawings of the 19th century French illustrator Gustave Doré, the impressionistic art of Monet and the expansive desert canvas of David Lean's *Lawrence of Arabia*.

● *Voices*: *Moses* Val Kilmer, *Rameses* Ralph Fiennes, *Tzipporah* Michelle Pfeiffer, *Miriam* Sandra Bullock, *Aaron* Jeff Goldblum, *Jethro* Danny Glover, *Pharaoh Seti* Patrick Stewart, *The Queen* Helen Mirren, *Hotep* Steve Martin, *Huy* Martin Short, *singing voice of Moses* Amick Byram, *singing voice of Miriam* Sally Dworsky, *singing voice of Yocheved* Ofra Haza, *singing voice of Jethro* Brian Stokes Mitchell, *singing voice of The Queen* Linda Dee Shayne, *Rameses' son* Bobby Motown.
● *Dir* Brenda Chapman, Steve Hickner and Simon Wells, *Pro* Penney Finkelman Cox and Sandra Rabins, *Ex Pro* Jeffrey Katzenberg, *Assoc Pro* Ron Rocha, *Screenplay* Philip Lazebnik and Nicholas Meyer, *Pro Des* Darek Gogol, *Ed* Nick Fletcher, *M* Hans Zimmer; songs: Stephen Schwartz; 'When You Believe' sung by Whitney Houston and Mariah Carey, 'I Will Get There' sung by Boyz II Men, *Costumes* Kelly Kimball, *Sound* Lon Bender and Wylie Stateman, *Animation* William Salazar, *Visual effects* Don Paul and Dan Philips.

Right: *Holy Moses! A typical scene from DreamWorks' moving and awe-inspiring* The Prince of Egypt *(from UIP)*

DreamWorks – UIP.
99 mins. USA. 1998. Rel: 18 December 1998. Cert U.

Prometheus ★★★★★

Totally stunning and unexpected is this highly cine-matic film poem, a first feature by the 60-year-old poet Tony Harrison. Contemporary in context, it yet draws on the ancient tale of Prometheus and of fire stolen from the gods. But, in a work surveying man's behaviour in the 20th century and ignoring neither Dresden nor Auschwitz, fire becomes a negative sym-bol (the smoke from the gas chambers, pollution) as well as a positive one (candles lit still represent hope). The film depicts a journey across Europe, yet centres on a duologue between Hermes (Michael Feast, speaking contemptuously on behalf of the gods) and a retired miner (Sparrow). The latter, despite being politically incorrect in his endorsement of smoking, is a truly affecting Everyman, who speaks for the indi-vidual and for ideals in a world where both are endan-gered. Add welcome humour and a magnificent score and, despite occasional obscurities, you have one of the finest and most imaginative avante-garde works ever made in Britain. [*Mansel Stimpson*]

● *Hermes* Michael Feast, *old man* Walter Sparrow, *Jack* Jonathan Waistnidge, *Io* Fern Smith, *Father* Steve Huison, *old woman* Audrey Haggerty, Catherine Pidd, Sue Barker, Dave Hill, Ian Clayton, Stewart Merrill.
● *Dir* and *Screenplay* Tony Harrison, *Pro* Andrew Holmes, *Ex Pro* Michael Kustow, *Ph* Alistair Cameron, *Pro Des* Jocelyn Herbert, *Ed* Luke Dunkley, *M* Richard Blackford, *Sound* Glenn Keiles.

Film Four/The Arts Council of England/Holmes Associates/National Lottery – Film Four.
130 mins. UK. 1998. Rel: 16 April 1999. Cert 15.

The Proposition ★½

Boston; 1935. A powerful lawyer, his liberated wife and an English priest find their destinies inexorably linked when an audacious plan is put into action. Unable to provide his wife with the child she so des-perately craves, the wealthy and arrogant Arthur Barret headhunts a young law student as his sexual surrogate ... Embracing such themes as sex, murder, scandal, religion, infidelity, big money and a crisis of faith, *The Proposition* is old-fashioned melodrama with a straight face. From Stephen Endelman's treacly score to Peter Sova's lush photography, the film plays like a Harlequin romance, underlined by a ripe, flow-ery voice-over from Kenneth Branagh. Nothing rings true, least of all the stars' sexual attraction for one another. Previously known as *Shakespeare's Sister*.

● *Father Michael McKinnon* Kenneth Branagh, *Eleanor Barret* Madeleine Stowe, *Arthur Barret*

William Hurt, *Roger Martin* Neil Patrick Harris, *Hannibal Thurman* Robert Loggia, *Syril Danning* Blythe Danner, *Father Dryer* Josef Sommer, Ken Cheeseman, Tom Downey, David Byrd, Willy O'Donnell, Frank T. Wells.
● *Dir* Lesli Linka Glatter, *Pro* Ted Field, Diane Nabatoff and Scott Kroopf, *Ex Pro* Lata Ryan, Co-*Ex Pro* Alessandro F. Uzielli, *Screenplay* Rick Ramage, *Ph* Peter Sova; Ralf Bode, *Pro Des* David Brisbin, *Ed* Jacqueline Cambas, *M* Stephen Endelman; Schubert, *Costumes* Anna Sheppard.

Interscope Communications – PolyGram.
114 mins. USA. 1997. Rel: 28 August 1998. Cert 12.

Psycho ★½

A bad girl on the run checks into the Bates Motel for a shower ... By literally re-filming every scene and line of dialogue from Alfred Hitchcock's 1960 classic, director Gus Van Sant (*Good Will Hunting*, *To Die For*) takes on more than he can animate. Constrained by a 38-year-old script, some rather good actors strug-gle to heat up roles that are frozen in time as they show greater service to the creaky dialogue than to the reality of the scene. It's like digging an out-of-date car-cass out of the deep freeze and serving it up as fresh food. In addition, part of the power of Hitchcock's version was its dismantling of sexual taboos, whereas this frigid imitation is about as thrilling as a diversion to the lingerie section in a department store. P.S. In his slavering devotion to the original, the director has not only kept the same number plates but has dressed an extra up as Hitchcock for the latter's traditional cameo! FYI: Before this colour-by-numbers update, the original *Psycho* had already suffered the ignominy of three sequels and countless parodies.

● *Norman F. Bates* Vince Vaughn, *Lila Crane* Julianne Moore, *Sam Loomis* Viggo Mortensen, *Milton Arbogast* William H. Macy, *Marion Crane* Anne Heche, *Dr Simon* Robert Forster, *Sheriff Chambers* Philip Baker Hall, *Mrs Chambers* Anne Haney, *Tom Cassidy* Chad Everett, *Mr Lowery* Rance Howard, *Caroline* Rita Wilson, *patrolman* James Remar, *car dealer* James LeGros, *Bob Summerfield* Flea, Marjorie Lovett, Ryan Cutrona, Ken Jenkins.
● *Dir* Gus Van Sant, *Pro* Van Sant and Brian Grazer, *Ex Pro* Dany Wolf, *Screenplay* Joseph Stefano, from the novel by Robert Bloch, *Ph* Christopher Doyle, *Pro Des* Tom Foden, *Ed* Amy Duddleston, *M* Bernard Herrmann, produced and adapted by Danny Elfman; songs performed by Rob Zombie, Slim Whitman, The Germs, and Jo Stafford, *Costumes* Beatrix Aruna Pasztor, *Titles* Saul Bass, *Mrs Bates design* Rick Baker, *Special thanks to* John Woo for his kitchen knife.

Universal Pictures/Imagine Entertainment – UIP.
104 mins. USA. 1998. Rel: 8 January 1999. Cert 15.

Above: The food of
love: Greta Scacchi
and Jason Flemyng
head for a musical
climax in Francois
Girard's beguiling
and seductive The
Red Violin (from
Film Four)

Quest For Camelot: The Magic Sword

See *The Magic Sword*.

The Real Howard Spitz ★★★

When the latest book by pulp crime novelist Howard Spitz is rejected by publishers, the writer turns to children's literature. Aided by a precocious seven-year-old girl, Spitz dreams up a bovine dick called Crafty Cow and sees his ill fortune quickly reversed. It's a shame, then, that he hates children so ... A perfect vehicle for the effortlessly sarcastic talents of Kelsey Grammer, *The Real Howard Spitz* should appeal to children and adults alike. Deftly milking the detective genre for a new generation, the film manages to be clever and funny without sacrificing any of its charm. [*Charles Bacon*]

● *Howard Spitz* Kelsey Grammer, *Laura* Amanda Donohoe, *Lou Gaddis* Joseph Rutten, *Roger* Patrick McKenna, *Samantha* Genevieve Tessier, Kay Tremblay, Lex Gigeroff, Cathy Lee Crosby.
● *Dir* Vadim Jean, *Pro* Paul Brooks and Christopher Zimmer, *Ex Pro* Alan Martin, *Screenplay* Jurgen Wolff, *Ph* Glen Macpherson, *Pro Des* Chris Townsend, *Ed* Pia Di Ciaula, *M* David A. Hughes and John Murphy; Johann Strauss, Tchaikovsky; songs performed by Ruth Allen, Jack Roberts, Kirsty McColl, Shane McGowan, Slam Dunk, etc, *Costumes* Martha Curry.

Writer's Block Ltd/Metrodome/Imagex/The Movie Network – The Mob.
101 mins. UK/Canada. 1997. Rel: 28 August 1998. Cert PG.

The Red Violin ★★★★¹/₂

Italy/Austria/England/Shanghai/Montreal; the 17th century to the present day. As his wife is about to bear him his first child, the Italian violin-maker Nicolo Bussotti is finishing the final touches to his own masterpiece, an acoustic marvel that truly bridges the gap between science and beauty. Over the next three centuries, Bussotti's 'red' violin passes through many different hands, its distinctive and magical properties transforming the lives of those it touches. Filmed in five countries in five different languages (Italian, German, French, Mandarin and English), *The Red Violin* is a one-off that defies categorisation. Cutting back and forth across time, the film artfully establishes the true nature of its subject's power in the tradition of a good detective novel, as the instrument itself – whether evoking feelings of spirituality, sexuality or greed – casts its own unique spell. Indeed, like the object of its drama, the film is a perfect marriage of beauty and technical accomplishment.

● *Nicolo Bussotti* Carlo Cecchi, *Anna Bussotti* Irene Grazioli, *Cesca* Anita Laurenzi, *Georges Poussin* Jean-Luc Bideau, *Kasper Weiss* Christoph Koncz, *Victoria Byrd* Greta Scacchi, *Frederick Pope* Jason Flemyng, *Xiang Pei/Xiang Pei's mother* Sylvia Chang, *Chou Yuan* Liu Zifeng, *Mme. Leroux* Monique Mercure, *Evan Williams* Don McKellar, *auctioneer* Colm Feore, *Charles Morritz* Samuel L. Jackson, *Mme Poussin* Clotilde Mollet, David Gant, Sandra Oh, Remy Girard.
● *Dir* Francois Girard, *Pro* Niv Fichman, *Line Pro*

Barbara Shrier, *Screenplay* Don McKellar and Francois Girard, *Ph* Alain Dostie, *Pro Des* Francois Seguin, *Ed* Gaetan Huot, *M* John Corigliano, *Costumes* Renee April.

New Line International/Channel Four/Telefilm Canada/ Rhombus Media/Mikado Prods/Sony Classical, etc – Film Four.
130 mins. Canada/Italy/USA/UK. 1998. Rel: 9 April 1999. Cert 15.

Return to Paradise ★★★★

Three American college graduates, having had the time of their lives in the tropical paradise of Malaysia, go their separate ways. Two years later in New York, Sheriff, a limo driver, and Tony, an architect, are approached by a lawyer with a devastating proposition: if they are willing to return to Penang to serve three years in prison, their friend – arrested for the possession of 140 grams of hash – will be spared his life ... Taking a moral hand grenade and exploding it in the lives of some very tangible, credible people, *Return to Paradise* is an emotionally complex drama that prompts some pretty harsh soul-searching. Unlike the facile *Red Corner* which covered similar ground, this Americanisation of the 1989 French film *Force Majeure* is intelligent, believable and uncompromising. There is also a sensational performance from Anne Heche as the tenacious, troubled lawyer and some splendid wide-screen photography. It's just a shame about the title, which conjures up unsavoury memories of the dreadful *Return to the Blue Lagoon*.

● *John 'Sheriff' Volgecherev* Vince Vaughn, *Beth Eastern* Anne Heche, *Lewis* Joaquin Phoenix, *Tony* David Conrad, *M.J. Major* Jada Pinkett Smith, Vera Farmiga, Nick Sandow, Ming Lee, Joel De La Fuente, Deanna Yussoff, Is Issariya, Elizabeth Rodriguez, Teoh Kah Yong, and *uncredited*: *Sheriff's father* Raymond J. Barry.
● *Dir* Joseph Ruben, *Pro* Alain Bernheim and Steve Golin, *Ex Pro* David Arnold and Ezra Swerdlow, *Screenplay* Wesley Strick and Bruce Robinson, *Ph* Reynaldo Villalobos, *Pro Des* Bill Groom, *Ed* Andrew Mondshein and Craig McKay, *M* Mark Mancina, *Costumes* Juliet Polcsa.

PolyGram/Propaganda Films/Tetragram – Polygram.
111 mins. USA. 1998. Rel: 16 April 1999. Cert 15.

Rien Ne Va Plus ★★★★

Michel Serrault is one of the world's most eminently watchable actors, whose every huff, bluster and edgy glance has been perfected to an art. Here, in Claude Chabrol's 50th film, he plays a small-time con man who pulls off his scams with complete success due to a resolute lack of greed. By leaving his victims the remaining two thirds of their spoils, he repeatedly manages to check both their wrath and belief and hence their pursuit. He is aided by Isabelle Huppert, a seductive siren who may or may not be in love with him and who may or may not stick by him. By presenting such an ambiguous central relationship, this deliciously perverse black comedy constantly keeps one step ahead of the viewer. And, like Hitchcock, Chabrol never labours his devices, allowing us the satisfaction of believing that we may not have seen what we thought we had. The climactic sequence, played out to the finale of Puccini's *Tosca*, is a masterpiece of sustained suspense.

● *Betty* Isabelle Huppert, *Victor* Michel Serrault, *Maurice* Francois Cluzet, *Monsieur K* Jean-Francois Balmer, Jackie Berroyer, Jean Benguigui, Mony Dalmes, Thomas Chabrol, Marie Dubois.
● *Dir* Claude Chabrol, *Pro* Marin Karmitz, *Screenplay* Claude Chabrol and Aurore Chabrol, *Ph*

Below: Deep-sixing seventh heaven: Anne Heche in Joseph Ruben's intelligent and uncompromising Return to Paradise *(from PolyGram)*

Right: *The gambler stumbles: Ewan McGregor (left) in James Dearden's small-scale, unconvincing* Rogue Trader *(from Pathe)*

Eduardo Serra, *Pro Des* Francoise Benoit-Fresco, *Ed* Monique Fardoulis, *M* Matthieu Chabrol, *Costumes* Corinne Jorry.

MK2 Prods/TFI Films/CAB Prods/Canal Plus,etc – Artificial Eye.
105 mins. France/Switzerland. 1997. Rel: 16 October 1998. Cert 15.

Rogue Trader ★★¹/₂

London/Jakarta/Singapore; the early 1990s. Before its ignominious collapse in 1995, Barings Bank, founded in 1763, was the oldest merchant bank in the world. Instrumental in financing the British war effort against Revolutionary and Napoleonic France and largely responsible for funding the Louisiana Purchase by the United States, it prided itself on being the chief monetary adviser to the royal family. Being strictly old-tie, the institution was not in the habit of hiring working class employees, but Margaret Thatcher changed all that. When Nick Leeson, a hard-drinking would-be trader from Watford, showed that he could turn a tidy profit in the 'Tiger' economy of South-East Asia, the London office let him get on with it. But then the figures refused to add up ... It would be hard to botch a story as extraordinary as Nick Leeson's, but writer-director James Dearden has a good try. While shedding a sympathetic light on Leeson's foolhardy operation (he was merely trying to cover his own mistakes) the film – based on Neeson and Edward Whitley's book of the same name – fails to convince on a human level. As Leeson, Ewan McGregor seems ill-at-ease, while the other characters stick out as stereotypes. Still, it's an extraordinary story.

● *Nick Leeson* Ewan McGregor, *Lisa Leeson* Anna Friel, *Pierre Bonnefoy* Yves Beneyton, *Brenda Granger* Betsy Brantley, *Ash Lewis* Caroline Langrishe, *Tony Hawes* Tim McInnerney, *Bonnie Lee* Irene Ng, *Danny Argyropoulos* Lee Ross, *Peter Norris* Simon Shepherd, *Peter Baring* John Standing, *Simon Jones* Pip Torrens, *George Seow* Tom Wu, Nigel Lindsay, Daniel York, Joanna David, Sarah Liew, Peter Quince, Jennifer Lim, Sharon Duce, Michelle Lee, Danny Argyropoulos.
● *Dir* and *Screenplay* James Dearden, *Pro* Dearden, Paul Raphael and Janette Day, *Ex Pro* David Frost, Pippa Cross and Claire Chapman, *Co-Ex Pro* William Tyrer and Chris Ball, *Ph* Jean-Francois Robin, *Pro Des* Alan McDonald, *Ed* Catherine Creed, *M* Richard Hartley; Mozart; songs performed by Andy Williams, Barrett Strong, Leftfield, Kula Shaker, Reef, The Clash, Jerry Lee Lewis, Praise, Blur, etc, *Costumes* Rachael Fleming.

Granada Film/Newmarket Capital/David Paradine – Pathe.
101 mins. UK/USA. 1998. Rel: 25 June 1999. Cert 15.

Ronin ★★¹/₂

France; the present. An unlikely ragbag of international undercover operatives are gathered together in Paris to plan the capture of a mysterious briefcase. Unaware of the contents of the case or even the identity of their employer, the mercenaries know only that should they fulfil their mandate – and stay alive – they will be handsomely rewarded ... Masquerading as a serious, hard-hitting international thriller in the packaging of *The Day of the Jackal*, John Frankenheimer's *Ronin* collapses under an increasingly improbable wel-

ter of double-crosses as ex-CIA, ex-KGB and ex-IRA agents join forces to kill as many innocent bystanders as humanly possible (in one scene, a duplicitous Stellan Skarsgard attempts to shoot the head off a little girl in a playground just 'to make a point'). However, the picturesque locations of Paris, Cannes, Nice and Arles and some genuinely thrilling car chases (often featuring the real actors in speeding vehicles) make up for much of the plot's senselessness and confusion. From the director of *The Manchurian Candidate* and *The Island of Dr Moreau* – go figure. FYI: Seventy-five vehicles were destroyed during filming. N.B. Ronin was the name given to samurai warriors deprived of a liege lord to serve.

● *Sam* Robert De Niro, *Vincent* Jean Reno, *Deirdre* Natascha McElhone, *Gregor* Stellan Skarsgard, *Spence* Sean Bean, *Seamus* Jonathan Pryce, *Larry* Skipp Sudduth, *Jean-Pierre* Michael Lonsdale, *Natacha Kirilova* Katarina Witt, Jan Triska, Ron Perkins, Feodor Atkine, Bernard Bloch.
● *Dir* John Frankenheimer, *Pro* Frank Mancuso Jr, *Ex Pro* Paul Kelmenson, *Assoc Pro* Ethel Winant, *Screenplay* J.D. Zeik and Richard Weisz, *Ph* Robert Fraisse, *Pro Des* Michael Z. Hanan, *Ed* Tony Gibbs, *M* Elia Cmiral; songs performed by Sarah Brightman and Andrea Bocelli, and Keith Carradine and Cady Huffman, *Costumes* May Routh.

United Artists/FGM Entertainment – UIP.
121 mins. USA. 1998. Rel: 20 November 1998. Cert 15.

Rounders ★★¹/₂

Apparently, the key to winning at poker is playing the man and not the cards. And Mike McDermott can read people's thoughts like subtitles stamped on their foreheads. Needless to say, poker is his life. But when he loses his law school tuition in one foolhardy game with a dangerous card shark, Mike calls it a day. Reduced to making his way as a delivery boy, Mike has become a conscientious student and loyal soul mate to his beautiful girlfriend, Jo. Then his best friend and gambling partner 'Worm' is released from prison ... An uncompromising portrait of the underground world of New York poker, *Rounders* is strong on grit and atmosphere but weak on story. And in spite of a sterling cast – Malkovich is particularly mesmerising as an oreo-chomping rounder (a professional poker player, to you) – the characters of Mike and Worm are too broadly drawn for plausibility. Besides their mutual obsession for poker, there seems little to bind the goody two-shoes law student and his irredeemable partner. And unless one knows one's poker, much of the film's 'action' will be largely redundant.

● *Mike McDermott* Matt Damon, *Worm* Edward Norton, *Joey Kinish* John Turturro, *Petra* Famke Janssen, *Jo* Gretchen Mol, *Teddy KGB* John Malkovich, *Professor Abraham Petrovsky* Martin Landau, *Grama* Michael Rispoli, *Barbara* Melina Kanakaredes, Josh Mostel, Lenny Clarke, Tom Aldredge, Goran Visnjic, Adam LeFevre.
● *Dir* John Dahl, *Pro* Joel Stillerman and Ted

Demme, *Ex Pro* Bob Weinstein, Harvey Weinstein, Bobby Cohen and Kerry Orent, *Screenplay* David Levien and Brian Koppelman, *Ph* Jean-Yves Escoffier, *Pro Des* Rob Pearson, *Ed* Scott Chestnut, *M* Christopher Young; songs performed by Counting Crows, Nat King Cole, Duke Ellington, Gene Krupa, Joan Jett & The Blackhearts, The Johnny Lewis Quartet, etc, *Costumes* Terry Dresbach.

Miramax/Spanky Pictures – Buena Vista.
121 mins. USA. 1998. Rel: 20 November 1998. Cert 15.

The Rugrats Movie ★¹/₂

Four toddlers and a new-born baby find themselves lost in a foreboding forest ... Conceived as a child's eye view of a *bourgeois* world, *The Rugrats* TV show is a disturbing cross between the crass, the scatological and what is a periodically insightful look at how a child grasps grown-up absurdities. So, following the success of such large-screen translations as *Casper* and *Beavis and Butt-Head Do America* (and bearing in mind the merchandising possibilities), the phenomenon was bound to end up on the big screen. The result, which is crudely drawn and even more crudely executed, is a poor excuse for a feature film and is likely to appal the uninitiated. Having said that, there are some wily flourishes that will please adult fans of the show and – needless to say – kids will love it (which, of course, is *really* scary). Favourite line: 'I can't wait till things get back to Norman'.

● Voices: *Tommy Pickles* E.G. Daily, *Chuckie Finster* Christine Cavanaugh, *Philip DeVille/Lillian DeVille/Betty DeVille* Kath Soucie, *Didi Pickles* Melanie Chartoff, *Stu Pickles* Jack Riley, *Howard DeVille* Phil Proctor, *Reptar Wagon* Busta Rhymes, *Rex Pester* Tim Curry, *Ranger Margaret* Whoopi Goldberg, *Ranger Frank* David Spade, Cheryl Chase, Tara Charendoff, Joe Alaskey, Cree Summer, Michael Bell, Tress MacNeille, Mary Gross, Andrea Martin, Edie McClurg, Roger Clinton, Margaret Cho, and *as*

the newborn babies: Beck, B Real, Jakob Dylan, Phife, Gordon Gano, Iggy Pop, Lenny Kravitz, Lisa Loeb, Lou Rawls, Patti Smith, Dawn Robinson, Fred Schneider, Kate Pierson, Cindy Wilson.
● *Dir* Norton Virgien and Igor Kovalyov, *Pro* Arlene Klasky and Gabor Csupo, *Ex Pro* Albie Hecht and Debby Beece, *Screenplay* David N. Weiss and J. David Stem. Art: Dima Malanitchev, *M* Mark Mothersbaugh and Jamshied Sharifi; songs performed by Lisa Loeb, Cheryl Chase and Cree Summer, Rakim and Danny Saber, Busta Rhymes, Blondie, Devo, etc.

Paramount/Nickelodeon – UIP.
80 mins. USA. 1998. Rel: 26 March 1999. Cert U.

Rush Hour ★★★

Hong Kong/Los Angeles; the present. When the best man in the Royal Hong Kong police force is teamed up with the LAPD's worst detective, some major mayhem is due to ensue. The 11-year-old daughter of the Chinese Consul has been kidnapped by a ruthless Hong Kong mastermind and the FBI want the case to themselves. So when the Consul calls on Detective Inspector Lee to aid the Feds, the latter is palmed off on Detective James Carter, a walking disaster zone ... Tapping into the twin niche audiences of chopsocky and broad Afro-American comedy, *Rush Hour* rustles up a winning formula that hits its marks with good-humoured pizzazz. By preserving the innocence and knockabout charm of Chan's Hong Kong *oeuvre* and injecting it with a healthy dash of Hollywood cynicism, the film has plenty to play with and does so at every opportunity. Whether parodying an armed showdown in the tradition of John Woo or getting Chan to sing along to Edwin Starr's 'War', the film is canny but unpretentious escapism that doesn't aspire to anything more than what it delivers. It's called good fun.

● *Detective Inspector Lee* Jackie Chan, *James Carter* Chris Tucker, *Thomas Griffin/Juntao* Tom Wilkinson, *Captain William Diel* Philip Baker Hall, *Agent Charles Warren Russ* Mark Rolston, *Consul Han* Tzi Ma, *Agent Whitney* Rex Linn, *Sang* Ken Leung, *Clive* Chris Penn, *Tania Johnson* Elizabeth Pena, *Soo Yung* Julia Hsu, Kai Lennox, Larry Sullivan Jr., Yan Lin, Clifton Powell, Albert Wong, Ai Wan, Lydia Look.
● *Dir* Brett Ratner, *Pro* Roger Birnbaum, Arthur Sarkissian and Jonathan Glickman, *Ex Pro* Jay Stern, *Co-Ex Pro* Leon Dudevoir, *Screenplay* Jim Kouf and Ross Lamanna, *Ph* Adam Greenberg, *Pro Des* Robb Wilson King, *Ed* Mark Helfrich, *M* Lalo Schifrin; songs performed by Michael Jackson, Maria Carey, Curtis Mayfield, James Brown, The Beach Boys, Edwin Starr, and KC & The Sunshine Band, *Costumes* Sharen Davis.

New Line Cinema – Entertainment.
98 mins. USA. 1998. Rel: 4 December 1998. Cert 15.

Below: Culture clash: Chris Tucker and Jackie Chan get on down in Brett Ratner's knockabout, good-humoured Rush Hour (from Entertainment)

Left: *Ryan's slaughter: Tom Sizemore and Tom Hanks do battle in Steven Spielberg's extraordinary, traumatising Saving Private Ryan (from UIP)*

Saving Private Ryan ★★★★¹/₂

France; 6-13 June, 1944. When three brothers are simultaneously killed in action in different parts of the world, a general decides to send a squadron into Nazi-occupied France to retrieve the sole surviving male of the family, Michael Francis Ryan. But the mission is fraught with unimaginable danger, and the soldiers begin to question why their lives are worth less than that of a greenhorn who may already be dead ... War is hell and people die in battle, but seldom has the sheer unadulterated horror of it been captured with such force. Once again Steven Spielberg has taken old conventions and turned them on their head, inverting cliches to take us by surprise. Whether using imperceptibly speeded-up film or whipping away the sound after a grenade explosion, Spielberg cranks up the surreal nightmare of warfare and then plies us with images we won't forget. He also invests his characters with a human credibility seldom found in Hollywood war films, showing us heroic men who are unafraid to cry and whose last words are often 'mama, mama...' FYI: A similar theme was previously explored in Lloyd Bacon's *The Sullivans* (1944), which was based on a true story.

● *Captain Miller* Tom Hanks, *Private Reiben* Edward Burns, *Pvt James Francis Ryan* Matt Damon, *Sergeant Horvath* Tom Sizemore, *Private Mellish* Adam Goldberg, *Private Caparzo* Vin Diesel, *T/4 Medic Wade* Giovanni Ribisi, *Corporal Upham* Jeremy Davies, *Captain Hamill* Ted Danson, *Pvt*

James Ryan Nathan Fillion, *General Marshall* Harve Presnell, *James Ryan as an old man* Harrison Young, Paul Giamatti, Dennis Farina, Joerg Stadler, Maximilian Martini, Dylan Bruno, Rolf Saxon, Nigel Whitmey, Dale Dye, David Wohl, Valerie Colgan, Amanda Boxer, Kathleen Byron.
● *Dir* Steven Spielberg, *Pro* Spielberg & Ian Bruce, Mark Gordon & Gary Levinsohn, *Co-Pro* Bonnie Curtis and Allison Lyon Segan, *Screenplay* Robert Rodat, *Ph* Janusz Kaminski, *Pro Des* Tom Sanders, *Ed* Michael Kahn, *M* John Williams, *Costumes* Joanna Johnston, *Sound* Gary Rydstrom.

DreamWorks/Paramount/Amblin/Mutual Film Co – UIP. 169 mins. USA. 1998. Rel: 11 September 1998. Cert 15.

Secret Defense ★★★¹/₂

Veteran French director Jacques Rivette shows all his mastery as he tells the story of a sister (Bonnaire) alerted by her brother (Colin) to the fact that the supposedly accidental death of their father could have been a murder perpetrated by his business partner (Radziwilowicz). The possibility of taking revenge echoes *Hamlet*, and there's something Ibsenite in the uncovering of hidden secrets from the past. Slow paced but admirably acted and characterised, this seems set to be a film to recommend to Rivette's admirers, who are unlikely to be daunted by a running length of 170 minutes. Unfortunately, though, no clear underlying theme emerges (as in *Paris Belongs To Us*), and the melodramatic climax leaves one dissatisfied. Rivette promises so much more that it's disconcerting to discover that *Secret Defense* is only as over-extended thriller. [*Mansel Stimpson*]

● *Sylvie Rousseau* Sandrine Bonnaire, *Walser* Jerzy Radziwilowicz, *Paul Rousseau* Gregoire Colin, *Veronique Lukachevski/Ludivine Lukachevski* Laure Marsac, *Marthe* Bernadette Giraud, *Sabine* Micheline Herzog, *Genevieve* Francoise Fabian.
● *Dir* Jacques Rivette, *Pro* Martine Marignac and Maurice Tinchant, *Screenplay* Rivette, Pascal Bonitzer and Emmanuelle Cuau, *Ph* William Lubtchansky, *Pro Des* Manu de Chauvigny, *Ed* Nicole Lubtchansky, *M* Jordi Savall, *Costumes* Anne Autran.

Pierre Grise Prods/La Sept Cinema/T&C Film/Canal Plus/Sofica Sofinergie 4/Eurimages, etc – Artificial Eye. 173 mins. France/Switzerland/Italy. 1997. Rel: 25 September 1998. Cert PG.

Seul contre tous – I Stand Alone ★★★

France; 1980. The unsmiling protagonist of this chilling film is the first to admit that this is 'the story of a sorry chump.' And that's about the most humour he's willing to concede, as his life of abuse, unemployment, penury, flight from the law, hunger and humiliation

inevitably spirals towards a horrific climax ... As an intellectual study of what drives a man to the abyss of an unspeakable act, *Seul contre tous* presents a powerful case. As a piece of stripped-to-the-bone cinema, with its staccato voice-over and gun-shot edits, it even attains an eloquent power. And, like *Henry: Portrait of a serial Killer* before it, it eschews the glamorisation of violence endemic in mainstream cinema – which, of course, is to be applauded. However, there are aspects of the piece that cast doubt on the moral integrity of its director: not least a 30-second warning before the film's most abhorrent sequence (talk about emotional manipulation) and then a false ending. A remarkable exercise by any standards, then, but a questionable one.

● *Jean Chevalier, the butcher* Philippe Nahon, *Cynthia, his daughter* Blandine Lenoir, *the mistress* Frankye Pain, *the mother-in-law* Martine Audrain, Zaven, Jean-Francois Rauger, Stephanie Sec, Gerard Ortega, Sylvie Raymond.
● *Dir*, *Pro* and *Screenplay* Gaspar Noe, *Ph* Dominique Colin, *Ed* Noe and Lucile Hadzihalilovic, *M* Thierry Durbet, Bruno Alexiu, Johann Pachelbel, etc.

Les Cinemas De La Zone/Canal Plus/Love Streams, etc – Alliance. 93 mins. France. 1998. Rel: 19 March 1999. Cert 18.

Shakespeare in Love ★★★★★

London; 1593. With the 'organ of his imagination' dried up, young playwright Will Shakespeare is looking for a new muse. Commissioned to write a comedy called *Romeo and Ethel, the Pirate's Daughter*, Shakespeare finds his creative juices unplugged when he espies the beautiful and aristocratic Viola De Lesseps. Confessing his secret ardour to the young actor playing Romeo, the wordsmith discovers that the latter is none other than Viola in disguise, who happens to be both a fan and frustrated performer. Yet not only is it an imprisonable offence for a woman to appear on stage, Viola is already betrothed to the arrogant Lord Wessex ... There is precious little known about the life of Shakespeare, but if one were to draw a line between the dry dots of historical fact one could not do so in a more vivid and entertaining way. Juggling genuine figures from the time with imagined characters and blending the strands of Shakespeare's own fiction with his life, this wonderful film is a marvel of invention and *chutzpah*. From the fascinating detail of the period (Viola brushing her teeth, Shakespeare spinning his quill), to the eloquent dialogue, striking sets, soaring music, magnificent Judi Dench and perfect symbiosis of the editing and camera moves, it would be hard to ask for anything more. An outstanding achievement on every level. FYI: *Shakespeare in Love* was originally due to be filmed in 1992 with Julia Roberts as Viola and Daniel Day-Lewis hoped for as Shakespeare. However,

Left: Drama queen: Judi Dench in her award-winning role as Elizabeth I in John Madden's vivid and eloquent *Shakespeare in Love* (from UIP)

when the latter turned the project down and both Ralph Fiennes and Colin Firth were rejected by Ms Roberts, the actress walked and the production folded.

● *Viola De Lesseps/ Thomas Kent* Gwyneth Paltrow, *William Shakespeare* Joseph Fiennes, *Philip Henslowe* Geoffrey Rush, *Lord Wessex* Colin Firth, *Ned Alleyn* Ben Affleck, *Queen Elizabeth* Judi Dench, *Tilney, Master of the Revels* Simon Callow, *Ralph Bashford* Jim Carter, *Richard Burbage* Martin Clunes, *Dr Moth* Antony Sher, *Nurse* Imelda Staunton, *Hugh Fennyman* Tom Wilkinson, *Wabash* Mark Williams, *Rosaline* Sandra Reinton, *John Webster* Joe Roberts, *Lady De Lesseps* Jill Baker, *Sam Gosse* Daniel Brocklebank, Steven O'Donnell, Steven Beard, Patrick Barlow, Barnaby Kay, Paul Bigley, Nicholas Le Prevost, Timothy Kightley, Mark Saban, Roger Frost, Martin Neeley, and *uncredited*: *Christopher Marlowe* Rupert Everett.
● *Dir* John Madden, *Pro* David Parfitt, Donna Gigliotti, Harvey Weinstein, Edward Zwick and Marc Norman, *Ex Pro* Bob Weinstein and Julie Goldstein, *Screenplay* Norman and Tom Stoppard, *Ph* Richard Greatrex, *Pro Des* Martin Childs, *Ed* David Gamble, *M* Stephen Warbeck, *Costumes* Sandy Powell, *Fights* William Hobbs.

Universal Pictures/Miramax/Bedford Falls – UIP. 123 mins. USA/UK. 1998. Rel: 29 January 1999. Cert 15.

She's All That ★¹/₂

Pacific Palisades, Los Angeles; the present. When Zack Siler, the most popular jock at Harrison High, is dumped by his girlfriend in favour of a TV personality, he boasts that he can transform any old student into the next prom queen. So his best friend takes him at his word and selects the nerdish, clumsy and anti-social Laney Boggs for the make-over of her life … Yet another teen romance updating a classic scenario – this time shades of *Cinderella* and *Pygmalion* pegged to the old wager routine (cf. *Cruel Intentions* and *10 Things I Hate About You*) – *She's All That* suffers dramatically from vacuous plotting and insipid direction. Which is a shame as the movie is chock-full of extremely talented players, from the winsome Rachael Leigh Cook (tomorrow's Winona Ryder) downwards. But it's all so vapid and old-hat that it's impossible to be seduced by the mechanics of the plot. If only they'd had the courage to cast someone *really* plain as Laney – who blossoms through personality alone – then we would have had something to believe in. As it is, Laney is the most perfectly beautiful creature on campus (with or without her horn-rim specs).

● *Zack Siler* Freddie Prinze Jr, *Laney Boggs* Rachael Leigh Cook, *Brock Hudson* Matthew Lillard, *Dean Sampson* Paul Walker, *Taylor Vaughan* Jody Lyn O'Keefe, *Wayne Boggs* Kevin Pollak, *Simon Boggs* Kieran Culkin, *Jesse Jackson* Elden Henson, *Mackenzie Siler* Anna Paquin, *Campus DJ* Usher Raymond, *Preston Harrison* Dule Hill, *Misty* Clea DuVall, *Harlan Siler* Tim Matheson, Kimberly 'Lil'Kim' Jones, Gabrielle Union, Tamara Mello, Debbie Morgan, Alexis Arquette, Chris Owen, Michael Milhoan, Vanessa Lee Chester, Patricia

Charbonneau, Sarah Michelle Gellar.
● *Dir* Robert Iscover, *Pro* Peter Abrams, Robert L.
Levy and Richard N. Gladstein, *Ex Pro* Bob
Weinstein and Harvey Weinstein, *Co-Ex Pro* Jeremy
Kramer and Jill Sobel Messick, *Line Pro* Louise
Rosner, *Screenplay* R. Lee Fleming Jr, *Ph* Francis
Kenny, *Pro Des* Charles Breen, *Ed* Casey O Rohrs,
M Stewart Copeland; songs performed by Remy
Zero, Liz Phair, Black Eyed Peas, Jurassic 5,
Allrighse, Stretch Princess, Sixpence, Girl Next
Door, Rick James, Superdag, The Afghan Wigs,
Goldie, Fat Boy Slim, etc, *Costumes* Denise Wingate.

Miramax/Tapestry Films/Filmcolony – Film Four.
95 mins. USA. 1998. Rel: 21 May 1999. Cert 12.

Side Streets ★★

Like Robert Altman's *Short Cuts*, Tony Gerber's feature
debut, made under the aegis of Merchant Ivory, weaves
together a number of stories. Since it sets out to por-
tray the multi-ethnic character of New York City, it
sounds like a good idea. But, although it puts Indians,
Italians, West Indians, Romanians and Puerto Ricans
side by side, its mini-dramas and mini-comedies are
just not memorable enough to sustain a duration of
over two hours. The plot lines, more often comic than
dramatic in intent, extend through a single day, but as
the film meanders on it grows wearisome due to lack
of real substance. The film's tragi-comic Indian tale,
with Shashi Kapoor as an ageing film star putting on
his relatives and denying that he is in eclipse, is broadly done but forceful. Disappointment is the overall
reaction. [*Mansel Stimpson*]

● *Sylvie Otti* Valeria Golino, *Vikram Raj* Shashi
Kapoor, *Errol Boyce* Leon, *Bipin Raj* Art Malik,
Chandra Raj Shabana Azmi, *Elena Iscovescu* Mirjana
Jokovic, *Ramon Yanes* John Ortiz, *Yuki Shimamura*
Miho Nikaido, *Manuel* Marc Tissot, David Vadim,
Rosario Dawson, Aunjanue Ellis, Victor Argo,
Jennifer Esposito, Mark Margolis.
● *Dir* Tony Gerber, *Pro* Bruce Weiss, *Ex Pro* Ismail
Merchant, Tom Borders and Gregory Cascante, *Co-
Pro* Victoria McGarry Lorino, *Screenplay* Gerber and
Lynn Nottage, *Ph* Russell Lee Fine, *Pro Des* Stephen
McCabe, *Ed* Kate Williams, *M* Evan Lurie; songs
performed by Machito and His Afro Cuban
Ensemble, Krosfyah, Black Stalin, Asha Bhosle, etc,
Costumes Kasia Walicka Maimone.

Merchant Ivory/Cornerstone – First Independent.
131 mins. USA. 1998. Rel: 23 April 1999. Cert 15.

The Siege ★¹/₂

New York City; today. When an unknown terrorist fac-
tion starts blowing up bits of the Big Apple, the FBI,
CIA and US army find themselves at a moral and strate-
gic crossroads ... If Hollywood is going to lay on another large-scale terrorist escapade, then there had better be
good reason for it. This formulaic, slackly paced foray
into the genre is so ill-conceived that it beggars belief.
Besides pawning us off with one-dimensional characters
(doesn't Denzel Washington have a home to go to?), a
flat linear narrative and predictable set-ups, the film features the year's most ridiculous villain (Bruce Willis as a
complete prat). And you know things are bad when a
leading character's death is greeted with relief over horror or glee. Previously known as *Martial Law*.

● *Anthony 'Hub' Hubbard* Denzel Washington, *Elise
Kraft/Sharon Bridger* Annette Bening, *General
William Devereaux* Bruce Willis, *Frank Haddad* Tony
Shalhoub, *Samir Nazhde* Sami Bouajila, *Sheik Ahmed
Bin Talal* Ahmed Ben Larby, Mosleh Mohamed,
Liana Pai, Mark Valley, David Proval, Peter
Schindler, Dakin Matthews, E. Katherine Kerr,
Jimmie Ray Weeks, Will Lyman, Victor Slezak, *him-
self* William Jefferson, Blythe Clinton.
● *Dir* Edward Zwick, *Pro* Zwick and Lynda Obst,
Ex Pro Peter Schindler, *Screenplay* Zwick, Lawrence
Wright and Menno Meyjes, *Ph* Roger Deakins, *Pro
Des* Lilly Kilvert, *Ed* Steven Rosenblum, *M* Graeme
Revell; songs performed by Little Buster & The Soul
Brothers, and Simple Minds, *Costumes* Ann Roth.

Fox – Fox.
116 mins. USA. 1998. Rel: 8 January 1999. Cert 15.

Simon Birch ★¹/₂

Gravestown, Maine; 1964. Born with a rare growth disorder, Simon Birch is ridiculed at school and virtually
ignored by his parents. But with the support of his best
friend, Joe, and the help of God, little Simon resolves
to be a hero ... You know you're in trouble when a film
opens with Jim Carrey standing over a gravestone.
Sweeping his comic history to one side, the star tells us
that it was Simon Birch who brought him to God.
Meanwhile, the camera swirls round him for no apparent reason while Marc Shaiman ups the ante by laying
on a treacly piano-driven score. Novice director Mark
Steven Johnson (who previously scripted the dreadful
Big Bully and *Jack Frost*) then lurches from one cliche to
the next (filtered lighting, naff pop songs), while laying
on the schmaltz with a JCB. Which is a shame as the
film's sentiments are commendable and young Ian
Michael Smith – all 3'1" of him – is quite winning
when not required to cry. Incidentally, Disney pushed
the American release of this atrocity in front of the sim-
ilarly-themed *The Mighty*, thus destroying the commercial chances of the latter infinitely superior film.

● *Joe Wenteworth* Joseph Mazzello, *Simon Birch* Ian
Michael Smith, *Rebecca Wenteworth* Ashley Judd, *Ben
Goodrich* Oliver Platt, *Reverend Russell* David
Strathairn, *Grandmother Wenteworth* Dana Ivey, *Hildie*

Grove Beatrice Winde, *Agnus Leavey* Jan Hooks, *Marjorie* Ceciley Carroll, *adult Joe Wenteworth* Jim Carrey, *Simon Wenteworth* John Mazzello, *Mr Birch* Peter MacNeil, *Mr Baker* John Robinson, Sumela-Rose Keramidopulos, Sam Morton, Holly Dennison, Roger McKeen, Sean McCann.
● *Dir* and *Screenplay* Mark Steven Johnson, 'suggested' by John Irving's novel *A Prayer for Owen Meany*, *Pro* Laurence Mark and Roger Birnbaum, *Ex Pro* John Baldecchi, *Co-Pro* Billy Higgins, *Ph* Aaron E. Schneider, *Pro Des* David Chapman, *Ed* David Finfer, *M* Marc Shaiman; numbers performed by Kenneth 'Babyface' Edmonds, The Newbeats, Smokey Robinson & The Miracles, Marvin Gaye, Peggy Lee, The Righteous Brothers, The Drifters, James Brown, Martha Reeves & The Vandellas, The Impressions, and Patti LaBelle & The Blue Belles, *Costumes* Betsy Heimann and Abram Waterhouse.

Hollywood Pictures/Caravan Pictures – Buena Vista. 113 mins. USA. 1998. Rel: 25 June 1999. Cert PG.

A Simple Plan ★★★¹⁄₂

According to all-round decent accountant Hank Mitchell, it is the simple things in life that make a man happy. And Hank has it all: a loving wife, a decent job and the respect of his neighbours. He also has a brother, Jacob, who's definitely on the simple side. Things then get far from simple when the siblings and Jake's hard-drinking buddy Lou stumble across a small plane in the woods and a bag containing $4,400,000 in crisp $100 bills ... Edging into territory already well explored by *Shallow Grave*, *Fargo* and *Affliction*, this character-driven drama's greatest surprise is that it is the work of Sam Raimi, the director who brought us such schlocky horror as *The Evil Dead* and *Army of Darkness*. Yet, in spite of the film's thematic familiarity there is much to admire: some intelligent pacing, evocative photography of snow-bound Minnesota and another subtly unrecognisable turn from Billy Bob Thornton, who imbues his village idiot with a genuine pathos and sense of reasoning. FYI: Bridget Fonda, a long-time fan of Raimi's, finally gets a role in one of his films (not counting her cameo in *Army of Darkness*).

● *Hank Mitchell* Bill Paxton, *Jacob Mitchell* Billy Bob Thornton, *Sarah Mitchell* Bridget Fonda, *Lou* Brent Briscoe, *Baxter* Gary Cole, *Nancy* Becky Ann Baker, *Carl* Chelcie Ross, Jack Walsh, Bob Davis, Peter Syvertsen, Tom Carey, John Paxton.
● *Dir* Sam Raimi, *Pro* James Jacks and Adam Schroeder, *Ex Pro* Gary Levinsohn and Mark Gordon, *Co-Pro* Michael Polaire, *Screenplay* Scott B. Smith, from his novel, *Ph* Alar Kivilo, *Pro Des* Patrizia Von Brandenstein, *Ed* Arthur Coburn and Eric L. Beason, *M* Danny Elfman; songs performed by Norman Greenbaum, Jolene, Imperial Crowns, and Tina and the B-Sides, *Costumes* Julie Weiss.

Mutual Film Company/BBC/Marubeni/Toho Towa/Paramount Pictures/Savoy Pictures, etc – UIP. 121 mins. USA/UK/Japan/Germany/France. 1998. Rel: 21 May 1999. Cert 15.

Sitcom ★★★¹⁄₂

While set up like a traditional sitcom – a suburban French household inhabited by clucking mother hen, newspaper-shielded father, randy teenage daughter and nerdy teenage son – Francois Ozon's debut feature quickly steps into the anarchic footsteps of Bunuel. At what at first appears to be a typical family dinner, the son, Nicolas, announces his homosexuality, setting in motion a chain of events underpinned by a variety of sexual deviance. Thus the daughter, after an unsuccessful suicide attempt, turns to sado-masochism, the maid's husband leaps out of the closet to join Nicolas and adultery, orgies and incest become a matter of course. Boasting a deftly deadpan tone and a deliciously subversive bite, *Sitcom* is satire that gleefully plucks the wings off the butterfly of the French bourgeoisie. FYI: To guide his actors, Ozon suggested various cinematic role models: Lana Turner for the mother, James Mason for the father, Bette Davis for Sophie, Sidney Poitier for Abdu, and so on.

● *Helene, the mother* Evelyne Dandry, *Jean, the father* Francois Marthouret, *Sophie, the daughter* Marina De Van, *Nicolas, the son* Adrien De Van, *David, the boyfriend* Stephane Rideau, *Maria, the maid* Lucia Sanchez, *Abdu, Maria's husband* Jules-Emmanuel Eyoum Deido, *psychotherapist* Jean Douchet.
● *Dir* and *Screenplay* Francois Ozon, *Pro* Olivier Delbosc and Marc Missonnier, *Ph* Yorick Le Saux, *Pro Des* Angelique Puron, *Ed* Dominique Petrot, *M* Eric Neveux; Mahler, Beethoven, Chopin, Mozart, Dvorak, etc, *Costumes* Herve Poeydemenge.

Fidelite Prods/Canal Plus – Alliance Releasing. 80 mins. France. 1997. Rel: 1 January 1999. Cert 18.

Below: *In the money: Billy Bob Thornton, Bill Paxton and Brent Briscoe succumb to greed in Sam Raimi's moody and gripping* A Simple Plan *(from UIP)*

Above: It happened one vacation: Anne Heche and Harrison Ford in Ivan Reitman's mildly diverting Six Days, Seven Nights (from Buena Vista)

Six Days, Seven Nights ★★¹/₂

She is the sassy, workaholic assistant editor of the lifestyle magazine *Dazzle*. He is the easy-going, fun-loving pilot of a careworn De Havilland Beaver. In the South Pacific to enjoy the vacation of a lifetime, the former finds herself stranded on a deserted island with the latter. And they don't like each other ... Attempting to recreate the screwball magic of such classic romantic comedies as *It Happened One Night* and *The African Queen*, *Six Days, Seven Nights* too often plays it for the obvious laugh. Harrison Ford and Anne Heche are enjoyable enough to spend an evening with, but they don't generate the chemistry expected of them. Ironically, it is David Schwimmer, in the distracting part of Heche's pathologically romantic boyfriend, who steals the most chuckles.

● *Quinn Harris* Harrison Ford, *Robin Monroe* Anne Heche, *Frank Martin* David Schwimmer, *Angelica* Jacqueline Obradors, *Jager* Temuera Morrison, *Marjorie* Allison Janney, Douglas Weston, Cliff Curtis, Danny Trejo, Amy Sedaris, Michael Chapman, Taj Mahal.
● *Dir* Ivan Reitman, *Pro* Reitman, Wallis Nicita and Roger Birnbaum, *Ex Pro* Joe Medjuck, Daniel Goldberg and Julie Bergman Sender, *Co-Pro* Gordon

Webb and Sheldon Kahn, *Screenplay* Michael Browning, *Ph* Michael Chapman, *Pro Des* J. Michael Riva, *Ed* Kahn and Wendy Greene Bricmont, *M* Randy Edelman; songs performed by Taj Mahal, Bob Marley, and Dreamhouse, *Costumes* Gloria Gresham, *Sound* John Pospisil.

Touchstone/Caravan Pictures/Northern Lights Entertainment – Buena Vista.
108 mins. USA. 1998. Rel: 3 July 1998. Cert 12.

Slam ★★¹/₂

Washington DC; today. In a conflict waged by drug pushers, users and cops, Ray Joshua is a lone casualty who finds temporary redemption in his rap poetry, or 'slamming' ... Strong on atmosphere and piquant visuals, *Slam* is another creditable slice-of-life urban testament in the tradition of Boaz Yakin's *Fresh* and Ernest Dickerson's *Juice*. First-time director Marc Levin certainly displays a raw emotional energy and coaxes wonderfully naked performances from his largely non-professional players. Even so, *Slam* feels more like a window of animosity than a film in its own right. Notwithstanding, it must have nudged a few nerves as it won the Grand Jury prize at Sundance and the Camera d'Or at Cannes. FYI: Former Washington DC mayor Marion Barry Jr – who was caught taking drugs while still in office – plays the judge who reprimands Ray for his misdemeanour.

● *Raymond Joshua* Saul Williams, *Lauren Bell* Sonja Sohn, *Hopha* Bonz Malone, *Jimmy Huang* Beau Sia, Lawrence Wilson, Andre Taylor, Dominic Chianese Jr.
● *Dir* Marc Levin, *Pro* Levin, Henri M. Kessler and Richard Stratton, *Ex Pro* Kessler and David Peipers, *Assoc Pro* Daphne Pinkerson. *Screenplay* Levin, Stratton, Bonz Malone, Sonja Sohn and Saul Williams, *Ph* Mark Benjamin, *Ed* Emir Lewis, *M* DJ Spooky; songs performed by DJ Spooky That Subliminal Kid, Love Unlimited, Earth Wind & Fire, Noreaga, Brass Construction, etc.

Offline Entertainment/Slam Pictures – Metro Tartan.
103 mins. USA. 1998. Rel: 9 April 1999. Cert 15.

Sling Blade ★★★★¹/₂

The fictional town of Millsburg, Arkansas; not so long ago. After spending 25 years in an asylum for the criminally insane, the partially retarded Karl Childers is released back into the community. Incarcerated for killing his mother and her lover when just a child, Karl is now a devotee of the Bible and knows the difference between right and wrong. But only a 14-year-old boy accepts him without judgement and so the beginning of an extraordinary friendship takes shape ... A beautifully observed moral fable, *Sling Blade* not only showcases a magnificent performance from Billy

Bob Thornton as a damaged angel of mercy, but some astutely judged direction and a perceptive script from the man as well. An ineffably touching experience. FYI: The character of Childers was originally developed by Thornton as part of a one-man show back in 1985. The film's other protagonists were written specially for the actors who play them.

● *Karl Childers* Billy Bob Thornton, *Doyle Hargraves* Dwight Yoakam, *Charles Bushman* J.T. Walsh, *Vaughan Cunningahm* John Ritter, *Frank Wheatley* Lucas Black, *Linda Wheatley* Natalie Canerday, *Karl's father* Robert Duvall, *Melinda* Christy Ward, James Hampton, Rick Dial, Brent Briscoe, Sarah Boss, Col. Bruce Hampton, Ret., Vic Chestnutt, Mickey Jones, Ian Moore, Jim Jarmusch.
● *Dir* and *Screenplay* Billy Bob Thornton, *Pro* Brandon Rosser and David L. Bushell, *Ex Pro* Larry Meistrich, *Ph* Barry Markowitz, *Pro Des* Clark Hunter, *Ed* Hughes Winborne, *M* Daniel Lanois; songs performed by Ali Jennings, Booker T. & The MGs, Tim Gibbons, Titty Twisters, Bambi Lee Savage, Emmylou Harris, and Daniel Lanois, *Costumes* Douglas Hall, *Sound* Jeff Kushner.

The Shooting Gallery – Buena Vista.
134 mins. USA. 1995. Rel: 10 July 1998. Cert 15.

Slums of Beverly Hills ★¹/₂

In an effort to provide his three kids with a decent education by keeping them within the vicinity of Beverly Hills, failed gambler and single father Murray Abramowitz drags his family – undercover of night – from one low-rent dive to the next. Meanwhile, Murray's daughter, Vivian, is forced to come to turns with her burgeoning sexuality and enormous breasts ... Like a sitcom stretched three times beyond its natural endurance, this first feature from former performance artist Tamara Jenkins all seems terribly irrelevant. Specifically set in 1976 in Beverly Hills, the film basks in its pop cultural references (there's Merv Griffin's house! listen to Freddy Fender on the soundtrack!) and lewd frankness (watch a 15-year-old girl masturbate! learn how to strap on a menstrual belt!). The wonder is that producer Robert Redford found something worthwhile in Jenkins' script that features yet another squabbling, all-American, dysfunctional Jewish family. Enough already.

● *Murray Abramowitz* Alan Arkin, *Vivian Abramowitz* Natasha Lyonne, *Eliot* Kevin Corrigan, *Doris* Jessica Walter, *Belle Abramowitz* Rita Moreno, *Ben Abramowitz* David Krumholtz, *Rickey Abramowitz* Eli Marienthal, *Mickey Abramowitz* Carl Reiner, *Rita* Marisa Tomei, Charlotte Stewart, Mary Portser, Jay Patterson, Sally Schaub.
● *Dir* and *Screenplay* Tamara Jenkins, *Pro* Michael Nozik and Stan Wlodkowski, *Ex Pro* Robert Redford,

Ph Tom Richmond, *Pro Des* Dena Roth, *Ed* Pamela Martin, *M* Rolfe Kent; songs performed by Ten Years After, Funkadelic, Perry Como, Parliament, Freddy Fender, Ike and Tina Turner, Bellamy Brothers, and Three Dog Night, *Costumes* Kirsten Everberg.

Fox Searchlight/South Fork Pictures/Sundance Institute – Fox.
91 mins. USA. 1998. Rel: 27 November 1998. Cert 15.

Small Soldiers ★¹/₂

Winslow Corners, Ohio; the present. For the soldiers of the Commando Elite, size really *doesn't* matter. With their technological savvy, tireless inventiveness and fearless disposition, these dedicated soldiers of misfortune have the potential to be the most deadly army in the world. Fortified by military microprocessor chips, the 12-inch-small elite don't even know that they are toys – yet they treat the rest of the world like their playground ... Taking the concept of Barry Levinson's *Toys* and marrying it to the mentality of Buzz Lightyear (from *Toy Story*), *Small Soldiers* is derivative and calculating. Aimed squarely at young-ish boys, the film benefits neither from the anarchic humour nor the genuine thrills of the same director's *Gremlins*. As for the amazing spe-

Above: The Lawnmower Man: Billy Bob Thornton as the socially challenged Karl Childers in his own beautifully observed Sling Blade (from Buena Vista)

cial effects (computer generated imagery mixed with live action), these days we have come to expect more from our dollar – the film is as mechanical as the merchandise it is trying to shift in the name of tie-in marketing.

● *Christy Fimple* Kirsten Dunst, *Alan Abernathy* Gregory Smith, *Larry Benson* Jay Mohr, *Phil Fimple* Phil Hartman, *Stuart Abernathy* Kevin Dunn, *Gil Mars* Denis Leary, *the voice of Archer* Frank Langella, *the voice of Chip Hazard* Tommy Lee Jones, *Irwin Wayfair* David Cross, *Joe* Dick Miller, *Irene Abernathy* Ann Magnuson, *Marion Fimple* Wendy Schaal, Alexandra Wilson, Robert Picardo, Belinda Balaski, Rance Howard, *and the additional voices of:* Ernest Borgnine, Jim Brown, Bruce Dern, George Kennedy, Clint Walker, Christopher Guest, Michael McKean, Harry Shearer, Jim Cummings, Sarah Michelle Gellar, Christina Ricci.
● *Dir* Joe Dante, *Pro* Michael Finnell and Colin Wilson, *Ex Pro* Walter Parkes, *Screenplay* Gavin Scott and Adam Rifkin, Ted Elliott and Terry Rossio, *Ph* Jamie Anderson, *Pro Des* William Sandell, *Ed* Marshall Harvey, *M* Jerry Goldsmith; Richard Strauss; songs performed by Bone Thugs-n-Harmony with Henry Rollins and Flea, Pat Benatar and Queen Latifah, The Pretenders, The Cult, Gary Glitter, Queen, Led Zeppelin, Cheap Trick, Spice Girls, Rush, and Billy Squier, *Costumes* Carole Brown-James, *Animation supervisor* David Andrews, *Visual effects* Stefen Fangmeier, *Action figure/animatronic design* Stan Winston.

DreamWorks/Universal Pictures/Amblin Entertainment – UIP.
110 mins. USA. 1998. Rel: 23 October 1998. Cert PG.

Snake Eyes ★★

Atlantic City Arena; New Jersey. Just as the world heavyweight champion is losing his title to an underdog, the US Secretary of Defence is assassinated in the crowd. Rick Santoro, boxing enthusiast and corrupt cop, smells a conspiratorial rat. He ain't cut out for

heroism, but a man's gotta do ... In spite of a script from David Koepp (*Jurassic Park*, *Carlito's Way*, etc), *Snake Eyes* offers little new and often plays like a Jean-Claude Van Damme vehicle with style. Nicolas Cage overacts outrageously, Gary Sinise hands in the intense, calculating performance he gave us in *Ransom* and a slew of familiar faces huff and puff in loyal support. Yet not one character projects a glimmer of sympathy. Earlier in his career, director Brian DePalma was likened to a modern-day Hitchcock – but Hitchcock made the audience care for *his* characters.

● *Rick Santoro* Nicolas Cage, *Kevin Dunne* Gary Sinise, *Gilbert Powell* John Heard, *Julia Costello* Carla Gugino, *Lincoln Tyler* Stan Shaw, *Lou Logan* Kevin Dunn, *Charles Kirkland* Joel Fabiani, *Cyrus* Luis Guzman, *Walt McGahn* Mike Starr, *Anthea* Tamara Tunie, Michael Rispoli, David Anthony Higgins, Chip Zien, Mark Camacho, Adam C. Flores, Christina Fulton, Byron Johnson, Peter McRobbie, Christian Napoli, James Whelan.
● *Dir* and *Pro* Brian De Palma, *Ex Pro* Louis A. Stroller, *Screenplay* David Koepp, from a story by De Palma and Koepp, *Ph* Stephen H. Burum, *Pro Des* Anne Pritchard, *Ed* Bill Pankow, *M* Ryuchi Sakamoto, *Costumes* Odette Gadoury, *Boxing choreography* James Gambina.

Touchstone Pictures/Paramount – Buena Vista.
99 mins. 1998. USA. Rel: 6 November 1998. Cert 15.

A Soldier's Daughter Never Cries
★★★

Like James Ivory's last film, *Surviving Picasso*, this account of an artist's life seems more preoccupied with the domestic than the creative, thus depriving the viewer of any true insight into the workings of the American writer James Jones (who penned the novels *From Here To Eternity*, *Some Came Running* and *The Thin Red Line*). True, Ivory and Ruth Prawer Jhabvala's screenplay is taken from the semi-autobiographical novel by Jones' daughter, Kaylie, and it is here that the film comes into its own – even as its pleasures are diluted by following in the wake of so many other recent nostalgia-tinged dramas. Set during the Sixties and Seventies, the film focuses on Kaylie's formative years in Paris and, as to be expected from the Merchant Ivory team, the look is exquisite and the acting laudable. But this is more a film of great moments than great scenes – a volcanic laugh from Kris Kristofferson, a sublime aria from Anthony Roth Costanzo – and the pace does drag.

● *Bill Willis* Kris Kristofferson, *Marcella Willis* Barbara Hershey, *Charlotte Anne 'Channe' Wallis* Leelee Sobieski, *Mrs Fortescue* Jane Birkin, *Candida* Dominique Blanc, *Billy Willis* Jesse Bradford, *Francis Fortescue* Anthony Roth Costanzo, *Keith Carter* Harley Cross, *Mamadou* Isaac de Bankole, *young*

Below: Punch drunk: Nicolas Cage takes a fall in Brian De Palma's over-baked Snake Eyes *(from Buena Vista)*

Channe Luisa Conlon, *Benoit/young Billy* Samuel Gruen, Virginie Ledoyen, Macha Meril, Nathalie Richard, Bob Swaim, Frederic Da, Michelle Fairley, Catriona McColl.
● *Dir* James Ivory, *Pro* Ismail Merchant, *Ex Pro* Richard Hawley and Nayeem Hafizka, *Screenplay* Ivory and Ruth Prawer Jhabvala, *Ph* Jean-Marc Fabre, *Pro Des* Jacques Bufnoir and Pat Garner, *Ed* Noelle Boisson, *M* Richard Robbins; Mozart, Puccini; songs performed by Tito Puente, Dalida, Bill Withers, Jane Birkin, Canned Heat, Deep Purple, Enrico Macias, 10cc, David Bowie, etc, *Costumes* Carol Ramsey.

Merchant Ivory/Capitol Films/British Screen – Roseland.
130 mins. UK. 1998. Rel: 9 October 1998. Cert 15.

Solomon & Gaenor ★★¹/₂

During a time of great hardship in the Welsh valleys of 1911, a handsome Jewish pacman (or peddler) befriends the daughter of a Welsh miner. Forbidden by their respective traditions to fraternise – let alone kiss – the young companions find themselves falling in love ... An old story transposed to a novel *milieu*, *Solomon & Gaenor* succeeds more as an illustration of time and place than as commanding emotional drama. The impoverished community of early 20th century Wales is keenly caught (and the surrounding countryside evocatively lit), while the telling minutiae of the every-day lives of the miners and Orthodox Jews are lovingly detailed. And, as the star-cross'd lovers, Ioan Gruffudd and Nia Roberts strike a credible note, even if the passion of their romance is dictated by the mandate of the story rather than by any on-screen chemistry.

● *Solomon* aka *Sam Livingstone* Ioan Gruffudd, *Gaenor Rhys* Nia Roberts, *Gwen Rhys* Sue Jones Davies, *Idris Rhys* William Thomas, *Crad Rhys* Mark Lewis Jones, *Rezl* Maureen Lipman, *Isaac* David Horovitch, *Noah Jones* Steffan Rhodri, Bethan Ellis Owen, Adam Jenkins, Cyril Shaps, Emyr Wyn, Rhys Evans, Derek Smith.
● *Dir* and *Screenplay* Paul Morrison, *Pro* Sheryl Crown, *Ex Pro* David Green and Andy Porter, *Ph* Nina Kellgren, *Pro Des* Hayden Pearce, *Ed* Kant Pan, *M* Ilona Sekacz, *Costumes* Maxine Brown, *Yiddish consultant* Barry Davies, *Accountant* David Mellor.

S4C/Film Four/Arts Council of England/Arts Council of Wales/APT/September Films – Film Four.
104 mins. UK. 1998. Rel: 30 April 1999. Cert 15.

Sour Grapes ★★

Cadging two quarters off his cousin Evan, sports shoe designer Richie Maxwell wins $436,214.50 from an Atlantic City slot machine. While not exactly needing the money himself, Evan – a brain surgeon by trade – resents that Richie doesn't offer him a percentage of his spoils. After all, he argues, those were *his* quarters that hit the jackpot. And so, on a whim, Evan decides to play a wicked prank on his cousin, a ruse that kick-starts a chain of disastrous events ... This, sadly, is a prime example of a great idea ruined by over-zealous direction. A witty and ingenious script from Larry David (co-creator of sitcom *Seinfeld*) is reduced to far-cical excess by the same man's insistence on playing every line for all it's worth. You can just picture David egging his actors on, 'come on guys, let's see some animation, this *is* a comedy.' In addition, the sound-track, cobbling together the most ebullient and over-used snatches of classical music ever heard in one sit-ting, just drowns the whole thing in bathos.

● *Evan Maxwell* Steven Weber, *Richie Maxwell* Craig Bierko, *Danny Pepper* Matt Keeslar, *Joan* Karen Sillas, *Roberta* Robyn Peterman, *Selma Maxwell* Viola Harris, *Digby* Orlando Jones, *Det. Crouch* Richard Gant, *Det. Frehill* James MacDonald, *Mr Bell* Philip Baker Hall, *TV producer* Larry David, Jennifer Leigh Warren, Sonya Eddy, Ann Guilbert, Harper Roisman, Michael Krawic, John Toley-Bey, Meredith Salenger.
● *Dir* and *Screenplay* Larry David, *Pro* Laurie Lennard, *Ex Pro* Barry Berg, *Ph* Victor Hammer, *Pro Des* Charles Rosen, *Ed* Priscilla Nedd-Friendly, *M* J.S. Bach, Brahms, Johann Strauss Jr, Beethoven, Mozart, Rossini, Prokofiev, Schubert, Grieg, Bizet, Mendellsohn, Von Suppe, Charles Gounod, Luigi Boccherini; 'Ain't That a Kick in the Head' sung by Dean Martin, *Costumes* Debra McGuire.

Castle Rock/Columbia – Warner.
92 mins. USA. 1997. Rel: 15 January 1999. Cert 15.

Southpaw ★★★

Without proper training facilities or even electricity and running water, Francis Barrett, a 19-year-old Traveller and amateur light welterweight boxer from Galway, reaches the highest level in amateur sport, fulfilling a lifelong dream by representing Ireland at the Olympic games in Atlanta in 1996. He then con-tinues his boxing career in London and attempts the double of Irish and English titles, a feat that hasn't been achieved in 43 years. A sort of real-life *Rocky*, this lovingly made little film unexpectedly delivers quite a punch. It's easy to find it all a bit sad and pathetic, but it's a tribute to Barrett that he emerges a victor – at least on points – over the desperate lack of promise his life seems to offer. [*Derek Winnert*]

● With Francis Barrett, Chick Gillen, Tom Humphries, Column Flynn, etc. *Narrator* Eamon Hunt.
● *Dir* Liam McGrath, *Pro* Robert Walpole and Paddy Breathnach, *Ex Pro* Clare Duignan and Rod Stoneman, *Line Pro* Lesley McKimm, *Ph* Cian de Buitlear, *Ed* James Dalton, *M* Dario Marianelli.

Right: *Con heir: Campbell Scott and Rebecca Pidgeon in David Mamet's artfully surprising* The Spanish Prisoner *(from Pathe)*

Treasure Films/Radio Telefis Erieann/Bord Scannan na hEireann/The Irish Film Board/Channel 4/Hillside Prods – Downtown.
80 mins. Ireland/UK. 1998. Rel: 12 March 1999. Cert 15.

The Spanish Prisoner ★★★¹/₂

Poised to become the next Bill Gates, Joe Ross is eager to have his unique 'process' evaluated by his company. But his boss repeatedly buys him off with nebulous promises that he will receive 'something big'. So, when Joe is befriended by an enigmatic millionaire in the Caribbean, he accepts the stranger's offer of legal help. But still the paranoia builds ... Returning to the tightly plotted manipulations of his first film, *House of Games*, writer-director David Mamet is back to what he does best: setting a chain of ingenious narrative traps for his audience. Never less than intriguing, *The Spanish Prisoner* deals its deck of cards with consummate skill, drawing the viewer deeper and deeper into its elaborate maze of false bottoms. Two quibbles: would the New York police really set up an airport roadblock for a single murder and what did Joe do with his FBI wire?

● *Joe Kline* Ben Gazzara, *Pat McCune* Felicity Huffman, *George Lang* Ricky Jay, *Jimmy Dell* Steve Martin, *Susan Ricci* Rebecca Pidgeon, *Joe Ross* Campbell Scott, J.J. Johnston, Tony Mamet, *FBI superior* Ed O'Neill, Lionel Mark Smith.
● *Dir* and *Screenplay* David Mamet, *Pro* Jean Doumanian, *Ex Pro* J.E. Beaucaire, *Co-Pro* Sarah Green, *Co-Ex Pro* Letty Aronson, *Ph* Gabriel Beristain, *Pro Des* Tim Galvin, *Ed* Barbara Tulliver, *M* Carter Burwell, *Costumes* Susan Lyall.

Jasmine Prods/Sweetland Films – Pathe.
110 mins. USA. 1997. Rel: 28 August 1998. Cert PG.

Species II ★★¹/₂

After NASA's first manned flight to Mars, a bizarre and deadly strain of DNA becomes manifest on earth. Seemingly intelligent, the demon strain reveals telepathic powers, a powerful ability to re-generate human tissue and an unbridled libido ... Where the first *Species* refused to recognise that it was just a cheesy monster movie, this engaging sequel lets its hair down with gay abandon. Yet for all its high camp and B-movie virtues it does make sense within the limits of its own premise (never underrate DNA). With plenty of nudity, gore and ingenious and inventive effects, *Species II* doesn't disappoint. As cheesy monster movies go this is Roquefort.

● *Press Lennox* Michael Madsen, *Eve* Natasha Henstridge, *Dr Laura Baker* Marg Helgenberger, *Dennis Gamble* Mykelti Williamson, *Colonel Carter Burgess Jr* George Dzundza, *Senator Ross* James Cromwell, *Patrick Ross* Justin Lazard, *Anne Sampas* Myriam Cyr, *U.S. President* Richard Belzer, Sarah Wynter, Baxter Harris, Scott Morgan, Nancy La Scala, Raquel Gardner, Henderson Forsythe, Felicia Deel, Susan Duvall, Sondra Williamson, Bill Boggs, and *uncredited*: *Herman Cromwell* Peter Boyle.
● *Dir* Peter Medak, *Pro* Frank Mancuso, Jr, *Ex Pro* Dennis Feldman, *Line Pro* Vikki Williams, *Screenplay* Chris Brancato, *Ph* Matthew F. Leonetti, *Pro Des* Miljen Kreka Kljakovic, *Ed* Richard Nord, *M* Edward Shearmur; songs performed by Tony! Toni! Tone!, B.B. King, and Apollo Four Forty, *Costumes* Richard Bruno, *Creature/make-up effects* Steve Johnson, *Species design* H.R. Giger.

MGM/FGM Prods – UIP.
93 mins. USA. 1998. Rel: 4 September 1998. Cert 18.

Star Trek: Insurrection ★★★

When the friendly android Data takes hostages during a routine survey of a New Age community, Captain Jean-Luc Picard must take decisive action. Discovering that the violated planet holds the key to eternal youth, the Captain realises that there could be some high-level chicanery afoot. Risking court martial, he takes the side of the persecuted hippies – the Ba'ku – and finds himself falling in love … Consolidating the series' traditional recipe of neat ideas, gentle humour, moral stance and self-parody, this is slight escapism with a knowing smile. More an extended TV episode than a film in its own right, this ninth instalment of the cinematic franchise offers plenty of diverting moments but still leaves one feeling shortchanged. Shame about the misleading title, too. *Star Trek: The New Age* might have been more fitting.

● *Captain Jean-Luc Picard* Patrick Stewart, *Commander William Riker* Jonathan Frakes, *android Lt. Commander Data* Brent Spiner, *Lt. Commander Geordi La Forge* LeVar Burton, *Lt. Commander Worf* Michael Dorn, *Dr Beverly C. Crusher* Gates McFadden, *Lt. Commander Deanna Troi* Marina Sirtis, *Ru'afo* F. Murray Abraham, *Anij* Donna Murphy, *Admiral Dougherty* Anthony Zerbe, *Gallatin* Gregg Henry, *Sojef* Daniel Hugh Kelly, *Artim* Michael Welch, Mark Deakins, Stephanie Niznik, Michael Horton.
● *Dir* Jonathan Frakes, *Pro* Rick Berman, *Ex Pro* Martin Hornstein, *Co-Pro* Peter Lauritson, *Assoc Pro* Patrick Stewart, *Screenplay* Michael Piller, from a story by Berman and Piller, *Ph* Matthew Leonetti, *Pro Des* Herman Zimmerman, *Ed* Peter E. Berger, *M* Jerry Goldsmith; Haydn, Mozart, Beethoven, Alan Silvestri; 'A British Tar', from Gilbert and Sullivan's *H.M.S. Pinafore*, *Costumes* Sanja Milkovic, *Make-up* Michael Westmore, *Special effects* Terry Frazee.

Paramount – UIP.
100 mins. USA. 1998. Rel: 1 January 1999. Cert PG.

Stepmom ★★★½

Jackie Harrison and Isabel Kelly are about as different as two women can get. But they love the same man, Luke Harrison. Ex-wife Jackie is the mother of Luke's two children, Anna and Ben, and Isabel is the young impostor trying to do the right thing. But when you're a stepmother nothing you can do is valid. It's a no-win situation: there are no right ways or wrong ways and the casualties are bound to be horrendous … The step-mother has never got a good press in Hollywood. So it seems perfectly acceptable that somebody as incandescently likeable as Julia Roberts gets to set the balance straight. As it happens, this project was personally developed by Ms Roberts in tandem with her friend, co-producer and co-star Susan Sarandon. And, as far as the acting goes, it is probably the best thing Roberts has done, while Sarandon turns in another

gritty, selfless portrayal of withering power. And for all the film's carefully crafted emotional button-pushing, it does address a bundle of genuine issues with some eloquence. Indeed, the script was actually based on a situation involving scenarist Gigi Levangie and her now-husband, top producer Brian Grazer.

● *Isabel Kelly* Julia Roberts, *Jackie Harrison* Susan Sarandon, *Luke Harrison* Ed Harris, *Anna Harrison* Jena Malone, *Ben Harrison* Liam Aiken, *Dr Sweikert* Lynn Whitfield, *Duncan Samuels* Darrell Larson, *Brad Kovitsky* Jason Maves, Mary Louise Wilson, Andre Blake, Russell Harper.
● *Dir* Chris Columbus, *Pro* Columbus, Mark Radcliffe, Michael Barnathan and Wendy Finerman, *Ex Pro* Julia Roberts, Susan Sarandon, Pliny Porter, Patrick McCormick, Ron Bass and Margaret French Isaac, *Screenplay* Gigi Levangie, Jessie Nelson, Steven Rogers, Karen Leigh Hopkins and Ron Bass, *Ph* Donald M. McAlpine, *Pro Des* Stuart Wurtzel, *Ed* Neil Travis, *M* John Williams; Rossini; songs performed by Queen & David Bowie, Five, Booker T. & The MGs, Marvin Gaye & Tammi Terrell, The Supremes, etc, *Costumes* Joseph G. Aulisi.

Columbia/1492 – Columbia TriStar.
125 mins. USA. 1998. Rel: 29 January 1999. Cert 12.

Still Crazy ★★½

Twenty-one years after divine intervention ended the reign of the British rock group Strange Fruit, keyboard player Tony Costello decides to get the band back together for a reunion concert. But can the strength of nostalgia overcome the bitter in-fighting that divided the group two decades earlier? And now, in advanced middle-age, do the musicians still have what it takes? A sort of English take on *This is Spinal Tap* – with a dash of *Leningrad Cowboys Go America* – *Still Crazy* has plenty of warmth and a few good laughs but just cannot keep up the momentum. Yet the performances linger well into the night: Timothy

Below: Games that intergalactic travellers play: Marina Sirtis and Jonathan Frakes in the latter's utterly agreeable Star Trek: Insurrection *(from UIP)*

Right: After all these years: Bill Nighy primps himself for a revival in Brian Gibson's funny if familiar Still Crazy (from Columbia TriStar)

Spall's rustic, farting drummer; Jimmy Nail's lugubrious, sardonic guitarist; and, perhaps best of all, Bill Nighy as the plummy, insecure and desperately befuddled lead singer. There's also a wonderful coup in securing the comeback of Bruce Robinson, the former actor who went on to write *The Killing Fields* and direct *Withnail & I*. However, the likelihood of such disparate figures ending up in the same band takes a stretch of the imagination that goes beyond The Traveling Wilburys. Good music, though.

● *Tony Costello* Stephen Rea, *Hughie* Billy Connolly, *Les Wickes* Jimmy Nail, *Beano Baggot* Timothy Spall, *Ray Simms* Bill Nighy, *Karen Knowles* Juliet Aubrey, *Brian Lovell* Bruce Robinson, *Astrid Simms* Helena Bergstrom, *Luke Shand* Hans Matheson, *Clare Knowles* Rachael Stirling, *Annabel* Zoë Ball, Phil Daniels, Phil Davis, Frances Barber, Andy Nichol, Frances Magee, Donna Air, Kerry Shale, Danny Webb, Daisy Donovan.
● *Dir* Brian Gibson, *Pro* Amanda Marmot, *Ex Pro* Dick Clement and Ian La Frenais, *Line Pro* Steve Clark-Hall, *Screenplay* Clement and La Frenais, *Ph* Ashley Rowe, *Pro Des* Max Gottlieb, *Ed* Peter Boyle, *M* Clive Langer; songs performed by Jimmy Nail, Bill Nighy, Bernie Marsden, Billy Connolly, and Hans Matheson, *Costumes* Caroline Harris.

Columbia Pictures/The Greenlight Fund/Marmot Tandy/ National Lottery/Arts Council of England – Columbia TriStar.
95 mins. USA/UK. 1998. Rel: 30 October 1998. Cert 15.

Swing ★★¹/₂

Swing music is back in fashion, isn't it? Real-life singer Lisa Stansfield lends her golden tones to this predictable musical/comedy/romance set in Liverpool. The man she loved (Hugo Speer) got put in the slammer so she went and married the anal cop what did him. But when he gets out, he's a man with a horn – saxophone, that is. In a spicy backing role, Alexei Sayle plays the Irish equivalent of a Blues Brother, as the hard man who doesn't like Speer but plays with him nevertheless. Soft-hearts will love this feel-good musical romp. Others, er, won't.
[Karen Krizanovich]

● *Martin Luxford* Hugo Speer, *Joan Woodcock* Lisa Stansfield, *Sid Luxford* Tom Bell, *Andy* Danny McCall, *Mighty Mac* Alexei Sayle, *Mags Luxford* Rita Tushingham, *Liam Luxford* Paul Usher, *Maria* Nerys Hughues, *Jack* Clarence Clemons, *Buddy* Scott Williams, Dermot Kierney, Tom Georgeson, James Hicks, Jon Huyton, Del Henney, Simon Selmon.
● *Dir* and *Screenplay* Nick Mead, *Pro* Su Lim and Louise Rosner, *Ex Pro* Robert L. Levy, Peter Abrams, J.P. Guerin, Peter Locke and Donald Kushner, *Ph* Ian Wilson, *Pro Des* Richard Bridgland, *Ed* Norman Buckley, *M* Ian Devaney; songs performed by Lisa Stansfield, Louis Prima, Georgie Fame, etc, *Costumes* Stephanie Collie, *Choreography* Simon Selmon.

Tapestry Films/Kushner – Locke – Entertainment.
97 mins. UK. 1998. Rel: 7 May 1999. Cert 15.

Tea With Mussolini ★★¹/₂

Florence, Italy; 1934-1945. To the expatriate Englishwomen who made up the social circle known as the 'Scorpioni' – so named for their mordant wit and critical eye – Mussolini was the nice gentleman who made the trains run on time. To young Luca, the illegitimate son of a local cloth merchant, the 'Scorpioni' were the women who opened his eyes to the wonders of art and Shakespeare. For a time, it was in Mussolini's interest to curry favour with the influential eccentrics from England, but the dark shadow of Fascism was about to change all that ... Loosely based on the childhood of its director Franco Zeffirelli, *Tea With Mussolini* is enriched by scintillating dialogue ('there are no illegitimate children in the world, only illegitimate parents') and a raft of dependable performances. Yet Zeffirelli's cloying insistence on underlining every emotional motif and a general heaviness of tone dampens the wit of a marvellous opportunity. Roberto Benigni covered similar territory in *Life is Beautiful* – the encroachment of Fascism on pre-war Italy, illuminated by unexpected comedy – with far greater style and effortlessness.

● *Elsa Morgenthall* Cher, *Arabella Delancey* Judi Dench, *Mary Wallace* Joan Plowright, *Lady Hester Random* Maggie Smith, *Georgina 'Georgie' Rockwell* Lily Tomlin, *Luca Innocenti, as a teenager* Baird Wallace, *Luca, as a child* Charlie Lucas, *Paolo* Massimo Ghini, *Vittorio* Paolo Seganti, *Connie* Tessa Pritchard, *Witham* Michael Williams, *Benito Mussolini* Claudio Spadaro, Paul Checquer, Mino Bellei, Pino Colizzi, Claudia Piccoli, Helen Stirling, Clarissa Fonda, Chris Larkin.

● *Dir* Franco Zeffirelli, *Pro* Riccardo Tozzi, Giovannella Zannoni and Clive Parsons, *Screenplay* Zeffirelli and John Mortimer, *Ph* David Watkin, *Pro Des* Carlo Centolavigna and Gioia Fiorella Mariani, *Ed* Tariq Anwar, *M* Alessio Vlad and Stefano Arnaldi; 'Smoke Gets In Your Eyes' sung by Cher, *Costumes* Jenny Beavan, Albertto Spiazzi and Anna Anni.

Medusa Film/Cattleya/Cineritmo/Film and General Prods – UIP.
116 mins. Italy/UK. 1998. Rel: 2 April 1999. Cert PG.

There's Something About Mary
★★★★★

Rhode Island/Miami; 1985-98. There's something about Mary that makes guys lie to her face just to impress her. But Mary values truth over money and success and is devoted to the elderly, the disabled and the mentally disadvantaged. Ted Stroehmann has been obsessed by Mary for 13 years – even though he hasn't seen her since their disastrous first date for the high school prom when he got his privates caught in his zipper. Now he's determined to find her again and so hires sleazy private investigator Pat Healy to track down her whereabouts. Healy not only finds her, but instantly falls in lust ... Farce is the hardest comedy to pull off, yet the writing-directing duo of Peter and Bobby Farrelly – the brothers responsible for making Hollywood a *Dumb and Dumber* place – have achieved the near-impossible with knobs on. Drawing their humour from character, unexpected plot turns and dialogue (and even some droll interactive songs), the Farrellys makes sure their film doesn't miss a single comic opportunity. Cameron Diaz is divine, Matt Dillon is a revelation (in his first out-and-out comic performance) and the tone is unapologetically juvenile (you'll never look at hair gel in the same light again). Where *Dumb & Dumber* will be remembered for the scene that elevated diarrhoea to a new comic low, *There's Something About Mary* presents a number of classic sequences – although Matt Dillon attempting to resuscitate Puffy (Lin Shaye's cannily discerning bearded collie) may be the most memorable of all.

● *Mary Jenson* Cameron Diaz, *Pat Healy* Matt Dillon, *Ted Stroehmann* Ben Stiller, *Tucker* Lee Evans, *Dom* Chris Elliott, *Magda* Lin Shaye, *Warren Jenson* W. Earl Brown, *Brett* Brett Favre, *Bob* Willie Garson, Jeffrey Tambor, Markie Post, Keith David, Sarah Silverman, Khandi Alexander, Marnie Alexenburg, Richard M. Tyson, Rob Moran, Hillary Matthews, David Goryl, Warren Tashjian, The Artist Formerly Known as Docky, Marianne Farrelly, Jonathan Richman, Tommy Larkins, James Gifford, Tracy Anne George, Jesse Farrelly, Anna Farrelly, Nancy Farrelly, Michael Murphy.
● *Dir* and *Ex Pro* Peter and Bobby Farrelly, *Pro* Frank Beddor, Michael Steinberg, Charles B. Wessler

Left: Mary had a little fan: Matt Dillon dog-sits (and burns, beats, etc) in Peter and Bobby Farrelly's outrageous and helplessly funny There's Something About Mary *(from Fox)*

Right: Stolen dreams: Misha Philipchuk in Pavel Chukhrai's rich and evocative The Thief (from Artificial Eye)

and Bradley Thomas, *Co-Pro* Marc C. Fischer and James B. Rogers, *Screenplay* Ed Decter, John J. Strauss, Peter and Bobby Farrelly, *Ph* Mark Irwin, *Ed* Christopher Greenbury, *M* Jonathan Richman; Mozart, Bizet; songs performed by Jonathan Richman, Ben Lee, Sally Stevens, The Push Stars, The Dandy Warhols, Zuba, John Cafferty, Ray Conniff, Joe Jackson, Tom Wolfe, The Lemonheads, Acker Bilk, Propellerheads, Lloyd Cole, The Foundations, Billy Goodrum, etc, *Costumes* Mary Zophres, *Visual consultant* Sidney J. Bartholomew Jr.

Fox/Farrelly Brothers – Fox.
118 mins. USA. 1998. Rel: 25 September 1998. Cert 15.

The Thief – Vor ★★★★

Born by the side of a dirt road in the unrelenting Russian tundra, young Sanya never knew his father. When, six years later, his mother befriends a dashing soldier on a train, Sanya is choked by mixed feelings. The soldier, who turns out to be nothing more than an inveterate thief, treats Sanya and his mother harshly, but he provides for them and supplies a figure of authority for the little boy. Gradually, almost against his will, Sanya finds himself beginning to depend on the stern imposter, much as his compatriots have learned to abide the austere regime of Stalin ... A characteristically grim tale of physical hardship and emotional numbness from Russia, *The Thief* is nonetheless a remarkable piece of film-making. Evocatively lit and richly scored, it is convincingly performed by the three main protagonists and paints a vivid portrait of the post-war, Stalinist Soviet

Union. Russian cinema may be but a shadow of its former self, but it still has immense talent to burn.

● *Tolyan* Vladimir Mashkov, *Katya* Ekaterina Rednikova, *Sanya, aged six* Misha Philipchuk, *Sanya, aged 12* Dima Chigarev, Amaliia Mordvinova, Lidiia Savchenko, Galina Petrova.
● *Dir* and *Screenplay* Pavel Chukhrai, *Pro* Igor Tolstunov, *Ex Pro* Sergei Kozlov, *Ph* Vladimir Klimov, *Pro Des* Victor Petrov, *Ed* Marina Dobryanskaya and Natalia Kucherenko, *M* Vladimir Dashkevich, *Costumes* Natalia Moneva.

NTV – Profit/Productions Le Pont/Roissy Films – Artificial Eye.
97 mins. Russia/France. 1997. Rel: 17 July 1998. Cert 15.

The Thin Red Line ★★★¹/₂

At the tail end of 1942 an American infantry unit lands in Guadalcanal – in the South Pacific's Solomon Islands – to seize the strategically vital site from the Japanese. Faced by a lethal and invisible enemy, the men of Charlie Company find that any hope of their physical and spiritual survival rests in their own sense of family ... It is unfortunate that, not having made a film since the stunningly realised *Days of Heaven* 20 years ago, Terrence Malick should choose to make his next venture a war film in the same year that *Saving Private Ryan* is released. By comparison, *The Thin Red Line*, for all its accomplishments, is slack and laboured cinema, lacking irony, a cohesive story and sheer visceral excitement. However, had Malick not been behind the cam-

era and had the subject not been the Second World War, expectations would have been markedly different. For here are some beautifully measured performances, plenty of ideas to chew on and the director's customary eye for a great shot. The downside is that the all-star cast is a distraction and the three-hour running time something of a trial on the patience. Filmed in the Daintree rainforest in Queensland, Australia. FYI: James Jones' 1962 novel, on which the movie is based, was previously filmed in 1964.

● *1st Sgt. Edward Welsh* Sean Penn, *Corporal Fife* Adrien Brody, *Pvt. Witt* Jim Caviezel, *Pvt. Bell* Ben Chaplin, *Captain Charles Bosche* George Clooney, *Captain John Gaff* John Cusack, *Sgt. Keck* Woody Harrelson, *Captain James 'Bugger' Staros* Elias Koteas, *Lt. Colonel Gordon Tall* Nick Nolte, *Sgt. Storm* John C. Reilly, *Pvt. 1cl. Doll* Dash Mihok, *Sgt. McCron* John Savage, *Brig. Gen. Quintard* John Travolta, *Pvt. 1cl. Dale* Arie Verveen, Penny Allen, Mark Boone Junior, Paul Gleeson, Don Harvey, Thomas Jane, Jared Leto, Miranda Otto, Larry Romano, Stephen Spacek, Nick Stahl, Steven Vidler.
● *Dir* and *Screenplay* Terrence Malick, *Pro* Robert Michael Geisler, John Roberdeau and Grant Hill, *Ex Pro* George Stevens Jr, *Ph* John Toll, *Pro Des* Jack Fisk, *Ed* Billy Weber, Leslie Jones and Saar Klein, *M* Hans Zimmer; Arvo Part, Gabriel Faure, etc, *Costumes* Margot Wilson.

Fox 2000/Phoenix Pictures – Fox.
170 mins. USA. 1998. Rel: 26 February 1999. Cert 15.

This Year's Love ★★½

Camden Town, London NW5; today. Thirty-five minutes into his wedding with Hannah, Glaswegian tattoo artist Danny finds out that his wife was unfaithful to him but a few weeks ago. Thus, over the next two years or so, Danny and Hannah and a cluster of locals find their paths and romantic destinies constantly intersecting ... There is much to commend this ensemble dramatic comedy, but due to a certain lack of structural discipline and the predictable curve of its dramatic trajectory, the film just doesn't gel. However, Kathy Burke is terrific ('I'm a bit of a sucker for sad bastards') and her up-and-coming co-stars all provide surprisingly rich characterisations, bringing their one-liners and one-on-one sketches to considerable life. Otherwise, with its trendy kitchen sink *milieu* and its endless musical montages it comes off like Mike Leigh re-packaged by K-Tel.

● *Marey* Kathy Burke, *Sophie Woods* Jennifer Ehle, *Liam* Ian Hart, *Danny* Douglas Henshall, *Hannah* Catherine McCormack, *Cameron* Dougray Scott, *Alice* Emily Woof, *Denise* Sophie Okonedo, *Carol* Bronagh Gallagher, *James Woods* Nicholas Jones, *Billie* Jamie Foreman, *Annabel Woods* Angela

Above: Poetry in action: Ben Chaplin and Woody Harrelson cower from the enemy in Terrence Malick's pensive and picturesque The Thin Red Line (from Fox)

Douglas, Annabelle Apsion, Gregg Prentice, Paul Blair, Matt Costello, Sacha Craise, Alastair Galbraith, Andy Gray, Elaine Lourdan, Eddie Marsan, Billy McElhaney.
● *Dir* and *Screenplay* David Kane, *Pro* Michele Camarda, *Ex Pro* Nigel Green, *Ph* Robert Alazraki, *Pro Des* Sarah Greenwood, *Ed* Sean Barton, *M* Simon Boswell; songs performed by Ocean Colour Scene, Finlay Quaye, Morcheeba, Mercury Rev, Buffy Sainte-Marie, Garbage, Labelle, Al Green, Stereophonics, Marc Bolan, Mandalay, etc, *Costumes* Jill Taylor, *Sound* Kevin Brazier and Stephen Griffiths, *Tattoo consultancy* Sacred Art.

Kismet Film Prods/Scottish Arts Council/National Lottery – Entertainment.
108 mins. UK. 1998. Rel: 19 February 1999. Cert 18.

Thursday ★★★¹/₂

Houston, Texas; today. Architect Casey Wells happens to be proud of his suburban life, spotless kitchen and range of meat substitutes. His wife may think he's becoming Fred MacMurray, but she doesn't know about his past. Then, one Thursday, his past comes to pay him a visit ... The nice thing about first films is that all of a writer-director's ideas are packed into one movie – and it often proves to be a hard act to follow. Here, Skip Woods' modish comic thriller recalls the economic, pictorially precise style of Steven Soderbergh (with an inevitable nod to Tarantino) and is as succinct as it is surprising. Woods – whose own past seems as mysterious as his leading protagonist's – certainly knows how to set up a scene and he writes tough, uncompromising dialogue. And the sequence in which Paulina Porizkova mounts Thomas Jane

Right: Shotgun honeymoon? Paulina Porizkova demands some favours from Thomas Jane in Skip Woods' economic, uncompromising Thursday (from PolyGram)

against his will is something of an erotic milestone.
● *Casey Wells* Thomas Jane, *Nick* Aaron Eckhart, *Dallas* Paulina Porizkova, *Billy* James Le Gros, *Christine Wells* Paula Marshall, *Mr Jarvis* Michael Jeter, *Rasta* Glenn Plummer, *Kasarov* Mickey Rourke, *Ballpeen* aka *Lester James* Gary Dourdan, *coffee cashier* Luck Hari, Bari K. Willerford, Shawn Michael Howard.
● *Dir* and *Screenplay* Skip Woods, *Pro* Alan Poul, *Ex Pro* Tim Clawson, *Co-Pro* Woods and Christine Sheaks, *Line Pro* W. Mark McNair, *Ph* Denis Lenoir, *Pro Des* Chris Anthony Miller, *Ed* Paul Trejo and Peter Schink, *M* Luna; songs performed by Unitone Hifi, and Glenn Plummer, *Costumes* Mark Bridges, *Sound* Frank Serafine.

PolyGram/Propaganda Films – PolyGram.
87 mins. USA. 1998. Rel: 25 September 1998. Cert 18.

Titanic Town ★★★

It is 1972 and Aidan and Bernie McPhelimy and their four children have just moved to the quiet residential estate of Anderstown, West Belfast. 'We thought we'd left The Troubles behind us,' says Annie McPhelimy, the eldest daughter. 'What we didn't know was that they were just beginning' ... Loosely adapted from the autobiographical novel by Mary Costello (who based the main character on her mother), *Titanic Town* rakes over old ground with a fresh plough. How the film succeeds to shock anew is that a) it brings the war to the manicured lawns of the suburbs (as opposed to the all too familiar battle-scarred streets of the inner city), and b) it uses comedy as a dramatic contrast to the horrors. However, after a very promising start the drama gets bogged down with social politics and one family squabble too many. Still, *Titanic Town* is memorable for showing the IRA as we've never seen them before – and the acting is first-rate.

● *Bernie McPhelimy* Julie Walters, *Aidan McPhelimy* Ciaran Hinds, *Annie McPhelimy* Nuala O'Neill, *Dino/Owen* Ciaran McMenamin, *Patsy French* Jaz Pollock, *Tony* Lorcan Cranitch, *Thomas McPhelimy* James Loughran, *Brendan McPhelimy* Barry Loughran, *Sinead McPhelimy* Elizabeth Donaghy, *Deirdre* Aingeal Grehan, *George Whittington* Oliver Ford Davies, *Nora* Doreen Hepburn, Caolan Byrne, Nicholas Woodeson, Des McAleer, Ruth McCabe, Veronica Duffy, Paula Hamilton, Jeananne Crowley, Tony Rohr, Tony Devlin, Catriona Hinds, Chris Parr, and *uncredited* Fiona Shaw.
● *Dir* Roger Michell, *Pro* George Faber and Charlie Pattinson, *Ex Pro* David Thompson, Robert Cooper and Rainer Mockert, *Screenplay* Anne Devlin, *Ph* John Daly, *Pro Des* Pat Campbell, *Ed* Kate Evans, *M* Trevor Jones; most songs performed by John Martyn, *Costumes* Hazel Pethig.

BBC Films/Hollywood Partners/Pandora Cinema/Arts Council of Northern Ireland/National Lottery/British Screen/Company Pictures – Alliance.
101 mins. UK/Germany/France. 1998. Rel: 26 February 1999. Cert 15.

To Have and To Hold ★ ¹/₂

Papua New Guinea; now. An expatriate Frenchman and dealer in illegal video reproduction, Jack has never got over the mysterious death of his wife. In Melbourne to purchase some new Van Damme and Chow Yun-Fat titles, he meets the romantic novelist Kate Henley. Intrigued by Jack's Gallic exoticism, Kate agrees to follow him back to his jungle retreat and share his tropical paradise. More fool her ... Both Tcheky Karyo (*Nostradamus*, *Bad Boys*) and Rachel Griffiths (*Muriel's Wedding*, *Divorcing Jack*) are very fine actors and the setting of the Papua New Guinea rainforest potentially enthralling. Unfortunately, not only is the film visually pedestrian but there is absolutely no chemistry between the stars. Besides, how can you sympathise with a woman who abandons her entire life after meeting an unshaven, greasy-haired foreigner for three minutes? The word we're looking for is 'risible'.

● *Jack* Tcheky Karyo, *Kate Henley* Rachel Griffiths, *Sal* Steve Jacobs, *Rose* Anni Finsterer, *Stevie* David Field, *Luther Yamu* Robert Kunsa, *James* Larry Laval, John Parinjo, Ura Eri, Mona Buie.
● *Dir* John Hillcoat, *Pro* Denise Patience, *Assoc Pro* Richard Hudson, *Line Pro* Sally Ayre-Smith, *Screenplay* Gene Conkie, *Ph* Andrew De Groot, *Pro Des* Chris Kennedy, *Ed* Stewart Young, *M* Nick Cave, Blixa Bargeld and Mick Harvey, *Costumes* Ross Wallace, *Sound* Dean Gawen.

Australian Film Finance Corporation/Small Man Prods/Calypso Films – Metro Tartan.
99 mins. Australia. 1996. Rel: 7 August 1998. Cert 18.

Topless Women Talk About Their Lives ★★ ¹/₂

Compulsive home movie-maker Harry Sinclair was so enamoured of the above title that he built his first feature around it. Writing on the run, he cast his friends in roles they'd already played in his shorts and then filmed the whole thing on weekends over a six-month period. Sinclair was above all determined to create a naturalistic portrait of twentysomething life in contemporary Auckland so integrated the genuine pregnancy of his leading lady into the plot. The result is a loose, fresh and sometimes inspired comedy of New Zealand manners (if there is such a thing) which just leaps off the screen. Ironically – or perhaps understandably – the least successful aspect of Sinclair's experiment is the eponymous film-within-the-film. P.S. The scene of Liz's labour (filmed shortly before the

actress's own) is one of the most realistic – and outrageous – depictions of childbirth ever captured on film.

● *Liz* Danielle Cormack, *Anthony 'Ant' Bainbridge* Ian Hughes, *Neil* Joel Tobeck, *Prue* Willa O'Neill, *Mike* Shimpal Lelisi, *Geoff* Andrew Binns, *Bryony* Josephine Davison, Stephen Lovatt, Oliver Driver, Peter Elliott, Tania Simon, Ian Mune, Frances Edmond.
● *Dir* and *Screenplay* Harry Sinclair, *Pro* Sinclair and Fiona Copland, *Ph* Dale McCready, *Ed* Cushla Dillon, *M* Flying Nun Records catalogue, including tracks by 3DS, The Clean, King Loser, etc, *Costumes* whatever the actors turned up in, *Sound* Chris Burt.

John Swimmer Ltd/New Zealand Film Commission/New Zealand On Air – NFT.
89 mins. New Zealand. 1996. Rel: 9 October 1998. No cert.

Touch ★★★

A former monk from an Amazonian monastery, Juvenal – aka Charles Lawson – now councils alcoholics at the Sacred Heart Rehabilitation Center in Los Angeles. Periodically, he also heals people. Then, when he restores the eyesight of a blind friend, his 'miracle' reaches the attention of conman Bill Hill, Catholic activist August Murray, newspaper reporter Kathy Worthington ... The carnival is ready to roll ... Fulfilling his mandate not to repeat himself, Paul Schrader ploughs his old themes of religious identity and spiritual redemption into light satire, adapted from the quirky and rakish novel by Elmore Leonard. However, satire of media manipulation and trivialisation is merely repeating the work of countless others, regardless of the curveballs you throw at it. Nonetheless, while treading uneasily between black comedy and full-out farce, *Touch* is constantly engaging, blessed by some tart dialogue and a charismatically serene performance from Skeet Ulrich as the pragmatic stigmatic.

● *Lynn Faulkner* Bridget Fonda, *Bill Hill* Christopher Walken, *Juvenal,* aka *Charles Lawson* Skeet Ulrich, *August Murray* Tom Arnold, *Debra Lusanne* Gina Gershon, *Antoinette Baker* Lolita Davidovich, *Artie* Paul Mazursky, *Kathy Worthington* Janeane Garofalo, *Elwin Worrel* John Doe, *Virginia Worrel* Conchata Ferrell, *Father Nestor* Mason Adams, *himself* LL Cool J, Breckin Meyer, Anthony Zerbe, Maria Celedonio, Richard Fancy, Tamlyn Tomita, Don Novello, Richard Schiff, O-Lan Jones, Brent Hinkley, Julie Condra, Kate Williamson, Dennis Burkley.
● *Dir* and *Screenplay* Paul Schrader, *Pro* Lila Cazes and Fida Attieh, *Co-Pro* Llewellyn Wells, *Ph* Ed Lachman, *Pro Des* David Wasco, *Ed* Cara Silverman, *M* David Grohl, *Costumes* Julie Weiss.

Initial Prods/Lumiere International – Pathe.
97 mins. USA/France. 1996. Rel: 10 July 1998. Cert 15.

Right: Scandal sheeter: James Woods ditches the dirt in Clint Eastwood's gritty and entertaining True Crime (from Warner)

True Crime ★★★★

In his prime, Steve Everett – newshound, womaniser and family man – brought down the mayor of New York City. Now he's scraping together a living at *The Oakland Tribune* writing human interest sidebars. Then, after a colleague is killed in a car crash, he's asked to follow through her story on Frank Beechum, a man convicted of killing a 23-year-old pregnant woman. With all appeals fallen through, Beechum is to face execution by lethal injection eight hours after Everett's interview. Then Everett gets a 'hunch' ... There's nothing like a colourful, rakish, flawed, complex and unrepentant character to carry a movie. Add a cracking good story, expert craftsmanship, some flavoursome dialogue and an incendiary social issue and you have some first-rate entertainment. *True Crime*, marking Clint Eastwood's 21st time behind

the camera, gamely goes after its cake and gets to swallow it whole. There's tension, laughs, social commentary and even a few tears, particularly in the scene between Everett and his long-suffering wife, superbly played by Diane Venora. But then everybody's pretty good (isn't James Woods always?) with a gold star going to Isaiah Washington as the noble Death Row inmate. And while Eastwood the actor continues to flourish, pensioners everywhere can rejoice.

● *Steve Everett* Clint Eastwood, *Frank Lewis Beechum* Isaiah Washington, *Bob Findley* Denis Leary, *Bonnie Beechum* Lisa Gay Hamilton, *Barbara Everett* Diane Venora, *Warden Luther Plunkitt* Bernard Hill, *Alan Mann* James Woods, *Reverend Shillerman* Michael McKean, *Dale Porterhouse* Michael Jeter, *Michelle Ziegler* Mary McCormack,

Angela Russel Hattie Winston, *Kate Everett* Francesca Fisher-Eastwood, *Patricia Findley* Laila Robins, *Cecilia Nussbaum* Frances Fisher, *Amy Wilson* Marissa Ribisi, *Bridget Rossiter* Christine Ebersole, *Tom Donaldson* Tom McGowan, Penny Bae Bridges, John Finn, Sydney Poitier, Erik King, Graham Beckel, Anthony Zerbe, Nancy Giles, William Windom, Don West, Lucy Alexis Liu, Dina Eastwood, Nicolas Bearde, Frances Lee McCain, Jack Kehler.
● *Dir* Clint Eastwood, *Pro* Eastwood, Richard D. Zanuck and Lili Fini Zanuck, *Ex Pro* Tom Rooker, *Screenplay* Larry Gross, Paul Brickman and Stephen Schiff, from the novel by Andrew Klavan, *Ph* Jack N. Green, *Pro Des* Henry Bumstead, *Ed* Joel Cox, *M* Lennie Niehaus; songs performed by Kenny Burrell, and Diana Krall.

Warner/Zanuck Company/Malpaso Prods – Warner.
127 mins. USA. 1999. Rel: 14 May 1999. Cert 15.

The Truman Show ★★★★

Seahaven Island; day 10,909. His life is the biggest TV soap opera in the world and he doesn't even know it. Literally born on camera, Truman Burbank has grown up on the world's largest sound stage and is constantly monitored by over 5,000 hidden cameras. As he sleeps, jokes and falls in love, a global audience stays tuned, watching 'real' life as never before. For Truman, it's the only reality he can identify with, so how should he know that his wife and best friend are just acting? With its original premise and polished execution, *The Truman Show* is so good that one feels it should have been even better. A number of inviting possibilities are thrown away and Truman's true confusion is never convincingly explored. Jim Carrey is very entertaining as the world's most famous Everyman, but you never believe him for a minute. Still, this is enormous fun and the last ten minutes feature some of the most exhilarating cinema seen in years. FYI: Carrey was so desperate to play Truman that he took a salary of $12 million, $8m less than his usual $20m.

● *Truman Burbank* Jim Carrey, *Meryl Burbank* Laura Linney, *Marlon* Noah Emmerich, *Lauren/Sylvia* Natascha McElhone, *Mrs Burbank* Holland Taylor, *Christof* Ed Harris, Paul Giametti, Adam Tommei, Harry Shearer, Brian Delate, Peter Krause, Heidi Schanz, Ron Taylor, Don Taylor, Judson Vaughn, Marcia DeBonis, Tony Todd, Una Damon, Philip Baker Hall, Philip Glass, O-Lan Jones, Krista Lynn Landolfi, *man in bath* Terry Camilleri.
● *Dir* Peter Weir, *Pro* Scott Rudin, Andrew Niccol, Edward S. Feldman and Adam Schroeder, *Ex Pro* Lynn Pleshette, *Screenplay*

Niccol, *Ph* Peter Biziou, *Pro Des* Dennis Gassner, *Ed* William Anderson, *M* Burkhard Dallwitz; Philip Glass (including his theme from *Mishima*); Mozart, Chopin, Brahms, David Hirschfelder, Wojcieh Kilar, *Costumes* Marilyn Matthews.

Paramount – UIP.
103 mins. USA. 1998. Rel: 9 October 1998. Cert PG.

Twilight ★★¹/₂

Los Angeles; the present. After 20 years on the force and five years in private investigation, reformed alcoholic Harry Ross has ended up as an odd job man for waning movie star Jack Ames. In exchange for free board, Ross carries out menial duties for his ailing friend and one day is asked to make a suspect delivery. After the simple mission backfires, Ross becomes a murder suspect; he pulls on his old investigative shoes and finds that the mire runs deep ... Strong on atmosphere and the wry sort of dialogue you only find in private eye thrillers, *Twilight* is the cinematic equivalent of a smooth malt matured in the wood. Paul Newman, while playing a cop well past his sell-by date, is still the sexiest 73-year-old around and brings a dry sparkle to his performance that should shame the cast of *Cocoon*. Notwithstanding, from the director of *Nobody's Fool* and *Kramer Vs Kramer* – and a star like Newman – this is slight work. Formerly known as *The Magic Hour*.

● *Harry Ross* Paul Newman, *Catherine Ames* Susan Sarandon, *Jack Ames* Gene Hackman, *Verna* Stockard Channing, *Mel Ames* Reese Witherspoon, *Reuben* Giancarlo Esposito, *Raymond Hope* James Garner, *Jeff Willis* Liev Schreiber, *Gloria Lamar* Margo Martindale, *Captain Phil Egan* John Spencer, *Lester Ivar* M. Emmet Walsh, Peter Gregory, Lewis Arquette, Clint Howard, Jeff Joy.
● *Dir* Robert Benton, *Pro* Arlene Donovan and Scott Rudin, *Ex Pro* Michael Hausman, *Screenplay* Benton and Richard Russo, *Ph* Piotr Sobocinski, *Pro Des* David Gropman, *Ed* Carol Littleton, *M* Elmer Bernstein; 'Blues Stay Away From Me' performed by The Notting Hillbillies, *Costumes* Jospeh G. Aulisi.

Paramount/Cinehaus – UIP.
94 mins. USA. 1998. Rel: 4 December 1998. Cert 15.

Twin Dragons – Shuanglong Hui ★¹/₂

Hong Kong; the present. A world famous conductor-cum-pianist and a rough-and-ready car mechanic with a mean kick discover that they are identical twins separated at birth. But how can their girlfriends and the pursuing Mafia tell them apart? Absurd, silly and logic-defying, *Twin Dragons* is minor fare even by Jackie Chan standards. The dubbing is risible, the story confusing and the premise itself ludicrous (not to mention scientifically impossible). However, there's enough comic buffoonery and ferocious choreography to keep the young of brain distracted. P.S. This is not to be confused with that classic pair of Jean-Claude Van Damme 'twin' movies *Double Impact* and *Maximum Risk*. FYI: With the exception of Maggie Cheung and Nini Li Chi, every actor in *Twin Dragons* is a film director!

● *Boomer/John Ma* Jackie Chan, *Barbara* Maggie Cheung, *Tyson* Teddy Robin, *John and Boomer's mother* Sylvia Chang, *car mechanic* Ringo Lam, *Tammy* Nina Li Chi, *Rocky* Jamie Luk, Philip Chan, Alfred Cheung, Jacob Cheung, Cheung Tung Jo, John Woo *priest*, Tsui Hark, James Wong, Kirk Wong.
● *Dir* Tsui Hark and Ringo Lam, *Pro* Teddy Robin, *Ex Pro* Ng Sze Yeun, *Screenplay* Tsui, Barry Wong, Cheung Tung Jo and Wong Yik, *Ph* Wong Wing Hang and Wong Ngor Tai, *Pro Des* Lun Chon-Hung and Lam Chun Fai, *Ed* Mak Che Sin, *M* Phe Loung, *Costumes* Chong Che Leung.

Dimension Films/Distant Horizon/Media Asia/Hong Kong Film Director's Guild/Miramax – Buena Vista.
89 mins. Hong Kong. 1991. Rel: 14 May 1999. Cert 12.

Two Girls and a Guy ★★★

Two girls waiting outside a Manhattan apartment building get talking and discover that they share the same boyfriend. Incensed by this turn of events, they break into the guy's flat and await his arrival ... A one-location three-hander, *Two Girls and a Guy* feels like a play yet is dramatically intense enough to overcome any sense of stasis usually associated with theatrical adaptations. In fact, the claustrophobia of the piece is perfectly in keeping with the trapped emotions of the three protagonists. And, as the routed bigamist, Robert Downey Jr is on terrific form, running the gamut of emotions from swaggering swain to snivelling wretch. He even gets to sing opera and recite *Hamlet*. FYI: Notch this up as the first mainstream film to depict an act of anilingus.

● *Blake Allen* Robert Downey Jr, *Carla Bennett* Heather Graham, *Lou* Natasha Gregson Wagner, Angel David, Frederique Van Der Wal.
● *Dir* and *Screenplay* James Toback, *Pro* Edward R. Pressman and Chris Hanley, *Ex Pro* Michael Mailer and Daniel Bigel, *Line Pro* Gretchen McGowan, *Ph* Barry Markowitz, *Pro Des* Kevin Thompson, *Ed* Alan Oxman, *M* Barry Cole; Vivaldi, Brahms; songs performed by Jackie Wilson, Dubcheck, and Robert Downey Jr, *Costumes* Renata Chaplynsky.

Fox Searchlight/Muse Prods – Fox.
84 mins. USA. 1997. Rel: 29 January 1999. Cert 15.

U

V

Left: Mythical madness: Natasha Gregson Wagner in Jamie Blanks' predictable and formulaic Urban Legend *(from Columbia TriStar)*

Urban Legend ★

According to Professor William Wexler, urban legend is contemporary folklore passed on as fact. You know the type: the Bill Gates e-mail promising a $1,000 reward, the burglars' photograph of the misappropriated toothbrushes, the gerbil and Richard Gere ... But at Pendleton University in Melbourne, New Hampshire, somebody is acting out somewhat more deadly versions of contemporary mythology ... Adopting the premise of *Copycat* and dropping it into the *milieu* of *Scream*, this slick, humourless and nasty thriller wins no points for originality. Besides the irritation of having to believe in twentysomething students, there are a minimum of six – count 'em – *six* false alarms in which characters accidentally bump into each other. How scary. Probably the most predictable, formulaic and unashamedly derivative 'lets-slash-and-dice a student' thriller ever made.

● *Paul* Jared Leto, *Natalie* Alicia Witt, *Brenda* Rebecca Gayheart, *Damon Brooks* Joshua Jackson, *Michelle Mancini* Natasha Gregson Wagner, *Reese* Loretta Devine, *Sasha* Tara Reid, *Parker* Michael Rosenbaum, *Tosh* Danielle Harris, *Dean Adams* John Neville, *Professor William Wexler* Robert Englund, Julian Richings, Vince Corrazza, Stephanie Mills, Danny Comden, Nancy McAlear, and *uncredited*: *MacDonald, the garage attendant* Brad Dourif.
● *Dir* Jamie Blanks, *Pro* Neal H. Moritz, Gina Matthews and Michael McDonnell, *Ex Pro* Brad Luff, *Screenplay* Silvio Horta, *Ph* James Chressanthis, *Pro Des* Charles Breen, *Ed* Jay Cassidy, *M* Christopher Young; songs performed by Bonnie Tyler, Ruth Ruth, Rob Zombie, Stabbing Westward, Paula Cole, Monster Magnet, Cherry Poppin' Daddies, Crystal Method, etc, *Costumes* Mary Claire Hannan.

Phoenix Pictures – Columbia TriStar.
96 mins. USA. 1998. Rel: 26 February 1999. Cert 18.

Velvet Goldmine ★½

Dublin/London/New York; 1854-1984, but mainly the early Seventies. It was a time of androgyny, platform boots, glitter make-up and the pervading personae of Ziggy Stardust, Alice Copper and T-Rex. One of the more popular exponents of Glam Rock, (the fictional) Brian Slade shoots his career in the foot when he fakes his own assassination on stage. Ten years later, English reporter Arthur Stuart is asked to do a story on Slade and his sudden disappearance ... If nothing else, writer-director Todd Haynes (*Poison*, *Safe*) captures the narcissistic excess and vulgarity of his subject with chilling conviction. Indeed, both a visual and sonic banquet, the film wallows in the decadent nihilism of the early Seventies with an exhibitionism that is totally in character with its superficial, self-obsessed protagonist. That may be the point, but it doesn't make *Velvet Goldmine* any less of a self-indulgent, disjointed and ultimately tedious experience.

● *Curt Wild* Ewan McGregor, *Brian Slade* Jonathan Rhys Meyers, *Mandy Slade* Toni Collette, *Arthur Stuart* Christian Bale, *Jerry Devine* Eddie Izzard, *Shannon* Emily Woof, *Cecil* Michael Feast, *female narrator* Janet McTeer, *Tommy Stone* Alastair Cumming, Don Fellows, Ganiat Kasumu, Jim Whelan, Sylvia Grant, Lindsay Kemp, Sarah Cawood, David Hoyle, Peter Bradley Jr, Brian Molko, Anthony Langdon, Steve Hewitt, Donna Matthews.
● *Dir* and *Screenplay* Todd Haynes, *Pro* Christine Vachon, *Ex Pro* Scott Meek, Michael Stipe and Sandy Stern, *Co-Pro* Olivia Stewart, *Co-Ex Pro* Chris J. Ball and William Tyrer, *Ph* Maryse Alberti, *Pro Des* Christopher Hobbs, *Ed* James Lyons, *M* Carter Burwell; Mahler; songs performed by Brian Eno, Shudder To Think, Slade, Lindsay Kemp, Gary Glitter, Freda Payne, The Venus in Furs, T-Rex,

Above: Salon kitty:
Nathalie Baye dishes
out cosmetic advice
in Tonie Marshall's
wry and touching
Venus Beauty
(from Gala)

Pulp, Roxy Music, Teenage Fanclub, Lou Reed, The Wylde Rattz, Placebo, Steve Harley, etc, *Costumes* Sandy Powell, *Make-up and hair* Peter King.

Zenith Prods/Killer Films/Single Cell Pictures/Film Four/ Newmarket Capital/Goldwyn Films/Miramax – Film Four. 123 mins. UK/USA. 1998. Rel: 23 October 1998. Cert 18.

Venus Beauty – Venus, Beaute (Institut) ★★★

Paris; the present. Angele Piane is not your typical beautician. While dedicated to her clientele's well being and the promotion of skin repair serums (not to mention the odd seaweed wrap), she avoids cosmetics herself and is sceptical of romance. Emotionally scarred by love, Angele has become adept at picking up men for a quickie in a hotel room or the back of a Citroen. But when a complete stranger professes his undying love for her, she retreats a mile … A wry contemplation of the various facets of female amour, sexuality and self-image, *Venus Beauty* is an unusual, touching and frequently amusing diversion. As the withdrawn, prickly heroine, Nathalie Baye – best known for her portrayals of sunny and sensible women – is quite remarkable, bringing enormous melancholy and selflessness to a complex character.

● *Angele Piane* Nathalie Baye, *Nadine* Bulle Ogier, *Antoine Dumont* Samuel LeBihan, *Samantha* Mathilde Seigner, *Marie* Audrey Tautou, *Jacques* Jacques Bonnaffe, *M. Lachenay, the pilot* Robert Hossein, *Antoine's girlfriend* Helene Filieres, *Madames Buisse* Claire Nebout, *Aunt Maryse* Micheline Presle, *Aunt Lyda* Emmanuelle Riva, Edith Scob, Marie Riviere, Brigitte Rouan, Claire Denis, Gilbert Melki, Sophie Grimaldi, Florence Derive, Martine Audrain, Joel Brisse.
● *Dir* Tonie Marshall, *Pro* Gilles Sandoz, Isabelle Pailley and Emmanuelle Pinet, *Screenplay* Marshall, Marion Vernoux and Jacques Audiard, *Ph* Gerard De Battista, *Pro Des* Michel Vandestien, *Ed* Jacques Comets, *M* Khalil Chahine, *Costumes* Nathalie Duroscoat and Claire Gerard-Hirne, *Beauty advisor* Charlotte Gratiot.

Agat Films & Cie/Arte France Cinema/Tabo Tabo Films/ Canal Plus, etc – Gala.
107 mins. France. 1998. Rel: 18 June 1999. Cert 15.

Very Bad Things ★

With his fiancée obsessing about the details of their wedding in one week's time, hen-pecked office worker Kyle Fisher cannot wait for his stag party in Las Vegas.

But, holed up in a hotel room with his four best friends, Kyle sees his day of bliss threatened when a stripper is killed during a moment of unbridled passion. Yet this is only the prologue to his nightmare ... The key to a film striding the fine line between helpless hilarity and downright tastelessness is pitch. Unfortunately, first-time director Peter Berg, working from his own script, pitches his film beneath parody and beyond credibility. Had Cameron Diaz and Jon Favreau's troubled bride and groom exhibited an iota of chemistry (or empathy), then the film might have had a leg to stand on. As it is, *Very Bad Things* charges out of the starting gate with all guns blazing, trampling over plausibility and quickly reaching a point of hysteria that is both objectionable and unbearably strident. Of course, even a suggestion of wit (or logic) might have helped.

● *Robert Boyd* Christian Slater, *Laura Garrety* Cameron Diaz, *Adam Berkow* Daniel Stern, *Lois Berkow* Jeanne Tripplehorn, *Keith Fisher* Jon Favreau, *Michael Berkow* Jeremy Piven, *Charles Moore* Leland Orser, *Mr Fisher* Lawrence Pressman, *Tina* Carla Scott aka Kobe Tai, Joey Zimmerman, Tyler Malinger, Russell B. Mckenzie, Byrne Piven, Bob Bancroft.

● *Dir* and *Screenplay* Peter Berg, *Pro* Michael Schiffer, Diane Nabatoff and Cindy Cowen, *Ex Pro* Ted Field, Scott Kroopf, Michael Helfant and Christian Slater, *Line Pro* Laura Greenlee, *Ph* David Hennings, *Pro Des* Dina Lipton, *Ed* Dan Lebental, *M* Stewart Copeland; songs performed by Willy Bobo, Hoi Polloi, White Zombie, Death in Vegas, Robbie Fulks, Tina and the B-Side Movement, The Chemical Brothers, Limp Bizkit, etc, *Costumes* Terry Dresbach.

PolyGram/Initial Entertainment/Interscope/Ballpark Prods – PolyGram.
100 mins. USA. 1998. Rel: 29 January 1999. Cert 18.

Victory ★¹/₂
The Dutch East Indies; 1913. Resigned to a life of solitude on the tropical island of Samburan, failed businessman Axel Heyst makes a rare visit to the Javanese port of Surabaya. There, he befriends Alma, a violinist from an all-ladies' orchestra who is about to be sold to the gruff owner of a local hotel. Against his better judgement, Axel agrees to smuggle Alma away to the relative security of his own remote hideaway ...

Above: My best friend's stag party: Cameron Diaz proves that she's not infallible when it comes to choosing scripts, seen here in Peter Berg's unendurable Very Bad Things (from PolyGram)

Like many celluloid versions of vintage literature, there is a leaden reverence here that stifles the life out of Joseph Conrad's 1915 novel. Nothing is credible. Willem Dafoe, made up like Van Gogh, is mannered and boring; Irene Jacob is lovely, but seems to be lost in a trance; Rufus Sewell is unconvincing with his variation of a 'cheeky chappy'; and Sam Neill exhibits none of the real danger that his part demands. Furthermore, devotees of Conrad will be angered by the liberties writer-director Peploe has taken with the original story (particularly the conclusion). Notwithstanding, the production design is exemplary.

● *Axel Heyst* Willem Dafoe, *Alma* Irene Jacob, *Mr Jones* Sam Neill, *Martin Ricardo* Rufus Sewell, *Schomberg* Jean Yanne, *Wang* Ho Yi, *Pedro* Graziano Marcelli, *Captain Davidson* Bill Paterson, *Ziangiacomo* Simon Callow, *Mrs Schomberg* Irm Hermann, Hansi Jochmann, Michael Lee, Patrick Field, Jack Galloway.
● *Dir* and *Screenplay* Mark Peploe, *Pro* Simon Bosanquet, *Ex Pro* Jeremy Thomas, Yves Attal and Ingrid Windisch, *Co-Ex Pro* Harvey Weinstein and Bob Weinstein, *Assoc Pro* Chris Auty, *Ph* Bruno de Keyzer, *Pro Des* Luciana Arrighi, *Ed* Tony Lawson and Michael Bradsell, *M* Richard Hartley; Faure, *Costumes* Louise Stjernsward.

UGC Images/Recorded Picture Co/Extrafilm/British Screen/Canal Plus, etc – Feature Film Co.
99 mins. UK/France/Germany. 1995. Rel: 27 November 1998. Cert 15.

Vigo – Passion For Life ★★¹/₂

Suffering from tuberculosis, young Jean Vigo is consigned to a forbidding sanatorium in the Pyrenees. There he meets the morose Elizabeth 'Lydu' Lozinska, a young French girl with spinal tuberculosis who, with grave dignity, has become resigned to her fate. Then, gradually, Vigo's passion for living – and his dream to become a film-maker – draws Lydu into his life ... Of course, stories about impoverished, dying French artists are two a centime. Yet the short, inspired history of Jean Vigo – who lived long enough to make the seminal masterpiece *L'Atalante* (1934) – is indeed a jewel amongst all the Hollywood paste. It is a shame, then, that this good-looking Euro-pudding lacks both the lyricism and passion to bring any distinction to the Vigo legend.

● *Elizabeth 'Lydu' Lozinska* Romane Bohringer, *Jean Vigo* James Frain, *Bonaventure* Jim Carter, *Emily* Diana Quick, *Marcel* William Scott-Masson, *Oscar Levy* Lee Ross, *Boris Kaufman* Nicholas Hewetson, Brian Shelley, James Faulkner, Paola Dionisotti, Frank Lazarus, Francine Berge, Vernon Dobtcheff, David Battley, Charles Collingwood, Kenneth Cranham, Donald Gee, Brian Petifer, John Quentin,

Juno Temple.
● *Dir* Julien Temple, *Pro* Amanda Temple and Jeremy Bolt, *Ex Pro* Kiki Miyake, *Co-Pro* Antoine De Clermont-Tonnerre, Mariela Besuievsky and Ulrich Felsberg, *Screenplay* Julien Temple, Peter Ettedgui and Anne Devlin, from the play *Love's a Revolution* by Chris Ward, *Ph* John Mathieson, *Pro Des* Caroline Greville-Morris, *Ed* Marie Therese Boiche, *M* Bingen Mendizabal; Maurice Jaubert, *Costumes* Roger Burton.

Channel Four/Little Magic Films/Impact Pictures/Nitrate Film/Canal Plus, etc – Film Four.
103 mins. UK/Japan/France/Spain/Germany. 1997. Rel: 4 June 1999. Cert 15.

Virus ★¹/₂

A catchy title, to be sure, but it has little to do with this generic mish-mash of recycled ideas. The virus here, in fact, is mankind himself, a species considered a threat to an intergalactic electrical intelligence. The latter, after lighting up the Mir space station, links via satellite to a Russian research vessel in the South Pacific and starts to adopt the mechanical and biological components of the ship in order to establish itself on earth ... Based on the Dark Horse comic book series of the same name, *Virus* suffers from that familiar malignancy of comic book adaptations: that is, a lack of identifiable characters. Here, the usual culturally diverse suspects are rounded up (to lend politically conventional ballast): a Canadian, Russian, Maori, Cuban, black American and two feisty women (although, thankfully, the requisite British villain is absent). At any rate, they can do little to breathe life into the habitual scenario of a menacing life force picking off its human prey in an enclosed space. And the miniature model effects are ropey to say the least. Not good. FYI: The Maori actor Cliff Curtis was last seen in *Deep Rising*, the story of a large ship taken over by an alien life form.

● *Kelly Fisher* Jamie Lee Curtis, *Steve Baker* William Baldwin, *Captain Robert Everton* Donald Sutherland, *Nadia* Joanna Pacula, *J.W. Woods Jr* Marshall Bell, *Squeaky* Julio Oscar Mechoso, *Richie* Sherman Augustus, *Hiko* Cliff Curtis, Yuri Chervotkin, Keith Flippen, Olga Rzhepetskaya-Retchin, Levani.
● *Dir* John Bruno, *Pro* Gale Anne Hurd, *Ex Pro* Mike Richardson, Chuck Pfarrer, Gary Levinsohn and Mark Gordon, *Screenplay* Pfarrer and Dennis Feldman, *Ph* David Eggby, *Pro Des* Mayling Cheng, *Ed* Scott Smith, *M* Joel McNeely, *Costumes* Deborah Everton, *Robotic effects* Steve Johnson and Eric Allard.

Universal/Mutual Film Company/Dark Horse Entertainment/Valhalla Motion Pictures – UIP.
99 mins. USA. 1998. Rel: 4 June 1999. Cert 18.

Left: Drinking problems: Adam Sandler dispenses the aqua in Frank Coraci's moronic and heavy-handed The Waterboy (from Buena Vista)

Waking Ned ★★★¹⁄₂

Sixty-three countries around the globe are united by their passion for the lottery. And the small community of Tullymore in Ireland is no less enthusiastic in its subscription to the get-rich-quick tradition. When one of their own wins the jackpot, Jackie and Annie O'Shea take it upon themselves to wheedle out the mysterious victor. In a village of 52 inhabitants, can the winner keep his secret for long? Book-ended by a priceless opening and climax, *Waking Ned* makes up for its relative slimness of plot with buckets of charm, sparkling performances and some eye-caressing photography of the Isle of Man (doubling for Ireland). Ian Bannen, seen commandeering a motorbike in his underpants, is a particular revelation. FYI: Fans of the BBC's *Ballykissangel* will find the film particularly appealing, as not only does it feature James Nesbitt from the series, it displays the same eccentric Irish charm, a familiar score from Shaun Davey and even the local pub – Fitzgerald's – with the same name. US title: *Waking Ned Devine.*

● *Jackie O'Shea* Ian Bannen, *Michael O'Sullivan* David Kelly, *Annie O'Shea* Fionnula Flanagan, *Maggie* Susan Lynch, *Pig Finn* James Nesbitt, *Maurice* Robert Hickey, *Pat Mulligan* Fintan McKeown, *Lizzy Quinn* Eileen Dromey, *Ned Devine* Jimmy Keogh, *Jim Kelly, the Lotto man* Brendan F. Dempsey, Maura O'Malley, Paddy Ward, James Ryland, Matthew Devitt, Kitty Fitzgerald, Dermot Kerrigan, Larry Randall, Eamonn Doyle, Rennie Campbell.
● *Dir* and *Screenplay* Kirk Jones, *Pro* Glynis Murray and Richard Holmes, *Ex Pro* Alexandre Heylen, *Co-Pro* Neil Peplow, *Co-Ex Pro* Stephen Margolis, *Assoc*

Pro Miara Martell, *Ph* Henry Braham, *Pro Des* John Ebden, *Ed* Alan Strachan, *M* Shaun Davey; 'Fisherman's Blues' performed by The Waterboys, *Costumes* Rosie Hackett.

Fox Searchlight/Tomboy Films – Fox.
91 mins. UK. 1998. Rel: 19 March 1999. Cert PG.

The Waterboy ★★

After 18 years' service as the 'water distribution engineer' and general whipping boy for Louisiana University's football team, Bobby Boucher is given the sack. Then, after signing on with the hapless Mud Dogs (for no wages), Bobby discovers an untapped skill as a formidable defensive tackler ... Following a string of unremarkable comedies (*Billy Madison, Happy Gilmore, Bulletproof*), Adam Sandler hit pay dirt with the critical and box-office triumph *The Wedding Singer.* Part of the latter film's success was due to Sandler's new persona of the acerbic clown with charm to spare, but here he's back to his old moronic devices. Saddled with an idiotic grimace and retarded drawl, Sandler's hero is both offensive and boorish. There are a few good jokes along the way (like the unintelligible coach and Kathy Bates' exotic road-kill cuisine), but the film's heavy-handed mockery of Southern hicks and the mentally challenged is both anachronistic and insulting.

● *Bobby Boucher* Adam Sandler, *Mama Boucher* Kathy Bates, *Vicki Vallencourt* Fairuza Balk, *Red Beaulieu* Jerry Reed, *Coach Klein* Henry Winkler, *Derek Wallace* Larry Gilliard Jr, *Farmer Fran* Blake Clark, *Professor* Robert Kokol, *Roberto* Frank

Above: Such stuff as dreams are made of: Robin Williams and Annabella Sciorra cosy up in the afterlife – in Vincent Ward's daring if unremittingly sentimental What Dreams May Come (from PolyGram)

Corachi, Peter Dante, Jonathan Loughran, Al Whiting, Clint Howard, Allen Covert, Rob Schneider, Todd Holland, Lee Corso, Dan Fouts, Brent Musburger, Lawrence Taylor.
● *Dir* Frank Coraci, *Pro* Robert Simonds and Jack Giarraputo, *Ex Pro* Adam Sandler, *Co-Pro* Ira Shuman, *Screenplay* Tim Herlihy and Adam Sandler, *Ph* Steven Bernstein, *Pro Des* Perry Andelin Blake, *Ed* Tom Lewis, *M* Alan Pasqua; songs performed by Creedence Clearwater Revival, Lenny Kravitz, Big Head Todd & The Monsters, Fastball, The Chemical Brothers, The Doors, The Candyskins, Eric Burdon, Earth Wind & Fire, Lifelong and Incident, John Mellencamp, Joe Walsh, Buckwheat Zydeco, Rush, The Allman Brothers, Goldfinger, etc, *Costumes* Tom Bronson.

Touchstone Pictures – Buena Vista.
89 mins. USA. 1998. Rel: 30 April 1999. Cert 12.

What Dreams May Come ★★¹/₂

When Chris Nielsen, a caring doctor, husband and father, is prematurely killed in an automobile collision he finds himself transported to an ethereal world resembling one of his beloved wife's paintings. But even after a happy reunion with his pet dog, Chris realises that he cannot continue in the afterlife without his wife – his soul mate – by his side ... This adaptation of Richard Matheson's 1978 eye-opening novel is such a bold, original undertaking that it's hard to judge whether it's a work of unparalleled genius or a complete crock. Visually, the film is nothing short of stunning, its digitally recreated landscapes of Monet, Turner and Caspar David Friedrich vividly and mirac-

ulously brought to life. Intellectually, though, the project ventures into stickier territory as its metaphysical design wobbles somewhere between Carlos Castaneda and *Heaven Can Wait*. Notwithstanding, there are some really neat ideas here: with his concept of Heaven still unformed, the recently deceased Chris finds the colours in his personal paradise sticking to him like wet paint, while a teacup literally folds in his hand. Ultimately, however, the film's unevenness of tone – its leap from slushy Hollywood romance to Biblical nightmare – sets the teeth on edge. An admirable, mind-blowing failure, then.

● *Chris Nielsen* Robin Williams, *Albert* Cuba Gooding Jr, *Annie Nielsen* Annabella Sciorra, *The Tracker* Max Von Sydow, *Marie Nielsen* Jessica Brooks Grant, *Ian Nielsen* Josh Paddock, *Leona* Rosalind Chao, Lucinda Jenney, Maggie McCarthy, Matt Salinger, Werner Herzog.
● *Dir* Vincent Ward, *Pro* Stephen Simon and Barnet Bain, *Ex Pro* Erica Huggins and Ron Bass, and Ted Field and Scott Kroopf, *Co-Pro* Alan C. Blomquist, *Screenplay* Ron Bass, *Ph* Eduardo Serra, *Pro Des* Eugenio Zanetti, *Ed* David Brenner and Maysie Hoy, *M* Michael Kamen, *Costumes* Yvonne Blake, *Visual effects* Ellen M. Somers.

PolyGram/Interscope Communications/Metafilmics – PolyGram.
113 mins. USA/New Zealand. 1998. Rel: 26 December 1998. Cert 15.

Who Am I?
See *Jackie Chan's Who Am I?*

The Wisdom of Crocodiles ★★★¹⁄₂

London; the present. Steven Grlsch (pronounced 'grilsh') is a mysterious young man without a social security number, a single vowel in his surname and, apparently, any fear. Following the death of his last girlfriend in a bizarre motoring accident, Grlsch steps forward to aid police investigate the murder of his subsequent girlfriend, Maria, whose body is found floating in the English Channel. Meanwhile, Grlsch befriends a beautiful structural engineer, Anne, who would seem to meet his singular needs ... By anchoring its mysticism in everyday reality, this fascinating, poetic thriller builds a depth and unease that is both chilling and quite beguiling. Jude Law's troubled, enigmatic and charming character is so multi-layered and unusual that one doesn't want to let him go. He also makes it easy for us to see how attractive he is to women, immaterial of his cutglass good looks. Oliver Curtis' stark, detailed photography, Paul Hoffman's intriguing, eye-opening dialogue and some deft performances from a believable cast add to the pleasure. FYI: The British-born Po Chih Leong previously made the London-set *Ping Pong* (1986) and has directed eleven other features in Cantonese.

● *Steven Grlscz* Jude Law, *Anne Levels* Elina Lowensohn, *Inspector Healey* Timothy Spall, *Maria Vaughn* Kerry Fox, *Detective Roche* Jack Davenport, *Martin* Colin Salmon, Joseph O'Conor, Anastasia Hille, Ashley Artus.
● *Dir* Po Chih Leong, *Pro* David Lascelles and Carolyn Choa, *Ex Pro* Scott Meek, Dorothy Berwin and Nigel Stafford Clark, *Line Pro* Laura Julian, *Screenplay* Paul Hoffmann, *Ph* Oliver Curtis, *Pro Des* Andy Harris, *Ed* Robin Sales, *M* John Lunn and Orlando Gough, *Costumes* Anna Sheppard.

Zenith Productions/Goldwyn Films/Film Foundry Partners/ Entertainment/Arts Council of England – Entertainment. 103 mins. UK. 1998. Rel: 27 November 1998. Cert 15.

Woo ★

New York; the present. A spirited and self-motivated beauty with a profound distrust of men, Darlene 'Woo' Bates reluctantly succumbs to a blind date with Tim Jackson, an insecure, straight-laced law clerk. Unnerved by Woo's catalogue of mischievous tricks, Jackson quickly finds his evening of romantic promise turn into a date from hell ... Encouraging her cast to over-act outrageously (eyes pop, mouths gape), director Mayer (*Party Girl*, *Madeline*) reduces a promising idea to tiresome slapstick. Even the lovely and talented Jada Pinkett Smith cannot rescue this overdone farce.

● *Darlene 'Woo' Bates* Jada Pinkett Smith, *Tim Jackson* Tommy Davidson, *Lenny* Dave Chappelle, *Claudette* Paula Jai Parker, *Darryl* LL Cool J, *Hop* Darrel M. Heath, *Frankie* Duane Martin, Michael Ralph, Foxy Brown, Aida Turturro, Dartanyan Edmonds, Lance Slaughter, Sam Moses, Girlina, Nick Corri, Orlando Jones, A.J. Johnson, and *uncredited* Billy Dee Williams.
● *Dir* Daisy V.S. Mayer, *Pro* Beth Hubbard and Michael Hubbard, *Ex Pro* John Singleton, Howard Hobson and Bradford W. Smith, *Co-Pro* Bill Carraro and David C. Johnson, *Screenplay* David C. Johnson, *Ph* Jean Lepine, *Pro Des* Ina Mayhew, *Ed* Nicholas Eliopoulos and Janice Hampton, *M* Michel Colombier; songs performed by M.C. Lyte and Nicci Gilbert, Chico DeBarge, Mona Lisa, Adina Howard and Jamie Foxx, Joi, Dark Latin Groove, Salt 'N' Pepa, Charli Baltimore, The O'Jays, Cam'Ron, Evelyn 'Champagne' King, Brownstone, Lost Boyz, Mint Condition, Simon Hines, Nate Dogg and Warren G, Atlantic Starr, etc, *Costumes* Michael Clancy.

New Deal/Gotham Entertainment – Entertainment. 84 mins. USA. 1998. Rel: 25 September 1998. Cert 15.

Left: Blood food: Jude Law samples Kerry Fox in Po Chih Leong's intriguing and poetic The Wisdom of Crocodiles *(from Entertainment)*

Above: Xecutive action: Gillian Anderson and David Duchovny in Rob Bowman's fun and cerebral The X-Files *(from Fox)*

The X-Files ★★★¹/₂

North Texas/Dallas/Washington DC/Somerset/London/Antarctica/Tunisia; 35,000 BC-1998 AD. A young boy stumbles across an ancient skull in North Texas and is stricken by a mysterious and deadly virus. An entire office block in the centre of downtown Dallas is blown up. FBI agents Fox Mulder and Dana Scully are singled out as scapegoats and ordered to go their separate ways. There's obviously a conspiracy afoot ... Aimed at introducing a new audience to the conspiratorial shenanigans of the cult TV series – and to tie up a few loose ends for diehard X-philes – this is one of the more successful TV-to-film transformations. Working from a budget of $70 million, director Rob Bowman and series creator Chris Carter introduce plenty of cinematic muscle (the scenes in Antarctica are particularly impressive), but sensibly remain true to the formula that has made the series so popular. Relying on brain over brawn, Mulder and Scully are as appealing as ever on the big screen, their dead-serious delivery bringing the tongue-in-cheek humour deliciously alive.

● *Agent Fox William 'Spooky' Mulder* David Duchovny, *Agent Dana Scully* Gillian Anderson, *Dr Alvin Kurtzweil* Martin Landau, *FBI Assistant Director Jana Cassidy* Blythe Danner, *Conrad Strughold* Armin Mueller-Stahl, *Dr Ben Bronschweig* Jeffrey DeMunn, *The Well-Manicured Man* John Neville, *The Cigarette-Smoking Man* William B. Davis, *Assistant Director Walter Skinner* Mitch Pileggi, Terry O'Quinn, Lucas Black, Dean Haglund, Bruce Harwood, Tom Braidwood, George Murdock, Gary Grubbs, Milton Johns, and *uncredited*: *barmaid* Glenne Headly.

● *Dir* Rob Bowman, *Pro* Chris Carter and Daniel Sackheim, *Ex Pro* Lata Ryan, *Co-Pro* Frank Spotnitz, *Screenplay* Carter, from a story by Carter and Spotnitz, *Ph* Ward Russell; Dick Pope, *Pro Des* Christopher Nowak, *Ed* Stephen Mark, *M* Mark Snow; songs performed by X, Noel Gallagher, and Foo Fighters, *Costumes* Marlene Stewart, *Visual effects* Mat Beck, *Make-up effects* Alec Gillis and Tom Woodruff Jr, *Alien blood consultant* Scott Michelson, *Wavelet weasel* Roy Edwards.

Fox/Ten Thirteen – Fox.
121 mins. USA. 1998. Rel: 21 August 1998. Cert 15.

Year of the Horse ★★

'Proudly filmed in Super 8', this is Jim Jarmusch's home-made tribute to Neil Young and his Crazy Horse band. Recording the group's 1996 tour in Europe and the US (with extra newsreel footage from 1976 and 1986), the movie is unpretentious to a fault. And this in spite of the fact that guitarist Frank 'Poncho' Sampedro accuses Jarmusch (on camera) of trying to capture thirty years of total insanity by asking two cutesy questions 'for some artsy film.' If your idea of a good time is watching four middle-aged men photographed through mud bopping to their guitars, then this is for you. Come on Jim, you can do better than this.

● With Ralph Molina, Frank (Poncho) Sampedro, Billy Talbot, Neil Young, Elliott Roberts, Scott Young (Neil's dad), Jim Jarmusch.
● *Dir* Jim Jarmusch, *Pro* and *Ph* L.A. Johnson, *Ex Pro* Bernard Shakey and Elliot Rabinowitz, *Ed* Jay Rabinowitz, *M* Neil Young & Crazy Horse.

Shakey Pictures – Artificial Eye.
107 mins. USA. 1997. Rel: 4 December 1998. Cert 15.

Your Friends & Neighbors ★★¹/₂

Six characters in an anonymous American city – two couples, a lesbian and a predatory lady-killer – find their private lives overturned by a series of startling revelations ... Neil LaBute, writer-director of the provocative, socially contentious *In the Company of Men*, notes, 'we humans are a fairly barbarous bunch, and I don't think we've changed much over the millennia'. His new film, which shows no mercy in its depiction of its self-serving urbanites, homes in on the battlefield of the bedroom, prising off the fingernails of sexual intimacy with some audacity. Yet for all its smart, tart dialogue ('nobody gives me more pleasure than me') and bold focus, the film doesn't ring true. People may be shits, but we're also remorseful, conciliatory and funny, too – and we have hearts. Notch this up as another cynical workout from a very incisive film-maker. FYI: Aaron Eckhart, who played the slick, handsome Chad in LaBute's first film, piled on 40 pounds here to transform himself into the oafish, cuckolded Barry.

● *Mary* Amy Brenneman, *Barry* Aaron Eckhart, *Terri* Catherine Keener, *Cheri* Nastassja Kinski, *Cary* Jason Patric, *Jerry* Ben Stiller.
● *Dir* and *Screenplay* Neil LaBute, *Pro* Steve Golin and Jason Patric, *Ex Pro* Alix Madigan-Yorkin and Stephen Pevner, *Co-Pro* Philip Steuer, *Ph* Nancy Schreiber, *Pro Des* Charles Breen, *Ed* Joel Plotch, *M* The songs of Metallica performed by Apocalyptica, *Costumes* April Napier.

Propaganda Films/Fleece Films – PolyGram.
100 mins. USA. 1998. Rel: 12 February 1999. Cert 18.

You've Got M@il ★★★

New York; December-spring, the present. Kathleen Kelly was brought up to cherish children's books and today she is the proud owner of the much-loved, 42-year-old The Shop Around the Corner. Joe Fox is a ruthless businessman who's opening up a rival warehouse with the accent on discounts, cappuccino and deep armchairs. Arch enemies in business, Kathleen and

Above: With neighbours like these: Ben Stiller, Aaron Eckhart and Jason Patric discuss intimate matters in Neil LaBute's cold, incisive Your Friends & Neighbors *(from PolyGram)*

Joe also happen to be carrying on an anonymous love affair by e-mail ... There are few things quite so dramatically potent as romantic destiny, and this cyber-update of Ernst Lubitsch's 1940 *The Shop Around the Corner* certainly knows which buttons to push. Mining the same formula as her *Sleepless in Seattle* – in which a man and woman fall in love without actually meeting – writer-director Nora Ephron reunites the same stars to rekindle the same magic. However, the magic only surfaces in fits and starts, the dialogue and supporting characters are not as sharp as they could be and the ending is entirely too rushed (after a very leisurely preamble). And it will take a forgiving audience indeed to overlook Joe Fox's unpunished deed. Still, this is a must for Meg Ryan devotees, AOL romantics and bibliophiles.

● *Joe Fox* Tom Hanks, *Kathleen Kelly* Meg Ryan, *Patricia Eden* Parker Posey, *Birdie* Jean Stapleton, *Kevin* Dave Chappelle, *George* Steve Zahn, *Frank Navasky* Greg Kinnear, *Christina* Heather Burns, *Gillian* Cara Seymour, *Miranda Margulies* Veanne Cox, *Charlie, the elevator operator* Michael Badalucco, Dabney Coleman, John Randolph, Hallee Hirsch, Jeffrey Scaperrotta, Katie Finneran, Deborah Rush, Bruce Jay Friedman, Kathryn Meisle, Lynn Grossman, and *uncredited*: *Henry* Jon Lovitz.
● *Dir* Nora Ephron, *Pro* Lauren Shuler Donner and Nora Ephron, *Ex Pro* Delia Ephron, Julie Durk and G. Mac Brown, *Screenplay* Nora and Delia Ephron, *Ph* John Lindley, *Pro Des* Dan Davis, *Ed* Richard Marks, *M* George Fenton; songs performed by Harry Nilsson, The Cranberries, Bobby Day, The Paulette Sisters, Bobby Darin, Louis Armstrong, Roy Orbison, Randy Newman, Stevie Wonder, Carole King, Billy Williams, and Sinead O'Connor, *Costumes* Albert Wolsky.

Warner – Warner.
120 mins. USA. 1998. Rel: 26 February 1999. Cert PG.

Zero Effect ★★★★½

Portland/Los Angeles; the present. Thanks to an uncanny memory and almost supernatural intuition, Daryl Zero has fashioned himself into the greatest private investigator in the world. As knowledgeable about chemicals as he is about beds – or anything – he can tell you your profession in 15 seconds flat. As he says, 'behaviour is always more revealing than language – if you know what to look for.' However, he is also paranoid, addicted to pretzels and terrified of human commitment ... Written, directed and co-produced by the son of filmmaker Lawrence Kasdan, *Zero Effect* heralds the most accomplished feature debut by a 22-year-old – *ever*. Intelligently written and ingeniously plotted, this gloriously confident film turns the gumshoe thriller on its head while presenting one of the most fascinating screen characters in recent memory. From the economic score to the crisp, atmospheric lensing of Bill Pope, this is a film which knows where it's coming from and where it's going. It's also extremely funny and flawlessly acted. A cinematic miracle.

● *Daryl Zero* Bill Pullman, *Steve Arlo* Ben Stiller, *Gregory Stark* Ryan O'Neal, *Gloria Sullivan* Kim Dickens, *Jess* Angela Featherstone, Hugh Ross, Sara Devincentis, Matt O'Toole, Robert Katmis.
● *Dir* and *Screenplay* Jake Kasdan, *Pro* Kasdan, Lisa Henson and Janet Yang, *Ex Pro* Jim Behnke, *Co-Pro* Naomi Despres, *Ph* Bill Pope, *Pro Des* Gary Frutkoff, *Ed* Tara Timpone, *M* The Greyboy Allstars; songs performed by Elvis Costello, Jamiroquai, Bill Pullman, Bond, Thermadore, Candy Butchers, Nick Cave & The Bad Seeds, Dan Bern, etc, *Costumes* Kym Barrett.

Columbia Pictures/Castle Rock/Manifest Film – Warner.
116 mins. USA. 1997. Rel: 7 August 1998. Cert 15.

Right: Love at first byte: Tom Hanks downloads his feelings in Nora Ephron's fitfully engaging You've Got M@il *(from Warner)*

Left: Doing good: Laurence Fishburne (right) in Michael Apted's powerful Always Outnumbered (from High-Fliers)

Video Releases
from July 1998 through to June 1999

Compiled by Charles Bacon

Additional reviews by James Cameron-Wilson
■: denotes films released theatrically in the US
★: denotes films of special merit

An Alan Smithee Film: Burn Hollywood Burn

See *Burn Hollywood Burn*.

■ Almost Heroes

Crass, inept farce in which Chris Farley and Matthew Perry are (mis)teamed as explorers determined to beat the legendary Lewis and Clark to discovering the Pacific Ocean in 1804. Sadly, this was Farley's last film appearance. Aka *Edwards and Hunt: The First American Road Trip*.
● Also with Eugene Levy, Bokeem Woodbine, Lisa B, Kevin Dunn, Hamilton Camp, Lewis Arquette. *Dir* Christopher Guest.
Columbia TriStar. June 1999. Cert 12.

★ Always Outnumbered

Based on the short stories of Walter Mosley, this powerful social drama features Laurence Fishburne as Socrates

Fortlow, an ex-con who tries to make up for lost time and do good in the neighbourhood. Fishburne is on particularly good form, as is singer Natalie Cole as the owner of a cafe with the hots for Fortlow.
● Also with Bill Cobbs, Bill Duke, Laurie Metcalf, Cicely Tyson, Bill Nunn, Isaiah Washington, Art Evans. *Dir* Michael Apted.
Hi-Fliers. October 1998. Cert 15.

And the Beat Goes On: The Sonny and Cher Story

Based on the autobiography by Sonny Bono, this is an insipid chronicle of Sonny and Cher's enduring career and partnership, with an uncanny performance from newcomer Renee Faia as Cher and, as Sonny, a rather weak interpretation from Jay Underwood.
● Also with Christian Leffler (*as Phil Spector*), Walter Franks (*as Little Richard*). *Dir* David Burton Morris.
Odyssey. May 1999. Cert PG.

■ Black Dog

Another dog for Patrick Swayze in which he plays a crook trying to go straight by hauling what he believes to be private conveniences. Wrong. The contraband is

actually a cargo of assault weapons. Bog standard.
● Also with Randy Travis, Meat Loaf, Gabriel Casseus, Stephen Tobolowsky, Charles S. Dutton. *Dir* Kevin Hooks, *M* George S. Clinton.
Universal. February 1999. Cert 12.

Breast Men

Moral fable-cum-pseudo docudrama in which two young medics embark on a career of breast enhancement. David Schwimmer is a revelation as Kevin Saunders, a cosmetic surgeon who sees the future in silicon bags. Spanning three decades, this decidedly black satire tires towards the end, but it's undeniably an original piece with a truly buxom premise.
● Also with Chris Cooper, Emily Procter, Matt Frewer, Louise Fletcher. *Dir* Lawrence O'Neil. *Screenplay* John Stockwell.
Hi-Fliers. September 1998. Cert 18.

■ Buddy

The true-life story of New York socialite Gertrude Lintz raising animals on her estate should appeal to children and drive some older viewers spare. The film certainly has its moments and Rene Russo, as Lintz, is very good, although the eponymous animatronic gorilla is less so.
● Also with Robbie Coltrane, Irma P. Hall, Alan Cumming, Paul Reubens. *Dir* and *Screenplay* Caroline Thompson. *Pro* Francis Ford Coppola, *M* Elmer Bernstein.
Columbia TriStar. July 1998. Cert U.

★ Buffalo Soldiers

Vivid, first-rate chronicle of the turbulent, violent clashes between black soldiers (led by a former slave superbly played by Danny Glover) and Apache Indians in the wake of the American Civil War. Pulling no punches in its depiction of torture and killing, this remarkable TV film is an object lesson in provocative drama. Acting, photography, direction and script are all superlative.
● Also with Lamont Bentley, Tom Bower, Timothy Busfield, Bob Gunton, Carl Lumbly, Glynn Turman, Michael Warren, Mykelti Williamson, Harrison Lowe. *Dir* Charles Haid.
Warner. July 1998. Cert 15.

■ Burn Hollywood Burn

What strived to be the ultimate satire of Hollywood turns in on itself and becomes a plodding in-joke. Director Arthur Hiller was so appalled by what the studios left of his project that he had his credit changed to, er, Alan Smithee. US title: *An Alan Smithee Film: Burn Hollywood Burn.*
● With Ryan O'Neal, Eric Idle, Coolio, Chuck D, Sandra Bernhard, Harvey Weinstein, Sylvester Stallone, Whoopi Goldberg, Jackie Chan, Cherie Lunghi, Stephen Tobolowsky, Billy Bob Thornton. *Screenplay* Joe Eszterhas.
Entertainment. February 1999. Cert 15.

David and Lisa

Accomplished, poignant TV remake of the 1962 romantic drama, with outstanding performances from Lukas Haas and Britanny Murphy as teenage misfits who find that love has a way. However, somewhat one-dimensional writing and the miscasting of Sidney Poitier as a psychiatrist ultimately rob the film of its potency.
● Also with Debi Mazar, Allison Janney. *Dir* Lloyd Kramer, *Ex Pro* Oprah Winfrey, *M* Marco Beltrami.
Odyssey. January 1999. Cert 12.

■ Dead Man On Campus

Stunningly ineffectual comedy about two students who try to push their room-mate into committing suicide so that they can earn a straight-A average in emotional compensation. Of course, Dan Rosen explored the same theme far more successfully with his *Dead Man's Curve.*
● With Tom Everett Scott, Mark Paul Gosselaar. *Dir* Alan Cohn.
CIC. May 1999. Cert 12.

Digging to China

Marking the directorial debut of actor Timothy Hutton this is an odd, sentimental trifle with poor character definition. Set in rural New Hampshire during the mid-Sixties, the drama focuses on the effect a retarded man has on a somewhat dysfunctional family. Still, it does look good and Hutton has drawn a winning performance from the young Evan Rachel Wood.
● Also with Kevin Bacon, Mary Stuart Masterson, Cathy Moriarty, Marian Seldes.
Entertainment. March 1999. Cert PG.

■ Dirty Work

Infantile and vulgar vehicle for the dubious talents of Norm MacDonald, the anchorman for TV's *Saturday Night Live*, in which he and Artie Lang set up their own unique company, Revenge For Hire. It hits more than it misses, but for those unoffended by bad taste there are a few sleazy laughs.
● Also with Jack Warden, Chevy Chase, Don Rickles, Christopher McDonald, Chris Farley, John Goodman, Adam Sandler, Gary Coleman. *Dir* Bob Saget, *M* Richard Gibbs.
MGM. April 1999. Cert 12.

Dream For an Insomniac

A self-satisfied, insipid romantic comedy, this follows the flirtation of an insomniac actress (Ione Skye) with a creatively blocked writer (Mackenzie Astin). Some of the dialogue shines, but the cliches are all too evident.
● Also with Jennifer Aniston (as a coffee shop waitress), Seymour Cassel. *Dir* and *Screenplay* Tiffanie DeBartolo.
Columbia TriStar. September 1998. Cert 15.

■★ The Driller Killer

The original video nasty, this accomplished piece of visceral horror finally gets a British re-release 25 years after it was made (just like *The Exorcist*). Like Travis Bickle in *Taxi Driver*, painter Reno Miller (played by Jimmy Laine aka Abel Ferrara) is driven mad by the irritations of New York City and embarks on a killing spree in which he shares his trusty electric drill with the homeless of the Big Apple. Shocking, unsettling and primal cinema.

● Also with Carolyn Marz. *Dir* Abel Ferrara.
Visual Film. June 1999. Cert 18.

★ Drive

Largely overlooked gem of an action-thriller martial arts extravaganza in which Mark Dacascos plays a killer who mends his ways to become a nightclub crooner. Packed with fabulous stunts and off-the-wall comedy, this is pure, unadulterated entertainment for overgrown schoolboys.

● Also with Kadeem Hardison, John Pyper-Ferguson, Brittany Murphy, Tracey Walter, James Shigeta. *Dir* Steve Wang.
Columbia TriStar. August 1998. Cert 18.

Edwards and Hunt: The First American Road Trip

See *Almost Heroes*.

The Ellie Nesler Story: Judgement Day

This is the true story of a woman who guns down her boyfriend in court after discovering that he molested her son. The script is a bit on the manipulative side, but some sterling performances (particularly from Christine Lahti and Mary Kay Place) and a balanced overview of complex issues make for engrossing drama.
● *Dir* Stephen Tolkin (brother of writer-director Michael Tolkin).
Odyssey. March 1999. Cert 18.

Everything That Rises

Somewhat sentimental directorial debut for Dennis Quaid in which he puts on his scowl mask to play a rancher coping with his son's confinement to a wheelchair. Actually, Quaid turns out to be a better director than actor here and carries off several difficult scenes with some intelligence.
● Also with Mare Winningham, Harve Presnell, Meat Loaf.
Warner. February 1999. Cert PG.

The Fall

Atmospheric if improbable thriller in which an American writer (Craig Sheffer) is 'befriended' by a beautiful and potentially deadly stranger (Helene De Fougerolles) on the old streets of Budapest. Thanks to a forceful performance from De Fougerolles, the film does hold together quite nicely.
● Also with Jurgen Prochnow, Kim Huffman. *Dir* Andrew Piddington.
Alliance. February 1999. Cert 18.

■ Firestorm

Mechanical action-thriller in which beefcake Howie Long plays a "smoke jumper" (a fireman who parachutes into forest fires) who locks horns with a melodramatic escaped convict (William Forsythe). While the conflagration is convincing, the dialogue is not.
● Also with Scott Glenn, Suzy Amis. *Dir* Dean Semler.
Fox Pathe. September 1998. Cert 15.

Home Fries

Much of the problem with this nasty black comedy is that there is no chemistry between Drew Barrymore's hapless pregnant cashier and Luke Wilson's infatuated Mama's boy. Which is odd as Drew and Luke dated for a while (they also starred together in *Best Men*). Anyway, on the headset of her restaurant's radio, Drew overhears Luke murder the father of her unborn child and so Luke's Bloody Mama sends him to ice her as well... On her own, Drew is good company, but she cannot help make sense of the convoluted plot.
● Also with Catherine O'Hara, Jake Busey, Shelley Duvall. *Dir* Dean Parisot, *M* Rachel Portman.
Warner. May 1999. Cert 12.

■ Hoodlum

Harlem, New York; 1934-5. While such underground figures as Al Capone, Lucky Luciano and Dutch Schultz are still well known today, the legend of Ellsworth 'Bumpy' Johnson (1906-68) is not. An amateur poet and keen chess player, Johnson was imprisoned for murder and on his release involved himself in the lucrative numbers' racket in Harlem. However, the scheming, volatile and openly racist Dutch Schultz was already moving in on the black franchise and was exercising considerable muscle to make it his own cash cow. But until Johnson no Harlem resident had dared face the deadly might of the white gangster... A handsome, brutal (and largely re-invented) portrait of a little-known slice of gangster history, *Hoodlum* lacks the poetic grandeur of *The Godfather* but holds the interest thanks largely to a terrific star cast. Perfectly capturing the nobility and inner turmoil of Johnson, Laurence Fishburne adds to his gallery of charismatic giants, while Tim Roth embezzles some uncomfortable laughs as the crass, despicable Dutch Schultz (played by Vic Morrow in the 1961 biography *Portrait of a Mobster*). FYI: Fishburne previously portrayed a character inspired by Johnson in Francis Coppola's *The Cotton Club*. [JC-W]
● Also with Vanessa L. Williams, Andy Garcia, Cicely Tyson, Chi McBride, Richard Bradford, William Atherton, Loretta Devine, Queen Latifah, Mike Starr. *Dir* Bill Duke, *Ex Pro* Fishburne, *M* Elmer Bernstein.

Right: Hush, Hush, Sweet Gwyneth: Jessica Lange lends some maternal advice to Gwyneth Paltrow in Jonathan Darby's Hush (from Columbia)

Hope

Marking the directorial debut of Goldie Hawn, this extremely well-acted, sensitive drama focuses on the paranoia surrounding the Cuban Missile Crisis and the growth of the Civil Rights Movement – as seen through the eyes of a 12-year-old girl in 1962 small-town Texas. While Kerry Kennedy's screenplay pushes its buttons a little obviously, Hawn counters this with a powerful sense of time and place.

● With Jena Malone, Christine Lahti, Catherine O'Hara, Jeffrey D. Samms, J.T. Walsh, Mary Ellen Trainor.

Warner. April 1999. Cert PG.

■ Hush

This routine thriller is a major disappointment considering that it unites two of America's finest actresses, Gwyneth Paltrow and Jessica Lange. The latter chews the handsome scenery as a vindictive mother-in-law who decides that life would be so much more agreeable should her son's wife disappear – *forever*. At least Ms Lange seems to be enjoying herself.

● Also with Johnathon Schaech, Nina Foch, Debi Mazar, Hal Holbrook. *Dir* Jonathan Darby, *M* Christopher Young.

Columbia. November 1998. Cert 15.

Jane Austen's Mafia!

See *Mafia!*

■ Leave It to Beaver

The model all-American Cleaver family of Fifties sitcomland get the update treatment in this pointless, mediocre family comedy. This sort of thing should be left to the Brady Bunch.

● With Christopher McDonald, Janine Turner, Erik von Detten, Cameron Finley (*as Theodore Cleaver the Beaver*), Barbara Billingsley, Ken Osmond, Frank Bank, Alan Rachins. *Dir* Andy Cardiff, *M* Randy Edelman.

Universal. January 1999. Cert PG.

■★ Lifebreath

A dark, sly and unusually accomplished thriller in which a Manhattan schoolteacher takes unusual (and morally questionable) steps to save the life of his beloved wife suffering from cystic fibrosis. An ample helping of twists and solid playing from a creditable cast help ease this intelligent shocker to its intriguing conclusion.

● With Luke Perry, Francie Swift, Gia Carides, David Margulies, Lisa Gay Hamilton. *Dir* P.J. Posner, *Screenplay* P.J. Posner and Joel Posner.

Hi-Fliers. November 1998. Cert 18.

★ The Lion King II: Simba's Pride

As *The Lion King* borrowed the template of Shakespeare's *Hamlet*, so its accomplished sequel is an obvious reworking of *Romeo and Juliet*. Here, Simba's pride and joy – Kiara (voiced by Neve Campbell) – grows up under the vigilant eye of her possessive father but, thanks to the ineptitude of Timon and Pumbaa, manages to meet (and befriend) the streetwise Kovu. The adopted son of the evil Scar, Kovu has been raised to despise the ruling pride, but is nonetheless taken by Kiara's spirit and natural beauty. Considering the film's strong story, handsome animation and musical numbers, it seems almost a shame that it was destined for VCR consumption. In video terms, then, this is a real treat. [JC-W]

● With the voices of: *Simba* Matthew Broderick, *Nuka* Andy Dick, *Rafiki* Robert Guillaume, *Mufasa* James Earl Jones, *Nala* Moira Kelly, *Timon* Nathan Lane, *Pumbaa* Ernie Sabella, *Kovu* Jason Marsden, *Zira* Suzanne Pleshette. *Dir* Darrell Rooney, *M* Nick Glennie-Smith.

Walt Disney. March 1999. Cert U.

Mafia!

This time director Jim Abrahams (*Airplane!*, *Hot Shots!*) turns his satirical magnifying glass onto *The Godfather* movies – with a pitiful lack of visual and verbal inspiration. Enough already.

● With Lloyd Bridges, Jay Mohr, Billy Burke, Olympia Dukakis, Christina Applegate, Pamela Gidley, Tony LoBianco, Joe Viterelli.

Touchstone. April 1999. Cert 12.

■★ The Maker

Refreshingly nuanced, textured drama in which ne'er-do-well Matthew Modine returns to his home town after ten years' absence and sets about embroiling his younger brother (Jonathan Rhys Meyers) into a life of crime. One of the year's better direct-to-video titles, distinguished by first-rate performances from Modine and Meyers and some tight, fast-paced direction from Tim Hunter (*River's Edge*).

● Also with Mary-Louise Parker, Michael Madsen, Fairuza Balk, Jesse Borrego.

Marquee. October 1998. Cert 15.

■ Manny and Lo

An endearing little comedy in which two runaways, a crabby 16-year-old and her earnest 11-year-old sister, kidnap the employee of a baby shop and find that they become this strangely mutually reliant family. A funny and well acted film marking the directorial debut of scenarist Lisa Krueger.
● With Mary Kay Place, Scarlett Johansson, Aleksa Palladino, Paul Guilfoyle, Cameron Boyd. *M* John Lurie.
CIC. September 1998. Cert 12.

Masterminds

In spite of its familiar set-up – a criminal mastermind finds his airtight hostage plan thwarted by a computer-friendly schoolboy – this witty and lively *Die Hard* rip-off keeps the action running smoothly. And Patrick Stewart is on exceptional form as the poised villain.
● Also with Vincent Kartheiser, Brenda Fricker, Bradley Whitford, Matt Craven. *Dir* Roger Christian.
Columbia TriStar. September 1998. Cert 12.

■ Meet the Deedles

Truly dreadful teen comedy about a pair of spaced-out twin brothers who are mistaken for Yellowstone park rangers. This is moronic humour dragged to an all-time low.
● With Steve Van Womer, Paul Walker, A.J. Langer, John Ashton, Dennis Hopper (get a new agent!), Eric Braeden, Richard Lineback, Robert Englund, Bart the Bear. *Dir* Steve Boyum.
Buena Vista. March 1999. Cert PG.

Men With Guns

Not to be confused with the John Sayles film of the same name (see Releases of the Year), this ultra-violent carbon copy of the Tarantino formula stars Donal Logue and Gregory Sporleder as two low-lifes who steal a stash of cocaine from a local crime lord. Mayhem, inevitably, ensues. Stocked with the customary cliches of the genre, this independent blood harvest at least benefits from some energetic direction and athletic editing.
● Also with Callum Keith Rennie, Max Perlich, Paul Sorvino. *Dir* Kari Skogland.
Hi-Fliers. August 1998. Cert 18.

Murder at Devil's Glen

Neat little campus thriller in which four ex-college friends find that an old murder of theirs is about to be discovered eight years after the event. All rather suspenseful until the script ties itself up in knots.
● With Rick Schroder, Jack Noseworthy, Jayce Bartok. *Dir* Paul Shapiro.
Odyssey. September 1998. Cert 18.

■ The Newton Boys

The first dud of Matthew McConaughey's sky-rocketing career (and a disappointment from director Richard Linklater), this is the 'true story' of the Newton Brothers, a gang of sibling bank robbers who made a point of not stealing from women or children or killing anybody. McConaughey and Skeet Ulrich turn in pleasing performances as Willis and Joe Newton but the film is lacklustre in most other departments, including its pacing and look.
● Also with Ethan Hawke, Vincent D'Onofrio, Julianna Margulies, Dwight Yoakam, Chloe Webb.
Fox. April 1999. Cert 15.

Nicholas' Gift

Gripping drama based on a true story in which a Mr and Mrs Green (Alan Bates and Jamie Lee Curtis) fight to save their child's life after an attempted car-jacking in Italy.
● *Dir* Robert Markowitz.
Odyssey. January 1999. Cert PG.

■ Nightwatch

Accomplished American remake of the Danish hit in which a law student takes a job as a morgue nightwatchman while a serial killer supplies the mounting corpses. Nick Nolte as the lugubrious cop on the case is on particularly good form.
● Also with Ewan McGregor, Patricia Arquette, Josh Brolin, John C. Reilly, Brad Dourif. *Dir* Ole Bornedal (director of the original), *Screenplay* Steven Soderbergh.
Buena Vista. October 1998. Cert 18.

★ Northern Lights

A quite endearing adaptation of John Hoffman's one-man off-Broadway play in which an eccentric New Yorker discovers that she is the beneficiary of a young boy in a New England backwater. Diane Keaton is on excellent form as the zany fish-out-of-water and is supported by a top-notch cast. A real original.
● Also with Maury Chaykin, Joseph Cross, Kathleen York, John Hoffman. *Dir* Linda Yellen, *Ex Pro* Keaton, Meg Ryan.
Alliance. October 1998. Cert PG.

■ Out to Sea

This is a bumpy voyage indeed for the nth teaming of Jack Lemmon and Walter Matthau as an odd couple of curmudgeons chasing women around a Caribbean cruise ship. A titanic waste of talent.
● Also with Dyan Cannon, Brent Spiner, Gloria De Haven, Elaine Stritch, Hal Linden, Donald O'Connor, Rue McClanahan. *Dir* Martha Coolidge, *M* David Newman.
Fox. December 1998. Cert 12.

■ Phantoms

An enjoyable and spooky if derivative horror yarn in which a community in Colorado is wiped out by Something Evil. Peter O'Toole pops up as a professor of ancient plagues and supplies some thespian dignity in the midst of a creditable cast of up-and-comers.
● Also with Rose McGowan, Joanna Going, Liev

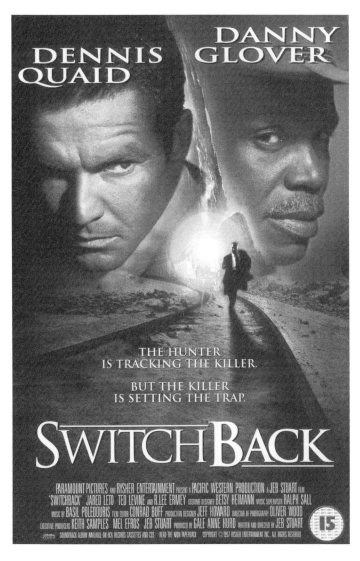

Schreiber, Ben Affleck, Nicky Katt. *Dir* Joe Chappelle, *Screenplay* Dean Koontz, from his own novel.
Buena Vista. February 1999. Cert 15.

Poodle Springs
Adapted by Tom Stoppard from Raymond Chandler's final (and unfinished) novel chronicling the exploits of his legendary private Philip Marlowe, this TV movie promises much. However, in spite of a confident turn from James Caan and some stylish direction from Bob Rafelson, the character has adapted poorly to late middle-age and it's hard to empathise with a no-hoper who's lost his edge. In short, Marlowe was not meant to grow old, become disillusioned or, Heaven forbid, get married. Shame.
● Also with Dina Meyer, David Keith, Tom Bower, Brian Cox, Joe Don Baker, Nia Peeples, Thomas F. Duffy. *Ex Pro* Sydney Pollack, *M* Michael Small.
Mosaic. April 1999. Cert 15.

★ Progeny
Desperate to be a father, low sperm-producer Arnold

Vosloo gets a little help from a repulsive alien... Capitalising on his knack for producing a gynaecological rush, director Brian Yuzna (*Society*, *Re-Animator 2*) pulls out all the stops in this gripping if well-trodden re-hash of *Rosemary's Baby*, *Alien* and their ilk. Gore fans will love it, although the squeamish should not even read the plot. A classic of its kind.
● Also with Jillian McWhirter, Brad Dourif, Lindsay Crouse, Wilford Brimley.
Pathe. April 1999. Cert 18 (funnily enough).

■ The Ringmaster
Crass re-working of the life and celebrity of infamous talk show host Jerry Springer, with Springer himself amazingly inept as an egotistical twerp called Jerry Farrelly. Dumb and witless.
● Also with Jaime Pressly, Molly Hagan, Michael Dudikoff, Michael Jai White, William McNamara. *Dir* Neil Abramson, *Pro* Jerry Springer.
Medusa. May 1999. Cert 18.

■★ She's So Lovely
A belated fruition of John Cassavetes' last screenplay – directed by his son – this is an extremely well-acted and darkly amusing look at an alcoholic who sets off to reclaim his ex-wife (now with three kids and re-married – to John Travolta) after ten years in a mental institution. Penn is quite remarkable as the psychotic wooer and deservedly won the best actor award at the 1997 Cannes festival.
● Also with Robin Wright Penn, Harry Dean Stanton, Debi Mazar, James Gandolfini, Gena Rowlands, Burt Young, Chloe Webb. *Dir* Nick Cassavetes, *Ex Pro* Penn, Travolta, Gerard Depardieu.
Buena Vista. October 1998. Cert 18.

Simba's Pride
See *The Lion King II: Simba's Pride*.

★ Suicide Kings
A gang of privileged kids abduct a retired gangster in order to prize information out of him leading to the whereabouts of a kidnapped friend. However, with a bit of psychological savvy their hostage turns them against each other in a caper that quickly gets way out of control. A neat idea is well played by Christopher Walken as the mobster and Denis Leary as his hitman, and there are some genuine surprises, to boot.
● Also with Henry Thomas, Sean Patrick Flanery, Jay Mohr, Jeremy Sisto, Johnny Galecki, Laura San Giacomo, Laura Harris, Cliff De Young. *Dir* Peter O'Fallon, *M* Graeme Revell.
Entertainment. April 1999. Cert 15.

■★ Switchback
Switching back and forth between two stories – one focusing on FBI agent Dennis Quaid tracking down a serial killer who's abducted his son, the other concerning lonely motorist Danny Glover picking up a

sullen hitchhiker (Jared Leto) – this gripping thriller marks the directorial debut of scenarist Jeb Stuart (*Die Hard*, *The Fugitive*). Excellent performances and a boffo climax on a speeding train add to the pedigree. Previously known as *Going West in America*.

● Also with R. Lee Ermey, William Fichtner, Ted Levine, Leo Burmester. *Screenplay* Jeb Stuart, *M* Basil Poledouris.

EV. July 1998. Cert 15.

■ Truth or Consequences N.M.

When a robbery backfires, a gang of ne'er-do-wells kidnap the owners of a motor home and wait for the cops and Mafia to turn up... Marking the directorial debut of Kiefer Sutherland, this quirky thriller leans too heavily on other heist-gone-wrong entries to get the blood going.

● With Vincent Gallo, Kim Dickens, Kiefer Sutherland, Mykelti Williamson, Grace Phillips, Kevin Pollak, Martin Sheen, Rod Steiger.

Columbia TriStar. July 1998. Cert 18.

The Versace Murder

Be warned, this is a truly dreadful, rushed attempt to capitalise on the murder of the legendary fashion designer Gianni Versace, scuppered by appalling performances and threadbare production values. Really tawdry.

● With Franco Nero, Steven Bauer. *Dir* Menahem Golan.

Arena. April 1999. Cert 18.

When the Trumpets Fade

Made prior to *Saving Private Ryan*, this extremely violent World War II story conjures up some impressive battle scenes but is marred by a Nineties sensibility that really jars. Still, Ron Eldard – as the sole survivor of a massacre – is very good indeed, as is Dwight Yoakam as a front-line colonel. Set during the 1944 Battle of Hurtgen Forest in Germany.

● Also with Zak Orth, Frank Whaley, Martin Donovan, Timothy Olyphant, Dan Futterman. *Dir* John Irvin.

Columbia TriStar. April 1999. Cert 15.

★ Wild America

A thoroughly winning family adventure that pits the innate charisma of its young cast against the spectacular backdrops of North America. Based on a true story, the film traces the escapades of three brothers who attempt to capture some of the US's rarest (and most ferocious) animals on film. Of course, some of the movie's magnificent photography will be lost on video, but this is still enormous fun.

● With Jonathan Taylor Thomas, Devon Sawa, Scott Bairstow, Frances Fisher, Jamie Sheridan, Tracey Walter, Don Stroud. *Dir* William Dear, *Ph* David Burr.

Warner. July 1998. Cert PG.

Other Video Releases:

Aberration Openly hokey horror fantasy with Pamela Gidley, Simon Bossell. *Dir* Tim Boxell. Marquee. August 1998. Cert 18.

Acts of Betrayal Dumb actioner with Maria Conchita Alonso, Matt McColm. Hi-Fliers. September 1998. Cert 18.

Addams Family Reunion Frenzied addition to the Gothic franchise with Tim Curry, Daryl Hannah, Ed Begley Jr, Ray Walston, Kevin McCarthy. *Dir* David Payne. Warner. November 1998. Cert U.

The Adventures of Slappy the Sea Lion Truly moronic kids' comedy with B.D. Wong, Bronson Pinchot, Sam McMurray. Columbia TriStar. August 1998. Cert U.

The Ages of Lulu Erotic drama with the divine Francesca Neri. *Dir* Bigas Luna. Tartan Video. July 1998. Cert 18.

Airborne Dumb but enjoyable actioner with Steve Guttenberg, Kim Coates, Sean Bean. *Dir* Julian Grant. Alliance. November 1998. Cert 18.

Aldrich Ames: Traitor Within True drama about the CIA agent who leaked secrets to the Russians, with Timothy Hutton, Joan Plowright. *Dir* John MacKenzie. CIC. May 1999. Cert PG.

Almost Dead Dippy and gruesome comic thriller with Shannen Doherty, Costas Mandylor, John Diehl, William R. Moses. *Dir* Ruben Preuss. Pathe. December 1998. Cert 18.

Ambushed Trite racist thriller with Courtney B. Vance, William Forsythe, Keith David, Chris Penn, Robert Patrick, Bill Nunn, Virginia Madsen. *Dir* Ernest Dickerson. Mosaic. November 1998. Cert 18.

Assault On Devil's Island Tepid actioner with Hulk Hogan, Shannon Tweed, Carl Weathers. Alliance. September 1998. Cert 15.

Atomic Dog Far-fetched canine thriller with Daniel Hugh Kelly, Cindy Pickett. CIC. September 1998. Cert PG.

Baby Monitor: Sound of Fear Dull crime thriller with Josie Bissett, Jason Beghe. CIC. October 1998. Cert 15.

Bionic Ever After? Banal romantic thriller featuring the Bionic duo Steve Austin and Jaime Somers, with (of course) Lindsay Wagner and Lee Majors. *Dir* Steven Stafford. Universal. March 1999. Cert PG.

Blackjack Slapdash action-thriller with Dolph Lundgren, Saul Rubinek, Fred Williamson, Kate Vernon. *Dir* John Woo. Hi-Fliers. August 1998. Cert 18.

Blade Squad Derivative action-thriller about a gang of roller-blading crime fighters, with Yancey Arias. *Dir* Peter Illif. Warner. May 1999. Cert 15.

Bone Daddy Suitably gory thriller about a serial killer extracting bones from his live victims, with Rutger Hauer, Barbara Williams. *Dir* Mario Azzopardi. Hi-Fliers. March 1999. Cert 18.

A Breed Apart Flaccid, eccentric zombie thriller

Above: Stephen Rea in Greg Yaitanes' classy Double Tap *(from High-Fliers)*

with Andrew McCarthy, Nick Mancuso, Robert Patrick. Mosaic. September 1998. Cert 18.

Carnival of Souls Surreal horror opus with Bobbie Phillips, Larry Miller, Shawnee Smith. *Dir* Adam Grossman. Hi-Fliers. March 1999. Cert 18.

A Chance of Snow Slushy domestic drama with JoBeth Williams, Michael Ontkean, Charles Durning. Odyssey. November 1998. Cert PG.

Children of the Corn IV: The Gathering Hair-raising and gory sequel to the Stephen King original, with Naomi Watts, Brent Jennings, William Windom, Karen Black. *Dir* Greg Spence. Hollywood Pictures. May 1999. Cert 18.

The Con OK crime comedy with Rebecca De Mornay, William H. Macy, Frances Sternhagen. *Screenplay* Macy. CIC. July 1998. Cert 12.

Countdown Sinewy crime thriller with Lori Petty, James LeGros, Jason London. *Dir* Keoni Waxman. Hi-Fliers. October 1998. Cert 18.

The Crow: Stairway To Heaven TV take on the Brandon Lee horror film, with Mark Dacascos. *Dir* Karl Skogland. PolyGram. February 1999. Cert 15.

David Searching Upbeat gay comedy with Anthony Rapp, Camryn Mannheim. *Dir* Leslie L. Smith. Millivres. May 1999. Cert 15.

Dead Husbands Flaky comedy about marital murder, with John Ritter, Nicolette Sheridan, Sonja Smits. *Dir* Paul Shapiro. Paramount. March 1999.

Cert 15.

Dearly Devoted The usual teenage slaughter drill with Rose McGowan, Alex McArthur. *Dir* Steve Cohen. Alliance. October 1998. Cert 18.

Death In the Shadows Gutsy drama allegedly based on the case that inspired *The Fugitive* TV series, with Peter Strauss, Henry Czerny, Lindsay Frost. *Dir* Peter Levin. Odyssey. June 1999. Cert 15.

Dennis Strikes Again Icky kids' farce with Justin Cooper, Don Rickles, George Kennedy, Betty White. *Dir* Charles T. Kangais. Warner. November 1998. Cert U.

The Dentist 2 Limp horror yarn about a sadistic dentist, with Corbin Bernsen, Jillian McWhirter. *Dir* Brian Yuzna. Hi-Fliers. May 1999. Cert 18.

Dirty Little Secret Workmanlike thriller with Tracey Gold, Jack Wagner. *Dir* Rob Fresco. CIC. December 1998. Cert 12.

Double Jeopardy Thriller with Frederic Forrest, Teri Garr, Joe Penny. CIC. July 1998. Cert 12.

Double Tap Stylish action-thriller with Heather Locklear, Stephen Rea, Peter Greene, Mykelti Williamson. *Dir* Greg Yaitanes. Hi-Fliers. July 1998. Cert 12.

Eden Unusual spiritual drama with Dylan Walsh, Joanna Going, Sean Patrick Flanery. *Dir* Howard Goldberg, *M* Brad Fiedel. CIC. October 1998.

Embrace the Darkness Playboy vampiric erotica with Kevin Spirtas. *Dir* Kelley Cauthern. Playboy. June 1999. Cert 12.

Every Mother's Worst Fear True thriller in which a girl gets caught up in slavery via the Internet, with Cheryl Ladd, Jordan Ladd. *Dir* Bill W.L. Norton. Universal. April 1999. Cert 12.

Evidence of Blood Elaborate, bookish thriller with David Strathairn, Mary McDonnell. *Dir* Andrew Mondshein. MGM. February 1999. Cert 12.

Final Justice Incisive true-life drama with Annette O'Toole, Michael McKean, Brian Wimmer, CCH Pounder. *Dir* Tommy Lee Wallace. Odyssey. July 1998. Cert 12.

The First 9 ¹/₂ Weeks Flaky erotic 'thriller' with Paul Mercurio, Frederic Forrest, Malcolm McDowell. *Dir* Alex Wright. Hi-Fliers. May 1999. Cert 12.

For Which He Stands Capable gangster thriller with William Forsythe, Robert Davi, Maria Conchita Alonso, Ernie Hudson. *Dir* Nelson McCormick. Mosaic. December 1998. Cert 12.

Futuresport Wooden futuristic malarkey with Dean Cain, Vanessa L. Williams, Wesley Snipes. *Dir* Ernest Dickerson. Columbia TriStar. May 1999. Cert 12.

Half Baked Druggy comedy with Dave Chappelle, Clarence Williams III. *Dir* Tamra Davis. Universal. March 1999. Cert 12.

Hav Plenty Uneven romantic comedy with Christopher Scott Cherot, Hill Harper. *Dir* Scott Cherot. Hollywood. January 1999. Cert 12.

Her Own Rules Clunky romantic drama with Melissa Gilbert, Jean Simmons, Jeremy Sheffield. *Dir* Bobby Roth. Odyssey. February 1999. Cert 12.

Hidden Agenda Standard thriller with Kevin Dillon, Andrea Roth, J.T. Walsh. *Dir* Iain Paterson. Alliance. April 1999. Cert 12.

His Bodyguard Standard thriller with Mitzi Rapture, Robert Guillaume. CIC. November 1998. Cert 12.

Hit and Run Poignant true-life drama with Margaret Colin, Lisa Vidal, Drew Pillsbury. *Dir* Don Lerner. Odyssey. February 1999. Cert PG.

The Hunchback of Notre Dame Workmanlike addition to the endless number of screen versions of Victor Hugo's tale, with Mandy Patinkin as Quasimodo, Richard Harris, Salma Hayek, Edward Atterton, Jim Dale. *Dir* Peter Medak, *M* Ed Shearmur. Alliance. November 1998. Cert 12.

The Hunted So-so thriller with Harry Hamlin, Madchen Amick. CIC. September 1998. Cert 12.

I Got the Hook Up Unintelligible 'comedic' shambles starring hip hop luminary Master P. *Dir* Michael Martin. Buena Vista. January 1999. Cert 12.

In God's Hands Surfing drama with Patrick Shane Dorian. *Dir* Zalman King. Columbia TriStar. May 1999. Cert 12.

In the Doghouse Family comedy with Matt Frewer, Rhea Perlman. *Dir* George Miller. CIC. April 1999. Cert PG.

It Came From the Sky Eccentric but captivating drama with Yasmine Bleeth, Christopher Lloyd, John Ritter, JoBeth Williams. *Dir* Jack Bender. Alliance. April 1999. Cert 12.

Last Rites Supernatural crime thriller with Randy Quaid, Embeth Davidtz. *Dir* Kevin Dowling. June 1999. Cert 12.

The Last Seduction 2 Ludicrous sequel to the John Dahl classic with Joan Severance, Con O'Neill, Beth Goddard. *Dir* Terry Marcel. PolyGram. October 1998. Cert 12.

Legion So-so horror film with Parker Stevenson, Terry Farrell, Corey Feldman, Rick Springfield. *Dir* Jon Hess. Hi-Fliers. December 1998. Cert 12.

Los Locos – see Posse II: Los Locos

Love is Strange OK real-life cancer melodrama with Ron Silver, Kate Nelligan, Julie Harris, Christopher Stack. *Dir* Annette Haywood-Carter. Odyssey. December 1998. Cert 12.

Love, Murder and Deceit Plodding thriller with Rachel Ward, Terry O'Quinn. *Dir* Mary Lambert. Odyssey. April 1999. Cert 12.

Mars Dull sci-fi thriller with Olivier Gruner, Shari Belafonte, Scott Valentine, Alex Hyde-White. *Dir* Jon Hess. Hi-Fliers. August 1998. Cert 12.

Mean Guns Slick and stylish action thriller with Christopher Lambert, Ice-T, Deborah Van Valkenburgh. *Dir* Albert Pyun. PolyGram. October 1998. Cert 18.

Mercenary 2 Dumb but vaguely enjoyable action-comedy with Claudia Christian, Olivier Gruner,

Above: Denis Leary and Colm Meaney in Ted Demme's Noose *(from High-Fliers)*

Robert Townsend. *Dir* Philippe Mora. Hi-Fliers. February 1999. Cert 12.

Meteorites! The meteorite movie that got away, with Roxanne Hart. *Dir* Chris Thomson. CIC. January 1999. Cert PG.

The Minion Low-budget Satanic actioner with Dolph Lundgren. *Dir* Jean-Marc Piche. Buena Vista. June 1999. Cert 12.

Mr Murder Sloppy sci-fi cloning thriller based on the Dean Koontz page-turner. With Stephen Baldwin, Julie Warner, Bill Smitrovich, Dan Lauria, James Coburn, Thomas Haden Church. *Dir* Dick Lowry. Odyssey. October 1998. Cert 12.

Ms Scrooge Unbearable black feminist update of Dickens' classic with Cicely Tyson, Katherine Helmond, Michael Beach. *Dir* John Korty. CIC. December 1998. Cert U.

My Husband's Secret Life Ludicrous New York drama with Anne Archer, James Russo, Maria Conchita Alonso. *Dir* Graeme Clifford. Universal. February 1999. Cert 12.

Naked City Engaging New York thriller with Scott Glenn, Courtney B. Vance. *Dir* Jeff Freilich. Universal. March 1999. Cert 12.

Naked City 2 Tired serial killer thriller with Scott Glenn, Courtney B. Vance. *Dir* Peter Bogdanovich (remember him?). CIC. April 1999. Cert 15.

No Laughing Matter Arresting domestic drama with Suzanne Somers. *Dir* Michael Elias. June 1999. Cert 12.

Noose Meditative Boston-set crime thriller with Denis Leary, Jason Barry, Billy Crudup, John Diehl, Noah Emmerich, Ian Hart, Famke Janssen, Colm Meaney, Martin Sheen, Jeanne Tripplehorn. Aka *Snitch. Dir* Ted Demme. Hi-Fliers. April 1999. Cert 12.

Not In This Town True-life racist drama with Kathy Baker, Adam Arkin, Ed Begley Jr, Max Gail. *Dir* Donald Wrye. CIC. August 1998. Cert 12.

Our Mother's Murder Powerful true-life TV thriller with Roxanne Hart, Holly Marie Combs, James Wilder. *Dir* Bill W.L. Norton. CIC. July

1998. Cert 12.

The Outsider Ludicrous sci-fi nonsense with Xavier DeClie. *Dir* David Bishop. Buena Vista. April 1999. Cert 12.

Overnight Delivery Mechanical road comedy with Paul Rudd, Reese Witherspoon, Christine Taylor. *Dir* Jason Bloom. Entertainment. January 1999. Cert 12.

The Pandora Project Loopy action-thriller with Daniel Baldwin, Erika Eleniak, Richard Tyson, Tony Todd. *Dir* Jim Wynorski, John Terlesky. First Independent. July 1998. Cert 12.

Past Perfect Inventive, compelling time-travelling sci-fi with Eric Roberts, Nick Mancuso, Saul Rubinek. *Dir* Jonathan Heap. Marquee. July 1998. Cert 12.

The Pentagon Wars Droll military comedy with Kelsey Grammer, Cary Elwes, John C. McGinley, Olympia Dukakis, Richard Benjamin. *Dir* Benjamin. Film Four. October 1998. Cert 12.

Police Story 4 Dubbed version of *Project S*. (qv).

Posse II: Los Locos Offbeat, engaging Western with Mario Van Peebles, Rene Auberjonois, Rusty Schwimmer. *Dir* Jean-Marc Vallee. Screenplay: Van Peebles. PolyGram. September 1998. Cert 12.

Project S Martial arts hokum with Michelle Yeoh as Inspector Wah and Jackie Chan in a cross-dressing cameo. *Dir* Stanley Tong. Hong Kong Classics. June 1999. Cert 12.

Promises and Lies Discerning and sympathetic true story of a homosexual father with Jean Smart, John Terry, Gretchen Corbett, Dorian Harewood. *Dir* Arvin Brown, *M* Patrick Williams. Odyssey. November 1998. Cert 12.

Purgatory Engaging supernatural Western with Sam Shepard, Eric Roberts, Peter Stormare, Donnie Wahlberg, Randy Quaid. *Dir* Uli Edel. June 1999. Cert PG.

Rescuers: Stories of Courage – Two Couples Double-bill of short stories about gentiles saving Jews in World War II. With Dana Delaney, Martin Donovan, Linda Hamilton, Alfred Molina. *Pro* Barbra Streisand. CIC. September 1998. Cert PG.

Rescuers: Stories of Courage – Two Families Another honourable double-bill from the files of the Holocaust, with Michael Rapaport, Robin Tunney, Daryl Hannah, Tim Matheson. *Pro* Barbra Streisand. CIC. November 1998. Cert 12.

The Revenant Genuinely unpleasant vampire trash with Casper Van Dien, Natasha Gregson Wagner, Kim Cattrall, Rod Steiger. *Dir* Richard Elfman. PolyGram. April 1999. Cert 12.

Richie Rich's Christmas Wish Broad, child-friendly follow-up to the Macaulay Culkin hit with David Gallagher, Martin Mull, Lesley Ann Warren, Eugene Levy. *Dir* John Murlowski. Cert U. Warner. December 1998.

Ride Smutty, predictable comedy with Malik Yoba, John Witherspoon. *Dir* Millicent Shelton. Buena Vista. January 1999. Cert 12.

The Ripper Rather interesting Victorian-era thriller with Patrick Bergin, Gabrielle Anwar, Samuel West, Michael York. *Dir* Janet Meyers. CIC. December 1998. Cert 12.

Scorpion Spring Bungled thriller set on the Mexican border with Alfred Molina, Ruben Blades, Esai Morales, Kevin Tighe, Matthew McConaughey. *Dir* Brian Cox. Hi-Fliers. December 1998. Cert 12.

Soldier Boyz Mechanical Vietnam actioner with Michael Dudikoff, Tyrin Turner, David Barry Gray, Don Stroud. *Dir* Louis Morneau. Marquee. October 1998. Cert 12.

Sometimes...They Come Back For More Flaccid, uninspired horror outing with Clayton Rohner, Chase Masterson, Damian Chapa, Max Perlich. *Dir* Daniel Berk. Hi-Fliers. Cert 12. January 1999.

Snitch – see *Noose*

Special Report: Journey To Mars Smart if somewhat emotionally remote sci-fi thriller with Keith Carradine, Judge Reinhold, Alfre Woodard. *Dir* Robert Mandel. Paramount. Cert U. January 1999.

The Spree Standard romantic thriller with Jennifer Beals, Powers Boothe, Rita Moreno. *Dir* Tommy Lee Wallace. MGM. July 1998. Cert 12.

Stand Off Routine action-thriller with Robert Sean Leonard, Keith Carradine, Natasha Henstridge, Dennis Haysbert. *Dir* Andrew Chapman. First Independent. July 1998. Cert 12.

The Substitute 2 A sort of *To Sir With Vengeance* starring Treat Williams, B.D. Wong. *Dir* Steven Pearl. Entertainment. December 1998. Cert 12.

Sunset Heights Irish gangland thriller with Toby Stephens, Patrick O'Kane, Jim Norton. *Dir* and *Screenplay* Colm Villa. Showcase. June 1999. Cert 18.

Talos the Mummy Muddled London-set horror opus with Jason Scott Lee, Louise Lombard, Christopher Lee, Sean Pertwee, Shelley Duvall. *Dir* Russell Mulcahy. Entertainment. June 1999. Cert 12.

A Town Has Turned To Dust Futuristic Western with Ron Perlman, Stephen Lang, Judy Collins. *Dir* Rob Nilsson, *Screenplay* Rod Serling. Odyssey. September 1998. Cert 12.

Trucks Foolish yet occasionally suspenseful action-thriller with Timothy Busfield, Brenda Bakke. First Independent. September 1998. Cert 12.

An Unexpected Life Domestic drama with Stockard Channing, Stephen Collins, Elaine Stritch. *Dir* David Jones. CIC. May 1999. Cert PG.

Viper TV sci-fi action-thriller with James McCaffrey, Dorian Harewood. CIC. August 1998. Cert 12.

When Danger Follows You Home Daffy thriller with JoBeth Williams, William Russ. *Dir* David Peckinpah. CIC. October 1998. Cert 12.

When the Bough Breaks 2: Perfect Prey Robotic serial killer thriller with Kelly McGillis, Bruce Dern, D.W. Moffett. *Dir* Howard McCain. Columbia TriStar. February 1999. Cert 12.

White Lies Chilling neo-Nazi drama from Canada with Sarah Polley, Tanya Allen, Lynn Redgrave. *Dir* Karl Skogland. Odyssey. October 1998. Cert 12.

Faces of the Year

Christian Bale

Christian Bale profited from the Jodie Foster syndrome in the most unexpected of ways. Following his instant exposure to celebrity as the 12-year-old star of Steven Spielberg's *Empire of the Sun* (1987), young Christian went quietly about his business slipping into predictable obscurity. Then, as a fully fledged adult, he won a variety of roles in a number of underwhelming projects while continuing to grow as an actor. In 1997 he landed the lead in Philip Saville's unadventurous *Metroland* – another distinguished flop – and played a brain-damaged young man in the intriguing disappointment *All the Little Animals*. He then tackled his second stab at Shakespeare on screen – playing Demetrius to Calista Flockhart's Helena – in, er, *William Shakespeare's A Midsummer Night's Dream*. But the real reason Bale is a Face of the Year is for snaring the title role in the troubled film version of Bret Easton Ellis's *American Psycho*. One of the most controversial and reviled novels in recent times, *American Psycho* was all set to roll with Bale ensconced in the part of Patrick Bateman, the misogynistic Yuppie who dismembers prostitutes and processes them in his liquidiser. But then the film's production company, Lion's Gate, got the idea of switching loyalties and offered Bateman to Leonardo DiCaprio instead – for a then-record $21 million. Leo immediately suggested that Oliver Stone replace the allotted director Mary Harron (who previously helmed *I Shot Andy Warhol*), but, according to producer Edward R. Pressman, he 'was obviously fascinated by the role, yet frightened by it.' Finally, the actor backed out and Christian Bale was back in. With Willem Dafoe, Samantha Mathis and Reese Witherspoon in support, *Psycho* promises to seal Bale's stardom if nothing else.

Born: 30 January 1974 in Pembrokeshire, Wales
TV: *Fay Weldon's Heart of the Country* (1986)
Film debut: *Empire of the Sun*
The other films: *Land of the Faraway, Anastasia: The Mystery of Anna* (TV movie), *Henry V, Treasure Island, Newsies* (aka *The News Boys*), *Swing Kids, Prince of Jutland* (aka *Royal Deceit*), *Little Women, Pocahontas* (voice only), *Joseph Conrad's The Secret Agent, The Portrait of a Lady, Velvet Goldmine*
Next up: *Psycho* mania
Significant others: Still single, he made a pass at Drew Barrymore when he was 12. 'I tried to kiss her,' he admits, but 'she ran'
Amazing fact: His popularity on the Internet rivals that of Leonardo DiCaprio (ironically)
Penetrating quote: 'Part of the enjoyment of acting is doing what you would never normally do'

Jim Caviezel

Few actors have had such an auspicious break as Jim Caviezel. A total unknown, he was chosen to play the lead role of the idealistic Private Witt in the $50 million war epic *The Thin Red Line*. This in itself was reason to crack open a case of Dom Perignon, but the film was to be directed by none other than Terrence Malick. The man behind *Badlands* and *Days of Heaven*, Malick garnered an instant reputation as a Hollywood legend in the Seventies and then completely vanished, fuelling his reputation as a cinematic Howard Hughes. When, 19 years later, he reappeared, every actor worth his weight in greasepaint wanted a bite of his next project. Indeed, the role of Pvt Witt itself was pursued by no less than Brad Pitt, Matthew McConnaughey and Johnny Depp. At the time Caviezel was on the verge of giving up acting and hadn't even heard of Malick. But, shortly after his audition for the reclusive film-maker, he was tracked down at his wife's hometown and hauled in for a talk – not about *The Thin Red Line* – but about baseball. Months later he landed the part and found himself supported by the likes of Sean Penn, Nick Nolte, John Travolta and George Clooney. The film went on to win extraordinary critical acclaim, numerous international awards and seven Oscar nominations. Caviezel, a darkly handsome actor of Irish-Swiss extraction, was on his way.

Born: 26 September 1968 in Conway, near Mount Vernon, Washington
TV: *Murder She Wrote, The Wonder Years*, the miniseries *Children of the Dust*
Film debut: an Italian ticket agent in *My Own Private Idaho*
The other films: *Diggstown* (aka *Midnight Sting*), *Wyatt Earp, The Rock, Ed, G.I. Jane, Ride With the Devil, Any Given Sunday*
Next up: The sci-fi drama *Frequency* with Dennis Quaid and Andre Braugher
Significant others: wife Carrie, a high-school English teacher
Amazing fact: He met his wife on a blind date and knew instantly that he was going to marry her
Penetrating quote: 'College is for smart guys. So I came to Hollywood'

Anna Friel

To the surprise of a large number of viewers and journalists, Anna Friel made the transition from cheeky soap starlet to critically applauded movie actress with accomplished ease. Pretty, perky and seductive (in a girl-next-door sort of way), Ms Friel confounded her critics and stunned her detractors. Until 15 December 1993, she was just another attractive thing in the murkier reaches of TV's kitchen sink when, as Beth Jordache in *Brookside*, she became the first actress to share a lesbian kiss on national prime time. The soap's viewing figures shot up to six million and Ms Friel was all over the tabloids.

But, far from capitalising on her new-born notoriety, she shed her housing estate Éclat and channelled her fame into surprisingly high-brow product. She played Bella Wilfer in the BBC's adaptation of Dickens' *Our Mutual Friend*, was Flora in Robert Louis Stevenson's *St Ives* and a spirited volunteer of the Women's Land Army in David Leland's picturesque *The Land Girls*. And she didn't stop there. Next, she played Hermia in *William*

Shakespeare's *A Midsummer Night's Dream* and headed for Broadway to star in Patrick Marber's *Closer*. Talk about a turnaround.

Born: 12 July 1976 in Rochdale, Lancashire
TV: *8.15 from Manchester, G.B.H.* (as Michael Palin's daughter), *Coronation Street, Emmerdale, Medics* (as Holly Jarrett), *Brookside, Reeves and Mortimer, Cadfael,* HBO's *Tales From the Crypt*
Film debut: Stephen Poliakoff's *The Tribe*
The other films: *Rogue Trader* (as Lisa Leeson), *All For Love, The Stringer, Mad Cows*
Next up: *Alfie,* with Ewan McGregor
Significant others: Robbie Williams, TV game show host Darren Day, Kate Moss (platonic)
Amazing fact: The notorious kiss with Nicola Stephenson in *Brookside* lasted eight seconds
Penetrating quote: 'The media has turned my private life into a soap, but I'm not going to let them turn me into a celebrity. I'm worth more than that'

Heather Graham

As pretty as a peach – and with a fashionably willowy body to match – Heather Graham shook off the bimbo girlfriend mould to find real stardom breathing down her neck. A whole decade after her initial 'breakthrough' role as the teenage runaway in Gus Van Sant's *Drugstore Cowboy*, Heather stumbled into a series of career-shaping films that ran the gamut from the idiotic box-office hit *Lost in Space* (in which she looked sensational in figure-hugging silverfoil) to the critically exalted *Boogie Nights*. But it was her performance in James Toback's daring, emotionally draining three-hander *Two Girls and a Guy* and her starring role as randy CIA operative Felicity Shagwell ('Shag-very-well by reputation') in the groovy, box-office juggernaut *Austin Powers: The Spy Who Shagged Me* that established her as a front-ranking actress.

Born: 29 January 1970 in Milwaukee, Wisconsin
TV: *O Pioneers!,* Annie Blackburn in *Twin Peaks*
Film debut: Mercedes in *License to Drive*
The other films: *I Love You To Death, Twin Peaks: Fire Walk With Me, Shout, Guilty as Charged, Diggstown* (aka *Midnight Sting*), *Six Degrees of Separation, The Ballad of Little Jo, Mrs Parker and the Vicious Circle, Even Cowgirls Get the Blues, Toughguy, Desert Winds, Kiss & Tell, Terrified, Don't Do It, Swingers, Nowhere, Entertaining Angels: The Dorothy Day Story, Scream 2, Alien Love Triangle, Bowfinger*
Next up: The Texas-set comedy-drama *Committed*, with Jon Stewart
Significant others: Stephen Hopkins (Australian director of *Lost in Space*), Edward Burns
What they say: 'Of all the actors, Heather had the most dedication to studying the pornos. It's, like, Drew Barrymore is a vixen and full of it. That's an act. Heather is a really pure, wonderful person.' Paul Thomas Anderson, director of the porno drama *Boogie Nights* 'The only good thing about Los Angeles is Heather Graham.' Edward Burns
Amazing fact: Her father was an FBI agent
Penetrating quote: 'Part of me wants to be kind of crazy. I have to make up for the time spent being productive'

Rhys Ifans

The British cinema is alive and well and featuring Rhys Ifans. Having given a head-turning performance as a substance-abusing, community-scaring car thief in the subversively entertaining *Twin Town*, Ifans bided his time. Then, two years later, he turned up opposite Meryl Streep and Catherine McCormack in Pat O'Connor's big-screen adaptation of Brian Friel's award-winning play *Dancing at Lughnasa*. However, it was his role as 'the scuzziest guy in the UK' – Hugh Grant's seedy lodger Spike in *Notting Hill* – that launched and then lodged him firmly into the minds of the public. Effortlessly stealing every scene he was in, he brought a committed, touching lunacy to the role that went well beyond the call of duty. Spike was a caricature, but one that seemed to have real blood running through his veins. This in itself seemed a guarantee of future success – at the very least, a string of parts in the *Worzel Gummidge* mould – but then Ifans did an about-face. In Jimmy McGovern's ferocious black comedy *Heart,* he played a smarmy womaniser; in *Rancid Aluminium* he was a troubled businessman and in *Janice Beard 45 wpm* he portrayed a double agent. He says he would like to play Macbeth and King Lear and, considering the range he has displayed in his portfolio to date, it's easy to believe he could do it.

Born: 1968, Ruthin, near Wrexham, Wales
TV: Michael Frederick Dunn in the two-part drama *Trial and Retribution*
Film debut: Griffiths in Anthony Hopkins' *August* (1996)
The other films: *You're Dead,* with John Hurt
Next up: The crime thriller *Love, Honour and Obey* with Ray Winstone, and *Kevin and Perry,* with Harry Enfield
Significant other: His brother Llyr Ifans, who played his brother in *Twin Town*
Amazing fact: At 13 he nationalistically changed his surname from Evans to Ifans
Penetrating quote: 'An immature culture can't laugh at itself'

Angelina Jolie

In Hollywood, being beautiful is not enough. Even having an Oscar-winning father is no guarantee of success. Or, for that matter, a famous husband. Angelina Jolie, the truly beautiful, bee-stung lipped daughter of Jon Voight and the ex-wife of Jonny Lee Miller, showed that she had 'It' when she teamed

up with Ellen Burstyn, Sean Connery, Dennis Quaid, Gena Rowlands and Madeleine Stowe and stole the entire picture from them.

The film was Willard Carroll's *Playing by Heart,* whose earlier title *Dancing About Architecture* is explained in its atmospheric first minutes. The movie opens on Angelina, who sets the mood for the whole piece as she talks conspiratorially to a listener off screen. They are in a nightclub and Angelina's humour is obviously softened by the sound of sultry jazz and a string of martinis. She is explaining the time she confronted a favourite musician and wanted to talk about music with him. But, she recalls, he said, 'talking about music is like talking about love. And talking about love is like dancing about architecture.'

Funny, wistful, petulant and profound, Angelina's character – a love-starved actress – was a part to die for. At least, a part to dance about. Since then she's gone on to star opposite Denzel Washington in the romantic crime thriller *The Bone Collector* and to play Nicolas Cage's girlfriend in the big-budget heist thriller *Gone in 60 Seconds.* Of course, it's downright unfair that so much talent and beauty has been compressed into one body.

Born: 4 June 1975 in Los Angeles
TV: the miniseries *True Women*
Film debut: *Lookin' to Get Out* (1982), with Jon Voight and Ann-Margret
The other films: *Cyborg 2: Glass Shadow, Without Evidence, Hackers* (with Jonny Lee Miller), *Mojave Moon, Foxfire, Love Is All There Is, George Wallace* (TV movie), *Playing God, Hell's Kitchen, Gia* (TV), *Pushing Tin*
Next up: The drama *Girl, Interrupted,* also starring Winona Ryder, Whoopi Goldberg and Vanessa Redgrave
Significant others: ex-husband Jonny Lee Miller, Timothy Hutton
What they say: 'No red-blooded male could fail to respond to her' Director Philip Noyce (*Patriot Games, The Bone Collector*)

Amazing fact: Her mother, Marcheline Bertrand, is part-Iroquois Indian
Penetrating quote: 'Things don't make me sick. I'm not afraid of death. Creepy rooms are kind of beautiful to me. And I love rats'

Rachael Leigh Cook

For a while there Rachael (that's pronounced 'Rachel') looked like nothing more than an extremely pretty clone of Winona Ryder. Then, in the surprise hit *She's All That,* she proved that she had the acting chops to accompany the most perfect set of brown eyes since *Bambi.* Creatively, the film wasn't much cop (not even Rachael as the 'ugly duckling' could hide her sensational looks under heavy-rimmed glasses) but she had enough drama to chew on to prove that she could shine with better material. And she displayed a natural comic timing uncanny in one so young.

Born: 4 October 1979 in Minneapolis, Minnesota
TV: *The Outer Limits,* Devon in *Dawson's Creek*
Film debut: Mary Anne Spier in

The Baby-Sitters Club
The other films: *26 Summer Street, Tom and Huck* (as Becky Thatcher), *Carpool, The House of Yes, The Eighteenth Angel, Strike!, Living Out Loud* (as the young Holly Hunter), *The Hi-Line*
Next up: *The Bumblebee Flies Away,* and the romantic comedy *Never Better*
Significant others: Rider Strong, Ryan Alosio
Amazing fact: The Minneapolis rock and blues band Budding Hollywood Starlet named themselves in her honour
Penetrating quote: 'I think avoiding anything set in high school would be a good move ... I don't remember a damn thing I learnt in high school' (on her future choice of roles)

Matthew Lillard

There is a demonic je-ne-sais-quois to Matthew Lillard. And he has certainly capitalised on it – either playing the rambunctious best friend or somebody entirely more sinister, as in *Scream* and *Dead Man's Curve*. While definitely not hewn from the same pretty-boy slate as such contemporaries as Freddie Prinze Jr and Skeet Ulrich, Lillard displays enough character to ensure a solid future. If he plays his card rights, he could graduate to a series of off-beat leading roles and end up a star in the James Woods mould.

Born: 24 January 1970 in Lansing, Michigan
TV: *Nash Bridges*
Film debut: *Ghoulies 3: Ghoulies Go to College*

The other films: *Serial Mom; Vanishing Son 4* (TV); *Ride For Your Life; Animal Room; Mad Love; Hackers; Scream; If These Walls Could Talk* (TV); *Tarantella; The Devil's Child* (TV); *Dead Man's Curve; Telling You; Senseless; Without Limits; Dish Dogs; S.L.C. Punk!; She's All That; Wing Commander*
Next up: The independent thriller *Spanish Judges*, in which he plays yet another slippery customer. He also produces
Significant others: Neve Campbell, his co-star in *Scream*
Amazing fact: He's a chess enthusiast
Penetrating quote: 'Actors should be given the chance to fuck up. To go on drug binges and sleep with prostitutes ... not that I've ever done that'

Alessandro Nivola

As one of America's fastest rising talents, Alessandro Nivola seems to have a peculiar aversion to American directors. A dark, brooding presence in the tradition of early Pacino, Nivola made his film debut in *Inventing the Abbots*, directed by the Irish-born Pat O'Connor. He then drew attention to himself as Nicolas Cage's slimy brother Pollux Troy in the smash-hit *Face/Off*, helmed by the Hong Kong veteran John Woo. After that he took the male lead in Michael Winterbottom's *I Want You* as an English ex-con and then played Nick, the wanderer with some exceedingly dubious *Best Laid Plans*, for the British-born film-maker Mike Barker.

Yet where one might expect Nivola to be put through his paces by an English director – in the Northamptonshire-set adaptation of Jane Austen's *Mansfield Park*, in which he plays the gaudy Henry Crawford – the film is actually directed by the Canadian Patricia Rozema. Nivola then turned to Shakespeare with *Love's Labour's Lost*, playing King Ferdinand under the tutelage of director Kenneth Branagh.

Hollywood superstar on her arm (Michael Douglas), this is one British actress who knows where she is going. Up, I'd say.

Born: 25 September 1969 in Swansea, Wales
TV: Mariette in *The Darling Buds of May*
Film debut: Sheherazade in *Les 1001 nuits* (1990)
The other films: *Out of the Blue* (TV movie), *Christopher Columbus: The Discovery*, *Splitting Heirs*, *Blue Juice*, *The Phantom*, *The Haunting*
Next up: Lee Tamahori's *The Tenth Victim*, in which she plays a government-endorsed executioner who falls in love with her sacrifice
Significant others: Blue Peter presenter John Leslie (one-time fiancé), film director Nick Hamm, Angus MacFadyen, David Essex, Mick Hucknall, Michael Douglas
What they say: "Inescapably radiant" – Kenneth Turan, *Newsday*
Amazing fact: She turned down the lead in *Anna and the King*, a role that was subsequently taken up by Jodie Foster
Penetrating quote: 'I go topless on the beach and sunbathing in the garden at home. As long as the nude scenes are in the context of the film, that is fine with me'

Born: 1973 in Boston, Massachusetts
TV: *Remember WENN* (1996)
Film debut: *The Almost Perfect Bank Robbery* (1996 TV movie); *Inventing the Abbots*
The other films: *Reach the Rock*
Next up: *Love's Labour's Lost*
Significant others: Rachel Weisz, for eight months
What they say: 'Michael Winterbottom and I saw Alessandro in *Face/Off* and there was one scene which he completely stole from Nicolas Cage. For a newcomer to be able to do that with an actor of that calibre was really impressive.' Andrew Eaton, producer of *I Want You*
Amazing fact: His idols happen to be the London-born Gary Oldman and Tim Roth
Penetrating quote: 'I'd grown up being a sort of Monty Python fanatic, obsessed with English films. Now I've kind of cornered the market in Yanks playing Brits'

Catherine Zeta-Jones

It's been aeons since an actress from Britain displayed such a heady combination of glamour, great looks, acting smarts and sheer sex appeal as Catherine Zeta-Jones. Sure, we have Kate Winslet on the one hand and Elizabeth Hurley on the other, but in the drop of two hit movies Ms Jones fulfilled all dreams to all men. While in *Entrapment* obviously too young for Sean Connery's roving libido, she gave the camera plenty to play with in one of the year's most erotic sequences. Dressed in a figure-hugging catsuit she undulates through, under and over a network of trip lasers, employing every curve and tendon of her body to devastatingly sensual effect. And in *The Mask of Zorro* she thrilled audiences with her skill with a rapier dressed in nothing but her underclothes. She was also the only cast member to bother with a Mexican accent (shaming even fellow Welshman Sir Anthony Hopkins). So, with the pick of Hollywood scripts cramming her letter-box and with a

Film World Diary
July 1998 – June 1999

JULY 1998

Right: Eddie Murphy talks to the animals in Dr Dolittle *(from Fox)*

After months of speculation, **Barbra Streisand** marries **James Brolin** at her home in Malibu, Los Angeles. Guests include **Tom Hanks**, **John Travolta** and **Roger Clinton** ● In his case against Warner Bros regarding the cancellation of his pet project, *Pinocchio*, **Francis Ford Coppola** is awarded $20 million in compensatory damages ● After eight years as a couple, **Eric Stoltz** and **Bridget Fonda** call it a day ● *As Good As It Gets* grosses $300m worldwide ● **Leonardo DiCaprio** – who was offered $21m to star in *American Psycho* and $22m to star in *A Farewell to Arms* – finally

commits to his first film since *Titanic*: **Danny Boyle**'s *The Beach* ● **Francis Ford Coppola** receives another $60m – for punitive damages – in his lawsuit against Warner Bros ● Producer **Robert Evans** marries for the fifth time – to the New York-born actress **Catherine Oxenberg** ● Single mother **Sandra Bernhard** gives birth to baby Cicely Yasin. Shortly afterwards, **Uma Thurman** and **Ethan Hawke** become the proud parents of baby Maya Ray (a girl) and **Will Smith** and **Jada Pinkett Smith** produce baby Jaden Christopher Syre Smith (a son) ● *Armageddon*

grosses $100m in the US – in under two weeks ● *Dr Dolittle* grosses $100m in the US ● *Mulan* grosses $100m in the US ● **Robert Evans** and **Catherine Oxenberg** terminate their marriage after two weeks. 'We both agreed to annul our marriage, but not our friendship,' Evans reveals ● **Gerard Depardieu** is slapped with a three-month suspended sentence for his drink-driving complication last May ● **Jodie Foster** gives birth to a baby boy, Charles, and still refuses to disclose the identity of the father ● *Lethal Weapon 4* grosses $100m in the US.

AUGUST 1998

Saving Private Ryan grosses $100m in the US ● *There's Something About Mary* grosses $100m in the US ● **Charlie Sheen** abuses his probation by partaking of illegal drugs, thus extending his probation for battery by another year. Next time, the judge says, the actor will be jailed ● A black caddy is suing **Michael Douglas** for $155 million after the actor allegedly hit him in the groin area with a golf ball. According to the plaintiff, James Parker, the actor walked up to him while he was bent double in agony, stuffed $60 into his back pocket and mumbled a racist insult ● **Anthony Hopkins** donates £1 million to the National Trust in an effort to preserve Snowdon, the highest mountain in Wales, as a public asset ● **Pierce Brosnan** becomes a grandfather for the first time after his stepdaughter, Charlotte, gives birth to a baby girl ● **Ewan McGregor**, local boy made good, is chosen to launch the Highland Games in his home town of Crieff, Perthshire. However, the star barely proves up to the task as he is not only unable to throw a 20ft caber but cannot even lift it.

SEPTEMBER 1998

Titanic grosses $600m in the US ● Three films concurrently in the US top ten – *Who Do Fools Fall In Love, How Stella Got Her Groove Back* and *Dance With Me* – are all starring African-American women, namely **Halle Berry**, **Angela Bassett** and **Vanessa L. Williams**. Is this a first? ● Can it be true? Separation is in the air as the tabloids announce the break-up of luvvy-duvvy couples **Matt Dillon** and **Cameron Diaz** and **Ben Affleck** and **Gwyneth Paltrow**. Now **Liam Neeson** and **Natasha Richardson** – who tied the knot in July of 1994 – are reportedly headed for the divorce courts because of 'irreconcilable differences caused by work pressure' ● Meanwhile, other couples are deciding to make it permanent: **David Arquette** and **Courteney Cox** have decided to make it official, as have **Johnathon Schaech** (Jimmy in *That Thing You Do!*) and **Christina Applegate** ● **Greta Scacchi** gives birth to a baby boy in Sydney, Australia. The father, Carlo Mantegazz, is the actress' first cousin ● **James Caan**, 59, and his wife Linda become the proud parents of a bouncing baby boy, Jacob Nicholas.

OCTOBER 1998

Armageddon grosses $400m worldwide ● **Tom Cruise** comes to the rescue of a woman mugged in London's Regent's Park. Hearing the victim scream as two men snatch a Cartier watch and ring worth £70,000 off her, Cruise – accompanied by two bouncers – chases the men 300 yards before they escape in a car ● **Kenneth Branagh** announces that he intends to film all of William Shakespeare's plays. Having already committed *Henry V, Much Ado About Nothing* and *Hamlet* to celluloid, the actor-director starts filming *Love's Labour's Lost* next February in England, with **Alicia Silverstone**, **Matthew Lillard** and **Natascha McElhone** in the cast. That just leaves another 33 adaptations, then ● Former judge Mara Thorpe is appealing against a decision made by the Manhattan Supreme Court that she is not owed $142,000 by **Macaulay Culkin**. Ms Thorpe was appointed guardian of Macaulay and his five siblings during their parents' custody battle and says she hasn't been paid for almost two years' work. The court argues that as the young star did not consent to the legal bill, he is not liable for it. However, Macaulay's parents don't have the money themselves, even though their son is worth over $17 million ● At the tender age of 66, **Joan Collins** becomes a grandmother ● The tabloid newspaper *The Mirror* pays out $85,370 in damages after 'unreservedly' admitting that their story about the marital crisis of **Liam Neeson** and **Natasha Richardson** was untrue. Neeson has decided to donate the money to a fund set up to help victims of the terrorist bombing in Omagh, Northern Ireland. Furthermore, the rumoured break-up of **Ben Affleck** and **Gwyneth Paltrow** also appears to be pure gossip ● **Alec Baldwin** reveals that he almost died in a plane crash recently when a small aircraft he was riding in with three friends crash-landed near Durban, South Africa, careening off the runway and down a hill. Baldwin admits that as the plane ploughed into some bushes he was thinking how tragic that he would be unable to finish smoking the contents of his prized box of Cuban cigars ● It's official: **Matt Dillon** and **Cameron Diaz** are no longer an item ● *Rush Hour* grosses $100m in the US ● To the collective sigh of millions of blokes everywhere, **Kate Winslet** announces her engagement to assistant director Jim Threapleton ● **Julia Roberts** is

to be paid in excess of $17 million for her part in *Runaway Bride*, the highest sum ever paid to an actress ● On Monday, 19 October, Britain's national critics watch *Velvet Goldmine*, *The Disappearance of Finbar* and *The Governess*, all featuring up-and-coming actor **Jonathan Rhys Meyers**. Has *any* performer ever been blessed with such an advantageous stroke of scheduling? ● *Armageddon* grosses $200m in the US, the first film since

Titanic to do so ● **Jennifer Aniston** is appalled to discover that her face has been used to sell condoms in Russia – without her consent ● **Tom Cruise** wins substantial damages from *The Express On Sunday* after the newspaper admits that its feature – which claimed the star's marriage to **Nicole Kidman** was a sham engineered to conceal their homosexuality – was entirely fabricated. Cruise and Kidman donate their winnings to charity.

NOVEMBER 1998

Above: Fragments of a deadly asteroid penetrate the atmosphere in Armageddon (from Buena Vista)

Tony Curtis, 74, marries for the fifth time. His new wife, Jill Vandenberg, a 6'2" lingerie model 46 years his junior, joins him at the altar in Las Vegas ● Director **James Orr** (*Man of the House*, *Mr Destiny*) is sentenced to 100 hours of community service and three months probation for assaulting his ex-girlfriend, **Farrah Fawcett** (*Man of the House*, *Poor Little Rich Girl*). Ms Fawcett wanted the film-maker jailed, but the judge argued that the actress had 'caused the fight in

a jealous rage' ● The long-awaited big-screen adaptation of ABC TV's *Charlie's Angels*, which was to have starred **Demi Moore**, **Nicole Kidman** and **Gwyneth Paltrow**, should now have **Cameron Diaz**, **Drew Barrymore** and **Angelina Jolie** as the trio of police academy graduates ● **Nick Moran**, who plays Eddy in *Lock, Stock and Two Smoking Barrels*, pleads guilty to assaulting a photographer at the film's London premiere last August. The actor is fined £350 and

ordered to pay £250 compensation ● **Carrie Fisher** checks into a detoxification programme – again ● British director **Tony Kaye** lodges a $200 million lawsuit against the Directors Guild of America and New Line Cinema for not allowing him to take his name off the credits of his film *American History X*. Kaye had tried to have his credit changed to Humpty Dumpty ● **Charlie Sheen** is released from drug rehab ● To the dismay of male fans everywhere, **Kate Winslet** marries assistant director Jim Threapleton at her family's parish church in Reading, Berkshire. The bride wears a creation by **Alexander McQueen**, complete with a pendant on her forehead ● *The Waterboy* grosses $100m in the US – in under three weeks ● **Michael J. Fox** reveals that he has been suffering from Parkinson's disease for the last seven years. He jokes that his hand now shakes so badly that he can 'mix a margarita in five seconds' ● Following her whirlwind 12-day marriage to producer **Robert Evans**, **Catherine Oxenberg** is now engaged to actor **Casper Van Dien**, star of *Starship Troopers* and TV's *Beverly Hills 90210* ● **Johnny Depp** and **Vanessa Paradis** announce that they are expecting a baby ● **Chuck Norris**, 58, marries Gena O'Kelley, 35, in Dallas, Texas.

DECEMBER 1998

Julie Andrews denies rumours that she will never sing again because of a throat ailment ● **Raquel Welch** reveals that she will marry pizza entrepreneur Richard Palmer – 16 years her junior – next May ● **James Cameron** faces an £80 million alimony pay-out as part of his divorce settlement with his estranged wife, the actress **Linda Hamilton** ● Reports suggest that after 29 years of marriage, **Julie Andrews** and her director husband **Blake Edwards** could be calling it a day. While Edwards prepares to

direct a new play in New York, his wife is recuperating from a throat operation at her home in the Swiss Alps ● *A Bug's Life* grosses $100m in the US, the twelfth movie in 1998 to do so ● **Sylvester Stallone** spends £26,000 on unusual Christmas presents for his wife Jennifer, her sister Trish and two of her closest friends. He buys them all breast implants ● DreamWorks and Twentieth Century Fox agree to bequeath approximately 16.5% of the *gross* receipts of their sci-fi thriller

Minority Report to the film's director **Steven Spielberg** and star **Tom Cruise**, a wage that could escalate to as much as 22.5% of the gross once the studios have recouped their costs ● **Sean Penn** announces to *The New York Times* that he intends to quit acting as soon as he's finished work on Woody Allen's *Sweet and Lowdown*. In future, he says, he will concentrate on writing and directing. Of course, Penn previously announced his retirement in 1989, a pledge he kept for three years.

JANUARY 1999

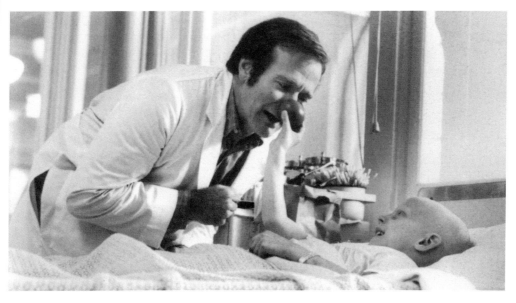

Left: Robin Williams treats the patient, not just the disease, in Patch Adams (from UIP)

Nigel Hawthorne is bestowed with a knighthood in the New Year's Honours. It is also revealed that **Vanessa Redgrave** turned down the opportunity to become a dame, refusing to accept the honour from a government run by **Tony Blair** ● **Cameron Diaz** agrees to take **Matt Dillon** back to her bosom on the condition that he places £500,000 into an account that will go to charity should he stray ● *Enemy of the State* grosses $100m in the US ● It's official: **Gwyneth Paltrow** and **Ben Affleck**

are no longer an item ● *Patch Adams* grosses $100m in the US ● News leaks out that **Alex Kingston** (*Croupier*, TV's *ER*) has tied the knot with her boyfriend Florian Haertel, a German journalist, in a secret ceremony held in Santa Fe, New Mexico. Two years ago the actress divorced **Ralph Fiennes** ● **Oliver Reed** is arrested during a drunken melee at Heathrow airport ● *You've Got M@il* grosses $100m in the US ● *Armageddon* grosses $500m worldwide ● In a move that has set

off alarm bells in Hollywood, Sony Pictures has offered a pool of 34 screenwriters a minimum of 2% of the *gross* receipts of their respective projects ● **Elizabeth Taylor** is rushed to hospital in Los Angeles for emergency treatment for an acute sinus infection. Doctors fear that the malady could lead to an infection of the brain ● **Johnny Depp** is held for four hours by police after a punch-up with photographers outside a London restaurant. The actor is let off with a caution for threatening behaviour.

FEBRUARY 1999

Sir Harry Secombe suffers a stroke at his home in Surrey ● **Jason Priestley** marries the make-up artist Ashlee Peterson on board a boat in Miami ● **Jonny Lee Miller** and **Angelina Jolie** are officially divorced ● *Saving Private Ryan* grosses $200m in the US ● Double Oscar nominee **Diane Ladd** (*Alice Doesn't Live Here Anymore, Rambling Rose*) marries entrepreneur Robert

Charles Hunter on St Valentine's Day. The actress's former husband **Bruce Dern** and daughter **Laura Dern** are in attendance ● **Christian Slater** is expecting his first child, courtesy of his girlfriend Ryan Haddon ● And it looks like perfect couple **Ryan Phillippe** (*54, Playing by Heart*) and **Reese Witherspoon** (*Twilight, Best Laid Plans*) are to become parents in the autumn ● **Oliver Reed** is arrested

during a drunken brawl in Hampstead, north London ● **Michael Douglas** and **Catherine Zeta-Jones** decide to shed the secrecy surrounding their romance. 'Michael is just adorable,' the Welsh beauty confirms ● **Jack Nicholson** disconnects himself from the Internet, admitting that it got so bad that he never left the house. 'There's so much darn porn on there,' he complains.

MARCH 1999

Above: *An anxious Laura Linney keeps the truth from Jim Carrey in* The Truman Show *(from UIP)*

Lynn Redgrave files for divorce from her husband of 32 years – and long-time manager – John Clark ● **Tom Hanks** is hospitalised after his leg becomes infected while filming *Cast Away* in Fiji. Following spells of dizziness and nausea, the actor discovered that he was suffering from cellulitis ● *The Truman Show* grosses $250m worldwide ● *The Rugrats Movie* grosses $100m in

the US. Scary ● When her limousine crashes on the freeway, **Catherine Zeta-Jones** is forced to hitch a lift to the Oscar ceremony – wearing a £10,000 Versace creation ● **Gwyneth Paltrow** sets a new record in saline-enhanced emotion when she accepts the Oscar for Best Actress. And **Roberto Benigni** – the Best Actor winner – breaks a few records of his own by leaping over the seats

at the Dorothy Chandler Pavilion and hopping on to the stage before offering to make love to the entire audience ● **Rufus Sewell**, 32, former paramour of **Kate Winslet** (see November), shatters the fantasies of his female fans by marrying Yasmin Abdullah, 23, at a London registry office ● After 22 weeks of release in the US, *Life is Beautiful* enters the American top ten box-office chart for the first time ● At a press conference for ShoWest, the annual convention for the National Association of Theater Owners in the US, **Sean Connery** storms off the rostrum, shouting backstage to a rowdy **Mike Myers**: 'Shut the fuck up!' ● **Richard Gere** puts his Malibu beach house on the market in order to raise funds for the Tibetan cause. The producer/star is asking $10 million ● As *Forces of Nature* enters its second week at the top of the American charts, one of its stars – **David Strickland** – is found hanging from the ceiling of his motel room. Strickland, 29, was most famous for playing Todd the music critic in *Suddenly Susan*, the sitcom starring **Brooke Shields** ● **Winona Ryder** is rushed to hospital from the set of *Girl, Interrupted*, after slipping on fake blood.

APRIL 1999

Susan Sarandon is arrested by New York police (along with 219 others) while protesting against the shooting of a 22-year-old immigrant. The actress is released after six hours ● Word has it that **Demi Moore** is now dating martial arts expert Oliver Whitcomb, who, at 29, is seven years her junior ● **Brooke Shields**, 33, and tennis ace **Andre Agassi**, 28, announce that they are filing for divorce after nearly two years of marriage ● After 17 weeks on release, *The Prince of Egypt* quietly passes the $100m mark in the US

● **Pamela Anderson**, goddess of the 37F cup, has her globes reduced to a size 34D. She turns down an offer from a Hollywood museum to have her abandoned implants put on show ● Six weeks before *Star Wars*: Episode I *The Phantom Menace* is due to open in Los Angeles, fans are queuing up for seats, armed with tents, sleeping bags, deck chairs and laptop computers ● Tabloid rumour has it that **Ben Affleck** is now dating the queen of American TV, *Ally McBeal*'s **Calista Flockhart** ● *Life is Beautiful* becomes the first for-

eign-language picture to pass the $50 million mark at the US box-office ● **Tom Cruise** and **Nicole Kidman** pitch a multi-million libel suit against the American magazine *The Star* after the latter suggests that they had to hire sex therapists in order to portray realistic scenes of intimacy in *Eyes Wide Shut*. The star couple are so incensed by the allegations that they are willing to reveal intimate details of their sex life ● *The Matrix* becomes the first 1999 release to pass the $100 million mark in the US.

MAY 1999

Having fallen out with **Edward Norton** over the actor's cut of *American History X*, British director **Tony Kaye** secures the services of **Marlon Brando** to star in his second film, *One Arm*. The latter project, about an amateur boxer who loses his arm in a car accident, is from a screenplay by the

late **Tennessee Williams** ● **Gina Lollobrigida**, 71, Italy's first postwar sex goddess, announces that she will stand for election to the European Parliament. 'I am the mother of Italy,' she declares, 'I'll be the most famous candidate standing' ● *Analyze This* grosses $100m in the US ● Following

relationships with **John Cusack**, **Matt Damon** and **Taylor Hawkins** (the drummer with Foo Fighters), **Minnie Driver** is to marry the stepson of **Barbra Streisand**. According to American tabloids, **Josh Brolin**, star of *Nightwatch* and *Best Laid Plans* and the son of actor **James**

Brolin, popped the question while on a Hawaiian holiday with the actress. The couple met while filming *Slow Burn* with **James Spader** ● The day before the start of the 52nd Cannes Film Festival, bomb disposal experts are called in to defuse a device discovered in the centre of the French resort ● **Richard Harris** refuses to attend the first night of Cannes because his leading role in the three-hour opening film, *The Barber of Siberia*, has been reduced to an extended cameo. 'I am pulsing with anger,' the actor tells *The Guardian* newspaper ● *Star Wars*: Episode I *The Phantom Menace* amasses $100 million in a record five days on release in the US ● *The Mummy* grosses $100m in the US – in just over two weeks ● **Johnny Depp** and his girlfriend **Vanessa Paradis** become the proud parents of a baby daughter, Lily ● *Star Wars*: Episode I *The Phantom Menace* grosses $200 million in the US in under two weeks. Records are a' falling.

JUNE 1999

Right: Sean Connery and Catherine Zeta-Jones in caper thriller Entrapment *(from Fox)*

Notting Hill grosses £7.8 million in its first seven days on general release in the UK, the most any British film has ever made on home turf in one week ● 'They're back together again now and are determined to stay that way,' reveals a friend of **Bruce Willis** and **Demi Moore**. The celebrity couple split up very publicly in June of last year ● Perfect couple **Ryan Phillippe** (*Cruel Intentions*) and **Reese Witherspoon** (*Cruel Intentions*) tie the connubial knot ● It's a great time for UK actors at the American box-office: the top-five films showing in the US all feature major British talent: **Liam Neeson** and **Ewan McGregor** in *Star Wars*: Episode I *The Phantom Menace*, **Hugh** Grant et al in *Notting Hill*, **Anthony Hopkins** in *Instinct*, **Rachel Weisz** and **John Hannah** in *The Mummy* and, at fifth place, **Sean Connery** and **Catherine Zeta-Jones** in *Entrapment* ● **David Arquette** and **Courteney Cox** tie the knot at a star-studded ceremony in San Francisco, with **Jennifer Aniston**, **Patricia Arquette**, **Rosanna Arquette**, **Lisa Kudrow**, **Matt LeBlanc**, **Liam Neeson**, **Matthew Perry**, **Brad Pitt**, **David Schwimmer** and **Kevin Spacey** in attendance ● Showing little sign of wear and tear at the US box-office, *Star Wars*: Episode I *The Phantom Menace* rakes in $250 million in a record 19 days ● Following eight weeks' work on the new **Paul Verhoeven** drama *The Hollow Man* – co-starring **Kevin Bacon** and **Josh Brolin** – **Elizabeth Shue** tears her Achilles tendon during a work-out at her gym. Some fear that Shue, who plays a scientist working on a serum that turns people invisible, might have to be replaced ● *Star Wars*: Episode I *The Phantom Menace* shatters more records as it grabs $300 million at the US box-office in a record 28 days – two weeks faster than *Titanic* managed to accumulate the same sum ● **Jean-Claude Van Damme** re-marries his third wife, Gladys Portugues, in Belgium. **Sylvester Stallone** looks on ● *Austin Powers: The Spy Who Shagged Me* grosses $100m in the US.

Film Soundtracks

Any year that can produce such distinctive and accomplished film albums as *Besieged*, *Cookie's Fortune*, *Gadjo Dilo*, *The Thin Red Line* and *Waking Ned* is not a total waste. Yet still there is the preponderance of rock-fuelled soundtracks that attract the shopper but ruin the movie. The cinema has always been a visual medium and the commercialism of film music continues to corrode the art form. Now it is almost a prerequisite to have a tacked-on musical montage, ostensibly to mark a passage of time in the narrative, but more likely installed to push up record sales. Yet it is the supposedly 'incidental' music that is really worrying me.

Even as distinguished a film as *William Shakespeare's A Midsummer Night's Dream* feels it needs a predominance of music to precipitate the mood. But to hear the Bard's words diluted by the background swelling of an orchestra constitutes a genuine ouch factor. Actors should be competent enough to generate the required emotions, without a string quartet underlining them – and distracting the viewer from the truth of the moment. Music is there to steer and add subliminal power to the action, not to laminate the dialogue. Three cheers then to *Funny Games* and *Your Friends & Neighbors*, two films which, discounting the opening and closing credit sequences, didn't use music at all.

SOUNDTRACKS OF THE YEAR

Back to Titanic

After the sheer repetition of **James Horner**'s musical behemoth (recycled at awards' ceremonies, McDonald's, etc), this reinvention of the soundtrack phenomenon is a refreshing change of pace. Not only do we have a magnificent 19-minute suite comprising a number of previously unheard themes, but a selection of familiar ballads and medleys heard in the film ('Alexander's Ragtime Band', a haunting violin rendition of 'Nearer My God To Thee,' etc) and the actual voices of Kate and Leo. Oh, yes, and Celine Dion sings something called 'My Heart Will Go On.'

Besieged

As culturally vibrant and entrancing as the characters featured in Bertolucci's underrated film, this rich mix showcases the articulate piano of Stefano Arnaldi provocatively juxtaposed with the raw, emotive singing of J.C. Olswang.

Best Laid Plans

A classy, laid-back and moody score from the suddenly ubiquitous **Craig Armstrong** (*Orphans*, *Plunkett and Macleane*), punctuated by a smattering of choice songs from Neneh Cherry, Mazzy Star, Gomez and, er, Patsy Cline.

Cinema Café

Simply one of the most enjoyable and satisfying compilations on the market, a 155-minute cornucopia of magnificent music from the cream of European cinema, including *Jean de Florette*, *Mon Oncle*, *Bilitis*, *A Man and a Woman*, *Emmanuelle*, *Diva*, *Betty Blue*, *Il Postino*, you name it. Buy.

Cookie's Fortune

A terrific collection of bluesy sounds crafted by **David A. Stewart**, a serious devotee of Delta Blues. Atmospheric, footstompin' and guitar-strummin' Mississippi nirvana.

Cousin Bette

A bit of a treat, this. A lush, majestic and bewitching score from the industrious, Cambridge-educated **Simon Boswell** (*Shallow Grave*, *Jack and Sarah*) – plus four choice songs from the previously undiscovered chanteuse Elisabeth Shue.

Cruel Intentions

Splendid collection of happening tracks that act as a killer exhibit for the names on show: Placebo, Fatboy Slim, Counting Crows, Kristen Barry, Skunk Anansie, et al. Only Blur really disappoint.

Dance With Me

Rocking Latin soundtrack bursting with swirling rhythms and hot flushes that refuses to let your feet rest. The Vanessa Williams/ Chayenne duos aside, this is a dance album to be proud of.

Elizabeth

An often difficult and challenging work, this masterly, brooding score from **David Hirschfelder** perfectly complements – and *enhances* – the atmosphere and historical context of Shekhar Kapur's powerful, vivid drama.

Firelight

A sweet, poignant score that both supports and illuminates its material, this is a fine achievement by composer **Christopher Gunning**. The piano refrain played by David Hartley and David Arch is particularly haunting.

Gadjo Dilo

A sublime celebration of the traditional music of the Romanian gypsy, this is an extraordinarily

Above left to right:
Hope Floats
Cookie's Fortune
Star Wars:
Episode I The
Phantom Menace

captivating album – rich, earthy, utterly consuming and drenched in undiluted emotion.

Gods and Monsters

A pensive, masterly score from **Carter Burwell** that perfectly captures the melancholy and power of the protagonist's monstrous ghosts. Hypnotic.

The Great Movie Scores: From the Films of Steven Spielberg

Splendid omnibus of timeless themes culled from some of the most influential hits of the last 25 years. Naturally, **John Williams** features heavily here (16 themes, from *The Sugarland Express* to *Saving Private Ryan*), but there's also **Jerry Goldsmith** (*Poltergeist*, *Twilight Zone*) and **Quincy Jones** (*The Color Purple*). Stirring.

Hilary and Jackie

The year's best classical soundtrack. A haunting, soaring medley of moods combining **Barrington Pheloung**'s complementary, cello-driven score (played by Caroline Dale in the manner of Jacqueline du Pre) with du Pre's own magnificent 30-minute performance of Elgar's *Concerto for Cello and Orchestra in E Minor*.

Hope Floats

One of the year's strongest compilations. A slickly packaged collection of stellar acts that packs an emotional and commercial wallop. Garth Brooks, Sheryl Crow, The Rolling Stones, Bryan Adams, Trisha Yearwood – every one a winner. Incidentally, this is now the top-selling Country soundtrack of all time.

The Impostors

A delightfully idiosyncratic, daft collection of vintage jazz numbers woven in with new compositions by **Gary DeMichele** (*Big Night*), creating a smorgasbord of period eccentricity. The sort of musical foolery that imprints a sheepish grin on the listener.

The Land Girls

A lush, lyrical, pastoral and uplifting score from **Brian Lock**. What more can the ear ask?

Life is Beautiful

A gently agreeable, touching work from **Nicola Piovani**, this won the Oscar for best dramatic score, cementing the stature of one of Italy's great unsung heroes. A genuine pleasure.

Little Voice

A splendid collection of classic ballads from the likes of Garland, Monroe, Bassey, Merman and Billie Holiday, but it's a shame not more use is made of Jane Horrocks' uncanny impersonations of the said stars. There's also a priceless (uncredited) cameo from Michael Caine drunkenly belting out Bill Dees and Roy Orbison's 'It's Over.'

Lock, Stock & Two Smoking Barrels

Dynamic cocktail of cheeky dialogue (Jason Flemyng: 'No can do.' Stephen Marcus: `What's that? A place near Katmandu?'), golden oldies (James Brown's 'The Payback'), creditable covers (Lewis Taylor and Carleen Anderson performing '18 With a Bullet') and new tracks from the likes of Ocean Colour Scene,

Robbie Williams and Skanga. Hip to the bone.

Mulan

Summoning up all the might and mystery of ancient China, **Jerry Goldsmith** creates another dynamic and majestic work for the Disney stable. The songs aren't bad, either.

The Mummy

For lovers of traditional film music, **Jerry Goldsmith**'s robust, swirling and mystical score is a magnificent homage to the legendary work of Alex North, Miklos Rozsa and early Maurice Jarre.

A vigorous, towering achievement that should pump four star into your camel.

My Name is Joe

Any CD that leaves one with a higher impression of a film in retrospect is a rare blessing. This muscular memento of Ken Loach's fine drama boasts a powerful score from **George Fenton**, plenty of hard-hitting dialogue (not for the faint-hearted) and a selection of miscellaneous music that ranges from Beethoven's violin concerto opus 61 to Status Quo and Norman Greenbaum's 'Spirit In the Sky.' Good stuff.

Notting Hill

Close call this. After dreadfully icky tracks from Another Level and Ronan Keating, the CD unleashes Elvis Costello and just gets better, with classic cuts from Al Green, Pulp and Spencer Davis Group, plus Lighthouse Family and Bill Withers observing that there 'Ain't No Sunshine.' It's just a shame we couldn't hear Julia

Roberts say 'I'm just a girl standing in front of a boy asking him to love me.'

Out of Sight

A gift to fans of Steven Soderbergh's hard-edged, testosterone-happy romantic thriller, this soundtrack is a comfortable balance of dialogue, a hip, jazzy score from **David Holmes** (*Resurrection Man*) and some appropriately upbeat tracks from The Isley Brothers, Dean Martin and such Latin acts as Willie Bobo and Mongo Santamaria.

Playing by Heart

Strongly influenced by the mellow, bittersweet playing of the legendary jazz trumpeter Chet Baker (who appears on three tracks), **John Barry**'s score is as seductive and classy as the film it complements. Pour the brandy.

The Prince of Egypt

Simply the best animation soundtrack of the year (1998), with stirring songs by Stephen Schwartz (*Godspell*, *Pocahontas*) and a thrilling, epic and exotic score from **Hans Zimmer**.

The Red Violin

While a bit heavy-going at times, this is nonetheless a virtuoso showcase for the range and power of the violin through the ages (and continents). Dark, moody, mournful and exultant, **John Corigliano**'s score follows the simple tune hummed by the violin maker's wife at the beginning of the film and whips into a variety of musical colours over the next 65 minutes. Soloist: Joshua Bell.

Saving Private Ryan

John Williams' finest score since *Schindler's List*, an elegant, plangent and powerfully seductive work which, considering its subject – war is hell – is strangely elegiac.

Shakespeare in Love

While **Stephen Warbeck**'s score for this sprightly, gushingly romantic film is largely a series of variations on the same theme, the theme is

strong enough to endure repetition. Still, the Oscar-winning music appeals most as a background distraction – for which it was intended – rather than as a work to be studied with any degree of concentration. Lovely, but repetitive.

Shostakovich: The Film Album

One of the miracle collections of the year, this is a 26-track, 78-minute epic capturing the astonishing, majestic range of Dmitri Shostakovich. You won't have heard of the films (*The Tale of the Silly Little Mouse* anyone?), but the CD is a major discovery for anybody interested in the Russian composer or hard-to-come-by film music. Played by the Royal Concertgebouw Orchestra.

A Soldier's Daughter Never Cries

A perfect memento of a pleasurable failure: **Richard Robbins**' splendid orchestral score mixed with an engagingly eclectic collection of songs, from Tito Puente and France Gall to Canned Heat and Deep Purple. This is how all soundtracks should be.

Star Wars: Episode I The Phantom Menace

If only for its presence in the soundtrack charts, this deserves a mention here. But unless you are a complete *Star Wars* devotee, it is something of a disappointment. **John Williams**' latest galactic extravaganza is just so much sonic bells and whistles.

10 Things I Hate About You

An unexpectedly fine collection of tracks, running the gamut from the upbeat and breezy (Letters To Cleo, Save Ferris) to the deeply felt and gut-wrenching (Joan Armatrading, Sister Hazel).

There's Something About Mary

In keeping with the Farrelly brothers' hilarious comedy, this is an appropriately idiosyncratic, upbeat and very funny collection of songs

that tie in uncannily with the film's distempered view of love. Thus cult-favourite Jonathan Richman observes that 'True Love is Not Nice' while Danny Wilson confesses that 'I made such a mistake when I was Mary's girl.' Great tracks, too, from Ben Lee, The Push Stars, The Lemonheads and, of course, The Foundations ('Build Me Up Buttercup').

The Thin Red Line

Hans Zimmer's most powerful score of the year, a mystical, pervasive work that contributes its own poetic piquancy to Terrence Malick's meditative canvas of war, sacrifice and redemption.

The Thin Red Line
Melanesian Choirs: The Blessed Islands

One of the year's more unexpected delights, a haunting companion piece to Hans Zimmer's score (*see above*), featuring the joyous, inspirational voices of native singers from Guadalcanal in the Pacific's Solomon Islands. Sung in pidgin English (the common language of the Solomons) by members of the All Saints Parish in Honiara and the Melanesian Brotherhood, these chants bring the beauty and spiritual purity of the South-West Pacific to soul-stirring life.

Ulee's Gold

This is the soundtrack to play when you've got a lot of thinking to do. A gentle, contemplative, piano-driven score from **Charles Engstrom**, *Ulee's Gold* empowers with its simplicity.

Waking Ned

One of the year's most outstanding soundtracks, an uplifting and melodic wallow in Irish whimsy from **Shaun Davey**. Complete with the usual compliment of uilleann pipes, fiddles and whistle, some haunting vocals from Liam O'Maonlai and Rita Connolly and brief but moving contributions from cast members James Nesbitt and Ian Bannen. The perfect film album.

Bookshelf

A round-up of the year's best film books

● **The Alien Quartet**, another in the A-Z series (see *Apocalypse Now*), this time focusing on the four *Alien* films, by David Thomson; **Bloomsbury; £10.99.**

● **Animated Short Films**, painstaking, picture-free A-Z of every cartoon short ever made (apparently), by Piotr Borowiec; **McFarland/Shelwing; £42.50.**

● **The Apartment**, the screenplay by Billy Wilder and I.A.L. Diamond; **Faber and Faber; £8.99.**

● **Apocalypse Now**, by Karl French; **Bloomsbury; £10.99;** 252 pages. In the past there have been some pretty flimsy excuses for a book, but this A-Z takes the biscuit. Running the gamut of entries from the novel *The Aardvark is Ready For War* (which features a review of *Apocalypse Now*) to Zoetrope (Coppola's production company) – and including segments on 'Disneyland' and 'women' – this is a blatant exercise in concept publishing gone awry. Unless you are an unquestioning fanatic of the film, you will find little point to this cumbersomely written brochure.

● **The Art of Nasty,** an unabashed look at the garish artwork of video nasties, by Nigel Wingrove and Marc Morris; **Salvation; £19.95.**

● **Audrey Style**, visually striking, fashion-orientated career analysis of Audrey Hepburn, by Pamela Clarke Keogh; **Aurum; £20.**

● **A-Z of Silent Film Comedy**, by Glenn Mitchell; **B.T. Batsford; £17.99;** 256 pages. Meeting a very real need in film reference, this exhaustive tome uncovers huge subterranean reservoirs of information relating to silent film comedy.

While necessarily covering the likes of Chaplin, Keaton, Lloyd and Langdon in some depth, film historian Glenn Mitchell (who previously penned encyclopedias on Chaplin, Laurel & Hardy and The Marx Brothers) casts his net extremely wide indeed. Here he explores the early days of cinema itself via Thomas Edison (and reveals the very first comedy to be a 1893 two-second short called *The Sneeze*), as well as taking in European cinema, a soft-pedalled account of Fatty Arbuckle's 'fabricated' attack of Virginia Rappe and the little known comic escapades of Douglas Fairbanks. As in his earlier books, Mitchell presents an alphabetical format that takes in stars, supporting players, directors, films and themes, but you do have to know your subject to find what you're looking for.

● **The Battle of Brazil**, the updated story of Terry Gilliam's conflict with Universal Pictures over the fight to release his version of *Brazil* intact, by Jack Matthews; **A&C Black; £14.99.**

● **Beneath Mulholland: Thoughts on Hollywood and Its Ghosts**, a series of sketches on the myth of Tinseltown, by David Thomson; **Abacus; £8.99.**

● **The Birds**, masterful account of Hitchcock's 1963 classic, by Camille Paglia; **BFI; £7.99.**

● **The Bond Files**, comprehensive companion to the whole James Bond phenomenon, by Andy Lane and Paul Simpson; **Virgin; £6.99.**

● **Bonnie and Clyde**, the screenplay by David Newman and Robert Benton; **Faber and Faber; £8.99.**

● **A Bug's Life: The Art and**

Making of an Epic of Miniature Proportions, a behind-the-scenes exploration of the making of *A Bug's Life*, by Jeff Kurtti; **Hyperion/Turnaround; £29.95.**

● **Cannibal Holocaust and the Savage Cinema of Ruggero Deodato**, a rundown of the sadistic cinema of the cult film-maker, by Harvey Fenton, Julian Grainger and Gian Luca Castoldi; **Fab Press; £13.99.**

● **Clint: The Life and Legend**, highly unauthorised pathography of Clint Eastwood, by Patrick McGilligan; **HarperCollins; £19.99.**

● **The Columbia Comedy Shorts**, well-researched tribute to the 526 comedy two-reelers produced by Columbia Pictures during 1933 and 1958, by Ted Okuda and Edward Watz; **McFarland/Shelwing; £22.50.**

● **Come By Sunday**, engaging biography of Diana Dors, by Damon Wise; **Pan; £5.99.**

● **The Complete Prose of Woody Allen**, the humorous articles of Woody assembled under one roof; **Picador; £7.99.**

● **Easy Riders, Raging Bulls**, the story of Seventies' Hollywood, by Peter Biskind; **Bloomsbury; £20.**

● **The Exorcist: Out of the Shadows**, thorough survey of the world's scariest celluloid phenomenon, by Bob McCabe; **Omnibus Press; £9.99.**

● **Film Follies: The Cinema Out of Order**, an examination of directorial megalomania, by Stuart Klawans; **Cassell; £13.99.**

● **Film Music Good CD Guide**, by Mark Walker; **Gramophone; £9.95;** 259 pages.

Third edition of the soundtrack guide, which reviews the best scores of everybody from Richard Addinsell to John Zorn. While retaining its coverage of the classic composers (Herrmann, Korngold, Steiner, Waxman) it also introduces the likes of John Debney and John Frizzell. Insightful if far from comprehensive.

● **Film Posters of the 70s**, by Tony Nourmand and Graham Marsh; **Aurum**; £14.95.

● **The Genius of the System: Hollywood Filmmaking in the Studio Era**, balanced examination of the studio system from 1920 to 1960, by Thomas Schatz; **Faber and Faber**; £14.99.

● **George Formby: A Troubled Genius**, definitive biography of the eukele-strumming comedian, by David Bret; **Robson**; £16.95.

● **Gilliam On Gilliam**, in-depth interview with Terry Gilliam (294 pages), by Ian Christie; **Faber and Faber**; £17.99.

● **Hollywood Hex**, round-up of misfortunes and curses that have plagued Tinseltown, by Mikita Brottman; **Creation**; £14.95.

● **I am Jackie Chan: My Life in Action**, the extraordinary story of the self-effacing action star, by Jackie Chan and Jeff Yang; **Pan**; £12.99.

● **James Cagney**, reprint of the informed biography by Richard Schickel; **Pavilion**; £4.99.

● **James Whale: A New World of Gods and Monsters**, biography of the gay director of *Frankenstein* and *The Bride of Frankenstein*, by James Curtis; **Faber and Faber**; £14.99.

● **John Barry: A Life in Music**, in-depth analysis of the career of British composer John Barry, by Geoff Leonard, Peter Walker and Gareth Bramley; **Simon & Company**; £24.99.

● **Leonard Maltin's 1999 Movie & Video Guide**; **Penguin**; £8.99; 1,632 pages. Still the most reasonably priced, comprehensive and accurate film guide around. Don't leave home without it.

● **The Macmillan International Film Encyclopedia**, third edition of the exhaustive, world-wise film Bible first published by Ephraim Katz in 1979, modestly updated here by Fred Klein and Ronald Dean Nolen; **Macmillan**; £35.

● **Making Movies**, a collection of the primitive but acerbic cartoons of director Alan Parker; **BFI Publishing**; £7.99.

● **Man on the Flying Trapeze: The Life and Times of W.C. Fields**, eye-opening, myth-destroying biography of the alcoholic comic, by Simon Louvish; **Faber and Faber**; £14.99.

● **Marilyn For Beginners**, entertaining comic book detailing the rise of Norma Jean Baker, by Kathryn Hyatt; **Writers and Readers**; £7.99.

● **Millennium Movies – End of the World Cinema**, exhaustive, intelligent and wry examination of Armageddon cinema by Kim Newman; **Titan**; £12.99.

● **Movies: A Crash Course**, pocket-size, surprisingly useful beginner's guide to the cinema, by John Naughton; **Simon & Schuster**; £9.99.

● **Of Gods and Monsters**, accomplished critical guide to the sci-fi and horror classics produced by Universal Pictures during the Thirties, by John T. Soister; **McFarland/Shelwing**; £58.50.

● **Peckinpah – a Portrait in Montage**, reprint of the definitive biography of the exacting film-maker, by Garner Simmons; **Gazelle/Limelight**; £14.99.

● **Peeping Tom**, the screenplay by Leo Marks; **Faber and Faber**; £8.99.

● **The Poe Cinema**, a critical filmography from the vaults of Edgar Allan Poe, by Don G. Smith; **McFarland/Shelwing**; £49.50.

● **The Power of Glamour**, bewitching survey of the lives of eleven women 'who defined the face of stardom' (Garbo, Dietrich, Swanson, Crawford, etc), by Annette Tapert; **Aurum**; £19.95.

● **The Prince of Egypt: A New**

Vision In Animation, another handsome, eye-opening 'the making of' book, by Charles Solomon; **Thames and Hudson**; £24.95.

● **Pure Drivel**, selection of comic essays from *The New Yorker* and other sources by Steve Martin; **Viking**; £9.99.

● **Quinlan's Film Directors**, by David Quinlan; **B.T. Batsford**; £25.00; 384 pages. A welcome (and substantial) update of Quinlan's essential and comprehensive 1983 tome, this painstakingly researched directory covers over 700 film-makers, from D.W. Griffith and Chaplin to Kieslowski and Tarantino. Handsomely produced and illustrated, the hardback comprises detailed biographies and complete filmographies (including shorts, TV movies and documentaries) and an index of actors who have directed. For once one can employ that over-used plaudit "a must" and really mean it. A must.

● **Rat Pack Confidential**, biography of the in-crowd comprised of Sinatra, Martin, Davis Jr, Lawford and Joey Fisher, by Shawn Levy; **Fourth Estate**; £12.

● **Robert Siodmak**, detailed chronology of the career of the atmospheric Germany-born director, by Deborah Lazaroff Alpi; **McFarland/Shelwing**; £49.50.

● **Sayles On Sayles**, extended interview with the acclaimed independent filmmaker John Sayles, edited by Gavin Smith; **Faber and Faber** (£9.99).

● **Screams and Nightmares**, diverting exploration of the cinema of mayhem maestro Wes Craven, by Brian J. Robb; **Titan**; £16.99.

● **Screencraft: Cinematography**, an in-depth, lavish look at the work of 17 cameramen (Jack Cardiff, Sven Nykvist, Janusz Kaminski, etc), by Peter Ettedgui; **RotoVision**; £27.50.

● **Seven**, intelligent in-depth analysis of the David Fincher thriller by Richard Dyer; **BFI**; £7.99.

● **Seventy Light Years: A Life in the Movies**, autobiography of Freddie Young, the Oscar-winning cinematographer; **Faber and Faber**; £17.99.

● **Star Wars: The Action Figure Archive**, seductively illustrated catalogue of the toys from the *Star Wars* treasury, by Stephen J. Sansweet and Josh Ling; **Virgin**; £25.

● **Star Wars Encyclopaedia**, by Stephen J. Sansweet; **Virgin**; £30.

● **Story**, an engrossing treatise on the art of constructing a screenplay, from the guru of such things, Robert McKee; **Methuen**; £16.99.

● **Superman: The Complete History**, a sumptuous chronicle of the Man of Steel, by Les Daniels and Chip Kidd; **Titan**; £19.99.

● **Sweet Smell of Success**, the screenplay by Clifford Odets and Ernest Lehman; **Faber and Faber**; £8.99.

● **The Three Colours Trilogy**, ardent account of Kieslowski's celebrated trinity, by Geoff Andrew; **BFI**; £7.99.

● **Time Out Film Guide**; **Penguin**; £13.99; 1,217 pages. The enormous advantage of this reference book is two-fold. One, it features an indispensable and exhaustive cross-referenced index of film subjects at the back, embracing such subjects as AIDS, Argentina and Jane Austen all the way to worms, Ziegfeld and Zimbabwean cinema. So, should you wish to recall the name of that Kevin Bacon film about those malevolent, subterranean worms, you can go straight to the thematic index and decide whether or not it was *Squirm, Tremors* or *The Worm Eaters* (or just look it up in the main bulk of the book). Or maybe you'd like to see how many films have been made with a golfing background or just want to browse through the titles of those movies dealing with Hinduism. And, secondly, unlike the other 13 A-Z film guides on the market, the *Time Out Film Guide* doesn't stint on foreign titles. So a Lebanese docudrama (however limited its British release) has as much priority as *Godzilla*. Where the book falls down, though, is through

the exclusion of older films that were not around during the 30-year reign of London's leading listings magazine. But even here, any golden oldie worth its salt will have been shown at some retrospective or other and hence will be included. Furthermore, the volume is more up-to-date than its rivals, including such spanking new titles as *The Truman Show, Primary Colors, My Name is Joe, Henry Fool* and *Happiness*, none of which had been released at the time of the book's publication. Perhaps more than any guide, this is the one that features the films that matter – all 12,000 of them.

● **TV Times Film & Video Guide**, by David Quinlan; **Batsford**; £9.99; 856 pages. A somewhat more manageable volume than its various cousins, this A-Z film guide offers slighter more in-depth reviews than your average synopsis, but at the expense of fewer titles: just over the 7,000 mark. However, the reviews are refreshingly contentious. Where Quinlan gives a cautious four stars to arguably the most critically exalted film of the Eighties, *Raging Bull*, he offers five to the Gene Hackman actioner *Bat 21*.

● **Vertigo: The Making of a Hitchcock Classic**, by Dan Auiler; **Titan**; £19.99.

● **VideoHound's Golden Movie Retriever 1999**, edited by Martin Connors and Jim Craddock; **Visible Ink**; £17.99; 1,815 pages. For sheer information value, this is the best film guide on the market. Boasting more than 23,000 movies, each with a decent compliment of credits and a breakdown of the plot, the Retriever gets better each year. It's also got an exhaustive cross section of genres, biographies, awards and even website addresses of the stars. Where else can you find a guide that gives you filmographies of Gerard Philipe, Ryan Phillippe and the composer John Phillips *and* which provides lists of movies clumped under headings like 'Dates From Hell', 'Great Death Scenes', 'Pure Ego Vehicles' and

'Torrid Love Scenes'? It's even got a sense of humour, in case you hadn't noticed.

● **VideoHound's World Cinema**, by Elliot Wilhelm; **Visible Ink**; £16.99; 551 pages. A welcome addition to the VideoHound library, this is a survey of over 800 films produced outside of the US. That leaves a cinematic spectrum running the gamut from *Secrets and Lies* and *Crash* to *Les Enfants du Paradis* and *Seven Samurai*, backed up by generous editorials, credits, awards, biographies (Pedro Almodovar, Gong Li, Nina Rota, etc), and over one hundred photographs. In addition, there's a helpful index at the back which supplies comprehensive tables of countries, stars, directors, writers, cinematographers, composers and various categories (such as "death and the afterlife", "Nazis", "nuns and priests" and "teen angst").

● **The Virgin Encyclopedia of Stage & Film Musicals**, a meaty and comprehensive A-Z that covers stars, composers, lyricists and, of course, the musicals themselves, both staged and filmed – by Colin Larkin; **Virgin**; £20.

● **Visions of Armageddon**, glossy book of the film, by Mark Cotta Vaz; **Titan**; £19.99.

● **Warner Bros Animation Art**, a lavish coffee table book by Jerry Beck and Will Friedwald; **Virgin**; £50.

● **Witness: The Making of Schindler's List**, expert 'making of the film' chronicle, by Franciszek Palowski; **Orion**; £9.99.

● **Women in Horror Films, 1930s**, a collection of 21 in-depth biographies of the leading 'scream queens' of the 1930s (Valerie Hobson, Gloria Stuart, Fay Wray), by Gregory William Mark; **McFarland**; £40.50.

● **Woody Allen: A Biography**, by John Baxter; **HarperCollins**; £19.99.

● **The Writer's Journey**, another 'how to' book for potential screenwriters (compare *Story*, by Robert McKee), by Christopher Vogler; **Pan**; £14.99.

Websites

Compiled by Marcus Hearn

The introduction of free Internet access by major service providers has had a huge impact over the last year. With more homes than ever on-line, the Internet is now regarded as a key marketing tool by UK distributors. It seems that no major movie poster is without the now obligatory www address, although even a cursory glance at those on offer will reveal that they are not all the same. Smaller production companies and independents generally offer simple sites in support of their movies, and even major distributors often don't try any harder than re-heating their electronic press kits. Basic sites sometimes offer intriguing insights into their films with information that is impossible to find elsewhere, and even the most vacuous major studio sites can often be admired for their state-of-the-art graphics and design. This section presents a broad overview of some of the year's most interesting official sites, both modest and lavish, with recommendations of what to look for in each one. All sites listed were active in September 1999.

STUDIO SITES

Most film websites nestle beneath the umbrella site of their production company or distributor. Studio sites are a good starting point to browse a broad range of films, read the corporate flannel and be first with details, pictures and downloaded trailers from new US releases. This year's major sites of special interest are listed below, and individual movie sites of distinction are listed underneath.

BUENA VISTA www.movies.go.com
DIMENSION FILMS
www.dimensionfilms.com
DREAMWORKS SKG
www.dreamworks.com
FOX SEARCHLIGHT
www.foxsearchlight.com
LION'S GATE ENTERTAINMENT
www.lionsgate-ent.com
MGM www.mgm.com
MIRAMAX www.miramax.com

NEW LINE CINEMA
www.newline.com
OCTOBER FILMS
www.octoberfilms.com
PARAMOUNT CLASSICS
www.paramountclassics.com
PIXAR www.pixar.com
SONY PICTURES ENTERTAINMENT
www.sonypictures.com
20th CENTURY FOX
www.foxmovies.com
UNITED INTERNATIONAL
PICTURES www.uip.com
UNIVERSAL PICTURES
www.universalpictures.com
WALT DISNEY PICTURES
www.disney.go.com/disneypictures/
WARNER BROS
www.movies.warnerbros.com

MOVIE SITES

● **THE ACID HOUSE** www.zeitgeist-film.com/current/acidhouse/
Includes a glossary of phrases and slang used in the film. Ranges from the obvious ('a soft touch' = 'a gullible person') to the baffling ('Super Mario' = 'very powerful LSD').

● **ARMAGEDDON**
www.movies.go.com/armageddon/
Download an 18-minute behind-the-scenes video following director Michael Bay during production of the film. Also features asteroid-busting games.

● **THE AVENGERS**
www.the-avengers.com
Fascinating behind-the-scenes pictures and storyboards. Offers a US version of the trailer, which – unlike its British counterpart – comprises footage actually included in the film.

● **BABE: PIG IN THE CITY**
www.babeinthecity.com
The little pig personally welcomes you to a site that includes vegetarian recipes from 'Babe's Country Cookbook'.

● **BLACK CAT WHITE CAT**
www.komuna.com
Gimmick-free site that offers a background to the pioneering Yugoslavian production company Komuna.

● **CUBE** www.cubethemovie.com
The usual cast, crew and look-at-what-awards-we-won routine, but presented in a refreshing style.

● **DR DOLITTLE** www.drdolittle.com
A disappointing site is redeemed by the opportunity to send a friend a 'Dolittle-gram'.

● **GODZILLA** www.godzilla.com
Instrumental in building the terrific hype that preceded this film, this site was later targeted by disgruntled movie-goers whose public criticisms weren't quite so good for PR. Downloads include a screensaver, an interview with director Roland Emmerich and, er, 'the new Godzilla roar'.

● **THE IDIOTS**
www.dogme95.dk/the_idiots/
An insight to the Dogma 95 philosophy from director Lars von Trier, who reveals that 'at first it was pretty distracting to have someone drooling down your trousers.'

● **JACK FROST** www.wb-jackfrost.com
Storyboards, clips and 'frosty facts' about the production of the films. Includes a game called 'Toboggan!'.

● **THE KING AND I**
www.thekingandi.com/

An inventive site clearly designed with children in mind, so the preponderance of unsolicited plugs for the home video is disappointing.

● LETHAL WEAPON 4 www.lw4.com
If you can get past the fiddly interface, you'll be rewarded with an exhaustive trawl through the film that even lets you peruse props and costume sketches.

● LIFE IS BEAUTIFUL
www.miramax.com/lifeisbeautiful/
A tasteful and easy-to-use site that features clips, interviews, the trailer and extracts from Nicola Piovani's score. Shame to see Orson Welles' name spelt wrong on the opening page.

● LITTLE VOICE
www.miramax.com/littlevoice/
Featuring clips, an interview with Michael Caine, the trailer and a TV spot. Sadly, there's little of the superb music available to download.

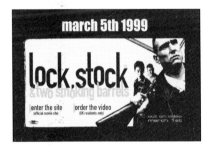

● LOCK, STOCK AND TWO SMOKING BARRELS
www.lockstock2barrels.com/
Stunning-looking site that dazzles with its presentation of trivia and goodies connected to the film. Make sure you send the children out of the room first, however – the slightest move of your mouse can unleash some quite naughty words from your speakers.

● THE MATRIX
www.whatisthematrix.com/

Great looking and sounding site, perfectly in keeping with the dour and paranoid feel of the movie. The screensaver is something of a disappointment.

● MESSAGE IN A BOTTLE
www.message-bottle.com/
The film's romantic premise is applied to the section of the site that allows you to send a digital webcard to a loved one.

● THE MUMMY
www.universalpictures.com/mummy/
Classy site that offers an evocative virtual journey through some of the film's most memorable scenes.

● NOTTING HILL
www.universalpictures.com/nottinghill/
Efficient site with lots of multimedia downloads in store for the curious. Opens with an unfamiliar version of the now-familiar pictures of Hugh Grant walking in front of the poster of Julia Roberts. Just how many times was the poor man made to do that?

● OUT OF SIGHT
www.outofsight.com/
Lots of well-presented details about the film, and a link to the official Elmore Leonard site.

● PAYBACK www.paybackmovie.com/
Distinguished only by a selection of photographs taken during the film's premiere at the Paramount Pictures lot.

● PERFECT BLUE
www.perfectblue.com/
Kicks off with an endorsement from Roger Corman and features a lengthy interview with director Satoshi Kon. Mercifully free from Hollywood-style bells and whistles.

● THE PRINCE OF EGYPT
www.prince-of-egypt.com/

Another chance to savour the exquisite animation and stirring score in one of the best-designed sites of the year. Features study guides suitable for parents, teachers and children of different faiths.

● PSYCHO www.psychomovie.com/
This comprehensive site gives director Gus Van Sant the opportunity to air yet another justification for remaking the Hitchcock classic, and they're always fun to read. Click on 'The Subconscious', however, and you'll be confronted with a disturbing series of animated sound and picture montages from the film's most unsettling scenes. Scary stuff.

● THE RUGRATS MOVIE
www.nick.com/rugrats_movie/
Play Baby Food Flingshot!

● THERE'S SOMETHING ABOUT MARY www.aboutmary.co.uk/
Notable for the chance it offers you to share your true life tales in the 'Cringe With Mary' section. Each week's most excruciating story wins a T-shirt – the ultimate winner is awarded the dubious accolade 'Unluckiest Person in the UK.'

● THE TRUMAN SHOW
www.truman-show.com/
An ingenious design invites you to click on the horizon of Truman Burbank's home town for movie information, or click on the surface of the moon for behind-the-scenes facts. Those familiar with the film will cotton on quicker than Jim Carrey's hapless hero.

● WHAT DREAMS MAY COME
www.whatdreamsmay.com/
Max Von Sydow's Tracker is your guide through this virtual journey through the after-life.

● THE X-FILES
www.fightthefuture.com/
Looks slick and sounds awesome, but much like the TV show of the same name this site doesn't live up to its early promise.

● YOU'VE GOT M@IL
www.youvegotmail.com/
Take a tour of the sights and sounds of the areas of New York that feature in the film.

Awards and Festivals

The 71st American Academy of
Motion Picture Arts and Sciences
Awards ('The Oscars') and
Nominations for 1998,
Los Angeles, 21 March 1999

Above: *Joseph Fiennes searches for inspiration in
the Oscar-winning Shakespeare In Love*

● **Best Film:** *Shakespeare In Love*.
Nominations: *Elizabeth*; *Life is Beautiful*;
Saving Private Ryan; *The Thin Red Line*.
● **Best Director:** Steven Spielberg, for
Saving Private Ryan. Nominations: Roberto
Benigni, for *Life is Beautiful*; John Madden,
for *Shakespeare In Love*; Terrence Malick,
for *The Thin Red Line*; Peter Weir, for *The
Truman Show*.
● **Best Actor:** Roberto Benigni, for *Life is
Beautiful*. Nominations: Tom Hanks, for
Saving Private Ryan; Ian McKellen, for *Gods
and Monsters*; Nick Nolte, for *Affliction*;
Edward Norton, for *American History X*.
● **Best Actress:** Gwyneth Paltrow, for
Shakespeare In Love. Nominations: Cate
Blanchett, for *Elizabeth*; Fernanda
Montenegro, for *Central Station*; Meryl
Streep, for *One True Thing*; Emily Watson,
for *Hilary and Jackie*.
● **Best Supporting Actor:** James Coburn, for
Affliction. Nominations: Robert Duvall, for *A
Civil Action*; Ed Harris, for *The Truman
Show*; Geoffrey Rush, for *Shakespeare In Love*;
Billy Bob Thornton, for *A Simple Plan*.
● **Best Supporting Actress:** Judi Dench, for
Shakespeare in Love. Nominations: Kathy
Bates, for *Primary Colors*; Brenda Blethyn, for
Little Voice; Rachel Griffiths, for *Hilary and
Jackie*; Lynn Redgrave, for *Gods and Monsters*.
● **Best Original Screenplay:** Marc Norman
and Tom Stoppard, for *Shakespeare In Love*.
Nominations: Warren Beatty and Jeremy
Pikser, for *Bulworth*; Vincenzo Cerami and

Roberto Benigni, for *Life is Beautiful*;
Robert Rodat, for *Saving Private Ryan*;
Andrew Niccol, for *The Truman Show*.
● **Best Screenplay Adaptation:** Bill
Condon, for *Gods and Monsters*.
Nominations: Scott Frank, for *Out of Sight*;
Elaine May, for *Primary Colors*; Scott B.
Smith, for *A Simple Plan*; Terrence Malick,
for *The Thin Red Line*.
● **Best Cinematography:** Janusz Kaminski,
for *Saving Private Ryan*. Nominations:
Conrad L. Hall, for *A Civil Action*; Remi
Adefarasin, for *Elizabeth*; Richard Greatrex,
for *Shakespeare in Love*; John Toll, for *The
Thin Red Line*.
● **Best Editing:** Michael Kahn, for *Saving
Private Ryan*. Nominations: Simona Paggi,
for *Life is Beautiful*; Anne V. Coates, for
Out of Sight; David Gamble, for *Shakespeare
in Love*; Billy Weber, Leslie Jones and Saar
Klein, for *The Thin Red Line*.
● **Best Original Score (musical or come-
dy):** Stephen Warbeck, for *Shakespeare in
Love*. Nominations: Randy Newman, for *A
Bug's Life*; Jerry Goldsmith, for *Mulan*;
Marc Shaiman, for *Patch Adams*; Hans
Zimmer, for *The Prince of Egypt*.
● **Best Original Score (dramatic):** Nicola
Piovani, for *Life is Beautiful*. Nominations:
David Hirschfelder, for *Elizabeth*; Randy
Newman, for *Pleasantville*; John Williams,
for *Saving Private Ryan*; Hans Zimmer, for
The Thin Red Line.
● **Best Original Song:** 'When You Believe'
from *The Prince of Egypt*, music and lyrics
by Stephen Schwartz. Nominations: 'I
Don't Want To Miss a Thing' from
Armageddon, music and lyrics by Diane
Warren; 'The Prayer' from *Quest For
Camelot*, music by Carole Bayer Sager and
David Foster, lyrics by Sager, Foster, Tony
Renis and Alberto Testa; 'A Soft Place to
Fall' from *The Horse Whisperer*, music and
lyrics by Allison Moore and Gwil Owen;
'That'll Do' from *Babe: Pig in the City*,
music and lyrics by Randy Newman.
● **Best Art Direction:** Martin Childs (art
direction), Jill Quertier (set direction),
for *Shakespeare in Love*. Nominations:
John Myhre (art), Peter Howitt (set), for
Elizabeth; Jeannine Oppewall (art), Jay
Hart (set), for *Pleasantville*; Tom Sanders
(art), Lisa Dean Kavanaugh (set), for
Saving Private Ryan; Eugenio Zanetti

(art), Cindy Carr (set), for *What Dreams
May Come*.
● **Best Costume Design:** Sandy Powell,
for *Shakespeare in Love*. Nominations:
Colleen Atwood, for *Beloved*; Alexandra
Byrne, for *Elizabeth*; Judianna
Makovsky, for *Pleasantville*; Sandy
Powell, for *Velvet Goldmine*.
● **Best Sound:** Gary Rydstrom, Gary
Summers, Andy Nelson and Ronald Judkins,
for *Saving Private Ryan*. Nominations: Kevin
O'Connell, Greg P. Russell and Keith A.
Wester, for *Armageddon*; Kevin O'Connell,
Greg P. Russell and Pud Cusack, for *The
Mask of Zorro*; Robin O'Donoghue, Dominic
Lester and Peter Glossop, for *Shakespeare in
Love*; Andy Nelson, Anna Behlmer and Paul
Brincat, for *The Thin Red Line*.
● **Best Sound Effects Editing:** Gary
Rydstrom and Richard Hymns, for *Saving
Private Ryan*. Nominations: George Watters
II, for *Armageddon*; David McMoyler, for
The Mask of Zorro.
● **Best Make-Up:** Jenny Shircore, for
Elizabeth. Nominations: Lois Burwell,
Conor O'Sullivan and Daniel C. Striepeke,
for *Saving Private Ryan*; Lisa Westcott and
Veronica Brebner, for *Shakespeare in Love*.
● **Best Visual Effects:** Joel Hynek, Nicholas
Brooks, Stuart Robertson and Kevin Mack,
for *What Dreams May Come*. Nominations:
Richard R. Hoover, Pat McClung and John
Frazier, for *Armageddon*; Rick Baker, Hoyt
Yeatman, Alan Hall and Jim Mitchell, for
Mighty Joe Young.
● **Best Animated Short Film:** *Bunny*.
Nominations: *The Canterbury Tales*; *Jolly
Roger*; *More*; *When Life Departs*.
● **Best Live Action Short Film:** *Election
Night*. Nominations: *Culture*; *Holiday
Romance*; *La Carte Postale*; *Victor*.
● **Best Documentary Feature:** *The Last
Days*. Nominations: *Dancemaker*; *The
Farm: Angola, U.S.A.*; *Lenny Bruce: Swear
To Tell the Truth*; *Regret To Inform*.
● **Best Documentary Short:** *The Personals:
Improvisations on Romance in the Golden
Years*. Nominations: *A Place in the Land*;
Sunrise Over Tiananmen Square.
● **Best Foreign-Language Film:** *Life is
Beautiful* (Italy). Nominations: *Central
Station* (Brazil); *Children of Heaven* (Iran);
The Grandfather (Spain); *Tango* (Argentina).
● **Career Achievement Award:** Elia Kazan.

The 40th Australian Film Institute Awards, Melbourne, November 1998

● **Best Film:** *The Interview*.
● **Best Actor:** Hugo Weaving, for *The Interview*.
● **Best Actress:** Deborah Mailman, for *Radiance*.
● **Best Supporting Actor:** John Polson, for *The Boys*.
● **Best Supporting Actress:** Toni Collette, for *The Boys*.
● **Best Director:** Rowan Woods, for *The Boys*.
● **Best Director of a Documentary:** David Goldie, for *The Big House*.
● **Best Original Screenplay:** Craig Monahan and Gordon Davie, for *The Interview*.
● **Best Screenplay Adaptation:** Stephen Sewell, for *The Boys*.
● **Best Short Screenplay:** Evan Clary, for *Mate*.
● **Best Cinematography:** Geoffrey Simpson, for *Oscar and Lucinda*.
● **Best Production Design:** Luciana Arrighi, for *Oscar and Lucinda*.
● **Best Editing:** Jill Bilcock, for *Head On*.
● **Best Music:** Thomas Newman, for *Oscar and Lucinda*.
● **Best Costumes:** Janet Patterson, for *Oscar and Lucinda*.
● **Best Sound:** Andrew Plain, Ben Osmo and Gethin Creagh, for *Oscar and Lucinda*.
● **Best Foreign Film:** *L.A. Confidential*, by Curtis Hanson (USA).
● **Best Animated Short:** *Vengeance*, by Wendy Chandler.
● **Best Documentary:** *The Dragons of Galapagos*.
● **The Byron Kennedy Award:** Alison Barrett, Arthur Cambridge.
● **The Raymond Longford Award:** Charles 'Bud' Tingwell, actor.
● **Open Craft Award:** *After Mabo*, for its visual design by John Hughes and Uri Mizrahi.

The 49th Berlin International Film Festival, 21 February 1999

● **Golden Bear for Best Film:** *The Thin Red Line* (USA).
● **Silver Bear, Special Jury Prize:** *Mifune* (Denmark).
● **Silver Bear for Best Director:** Stephen Frears, for *The Hi-Lo Country* (USA).
● **Silver Bear, Best Actor:** Michael Gwisdek, for *Night Shapes* (Germany).

● **Silver Bear, Best Actress (shared):** Juliane Koehler and Maria Schrader, for *Aimee & Jaguar* (Germany).
● **Silver Bear for Outstanding Single Achievement:** Marc Norman and Tom Stoppard, scenarists of *Shakespeare In Love*.
● **Blue Angel Prize:** *Journey To the Sun* (Turkey/The Netherlands/Germany).
● **Alfred Bauer Prize:** *Karnaval* (France/Belgium/Switzerland).
● **Golden Bear for Best Short Film (shared):** *Faraon* (Russia); and *Masks* (Germany/Poland).
● **Silver Bear for Best Short Film:** *Desserts* (UK).
● **Ecumenical Jury Prize:** *It All Starts Today* (France).
SPECIAL MENTIONS:
● **Young actress:** Iben Hjejle, for *Mifune*.
● **Cinematographer:** John Toll, for *The Thin Red Line*.

FIPRESCI Prizes (International Film Critics' Association):

● **Best Film:** *It All Starts Today*.
● **Panorama:** *Wait and See* (Japan).
● **International Forum:** *Dealer* (Germany).
● **Wolfgang Staudte Prize:** *The Cruise* (USA).
● **CICAE (international confederation of art cinemas):** *The War Zone* (UK).
● **German Arthouse Cinemas Guild:** *Cookie's Fortune* (USA).
● **Gay Teddy Bear Award, Best Feature:** *Fucking Amal* (Sweden).
● **Peace Film Prize:** *Journey To the Sun*.
● **Panorama Audience Award:** *Alone* (Spain).

Jury: Angela Molina (president); Ken Adam; Paulo Branco; Assi Dayan; Pierre-Henri Deleau; Katja von Garnier; Hellmuth Karasek; Jeroen Krabbé; Michelle Yeoh

The 1998 British Academy of Film and Television Arts Awards ('BAFTAs'), 11 April 1999

● **Best Film:** *Shakespeare in Love*.
● **David Lean Award for Best Direction:** Peter Weir, for *The Truman Show*.
● **Best Original Screenplay:** Andrew Niccol, for *The Truman Show*.
● **Best Adapted Screenplay:** Elaine May, for *Primary Colors*.
● **Best Actor:** Roberto Benigni, for *Life is Beautiful*.

● **Best Actress:** Cate Blanchett, for *Elizabeth*.
● **Best Supporting Actor:** Geoffrey Rush, for *Shakespeare in Love*.
● **Best Supporting Actress:** Judi Dench, for *Shakespeare in Love*.
● **Best Cinematography:** Remi Adefarasin, for *Elizabeth*.
● **Best Production Design:** Dennis Gassner, for *The Truman Show*.
● **Best Editing:** David Gamble, for *Shakespeare in Love*.
● **The Anthony Asquith Award for Best Music:** David Hirschfelder, for *Elizabeth*.
● **Best Costumes:** Sandy Powell, for *Velvet Goldmine*.
● **Best Sound:** Gary Rydstrom, Gary Summers, Andy Nelson and Ronald Judkins, for *Saving Private Ryan*.
● **Best Special Visual Effects:** Steven Fangmeier, Roger Guyett and Neil Corbould, for *Saving Private Ryan*.
● **Best Make-up/hair:** Jenny Shircore, for *Elizabeth*.
● **Alexander Korda Award for Best British Film:** *Elizabeth*.
● **Best Foreign Language Film:** *Central Station* (Brazil).
● **Best Short Film:** *Home*.
● **Best Animated Short:** *The Canterbury Tales*.
● **Carl Foreman Award for British Newcomer:** Richard Kwietniowski, writer-director of *Love and Death On Long Island*.
● **Michael Balcon Award for Outstanding British Contribution to the Cinema:** Michael Kuhn.
● **BAFTA Fellowship:** Elizabeth Taylor.
● **The Orange Audience Award:** *Lock, Stock and Two Smoking Barrels*.

The 19th Canadian Film Awards ('Genies'), Mississauga, Ontario, 4 February 1999

● **Best Film:** *The Red Violin*.
● **Best Director:** Francois Girard, for *The Red Violin*.
● **Best Actor:** Roshan Seth, for *Such a Long Journey*.
● **Best Actress:** Sandra Oh, for *Last Night*.
● **Best Supporting Actor:** Callum Keith Rennie, for *Last Night*.
● **Best Supporting Actress:** Monique Mercure, for *Conquest*.
● **Best Screenplay:** Girard and Don McKellar, for *The Red Violin*.
● **Best Cinematography:** Alain Dostie, for *The Red Violin*.

● **Best Editing:** Jeff Warren, for *Such a Long Journey*.
● **Best Art Direction:** François Séguin, for *The Red Violin*.
● **Best Music:** John Corigliano, for *The Red Violin*.
● **Best Original Song:** Suzie Ungerlieder, for 'River Blue' from *The Fishing Trip*.
● **Best Costumes:** Renée April, for *The Red Violin*.
● **Best Sound Editing:** David Evans, Rick Cadger, Donna Powell, Paul Shikata, Phong Tran and Clive Turner, for *Such a Long Journey*.
● **Best Overall Sound:** Claude La Haye, Jo Caron, Bernard Strobl and Hans Peter Strobl, for *The Red Violin*.
● **Claude Jutra Award for Best First Feature:** *Last Night*.
● **Best Feature-length Documentary:** *A Place Called Chiapas*, by Betsy Carson, Kirk Tougas and Nettie Wild.
● **Best Short Documentary:** *Shadow Maker: Gwendolyn MacEwen, Poet*, by Anita Herczeg and Brenda Longfellow.
● **Best Animated Short:** *Bingo*, by Andy Jones, Chris Landreth and Kevin Tureski.
● **Best Live-Action Short:** *When Ponds Freeze Over*, by Mary Lewis.
● **The Golden Reel Award for Box-Office Performance:** *Les Boys*.

The 52nd Cannes Film Festival Awards, 23 May 1999

● **Palme d'Or for Best Film:** *Rosetta*, by Luc and Jean-Pierre Dardenne (Belgium).
● **Grand Prix du Jury:** *L'Humanite* (France).
● **Best Actor:** Emmanuel Schotte, for *L'Humanite*.
● **Best Actress (shared):** Emilie Dequenne, for *Rosetta*; and Severine Caneele, for *L'Humanite*.
● **Best Director:** Pedro Almodovar, for *All About My Mother* (Spain/France).
● **Best Screenplay:** Yuri Arabov and Marina Koreneva, for *Moloch* (Russia/Germany).
● **Palme d'Or for Best Short:** *When the Day Breaks*, by Wendy Tilby and Amanda Forbis (Canada).
● **Jury Prize for Best Short:** *So-Poong*, by Song Ilgon (South Korea); shared with *Stop*, by Rodolphe Marconi (France).
● **Camera d'Or for First Feature:** *Throne of Death* (India), by Murali Nair.
● **Grand Prix Technique:** Tu Juhua, production designer of *The Emperor and the Assassin* (China/Japan/France).

● **Fipresci International Critics' Award:** *New Dawn*, by Emilie Deleuze (France).
● **Out of competition:** *M/Other*, by Nobuhiro Suwa (Japan).
● **Ecumenical Prize:** *All About My Mother*.
● **Special mention:** *Rosetta*.
CRITICS' WEEK:
● **Feature:** *Flowers From Another World*, by Iciar Bollain (Spain).
● **Short:** *Shoes Off!*, by Mark Sawers (Canada).
CINEFONDATION AWARDS:
● **First Prize:** *Second Hand*, by Emily Young (UK/Poland).
● **Second Prize:** *Im Hukim*, by Dover Kosashvili (Israel/Georgia); shared with *La Puce*, by Emmanuelle Bercot (France).
● **Prix du Jury:** Manoel de Oliveira.

Jury: David Cronenberg (president); Andre Techine, George Miller, Maurizio Nichetti and Doris Dorrie, playwright Yasmina Reza, opera singer Barbara Hendricks and the actors Dominique Blanc, Holly Hunter and Jeff Goldblum

The 42nd David di Donatello Awards ('Davids'), Rome, July 1998

● **Best Film:** *Life is Beautiful*, by Roberto Benigni.
● **Best Director:** Roberto Benigni, for *Life is Beautiful*.
● **Best Actor:** Roberto Benigni, for *Life is Beautiful*.
● **Best Actress:** Valeria Bruni Tedeschi, for *La Parola amore esiste*.
● **Best Supporting Actor:** Silvio Orlando, for *Aprile*.
● **Best Supporting Actress:** Nicoletta Braschi, for *Ovosodo*.
● **Best Screenplay:** Roberto Benigni and Vincenzo Cerami, for *Life is Beautiful*.
● **Best Music:** Nino D'Angelo, for *Tano da morire*.
● **Best Sound:** *Ovosodo*.
● **Best New Director:** Roberta Torre, for *Tano da morire*.

The 24th Deauville Festival of American Cinema, 13 September 1998

● **Grand Prix for Best Film:** *Next Stop, Wonderland*, by Brad Anderson.
● **Jury Prize:** *High Art*, by Lisa Cholodenko.
● **Prix du Public:** *Next Stop, Wonderland*.

● **International Critics' Grand Prix:** *Gods and Monsters*, by Bill Condon.
● **Youth Jury Award:** *Very Bad Things*, by Peter Berg.
● **Best short:** *Whacked*, by Rolf Gibbs.

The 11th European Film Awards ('The Felixes'), London, 4 December 1998

● **Best European Film:** *Life is Beautiful* (Italy), by Roberto Benigni.
● **Best Actor:** Roberto Benigni, for *Life is Beautiful*.
● **Best Actress:** Elodie Bouchez and Natacha Regnier, for *The Dream Life of Angels* (France).
● **Best Screenplay:** Peter Howitt, for *Sliding Doors*.
● **Best Cinematography:** Adrian Biddle, for *The Butcher Boy*.
● **Best Short Film:** *Un Jour*, by Marie Paccou.
● **Discovery of the Year (Fassbinder Award):** Thomas Vinterberg, director of *Festen*; and Erick Zonca, director of *The Dream Life of Angels*.
● **Best Documentary (Prix Arte):** *Tableau avec chute*, by Claudio Pazienza.
PEOPLE'S AWARDS:
● **Best Actor:** Antonio Banderas, for *The Mask of Zorro*.
● **Best Actress:** Kate Winslet, for *Titanic*.
● **Best Director:** Roland Emmerich, for *Godzilla*.
● **Best Non-European Film:** *The Truman Show* (USA).
● **Achievement in World Cinema:** Stellan Skarsgaard, for his performances in *Amistad* and *Good Will Hunting*.
● **FIPRESCI Award:** Goran Paskaljevic, for *Bure Baruta* (aka *The Powder Keg*).
● **Lifetime Achievement Award:** Jeremy Irons.

Hosts: Carole Bouquet, Mel Smith.

The 24th French Academy ('Cesar') Awards, 6 March 1999

● **Best Film:** *The Dream Life of Angels*.
● **Best Director:** Patrice Chereau, for *Those Who Love Me Can Take the Train*.
● **Best Actor:** Jacques Villeret, for *Le Diner de Cons*.
● **Best Actress:** Elodie Bouchez, for *The Dream Life of Angels*.
● **Best Supporting Actor:** Daniel Prevost, for *Le Diner de Cons*.
● **Best Supporting Actress:** Dominique

Below: Fine young criminals: Elodie Bouchez and Natacha Regnier in The Dream Life of Angels, winner of the best film award at the French 'Cesars'

Blanc, for *Those Who Love Me Can Take the Train*.
● **Best New Director:** Bruno Podalydès, for *Dieu seul me voit*.
● **Most Promising Young Actor:** Bruno Putzulu, for *Petits désordres amoureux*.
● **Most Promising Young Actress:** Natacha Regnier, for *The Dream Life of Angels*.
● **Best First Film:** *Only God Sees Me*.
● **Best Screenplay:** Francis Veber, for *Le Diner de Cons*.
● **Best Photography:** Eric Gautier, for *Those Who Love Me Can Take the Train*.
● **Best Production Design:** Jacques Rouxel, for *Lautrec*.
● **Best Editing:** Véronique Lange, for *Taxi*.
● **Best Music:** Tony Gatlif, for *Gadjo Dilo*.
● **Best Costumes:** Pierre-Jean Larroque, for *Lautrec*.
● **Best Sound:** Vincent Tulli and Vincent Amardi, for *Taxi*.
● **Best Short:** *L'Interview*, by Xavier Giannoli.
● **Best Foreign Film:** *Life is Beautiful* (Italy).
● **Honorary Cesars:** Jean Rochefort, Johnny Depp, Pedro Almodovar.

Host: Isabelle Huppert

The 56th Hollywood Foreign Press Association ('Golden Globes') Awards, 24 January 1999

Above: Central Station, the Brazilian movie that won the Best Foreign Language Film award at the Golden Globes

● **Best Film – Drama:** *Saving Private Ryan*.
● **Best Film – Comedy or Musical:** *Shakespeare in Love*.
● **Best Actor – Drama:** Jim Carrey, for *The Truman Show*.
● **Best Actress – Drama:** Cate Blanchett, for *Elizabeth*.
● **Best Actor – Comedy or Musical:** Michael Caine, for *Little Voice*.
● **Best Actress – Comedy or Musical:** Gwyneth Paltrow, for *Shakespeare in Love*.
● **Best Supporting Actor:** Ed Harris, for *The Truman Show*.
● **Best Supporting Actress:** Lynn Redgrave, for *Gods and Monsters*.
● **Best Director:** Steven Spielberg, for *Saving Private Ryan*.
● **Best Screenplay:** Marc Norman and Tom Stoppard, for *Shakespeare in Love*.
● **Best Original Score:** Burkhard Dallwitz and Philip Glass, for *The Truman Show*.
● **Best Original Song:** 'The Prayer', music and lyrics by David Foster and Carole Bayer Sager, from *Quest For Camelot: The Magic Sword*
● **Best Foreign Language Film:** *Central Station* (Brazil), by Walter Salles.
● **Best TV Film or miniseries:** *From the Earth to the Moon*.
● **Cecil B. De Mille Award for Lifetime Achievement:** Jack Nicholson.

The 14th Independent Spirit Awards, Santa Monica, 20 March 1999

● **Best Film:** *Gods and Monsters*.
● **Best First Film:** *The Opposite of Sex*.
● **Best Director:** Wes Anderson, for *Rushmore*.
● **Best Actor:** Ian McKellen, for *Gods and Monsters*.
● **Best Actress:** Ally Sheedy, for *High Art*.
● **Best Supporting Actor:** Bill Murray, for *Rushmore*.
● **Best Supporting Actress:** Lynn Redgrave, for *Gods and Monsters*.
● **Best Debut Performance:** Evan Adams, for *Smoke Signals*.
● **Best Screenplay:** Don Roos, for *The Opposite of Sex*.
● **Best First Screenplay:** Darren Aronofsky, for *Pi*.
● **Best Cinematography:** Maryse Alberti, for *Velvet Goldmine*.
● **Best Foreign Film:** *Festen* (Denmark).
● **Someone To Watch Award:** David Williams, director, writer and editor of *13*.
● **Ralph Lauren Producers' Award:** Susan A. Stover.

The 19th London Film Critics' Awards ('The Alfs'), The Dorchester, London, 4 March 1999

● **Best Film:** *Saving Private Ryan*.
● **Best Actor:** Jack Nicholson, for *As Good As It Gets*.
● **Best Actress:** Cate Blanchett, for *Elizabeth*.
● **Best Director:** Steven Spielberg, for *Saving Private Ryan*.
● **Best Screenwriter:** Andrew Niccol, for *Gattaca* and *The Truman Show*.
● **Best British Film:** *Lock, Stock and Two Smoking Barrels*.
● **Best British Producers:** Alison Owen, Tim Bevan and Eric Fellner, for *Elizabeth*.
● **Best British Director:** John Boorman, for *The General*.
● **Best British Screenwriter:** Guy Ritchie, for *Lock, Stock and Two Smoking Barrels*.
● **Best British Actor:** Brendan Gleeson, for *The General*.
● **Best British Actress:** Helena Bonham Carter, for *The Wings of the Dove*.
● **Best British Supporting Actor:** Nigel Hawthorne, for *The Object of My Affection*.
● **Best British Supporting Actress:** Kate Beckinsale, for *The Last Days of Disco*; and Minnie Driver, for *Good Will Hunting*.
● **Best British Newcomer:** Peter Mullan, star of *My Name is Joe*.
● **Best Foreign Language Film:** *Shall We Dance?* (Japan).
● **Dilys Powell Awards:** Albert Finney, John Hurt
● **Lifetime Achievement Awards:** John Boorman, production designer John Box

Presenters: Christopher Tookey, James Cameron-Wilson, Mariella Frostrup, Paul Gambaccini, Marianne Gray, Tom Hutchinson, Karen Krizanovich, John Marriott, George Perry, Simon Rose, etc

The Los Angeles Film Critics' Association Awards, 12 December 1998

● **Best Film:** *Saving Private Ryan*.
● **Best Actor:** Ian McKellen, for *Gods and Monsters*.
● **Best Actress:** Fernanda Montenegro, for *Central Station*; and Ally Sheedy, for *High Art*.
● **Best Supporting Actor:** Bill Murray, for *Rushmore* and *Wild Things*; and Billy Bob Thornton, for *A Simple Plan*.
● **Best Supporting Actress:** Joan Allen, for *Pleasantville*.
● **Best Director:** Steven Spielberg, for

Saving Private Ryan.
- **Best Screenplay:** Warren Beatty and Jeremy Pikser, for *Bulworth.*
- **Best Cinematography:** Janusz Kaminski, for *Saving Private Ryan.*
- **Best Production Design:** Jeannine Oppewall, for *Pleasantville.*
- **Best Music:** Elliot Goldenthal, for *The Butcher Boy.*
- **Best Foreign Film:** *Festen* (Denmark). Best Animated Feature: *A Bug's Life* by John Lasseter and Andrew Stanton; and *T.R.A.N.S.I.T.* by Piet Kroon.
- **Best Documentary:** *The Farm: Angola USA,* by Jonathan Stack, Liz Garbus and Wilbert Rideau.

The 90th National Board of Review of Motion Picture Awards, New York, 8 December 1998

- **Best Film:** *Gods and Monsters.*
- **Best Actor:** Ian McKellen, for *Gods and Monsters.*
- **Best Actress:** Fernanda Montenegro, for *Central Station.*
- **Best Supporting Actor:** Ed Harris, for *Stepmom* and *The Truman Show.*
- **Best Supporting Actress:** Christina Ricci, for *Buffalo 66, The Opposite of Sex* and *Pecker.*
- **Best Director:** Shekhar Kapur, for *Elizabeth.*
- **Best Directorial Debut:** Kasi Lemmons, for *Eve's Bayou.*
- **Best Ensemble Cast:** *Happiness.*
- **Best Documentary:** *Wild Man Blues,* by Barbara Kopple.
- **Best Foreign Film:** *Central Station* (Brazil), by Walter Salles.
- **Breakthrough Performance:** Bai Ling, for *Red Corner.*
- **Special Achievement in Filmmaking Award:** Roberto Benigni, for producing, writing, directing and starring in *Life is Beautiful.*
- **The Billy Wilder Award for Excellence:** Martin Scorsese.
- **Freedom of Expression Award:** Bernardo Bertolucci.
- **Career Achievement Award:** Michael Caine.

The 33rd National Society of Film Critics' Awards, New York, January 1999

- **Best Film:** *Out of Sight.*
- **Best Actor:** Nick Nolte, for *Affliction.*

- **Best Actress:** Ally Sheedy, for *High Art.*
- **Best Director:** Steven Soderbergh, for *Out of Sight.*
- **Best Supporting Actor:** Bill Murray, for *Rushmore.*
- **Best Supporting Actress:** Judi Dench, for *Shakespeare in Love.*
- **Best Screenplay:** Scott Frank, for *Out of Sight.*

The 64th New York Film Critics' Circle Awards, 16 December 1998

- **Best Film:** *Saving Private Ryan.*
- **Best Actor:** Nick Nolte, for *Affliction.*
- **Best Actress:** Cameron Diaz, for *There's Something About Mary.*
- **Best Supporting Actor:** Bill Murray, for *Rushmore.*
- **Best Supporting Actress:** Lisa Kudrow, for *The Opposite of Sex.*
- **Best Director:** Terrence Malick, for *The Thin Red Line.*
- **Best Screenplay:** Marc Norman and Tom Stoppard, for *Shakespeare in Love.*
- **Best Cinematography:** John Toll, for *The Thin Red Line.*
- **Best Foreign Film:** *Festen* (Denmark).
- **Best Non-Fiction Film:** *The Farm: Angola USA,* by Jonathan Stack, Liz Garbus and Wilbert Rideau.
- **Best First Film:** *Love and Death on Long Island* (Canada/UK), by Richard Kwietniowski.
- **Special Award:** October Films and Universal Pictures for the newly edited version of Orson Welles' *Touch of Evil.*

The 15th Sundance Film Festival, Park City, Utah, 30 January 1999

- **The Grand Jury Prize (best feature):** *Three Seasons,* by Tony Bui.
- **The Grand Jury Prize (best documentary):** *American Movie,* by Chris Smith.
- **Best Performance:** Steve Zahn, for *Happy, Texas.*
- **Best Direction:** Eric Mendelsohn, for *Judy Berlin.*
- **Best Direction (documentary):** Barbara Sonnenborn, for *Regret to Inform.*
- **Best Cinematography:** Lisa Rinzler, for *Three Seasons.*
- **Best Cinematography (documentary):** Emiko Omori, for *Rabbit in the Moon* and *Regret to Inform.*
- **Audience Award (best feature):** *Three*

Seasons, by Tony Bui.
- **Audience Award (best documentary):** *Genghis Blues,* by Roko Belic.
- **Filmmakers' Trophy (best feature):** *Tumbleweeds,* by Gavin O'Connor.
- **Filmmakers' Trophy (best documentary):** *Sing Faster: The Stagehands' Ring Cycle,* by Jon Else.
- **Short Filmmaking Award:** *More,* by Mark Osborne.
- **Waldo Salt Screenwriting Award:** Audrey Wells, for *Guinevere*; and Frank Whaley, for *Joe the King.*
- **Freedom of Expression Award:** *The Black Press: Soldiers Without Swords,* by Stanley Nelson.
- **Special Jury Award (documentary):** *On the Ropes,* by Nanette Burstein and Brett Morgan.
- **Latin American Cinema Award:** *La Vida es silbar,* by Fernando Perez.
- **World Cinema:** *Lola rennt,* by Tom Tykwer; and *Train de vie,* by Radu Mihaileanu.

The 55th Venice International Film Festival Awards, September 1998

- **Golden Lion for Best Film:** *The Way We Laughed,* by Gianni Amelio (Italy).
- **Special Jury Grand Prix:** *Last Stop Paradise,* by Lucian Pintilie (France/Romania).
- **Best Actor:** Sean Penn, for *Hurlyburly* (USA).
- **Best Actress:** Catherine Deneuve, for *Place Vendome* (France).
- **Marcello Mastroianni Award for Emerging Actor:** Niccoli Senni, for *Shooting the Moon* (Italy).
- **Best Director:** Emir Kusturica, for *Black Cat, White Cat* (France/Germany/Yugoslavia).
- **Best Screenplay:** Eric Rohmer, for *An Autumn Tale* (France).
- **Best Photography:** Luca Bigazzi, for *Shooting the Moon* and *The Way We Laughed.*
- **Best Music:** Gerardo Gandini, for *The Cloud* (Argentina/France/Italy/Germany).
- **Gold Medal (for a film which emphasises civil progress and human solidarity):** *The Silence,* by Mohsen Makhmalbaf (Iran/France).
- **Fipresci Award:** *The Powder Keg,* by Goran Paskaljevic (France/Yugoslavia/Greece/ Macedonia/Turkey).
- **Fipresci Award for best first or second feature:** *Train of Life,* by Radu Mihaileanu (France/Belgium/Romania/The Netherlands).
- **Golden Lion for lifetime achievement:** Warren Beatty.

In Memoriam

JOHN ADDISON

Born: 16 March 1920 in West Chobham, Surrey, England. **Died:** 7 December 1998 in Vermont of a stroke.

● A prolific composer of British films, John Addison will probably be best remembered for his ebullient, Oscar-winning score to *Tom Jones* (1963). Other credits include *Reach for the Sky* (1956), *Look Back in Anger*, *The Entertainer*, *A Taste of Honey*, *The Loneliness of the Long Distance Runner*, Hitchcock's *Torn Curtain*, *The Charge of the Light Brigade*, *Sleuth* and *A Bridge Too Far*. The playwright John Osborne, a close friend, based two characters from his 1968 play *The Hotel in Amsterdam* on Addison and his wife Pamela.

KIRK ALYN

Born: 8 October 1910 in Oxford, New Jersey. **Died:** 14 March 1999 of 'natural causes'. **Real name:** John Feggo Jr.

● A supporting player in B-movies, Alyn won fame at the age of 37 when he was cast as the first Man of Steel in the serials *Superman* (1948) and *Atom Man vs Superman* (1950). Initially reluctant to take on the mantle of the superhero, Alyn lived to regret his change of heart, saying that the part destroyed his career. His other credits include such films as *Federal Agents vs Underworld Inc* (1949), *Radar Patrol vs Spy King* (1950) and *The Eddy Duchin Story* (1956). He was also cast as Lois Lane's father in the 1978 *Superman – The Movie*, but was dropped from the finished print. He was married to the actress Virginia O'Brien (1943-49) and wrote an autobiography, *A Job for Superman*.

GENE AUTRY

Born: 29 September 1907 in Tioga, Texas. **Died:** 2 October 1998 in Studio City, California, after a long illness. **Real name:** Orvon Gene Autry.

● Through sheer hard work and determination, Gene Autry became the first singing cowboy star of the movies, laying the trail for the likes of Roy Rogers and Tex Ritter. With his trusty steed Champion, comic sidekick 'Frog' (played by Smiley Burnette) and signature theme song 'Back in the Saddle Again', Autry became an American institution, baf-

fling the critics and stirring the imagination of clean-cut boy scouts everywhere. Indeed, such was his enduring popularity that the town of Berwyn, Oklahoma, changed its name to – Gene Autry. The son of a poor tenant farmer, little Gene learned to ride young and at 15 joined a patent medicine show. He then bought a guitar and, after a chance encounter with Will Rogers, tried his luck with a studio test in New York. This led to a series of RCA Victor recordings which, in turn, landed him his own radio show, *The Oklahoma Yodelling Cowboy* – and his first million-selling record. In 1934 he made his film debut in *In Old Sante Fe* and received so much fan mail that he was assigned his own series, *Phantom Empire*. This led to his first starring film role, in *Tumbling Tumbleweeds* (1935), and he was off. He was featured in 93 films in all and was always a paradigm of virtue, a non-smoking teetotaller who never hit or shot a man first. He was also the first Western star to become a top-ten box-office attraction and went on to amass one of the largest fortunes in showbusiness. In the early Fifties he starred in his own TV series and produced several others, while his weekly radio show *Melody Ranch* (sponsored by Wrigley's chewing gum) was a phenomenal success. As a recording star, his song 'Rudolph the Red-nosed Reindeer' (1949) became the second highest selling record of all time (after 'White Christmas'). Ever the shrewd businessman, Autry purchased the California Angels baseball franchise and, in the early Eighties, set up The Gene Autry Western Heritage Museum with former banker Jacqueline Ellam, who became his second wife. He also penned an autobiography, *Back in the Saddle Again*, published in 1978.

ROBIN BAILEY

Born: 5 October 1919. **Died:** January 1999.

● A well-known face on the British stage and on TV – usually as cricket-loving brigadier types – Robin Bailey made occasional forays into film, including *Private Angelo* (1949), *Catch Us If You Can* (1965), *The Whisperers* (1966), *You Only Live Twice* (1967), *Blind Terror* (1971) and *Jane and the Lost City* (1987).

BINNIE BARNES

Born: 25 March 1903 in Finsbury, north London. **Died:** 27 July 1998 of natural causes at her home in Beverly Hills. **Real name:** Gertrude Maude Barnes.

● A sophisticated, self-assured presence in many British films – and then in Hollywood – Binnie Barnes was typecast as 'the other woman' but made a virtue of her roles as acerbic mistresses and wise-cracking girlfriends. She made her mark as a seductive Catherine Howard in Alexander Korda's *The Private Life of Henry VIII* (1933) and went on to appear in *Diamond Jim*, *The Last of the Mohicans*, *The Adventures of Marco Polo*, *The Three Musketeers*, *The Divorce of Lady X* and *Three Girls About Town*. During a poker game with Clark Gable she was introduced to former football star Mike Frankovich, fell in love, married and retired from the screen in 1955. However, she returned to make three more films, namely *The Trouble With Angels* (1966), *Where Angels Go...Trouble Follows* (1968) and *Forty Carats* (1973). In her later years she devoted much of her time to charity fund-raising.

EVA BARTOK

Born: 18 June 1926 in Kecskemet, Hungary. **Died:** 1 August 1998 in a London hospital. **Real name:** Eva Martha Szoke.

● Something of a tabloid's darling, Eva Bartok exercised a powerful grip on the public's imagination via a string of husbands, lovers and stylish material accessories. Indeed, by the time she was 32 she had been divorced no less than four times. At 16 she married a Hungarian SS officer (apparently against her will), had the liaison annulled after the war and then threw herself into an acting career. She wrote to the Hungarian producer Alexander Paal in Hollywood asking for an American visa, but was summarily turned down. Instead, Paal returned to Europe and married her, a union that lasted three years. She then settled down to a period of domestic bliss with the publicist William Wordsworth (the great grandson of the poet), before marrying the German star Curt Jurgens, whom she divorced a year later. Next, she embarked on a torrid affair with Frank Sinatra, became pregnant and claimed that he was the father. Of her 40 films, most were immediately forgettable, although Robert Siodmak's *The Crimson Pirate* (1952) was a success and one critic liked *Front Page Story* (1954), a British drama with Jack Hawkins. Eventually tiring of her regular commute between Rome and London's Mayfair, the actress opted for a life of retirement in Indonesia, but later returned to London where she was found wandering the streets. She published an autobiography, *Worth Living For*, in 1959.

DIRK BOGARDE

Born: 28 March 1920 in London. **Died:** 8 May 1999 of a heart attack at home in London.
Real name: Derek Jules Gaspard Ulric Niven van den Bogaerde.
● Dirk Bogarde had so many facets to his career that it was hard to believe that the teen idol, art-house actor and writer all resided within the same man. The son of Ulric Van Den Bogaerde, the arts editor of *The Times*, Bogarde resisted his father's attempts to start him on a course of journalism and joined the theatre instead. Even as a boy he had written plays to amuse his sister and was an enthusiastic participant in school productions. After service in the war, Bogarde's dark good looks attracted talent scouts at Rank and soon he was being groomed for screen stardom. Following his debut as a young policeman in *Dancing With Crime* (1947), starring Richard Attenborough, he attracted enthusiastic reviews for his portrayal of Tom Riley, a petty crook in Basil Dearden's *The Blue Lamp* (1949). He followed this with increas-

ingly impressive roles in such British pictures as *Hunted*, *The Gentle Gunman* (both 1952) and *They Who Dare* (1953), until his performance as the romantically befuddled Simon Sparrow in *Doctor in the House* (1954) heralded a new period of popularity. In fact, such was his appeal to young women that at public engagements he was forced to sew up his fly buttons. Bogarde himself noted (in *The Sunday Telegraph*), 'I never looked a conventional romantic hero. And I think it was only because the producer was a woman, Betty Box, that she could see I had sex appeal, though not of the orthodox kind.' Now Bogarde was a certified box-office star and the only Rank player to have script approval. His career took another turn when he courageously took on the role of a bisexual lawyer in Dearden's ground-breaking *Victim* (1961), the first British picture to openly tackle the question of homosexuality and which partly led to the decriminalisation of the practice in England. Bogarde himself was fiercely guarded about his own homosexuality and, indeed, of any probing into his private life. Anyhow, *Victim* dramatically changed his image as a romantic leading man and he embarked on a series of films with the expatriate American director Joseph Losey, the first of which was the critically acclaimed *The Servant* (1963) in which, again, the actor played a character with gay undertones. However, by the late Sixties Bogarde had become disillusioned by the British cinema and he moved to Rome and then Provence for a fresh start in some noteworthy European features, including Luchino Visconti's celebrated *Death in Venice* (1971), in which he played an ageing composer obsessed by a young boy. He also starred in Liliana Cavani's controversial *The Night Porter* (as a sadomasochistic concentration camp guard obsessed by a Jewish inmate), Alain Resnais' *Providence* (1977), Rainer Werner Fassbinder's *Despair* (1978) and Bertrand Tavernier's *Daddy Nostalgie* (1990). Meanwhile, in 1976 he was approached by the publisher Chatto and Windus to pen his autobiography, *A Postillion Struck by Lightning*, a book that was met with such critical praise that he took to writing a series of autobiographical volumes, destroying all relevant letters and memorabilia after the completion of each title. Then, when his companion and manager Tony Forwood fell seriously ill in the early Eighties, he was forced to sell his French estate and move back to London. He was knighted in 1992.

BETTY BOX

Born: 25 September 1915 in Beckenham, Kent. **Died:** 15 January 1999.
● Betty Box produced so many successful pictures in her day that she acquired the nickname of Miss Box-Office. Yet her films – which regularly featured budding Rank stars – never attempted to be anything other than meat-and-two-veg productions, with little regard for artistic pretension or overseas appeal. Starting out as an assistant to her twin brother, the writer-producer Sydney Box, she went on to team up with Ralph Thomas to produce 30 productions between 1950 and 1974, usually broad comedies and Boy's Own adventures. Interestingly, in what appeared to be an increasingly incestuous business, her partner was the brother of Gerald Thomas, the producer of the *Carry On* films which were produced by Peter Rogers, her second husband. She was made a CBE in 1958.

RORY CALHOUN

Born: 8 August 1922 in Los Angeles. **Died:**

28 April 1999 in Los Angeles, from complications involving emphysema and diabetes.
Real name: Francis Durgin.
● A handsome, rugged-looking actor, Rory Calhoun found fame as Bill Longley in NBC's *The Texan* (1958-60), then went on to feature in a string of outdoorsy vehicles, including *Marco Polo* (1962), in which he played Marco Polo, *Apache Uprising* (1965), *Dayton's Devils* (1968) and *Pure Country* (1992). He was married to the actress-singer Lita Baron from 1949 to 1970.

IRON EYES CODY

Born: 3 April 1907. **Died:** 4 January 1999 in Los Angeles of natural causes.
● One of the most recognisable Indian faces in American cinema, Cody appeared in over one hundred film and TV shows, from his

reputed debut in D.W. Griffith's *The Massacre* (1912) to Howard Zieff's affectionate homage to the cowboy film, *Hearts of the West* (1975). The son of a Cherokee (his father) and a Cree (his mother), both of whom performed in Wild West shows, Cody caught the showbiz bug early. He was just seven when he danced on screen in Cecil B. DeMille's *The Squaw Man*, going on to appear in such silents as *The Covered Wagon* (1923), John Ford's *The Iron Horse* (1924) and *War Paint* (1926). An ardent supporter of his own culture, he served as technical advisor on a number of films, including *Union Pacific* (1939), *North West Mounted Police* (1940) and *Unconquered* (1947), in which he co-starred. He achieved even greater recognition when he agreed to front an anti-litter campaign in the Seventies, in which his stoic features were seen to shed a single tear (although he argued that 'Indians don't cry'). He also wrote a number of books, including an autobiography, and maintained a museum full of Indian artifacts, costumes and paintings.

VITTORIO COTTAFAVI

Born: 30 January 1914 in Modena, northern Italy. **Died:** 13 December 1998 in Anzio, near Rome.

● Noted more for his stylish direction than for the quality of his films, Cottafavi specialised in sword and sandal 'epics' like *Revolt of the Gladiators* (1958), *Goliath and the Dragon* (1960) and *Hercules Conquers Atlantis* (1961). Apparently, he was an inspiration for Francois Truffaut.

MICHAEL DENISON

Born: 1 November 1915 in Doncaster, Yorkshire. **Died:** 22 July 1998 of cancer at his home in Amersham, Bucks.

● Cast as debonair, jolly decent chaps, Michael Denison was an enormously popular star in British films after the war. Trained at the Webber Douglas Academy of Dramatic Art, he made his professional debut in 1938 – as Lord Fancourt Babberley in *Charley's Aunt* at Frinton-on-Sea, Essex – and a year later was in his first film, Walter Forde's *Inspector Hornleigh On Holiday*. That same year he married the actress Dulcie Gray and so began one of the sturdiest husband-and-wife partnerships in British entertainment. His other films included *Tilly of Bloomsbury*, *Hungry Hill*, *My Brother Jonathan*, *The Glass Mountain*, *The Magic Box*, *The Franchise Affair*, *Angels One Five*, *The Importance of Being Earnest* (in which he

played Algernon Moncrieff), *Contraband Spain*, *Faces in the Dark* and Richard Attenborough's *Shadowlands*. He and his wife co-authored *The Actor and His World* in 1964 and were jointly appointed the CBE in 1983. He also wrote two memoirs, *Overtures and Beginners* (1973) and *Double Act* (1985).

FAITH DOMERGUE

Born: 16 June 1925 in New Orleans.
Died: 4 April 1999 of cancer.

● A starlet of dubious acting merit and sultry good looks, Domergue was the protege of Howard Hughes. Spotted by the tycoon on a Warner Bros publicity cruise, the contracted player was duly courted and moved in with him on her 16th birthday. After building her a villa and cementing her confidence with extravagant gifts and acting lessons, Hughes cast her in the Jane Russell vehicle *Young Widow* (1946) and then in her own picture, *Vendetta* (1950). Following withering reviews and Hughes' new infatuation with Ava Gardner, Domergue looked like history but emerged as the star of a series of low-budget films with titles like *It Came From Beneath the Sea* (1955), *Prehistoric Planet Women* (1966) and *The House of Seven Corpses* (1974). She never won an Oscar, though.

MEREDITH EDWARDS

Born: 10 June 1917 in Rhosllannerchrugog, Clwyd, Wales. **Died:** 8 February 1999.

● Adept at playing resourceful Welshmen and benevolent officers of the law, Meredith Edwards brightened up a fair number of films from Ealing Studios' *A Run For Your Money* in 1949 (in which he was supported by Alec Guinness) to the 1994 *A Christmas Reunion* directed by David Hemmings. He was also a steadfast supporter of Welsh nationalism.

PENNY EDWARDS

Born: 24 August 1928 in Jackson Heights, New York. **Died:** 26 August 1998 of lung cancer in Friendswood, Texas.

Real name: Millicent Edwards.

● A blonde staple of Roy Rogers programmers, Penny Edwards failed to break out of the saddle that Republic had hitched her to. A member of the Ziegfeld Follies by the age of 12, she made her film debut at 19 in the Ronald Reagan/Shirley Temple drama *That Hagen Girl* and three years later signed up with Republic and a future of sagebrush. She was married to the Universal casting director Ralph Winters and is the mother of the actress Deborah Winters.

NORMAN FELL

Born: 24 March 1924 in Philadelphia.
Died: 14 December 1998 of cancer in Woodland Hills, Los Angeles.

● A character actor with lugubrious looks, Norman Fell was equally at home in drama and comedy and made a name for himself as the impotent landlord Stanley Roper on ABC TV's *Three's Company* (1977-79) and the spin-off *The Ropers* (1979-80). His film credits were numerous and included *Ocean's Eleven*, *Inherit the Wind*, *The Killers*, *Bullitt*, *The Graduate*, *Catch 22*, *Charley Varrick*, *For the Boys* and *The Destiny of Mary Fine*.

EDWIGE FEUILLERE

Born: 29 October 1907 at Vesoul, in the Jura. **Died:** 14 November 1998.

Real name: Caroline Vivette Edwige Cunati.

● A leading light of the Comedie Francaise, Mlle Feullere brought a grace, eroticism and warmth to her performances that made her one of the greatest actresses of the French theatre. It all began in 1931 when she married the stage actor Pierre Feullere (and took his name, although they divorced two years later), joined the Comedie Francaise and made her film debut (complete with nude scene) in the Fernandel short *La Fine Combine*. She appeared in one British film – *Woman Hater* (1948) with Stewart Granger – and numerous French productions, notably such costume dramas as *Lucrece Borgia* (1935), *De Mayerling a Sarajevo* (1940), *L'Idiot* (1946) and *L'Aigle a deux tetes* (1948), the last named being a role written especially for her by Jean Cocteau. She penned her autobiography in 1977 and received an honorary Cesar seven years later.

CHRISTOPHER GABLE

Born: 13 March 1940 in the East End of London. **Died:** 23 October 1998 of cancer in London.

● A leading dancer with the Royal Ballet, Gable made his mark internationally as an actor in the films of Ken Russell. Following supporting roles in Russell's *Women in Love* (1969) and *The Music Lovers* (1971), he went on to play the all-dancing romantic male lead in *The Boyfriend* (1971), opposite Twiggy. He was also featured in *The Slipper and The Rose* (1975) and in Russell's *The Lair of the White Worm* (1988) and *The Rainbow* (1989).

ERNEST GOLD

Born: 13 July 1921 in Vienna. **Died:** 17 March 1999 from complications following a stroke.

● A year after emigrating to New York with his family in 1938, Gold composed his first symphony, which was broadcast by NBC. Six years later he moved to Hollywood and embarked on a fruitful career scoring movies. Among his more notable credits are *On the Beach*, *Inherit the Wind*, *It's a Mad, Mad, Mad, Mad World*, *The Secret of Santa Vittoria*, *Tom Horn* and his popular, Oscar-winning score for Otto Preminger's *Exodus* (1960). He was married to the actress-singer Marnie Nixon (most famous for dubbing Audrey Hepburn's singing in *My Fair Lady*) and was the first film composer to win a place on Sunset Boulevard's Walk of Fame.

JAMES GOLDMAN

Born: 30 June 1927 in Chicago.
Died: 28 October 1998 of a heart attack in Manhattan, New York.
● A celebrated playwright, scenarist and novelist, James Goldman will be best remembered for the Oscar-winning adaptation of his own stage success, *The Lion in Winter*. He also penned the screenplays *They Might Be Giants* (again, from his own play), *Nicholas and Alexandria*, *Robin and Marian* and *White Nights*, and was the author of the book of the stage musical *Follies*, for which Stephen Sondheim wrote the songs. His brother is the successful screenwriter and Hollywood commentator William Goldman.

MARIUS GORING, CBE

Born: 23 May 1912 in Newport, Isle of White. **Died:** 30 September 1998.
● While today best remembered for his portrayal of Julian Craster, the struggling composer married to Moira Shearer's ballerina in Powell and Pressburger's *The Red Shoes* (1948), Marius Goring was actually typecast in the cinema as smooth and dangerous bounders, frequently with German accents. He was a Nazi stormtrooper in *Pastor Hall* (1940), the German governor of Crete in *Ill Met By Moonlight* (1956) and a Nazi spy in *I Was Monty's Double* (1958). He was also the voice of Hitler in the 1935 radio series *The Shadow of the Swastika*. However, he proved more versatile on the stage, triumphing in Shakespeare and later starring in a very successful West End run of Anthony Shaffer's *Sleuth*. Then on television he found a loyal following in the late Sixties with his portrayal of Dr John Hardy, *The Expert*, a red-bearded forensic scientist unravelling clues in Warwickshire. He was also an active force in British Equity, having been a founding

member of the union in 1929, becoming vice-president in the Sixties.

LEW GRADE

Born: 25 December 1906 in Tokmak, the Ukraine. **Died:** 13 December 1998 from heart failure in a London hospital.
Real name: Louis Winogradsky.
● Always brandishing his trademark nine-inch cigar and ready with a quip, Lew Grade was a colourful figure in the British entertainment industry. A tireless worker, he was famous for his outsize *chutzpah*, instant deals and business catastrophes. Yet he struggled on, becoming the founding father of independent television and producing a string of big-budget, international extravaganzas. Among his more unusual achievements was his winning of the World Charleston championship (in 1926) and his offer to sign up one of his own clients at a hugely inflated rate. He also established Associated Television, the theatrical agency The Grade Organisation and ITC Entertainment. Among his credits as producer were such high-profile films as *The Cassandra Crossing*, *The Boys From Brazil*, *Raise the Titanic*, *On Golden Pond* and *Sophie's Choice*. In 1976 he was created a Life Peer and in 1987 wrote his autobiography, *Still Dancing*. Contrary to popular legend, when asked by a little girl how much two and two made, Grade did not respond, 'it depends if you're buying or selling.' However, he did say, 'all my shows are great. Some of the them are bad. But they are all great.' His brother was Lord Delfont, another indefatigable, cigar-chomping entertainment tycoon.

HUNTZ HALL

Born: 15 August 1920 in Boston, Massachusetts. **Died:** 30 January 1999 of heart failure in North Hollywood.
Real name: Henry Hall.
● A bug-eyed, broken-nosed character actor, Huntz Hall originated the role of the buffoonish Dippy in the stage version of *Dead End* (1935). He went on to play the character's various transformations in a series of films featuring the Dead End Kids and their replacements the East End Kids and the Bowery Boys, by which time Dippy had become Satch. In his later years, Hall became a regular nightclub performer as well as playing the judge in Disney's *Herbie Rides Again* (1974) and the movie mogul Jesse Lasky in Ken Russell's *Valentino* (1977).

HURD HATFIELD

Born: 7 December 1918 in New York City.
Died: 25 December 1998 at a friend's house in Ireland.
Real name: William Rukard Hurd Hatfield.
● Much like the ageless, handsome character he played in the poignant film of Oscar Wilde's *The Picture of Dorian Gray* (1945), Hatfield retained his icy good looks into advanced middle age. However, in spite of the success of the actor's second film, his career quickly slid downhill and he rapidly found himself in tosh like *Tarzan and the Slave Girl* and *Destination Murder* (both 1950). Theatre, TV movies and supporting roles in films followed, his last feature being the abysmal Tom Selleck romp *Her Alibi* (1989).

PATRICIA HAYES

Born: 22 December 1909 in London.
Died: 19 September 1998 in London.
● An irrepressible character actress, most at home in raucous Cockney roles, Patricia Hayes found her niche in television, particularly as *Edna, the Inebriate Woman* (1972), for which she won the BAFTA award as Best Actress. Her numerous film credits include *Broken Blossoms* (1936), *Nicholas Nickleby*, *A Hard Day's Night*, *Help!*, *Goodbye Mr Chips* (1969), *The Never Ending Story*, *Little Dorrit* (as Affery Flintwinch), *Willow*, *A Fish Called Wanda*, *The Fool* and *The Steal*.

JOAN HICKSON

Born: 5 August 1906 in Kingsthorpe, Northampton. **Died:** 17 October 1999 in Colchester.
● While beginning her career as a 21-year-old Lady Shoreham in a tour of *His Wife's Children* (1927), Joan Hickson won her greatest acclaim at the age of 78. Bringing a fresh note of acuity and level-headedness to the role of Agatha Christie's Miss Marple in the 1984-92 BBC series, Miss Hickson suddenly became a household name. Film buffs, however, knew her from a variety of comic cameos in countless films, from the 1933 *Trouble in Store* to Stephen Poliakoff's *Century* (1993).

VALERIE HOBSON

Born: 14 April 1917 in Larne, Northern Ireland. **Died:** 13 November 1998 of a heart attack in London.
● An elegant leading lady of British films, Valerie Hobson will forever be remembered as the grown-up Estella in David Lean's *Great Expectations* (1946) and as the serenely aristocratic Edith D'Ascoyne in the Ealing classic *Kind Hearts and Coronets* (1949). However,

her name is equally linked to that of her husband, the Conservative MP John Profumo, whose affair with the call girl Christine Keeler ostensibly toppled the British Cabinet in 1963 (and provided the scenario for the 1988 film *Scandal*). The actress was previously married to the producer Anthony Havelock-Allan, but retired after falling in love with Profumo, with whom she stayed married until her death. Her other notable film credits include the American movies *The Mystery of Edwin Drood*, *The Werewolf in London* and *Bride of Frankenstein* as well as the British *Q Planes*, *The Rocking Horse Winner*, *Contraband* and *The Card*. She also originated the role of Anna in the 1953 London stage version of *The King and I*.

MEGS JENKINS

Born: 21 April 1917 in Cheshire.
Died: 5 October 1998.

● A plump, useful character actress, Megs Jenkins graced a considerable number of British pictures from her debut in the George Arliss vehicle *Dr Syn* (1937) to the entirely less commendable *The Amorous Milkman* (1974). Among her more memorable portrayals were the nurse in Launder and Gilliat's sublime *Green for Danger* (1946) and the jolly landlady in *The History of Mr Polly* (1949).

ROSAMUND JOHN

Born: 19 October 1913 in Tottenham, London.
Died: 27 October 1998.
Real name: Nora Rosamund Jones.

● A striking reddish-blonde, Rosamund John was encouraged by Robert Donat to pursue a career in films and at the age of 29 played the wife of Leslie Howard's aircraft designer R.J. Mitchell in his *The First of the Few* (1942). She soon became a solid and popular star, appearing in such Forties' favourites as *The Lamp Still Burns*, *The Way to the Stars* (as the stoically grieving wife of Michael Redgrave), *Green for Danger*, *The Upturned Glass* and *Fame is the Spur*. She excelled in a variety of roles, although she was at her best playing gracious and sensible pillars of the British community. Later, she turned her attention to politics and, in 1950, married the Labour MP John Silkin.

HENRY JONES

Born: 1 August 1912 in Philadelphia.
Died: 17 May 1999 from a fall in his Santa Monica home, California.

● Small, pugnacious and chinless, Henry Jones was a useful and adaptable character actor, at home on the big screen, on TV and

on stage playing anything that was thrown at him. In the theatre he won a Tony for his part as Louis Howe in *Sunrise at Campobello* and on screen he appeared in *The Bad Seed*, *Vertigo* (as the coroner), *Butch Cassidy and the Sundance Kid*, *Arachnophobia* and *The Grifters*.

GARSON KANIN

Born: 24 November 1912 in Rochester, New York. **Died:** 13 March 1999 of heart failure in Manhattan.

● A playwright, actor, film director and documentarist, Garson Kanin will be best remembered for his screenplays to *A Double Life* (1947), *Adam's Rib* (1949) and *Pat and Mike* (1952), all of which were directed by George Cukor, nominated for Oscars and co-scripted by his wife, the actress-writer Ruth Gordon. He and Gordon also wrote two vehicles for the actress Judy Holliday (who had starred in Cukor's adaptation of Kanin's hit Broadway play, *Born Yesterday*), *The Marrying Kind* and *It Should Happen To You*. In 1946 he won an Oscar for his feature documentary on the Liberation of Europe, *The True Glory*.

DeFOREST KELLEY

Born: 20 January 1920 in Atlanta, Georgia. **Died:** 11 June 1999 of stomach cancer in Los Angeles.
Real name: Jackson DeForest Kelley.

● Although he had good roles in such movies as *Fear in the Night* (1947), *Gunfight at the OK Corral* (1957; as Morgan Earp), *Warlock* (1959) and *Apache Uprising* (1966), DeForest Kelley found his niche as the down-to-earth Dr Leonard 'Bones' McCoy in the *Star Trek* TV and movie series. It made him one of the most recognisable faces in the galaxy and his prognosis, 'he's dead, Jim,' an international catch phrase.

PERSIS KHAMBATTA

Born: 2 October 1950 in Bombay. **Died:** 18 August 1998 of a heart attack in Bombay.
● Arguably one of the most stunningly beautiful actresses to make a name for herself outside her native India, Persis shot to fame as the bald alien Ilia in *Star Trek – The Motion Picture* (1979). A former Miss India, the actress went on to grace such English-speaking pictures as *Nighthawks*, *Megaforce* and *Phoenix the Warrior*.

RICHARD KILEY

Born: 31 March 1922 in Chicago. **Died:** 5 March 1999 in Warwick, New York.
● It was Richard Kiley who originated the resounding blast of 'I am I – the Man of La

Mancha!' in the Broadway musical of 1965 and went on to win a Tony for his pains. He also won three Emmys – for *The Thorn Birds*, *A Year in the Life* and *Picket Fences* – and appeared in such films as *The Blackboard Jungle*, *The Little Prince*, *Looking for Mr Goodbar*, *Phenomenon* and *Patch Adams*. He was also the distinguished voice ('no expense spared') that welcomed visitors to *Jurassic Park* in the film of the same name.

KEISUKE KINOSHITA

Born: 5 December 1912 in Hamamatsu, Japan. **Died:** 30 December 1998 of a stroke, in Tokyo, Japan.
● A prolific master of Japanese cinema, Kinoshita directed 46 films over a period of 43 years, including Japan's first colour film, *Carmen Comes Home* (1951), and *Morning for the Osone Family* (1946), *She Was Like a Wild Chrysanthemum* (1955), *The Ballad of Narayama* (1958) and *Children of Nagasaki* (1983). Little known outside his own country, Kinoshita was praised for his range and visual purity, although some criticised him for sentimental excess.

STANLEY KUBRICK

Born: 26 July 1928 in the Bronx, New York City. **Died:** 7 March 1999 of a heart attack at his home in Hertfordshire, England.
● Like Howard Hughes and J.D. Salinger, Stanley Kubrick was a recluse. When he moved to England in 1961, he was never to return to his native America. And, in a period of 35 years, he directed only eight films, refusing to publicise any of them. Instead, he holed himself up in Childwickbury Manor, his magnificent pile in Hertfordshire, and regardless of the subject of his projects – the intergalactic universe of *2001: A Space Odyssey*, the Vietnamese killing fields of *Full Metal Jacket* –

he shot them all in Britain. A technical innovator and an emotional cynic, Kubrick produced a body of work that beguiled the eye, excited the mind yet left the heart cold. His critics were many, and then so were his admirers. The son of a doctor, he sold a photograph of a news vendor to *Look* when he was just 16. The magazine paid him a mere $25 but hired him on the spot. Two years later Kubrick discovered the seduction of the cinema and, after leaving *Look* at 21, actively pursued a career as a film-maker. His first venture, a short called *Day of the Fight* (1951), saw him take on the duties of director, producer, cameraman, editor and soundman. On his last film, *Eyes Wide Shut*, he was similarly involved, being the director, producer, editor and co-writer. His submersion in and control of his own pictures extended from years of pre-production and subjugation of various writers right down to the marketing and quality of prints. Today, the films speak for themselves: *Fear and Desire* (1953), *Killer's Kiss* (1955), *The Killing* (1956), *Paths of Glory* (1957), *Spartacus* (1960), *Lolita* (1962), *Dr Strangelove* (1963), *2001: A Space Odyssey* (1968), *A Clockwork Orange* (1971), *Barry Lyndon* (1975), *The Shining* (1980), *Full Metal Jacket* (1987) and *Eyes Wide Shut* (1999). Such was Kubrick's reputation and influence that he felt free to call up anybody in the world and ask a favour – whether he knew them or not. And, as in the case of geniuses, he would usually get his way (generally free of charge). Oliver Stone called him 'the single greatest American director of his generation,' but by most accounts he was neither a likeable nor gracious man. According to his former housekeeper, the only clothes he wore were 'a crumpled shirt, baggy cords and a jacket held together with safety pins' (although, she added, he did own one spare pair of underpants). Yes, he was a total original. Famously, he noted: 'the great nations have always acted like gangsters, the small nations like prostitutes.'

AKIRA KUROSAWA

Born: 23 March 1910 in Tokyo, Japan. **Died:** 6 September 1998 of a stroke, in Setagaya, Tokyo.
● Categorically the most famous film-maker ever produced by Japan, Akira Kurosawa will forever be associated with his 16th century epic *Seven Samurai* (1954), later remade by United Artists as the 1960 Western *The Magnificent Seven*. The youngest son (of seven children) of an army officer, Kurosawa revealed an early faculty for painting but, unable to support himself as a commercial artist, he turned to the cinema. By 1941 he

was writing scripts and directing entire sequences for the films of Kajiro Yamamoto and two years later made his directorial debut with *Judo Saga*. In 1950 his *Rashomon*, an incisive exploration of human nature as filtered through four disparate reports of a rape and murder, won the Oscar for best foreign film and put Japanese cinema on the map. Having attended an art school that celebrated occidental form, Kurosawa drew liberally from Western thematic sources, basing his *Throne of Blood* (1957) on *Macbeth*, his *The Bad Sleep Well* (1959) from elements of *Hamlet* and *Ran* (1985) on *King Lear*, as well as directing adaptations of Dostoevsky's *The Idiot* (1951), Gorky's *The Lower Depths* (1959) and frequently emulating the style of the American film-maker John Ford. In turn, many Western directors plundered Kurosawa's own oeuvre, including George Lucas, whose *Star Wars* was in part inspired by *The Hidden Fortress* (1958). Revealing a strong visual style and economic narrative sensibility, Kurosawa was unarguably one of the greatest directors of his generation – and even that may be an understatement. In 1990 he was awarded an honorary Oscar, for 'accomplishments that have inspired, delighted, enriched and entertained audiences and influenced film-makers throughout the world.'

JOSEPH MAHER

Born: 29 December 1933. **Died:** 17 July 1998 of a brain tumour at his home in Los Angeles.
● Maher was a fleshy character actor equally adept at playing friendly eccentrics (*I.Q.*) and sinister monsters (*The Evil That Men Do*). He also appeared in such films as *Heaven Can Wait* (1978), *Sister Act*, *The*

Shadow and *Surviving Picasso*. On Broadway he received Tony nominations for *Spokesong*, *Night and Day* and *Loot*.

DAVID MANNERS

Born: 30 April 1901 in Halifax, Nova Scotia. **Died:** 23 December 1998 of 'natural causes' in Santa Barbara, California.
Real name: Rauff de Ryther Duan Acklom.
● A leading Hollywood man of the Thirties, Manners (whose publicist claimed was a descendant of William the Conqueror) will be best remembered for his role as Jonathan Harker to Bela Lugosi's *Dracula* (1931). He also played Raleigh in the 1930 screen version of *Journey's End* (his first film), starred opposite Boris Karloff in *The Mummy* (1931), was the love interest of Katharine Hepburn in *A Bill of Divorcement* and romanced Gloria Stuart in *Roman Scandals* (both 1932). In 1936 he retired from the cinema and became the author of several novels and two works of philosophy.

JEAN MARAIS

Born: 11 December 1913 in Cherbourg, France. **Died:** 8 November 1998 in Cannes of a pulmonary disorder.
● An icon of the French cinema, Jean Marais displayed the countenance of a Greek god and appeared in over a hundred films between 1933 and 1996. The son of a veterinarian, Marais was, apparently, a difficult child and a poor student: he failed to earn a place in the Conservatoire, but, due to his good looks, he secured a series of bit parts in the films of Marcel L'Herbier. In 1937 he met the poet and film-maker Jean Cocteau at an audition and not long afterwards the two men moved in together. Cocteau, who had abandoned the cinema since making his surrealist fantasy *The Blood of the Poet* in 1930, was inspired to return, gave up drugs and directed Marais in his four most famous films: *La Belle et la bete* (1946), *Les Parents terribles* (1948), *Oprhee* (1949) and *Le Testament d'Orphee* (1960). Marais also cut a dash in costume epics, becoming the French equivalent of Errol Flynn, and worked for Jean Renoir in *Elena et les Hommes* (1956) and for Visconti in *White Nights* (1957). When, at 83, he was asked by Bernardo Bertolucci to play the crotchety antique dealer in *Stealing Beauty* (1996) Marais marvelled, 'I was so flattered that he should know who I am – I was astonished he even knew I was alive.' In a cast that included Jeremy Irons, Liv Tyler and Joseph Fiennes, Marais made his presence felt, giving due profundity to his most telling line: 'There's not

love – only proof of love.' In 1975 he wrote his autobiography, *Histoires de Ma Vie*.

E.G. MARSHALL

Born: 18 June 1910 in Owatonna, Minnesota. **Died:** 24 August 1998 in Bedford, New York. **Real name:** Edda Gunna Marshall.

● A square-jawed character actor who excelled in serious parts, Marshall proved to be an indispensable figure of authority in Hollywood films. Following a lengthy stage career that blossomed in 1938 with the New York production *Prologue to Glory*, Marshall made his cinematic mark in the Fifties with such roles as Lt. Commander Challee in *The Caine Mutiny* (1954) and as the unflappable 'juror No. 4' in *Twelve Angry Men* (1957). Other roles of note included the book-keeper in *Bachelor Party* (1957), the state attorney in *Compulsion* (1959), Lt. Col. Bratton in *Tora! Tora! Tora!* (1970), the father in Woody Allen's *Interiors* (1978), the president of the United States in *Superman II* (1980), John Mitchell in *Nixon* (1995) and the ruthless billionaire Walter Sullivan in Clint Eastwood's *Absolute Power* (1996). On television he made a name for himself as the imperial lawyer Lawrence Preston in CBS TV's controversial legal series *The Defenders* (1961-65). He was also an outspoken campaigner for health care.

RODDY McDOWALL

Born: 17 September 1928 in Herne Hill, London. **Died:** 3 October 1998 of brain cancer in Studio City, California.

● As child star, photographer, charity patron, raconteur, photographer, friend of Elizabeth Taylor and tireless collector of film memorabilia, Roddy McDowall was a notable fixture in Hollywood circles. Born in South London

to a Scottish merchant seaman, young Roddy embarked on commercial modelling at the age of four and made his film debut aged nine in *Scruffy* (1938), which was followed by a further 15 British pictures, including *Convict 99* (with Will Hay), *Murder in the Family*, *The Outsider*, *Dead Man's Shoes* and *Just William*. Then, when his family was evacuated from London during the Battle of Britain, he caught the eye of Twentieth Century Fox and was signed up to play the leading part of Huw Morgan in John Ford's Oscar-winning hymn to Welsh village life, *How Green Was My Valley* (1941). This was followed by a long-term contract, *Lassie Come Home* (1943) and an introduction to fellow London-born child star Elizabeth Taylor. Subsequent films included *My Friend Flicka*, *The Keys of the Kingdom*, *The White Cliffs of Dover*, *Son of Flicka* and *Kidnapped*. As a young leading man McDowall concentrated on the stage and then turned to television, before edging back into the movies in the early Sixties. In 1968 his career received a fresh boost when he played a monkey – Cornelius – in the hugely successful *Planet of the Apes*. As a character actor, his later films included *Bedknobs and Broomsticks*, *The Poseidon Adventure*, *The Legend of Hell House*, *Funny Lady*, *Evil Under the Sun*, *Fright Night*, *Overboard* and, as the voice of Mr Soil, *A Bug's Life*. He also dabbled in direction, marking his sole territory behind the camera with the odd Ava Gardner vehicle *Tam Lin* (aka *The Devil's Widow*). In 1966 he published *Double Exposure*, the first of four volumes of celebrity photographs.

ANTHONY NEWLEY

Born: 24 September 1931 in Hackney, East London. **Died:** 14 April 1999 of cancer in Jensen Beach, Florida.

● An all-round entertainer, Anthony Newley was an actor, singer, songwriter and director who began his career as a child star, playing the Artful Dodger to huge acclaim in David Lean's *Oliver Twist* (1948). At the time, he recalled, he lost his virginity to Diana Dors (who played Charlotte in the film) and went on to gain something of a reputation as a playboy. In 1963 he married Joan Collins (the second of three wives), whom he met when she saw him on stage in the musical *Stop the World, I Want To Get Off*. 'I had drooled over pictures of Joan,' he recalled, 'and there she was backstage.' After appearing together in the critically lambasted *Can Hieronymus Merkin Ever Forget Mercy Humpee and Find True Happiness?* (which he also wrote, directed and scored), the couple divorced in 1973.

Apparently, Newley wrote his first musical, *Stop the World...*, in just seven days (in collaboration with Leslie Bricusse), and went on to pen *The Roar of the Greasepaint, the Smell of the Crowd*, *The Good Old Bad Old Days* and *Chaplin*. He also achieved some fame as a pop singer, climbing to the top of the British charts with such hits as 'I've Waited So Long', 'Personality', 'Why', 'Do You Mind' and 'Strawberry Fair'. As an actor, his more celebrated film credits include *Cockleshell Heroes* (1955), *The Good Companions* (1957) and *Doctor Dolittle* (1967). More recently, he played a second hand car salesman in the TV soap *Eastenders* and was an amoral bishop in the BBC series *The Lakes*.

DICK O'NEILL

Born: 29 August 1928 in New York City. **Died:** 17 November 1998 of heart failure in Santa Monica, Los Angeles.

● A rubber-faced, usually dour-looking, bloodhound type, O'Neill was a character actor of ubiquitous presence, cropping up as harried police captains, distracted grandfathers and anxious military types. His films included *Pretty Poison* (1968), *Hail to the Chief*, *The Taking of Pelham 1-2-3*, *The Front Page*, *McArthur*, *House Calls*, *The Jerk*, *Wolfen*, *Prizzi's Honor*, *The Mosquito Coast* and many others.

ALAN J. PAKULA

Born: 7 April 1928 in New York City. **Died:** 19 November 1998 in Long Island, New York, after a steel pipe hit by a car ricocheted through the windscreen of his own car, sending him off the road and crashing into a barrier.

● One of the more intelligent directors working in mainstream Hollywood, Pakula attracted major talent to discriminating projects and regularly procured his stars Oscar commendation. He himself was nominated for his production of *To Kill a Mockingbird* and for his direction of *All the President's Men* and *Sophie's Choice*. His other credits, following his start as a producer on such films as *Fear Strikes Out* and *Inside Daisy Clover*, include *Klute*, *The Parallax View*, *Starting Over*, *Rollover*, *Orphans*, *Presumed Innocent*, *The Pelican Brief* and *The Devil's Own*.

BOB PECK

Born: 23 August 1945 in Leeds, Yorkshire. **Died:** 4 April 1999 of cancer in London.
● A muscular British character actor with a purposeful air, Bob Peck made his name in the critically acclaimed *film noir* BBC serial, *Edge of Darkness*, playing a cop investigating his daughter's murder. On film, he appeared in *The Kitchen Toto*, *On the Black Hill*, *Slipstream* and *Lord of the Flies* and made the big time as the game warden Robert Muldoon in *Jurassic Park*. After that he co-starred in *Surviving Picasso*, *Smilla's Sense of Snow*, *The Opium War* and *Fairy Tale: A True Story*.

LEO PENN

Born: 1921. **Died:** 5 September 1998 of cancer in Los Angeles.
● An Emmy-winning director and occasional actor, Leo Penn was responsible for helming over 400 hours of primetime television. He also directed a number of TV movies and a couple of theatrical features, namely *A Man Called Adam* (1966), with Sammy Davis Jr, and *Judgment in Berlin* (1988), with Martin Sheen and his son Sean. Leo met his wife, the actress Eileen Ryan, when they appeared in the Fifties' production of *The Iceman Cometh* and together they bore three sons: Sean and Chris, both successful actors, and the singer-songwriter Michael Penn.

OLIVER REED

Born: 13 February 1938 in Wimbledon, South London. **Died:** 2 May 1999 of a heart attack following a drinking spree in a Maltese bar.
● While best known to the public for his public displays of drunken tomfoolery, Oliver Reed was an actor of some substance, revealing both danger and a brutish animal magnetism. Yet, had it not been for the support of three film directors he probably would have disappeared from the neon far quicker than he did. Following a chequered academic history at 13 schools, Reed shuffled through odd jobs

as a strip club bouncer, fairground boxer and soldier (in the Royal Army Medical Corps), before drifting into films via extra work. Then, in 1960, he got a speaking role in the Tony Hancock comedy *The Rebel* and embarked on a succession of parts playing rogues and bullies, co-starring in Hammer's *The Curse of the Werewolf* (1961) as the lycanthropic anti-hero. In 1964, Michael Winner cast him in the part of a womanising photographer in *The System* and a fruitful actor-director relationship was born. Reed's standing as a star increased in Winner's *The Jokers* and *I'll Never Forget What's 'is Name* and was cemented when his uncle, Sir Carol Reed, cast him as Bill Sikes in the Oscar-winning musical *Oliver!* (1968). Reed then entered the record books when he became the first actor (along with Alan Bates) to expose his manhood on screen in the notorious nude wrestling match in Ken Russell's *Women in Love* (1969). In fact, it was Russell who revealed Reed's depths as an actor, having previously cast him as Debussy and Rossetti in the highly-praised TV productions *The Debussy Film* (1965) and *Dante's Inferno* (1967). Meanwhile, Reed's stature as an international star rose with the brutal Western *The Hunting Party* (in which he raped both Candice Bergen and the American dialect), Ken Russell's highly controversial *The Devils* (which was repeatedly banned) and the all-star *The Three Musketeers* (1973), with Reed top-billed as Athos. By this time he was Britain's highest paid actor and he went on to star in *The Four Musketeers* (1974), Russell's *Tommy* (1975) and *The Prince and the Pauper* (1977), although his increasing girth and all-night drinking binges seriously damaged his career. His garnered more notoriety when, in 1985, he married his companion of five years, Josephine Burge, who was still only 21 – 26

years his junior. His later films included David Cronenberg's *The Brood* (1979), *Lion of the Desert* (1981), *Castaway* (1986) and *Funny Bones* (1995). He was halfway through filming Ridley Scott's *Gladiator* when he died.

BERT REMSEN

Born: 25 February 1925 in Glen Cove, New York. **Died:** 22 April 1999 'of natural causes' in the San Fernando Valley, Los Angeles.
● A grumpy looking character actor, Remsen was restricted to playing somewhat incapacitated characters after a crane fell on him in 1965, breaking his leg and back. Notwithstanding, he racked up an impressive array of credits, including *Brewster McCloud*, *McCabe and Mrs Miller*, *Thieves Like Us*, *California Split*, *Nashville*, *Buffalo Bill and the Indians*, *A Wedding* and *The Player* (all for Robert Altman) and, more recently, *Jack the Bear*, *Maverick*, *Conspiracy Theory*, *Forces of Nature* and *The Sky is Falling*. In 1945 he received the Purple Heart for wounds sustained in the Okinawa campaign.

CHARLES 'BUDDY' ROGERS

Born: 13 August 1904 in Olathe, Kansas. **Died:** 21 April 1999 at his home near Rancho Mirage, California.
● Once dubbed 'America's Boyfriend', Buddy Rogers had the distinction of starring in the first movie to win a 'Best Picture' Oscar – the World War I drama *Wings* (1927). He was also the husband of Mary Pickford ('America's sweetheart') – from 1937 until her death in 1979 – and brightened many silent films with his boyish, amiable energy. With the advent of sound he sang in the Hollywood musicals *Paramount on Parade* and *Heads Up* (both 1930) and, in England, *Once in a Million* (1936) and *Let's Make a Night Of It* (1937). He left the cinema in 1948 for TV and radio but made an incongruous comeback in 1957 in the Western *The Parson and the Outlaw*, which he also produced. He also toured extensively with his own band, The California Cavaliers, which featured the singer Mary Martin with Gene Krupa on drums.

ROY ROGERS

Born: 5 November 1912 in Duck Run, Ohio. **Died:** 6 July 1998 of congestive heart failure in Apple Valley, California.
Real name: Leonard Slye.
● Before testosterone and cynicism replaced gallantry and singalongs in the West, Roy Rogers was the undisputed King of the Cowboys. A former fruit picker, Rogers – who

initially jumped from being Leonard Slye to Dick Weston – was America's top box-office Western star at a time when such things mattered. Outfitted in colourful, garish costumes, he was accompanied by his equally famous horse Trigger (who could perform 52 equestrian tricks) and his loyal sidekick George 'Gabby' Hayes. Breaking out in the 1938 *Under Western Stars*, Rogers was an immediate success with the public and critics alike, prompting *The New York Times* to enthuse that he 'has a drawl like Gary Cooper, a smile like Shirley Temple and a voice like Tito Guizar.' He went on to reign at the box-office for a further 17 years, knocking out such films as *Dark Command*, *Heart of the Golden West*, *San Fernando Valley*, *My Pal Trigger* and, with Bob Hope, *Son of Paleface*. In 1947 he married Dale Evans, the proclaimed 'Queen of the West' and his co-star in 20 films. Later, he successfully turned his attention to TV and business matters and became one of the richest men in showbusiness.

ESTHER ROLLE

Born: 8 November 1922 in Pompano Beach, Florida. **Died:** 17 November 1998 from diabetes in Culver City, California.

● A character actress who specialised in playing no-nonsense maids, Rolle will be best remembered as Florida Evans, the maid in the CBS sitcom *Maude* (1972-74). She also appeared in the films *Driving Miss Daisy*, *House of Cards*, *Rosewood* and *Down in the Delta* and won an Emmy in 1978 for her role as the housekeeper in the TV movie *The Summer of My German Soldier*. She was also an ardent campaigner against the stereotyping of blacks in Hollywood.

NORMAN ROSSINGTON

Born: 24 December 1928 in Liverpool. **Died:** 20 May 1999.

● A squat, lantern-chinned character actor, Rossington specialised in playing cheeky sidekicks and comic Jack-the-lads. Making his name as Private 'Cupcake' Cook in Granada TV's *The Army Game* (1957-61), he became a familiar face in such films as *Saturday Night and Sunday Morning*, *The Longest Day*, *Lawrence of Arabia*, *A Hard Day's Night*, *Double Trouble*, *Young Winston*, *Digby the Biggest Dog in the World*, *The Krays*, *Let Him Have It* and several Carry On entries.

SHIRLEY STOLER

Born: 30 March 1929 in Brooklyn, New York. **Died:** 17 February 1999 of heart failure in New York.

● While best remembered for her role as the homicidal, overweight nurse in the chilling *The Honeymoon Killers* (1970), Shirley Stoler played a wide variety of roles in such films as Lina Wertmuller's *Seven Beauties* (as the Nazi commandant), *The Deer Hunter*, *Miami Blues*, *Frankenhooker*, *Malcolm X* and John Turturro's *Mac*.

SUSAN STRASBERG

Born: 22 May 1938 in New York City. **Died:** 21 January 1999 of breast cancer in her apartment in New York City.

● The daughter of the acting guru Lee Strasberg, Susan Strasberg looked set for a promising vocation in the Fifties, but her career quickly shifted to Italian B-movies and trendy Sixties flotsam (*The Trip*, *Psych-Out*). Her more notable credits include *Picnic* (1955), *Stage Struck*, *The Manitou*, *Rollercoaster* and *In Praise of Older Women*. In 1966-1968 she was married to the actor Christopher Jones (*Wild in the Streets*, *Ryan's Daughter*) and wrote her autobiography, *Bittersweet*, in 1980.

KAY THOMPSON

Born: 9 November 1912 in St Louis, Missouri. **Died:** 2 July 1998 in New York City.

● While best known as the creator of the mischievous Eloise in her four best-selling children's books, Ms Thompson dabbled in many other pursuits. At 15 she played the piano with the St Louis Symphony Orchestra and then embarked on a career as a diving instructor. After that she sang with Bing Crosby on the radio and ended up with her own show, *Kay Thompson and Company*. She was also a businesswoman, clothes designer, composer, dancer, songwriter and the godmother of Liza Minnelli. However, to film buffs she will be best remembered as Maggie Prescott, the fashion editor in Stanley Donen's *Funny Face* who sings the classic Gershwin numbers 'Think Pink' and 'Bonjour Paris'. As an actress, she also appeared as Miss Gregory in Otto Preminger's *Tell Me That You Love Me, Junie Moon* (1970).

ERNIE WISE

Born: 27 November 1925 in Leeds, West Yorkshire. **Died:** 21 March 1999 following a triple heart bypass.

● The straight man 'with the short, fat, hairy legs' to Eric Morecambe's bespectacled clown, Ernie Wise appeared with his friend and colleague in three films, *The Intelligence Men* (1964), *That Riviera Touch* (1966) and *The Magnificent Two* (1967).

JOHN WOOLF

Born: 15 March 1913 in Cricklewood, north London. **Died:** 28 June 1999.

● John Woolf was one of the most successful of British film producers, famously investing his own money in the box-office hits *The African Queen* and *Room at the Top*. He also produced such pictures as *Pandora and the Flying Dutchman*, *Moulin Rouge*, *Richard III*, *Oliver!*, *The Day of the Jackal* and *The Odessa File*. In 1949 he founded Romulus Films with his brother James, helped to set up Anglia Television in 1958 and was knighted in 1975.

FREDERICK A. YOUNG

Born: 9 October 1902 in London. **Died:** 1 December 1998 of 'natural causes' in London.

● At his peak the world's most famous cinematographer, Freddie Young (as he was universally known) will be best remembered for his spectacular, Oscar-winning work on David Lean's *Lawrence of Arabia*, *Doctor Zhivago* and *Ryan's Daughter*. He also directed one film, the 1985 *Arthur's Hallowed Ground*, aged 82.

ROBERT YOUNG

Born: 22 February 1907 in Chicago, Illinois. **Died:** 21 July 1998 of respiratory failure in Westlake Village, California.

● Admitting that he was 'an introvert in a field of extroverts,' Robert Young elevated blandness to an art form. Yet, when playing against his own grain, he was an actor to be reckoned with, particularly as the womaniser in *They Won't Believe Me* and as the laconic detective in Edward Dmytryk's excellent, hard-hitting *Crossfire* (both 1947). More often, though, he was cast as the unthreatening support in major features (*Tugboat Annie*; *Hell Below*) and as an amiable romantic in B-films. On television, a medium which seemed to suit his unspectacular talents better, he won the Emmy twice for playing the buoyant insurance agent Jim Anderson in *Father Knows Best* (1954-1962) and a third time for his portrayal of the genial medic *Marcus Welby, M.D.* (1969-1976). Then, after becoming a TV fixture, Young retired in the early Eighties only to be coaxed back to play Roswell Gilbert, a real-life, genial wife-killer, in the so-so docudrama *Mercy or Murder?* (1987). Four years later, Young, a heavy drinker, attempted to kill himself by carbon monoxide poisoning (the old hose in the exhaust pipe routine) and admitted himself for psychiatric treatment.

Index

Names of films and videos appear in the index in *italics*. Page references for illustrations are shown in **BOLD**. The last separate word of an individual's name is used as the index entry; thus Jean-Claude Van Damme appears under 'D' as Damme, Jean-Claude Van.

Aberration, 150
Acid House, The, 10-11, 172
Acts of Betrayal, 150
Adams, Jane, 57
Addams Family Reunion, 150
Addison, John, 179
Adefarasin, Remi, 174
Adventures of Slappy the Sea Lion, The, 150
Affleck, Ben, 15-16, **48**, 49-50, 115-116, 160, 160-161, 162, 164
Affliction, 11, 174
Agassi, Andre, 164
Ages of Lulu, The, 150
Air Bud, 11
Airborne, 150
Alan Smithee Film, An: Burn Hollywood Burn see *Burn Hollywood Burn*
Albinus, Jens, 64, **64**
Aldrich Ames: Traitor Within, 150
Alf Awards 1999, 177
Alien Quartet, The (book), 169
Allen, Joan, 103-104, **104**
Allen, Ray, 58
Allen, Tim, 50
Allen, Woody, 13-14, 28
Alley, Kirstie, 50
Almost Heroes, 144
Altman, Robert, 52
Always Outnumbered, 144, **144**
Alyn, Kirk, 179
Ambushed, 150
American Academy of Motion Picture Arts and Science Awards 1998, 174
American History X, 6, **10**, 11-12, 161, 164, 174
American Perfekt, 12
Among Giants, 12
Almost Dead, 150
Analyze This, 164
And the Beat Goes On: The Sonny and Cher Story, 144
Anderson, Gillian, 141, **141**
Anderson, Pamela, 164
Andrews, Julie, 162
Angel Dust, 13
Angelopoulos, Theo, 44
Animated Short Films (book), 169
Aniston, Jennifer, 161
Annis, Francesca, 35
Antz, 8, 9, 13-14, **13**
Apartment, The (book), 169
Apocalypse Now (book), 169
Apple, The – Sib, 14
Applegate, Christina, 21-22, 160
Aprile, 14
Apt Pupil, 14
Araki, Gregg, 39-40
Ardent, Fanny, 42-43
Arditi, Pierre, 95
Arkin, Adam, 56
Arkin, Alan, 120
Arlington Road, 14-15, **15**
Armageddon, 8, 15-16, 159, 160, 161, 162, 172, 174
Aronofsky, Darren, 102-103
Arquette, Alexis, 66-67
Arquette, David, 160, 165
Art of Nasty, The (book), 169
Artemisia, 16
As Good As It Gets, 159
Ashley, Elizabeth, 57
Assault on Devil's Island, 150
Assignment, The, 16
At First Sight, 16-17
Atomic Dog, 150
Attenborough, Richard, 42-43
Audrey Style (book), 169

August, Billie, 87-88
Austin Powers: The Spy Who Shagged Me, 165
Australian Film Institute Awards 1998, 175
Auteuil, Daniel, 24, 77-78, **78**
Autry, Gene, 179
Autumn Tale, An – Conte d'Automne, 17
Avengers, The, 17, **17**, 172
Avital, Mili, 69-70
Aykroyd, Dan, 13-14
A-Z of Silent Film Comedy (book), 169
Azaria, Hank, 28, 54-55, **55**
Azema, Sabine, 95
Azmi, Shabana, 49

Babe: Pig in the City, 18, 172, 174
Baby Monitor: Sound of Fear, 150
Babymother, 19
Back to Titanic, 166
Bacri, Jean-Pierre, 95
BAFTA Awards for 1998, 175
Bailey, Robin, 179
Baker, Dylan, 57
Baldwin, Alec, 84, 161
Baldwin, William, 137
Bale, Christian, 86, 154
Balk, Fairuza, 11-12, 12
Bancroft, Anne, 13-14
Bancroft, Tony, 89-90
Banderas, Antonio, 82
Bannen, Ian, 138
Barber of Siberia, The, 165
Bardem, Javier, 101
Barker, Mike, 21
Barnes, Binnie, 179
Barney's Great Adventure, 19
Barrett, Francis, 122-123
Barrymore, Drew, 44-45
Bartok, Eva, 179-180
Bassett, Angela, 62, 160
Bates, Kathy, 138-139, 174
Battle of Brazil, The (book), 169
Bay, Michael, 15-16
Baye, Nathalie, 135, **135**
Beatty, Warren, 26, 174
Becker, Harold, 84
Becker, Wolfgang, 74
Beckinsale, Kate, 72-73
Bedrooms & Hallways, 19
Bello, Maria, 100
Belmont, Vera, 81-82
Beloved, **18**, 19-20
Belushi, James, 51-52
Beneath Mulholland: Thoughts on Holloywood and its Ghosts (book), 169
Benigni, Roberto, 74, **75**, 163, 174
Bening, Annette, 65, 117
Bennett, Bill, 70
Benton, Robert, 133
Berg, Peter, 135-136
Bergh, Clement Van Den, 30
Berlin International Film Festival 1999, 175
Bernhard, Sandra, 159
Berry, Halle, 26, 160
Bertolucci, Bernardo, 20-21
Besieged, 20-21, **20**, 166
Best Laid Plans, 21, 166
Beyond Silence – Jenseits der Stille, 21
Bierko, Craig, 122
Big Hit, The, 21-22
Bionic Ever After?, 150
Birds, The (book), 169
Bisset, Jacqueline, 61
Black Cat White Cat, 22, **22**, 172

Black Dog, 144-145
Blackjack, 150
Blackwood, Vas, 76-77, 77
Blade, 23, **23**
Blade Squad, 150
Blanchett, Cate, 42-43, **43**, 63, **63**, 174
Blanks, Jamie, 134
Blast From the Past, 23
Blethyn, Brenda, 74-76, 174
Bluteau, Lothaire, 96
Bogarde, Dirk, 180, **180**
Bohringer, Romane, 137
Bond Files, The (book), 169
Bone Daddy, 150
Bonet, Lisa, 43-44
Bonnaire, Sandrine, 115
Bonneville, Hugh, 94
Bonnie and Clyde (book), 169
Bossu, Le, 6, 7, 24, **24**
Bouchez, Elodie, 40, **177**
Bowman, Rob, 141
Box, Betty, 180
Boyle, Lara Flynn, 57
Boys, The, 24
Branagh, Kenneth, 28, **28**, 52, 108, 160
Brando, Marlon, 164
Brandy, 66, **66**
Braschi, Nicoletta, 74
Brassard, Marie, 93
Breast Men, 145
Breed Apart, A, 150-151
Bremner, Ewen, 10-11
Brenneman, Amy, 142
Brest, Martin, 83-84
Brewster, Jordana, 46
Bride of Chucky, 6, 24-25
Bridges, Jeff, 14-15, **15**
Briscoe, Brent, 118, **118**
British Academy of Film and Television Arts Awards for 1998, 175
Brittain, Charlotte, 52
Broca, Philippe De, 24
Broderick, Matthew, 54-55
Brody, Adrien, 127-128
Brolin, James, 159
Brolin, Josh, 21, 164-165
Broomfield, Nick, 71
Brosnan, Pierce, 160
Bruno, John, 137
Brylcreem Boys, The, 25
Buddy, 145
Buena Vista (website), 172
Buffalo 66, 25
Buffalo Soldiers, 145
Bug's Life, A, 8, **8**, 9, 26, **26**, 162, 174
Bug's Life, A: The Art and Making of an Epic of Miniature Proportions (book), 169
Bullock, Sandra, **48**, 49-50, 61, 105, 107-108
Bulworth, 26, 174
Bunny, 174
Burke, Kathy, 42-43, 128-129
Burn Hollywood Burn, 145
Burns, Edward, 114-115
Buscemi, Steve, 65
Butterworth, Jez, 88

Caan, James, 160
Cadieux, Anne-Marie, 93
Caffrey, David, 38
Cage, Nicolas, 9, 42, **42**, 121, **121**
Caine, Michael, 74-76, **76**
Calhoun, Rory, 180, **180**
Cameron, James, 162
Campbell, Bill, 25

Campbell, Martin, 82
Canadian Film Awards 1999, 175-176
Cannes Film Festival Awards 1999, 176
Cannibal Holocaust and the Savage Cinema of Ruggero Deodato (book), 169
Cannon, Danny, 66
Cantarini, Giorgio, 74, **75**
Canterbury Tales, The, 174
Captain Jack, 27, **27**
Carlyle, Robert, 104-105, **105**
Carnival of Souls, 151
Carrey, Jim, 9, 132-133
Carte Postale, La, 174
Cassel, Vincent, 38-39
Castle, The, 27-28
Caton, Michael, 27-28
Caviezel, Jim, 127-128, 154
Cecchi, Carlo, 109-110
Celebrity, 28, **28**
Central Station – Central do Brasil, 28-29, 174
Cerami, Vincenzo, 174
Cervi, Valentina, 16
Cesar Awards 1999, 176-177
Chabrol, Claude, 110
Chambers, Emma, 94
Chan, Benny, 68
Chan, Jackie, 68, 89, 113, **113**, 133
Chance of Snow, A, 151
Chaplin, Ben, 127-128, **128**
Chapman, Brenda, 107-108
Character – Karakter, 29
Charlie's Angels, 161
Chart, Paul, 12
Chau, Frederick Du, 81
Chayanne, 33-34
Cheadle, Don, 26
Chechik, Jeremiah, 17
Chelsom, Peter, 86
Cher, 126
Chikezie, Caroline, 19
Children of Heaven, 174
Children of the Corn IV: The Gathering, 151
Cholodenko, Lisa, 59-60
Christopher, Mark, 47-48
Chukhrai, Pavel, 127
Cinema Cafe, 166
Civil Action, A, 29-30, **29**, 174
Clapczynski, Stefan, 50, **50**
Class Trip – La Classe de Neige, 30
Clayton, Sue, 37
Cleese, John, 99
Clint: The Life and Legend (book), 169
Clockwatchers, 30
Clooney, George, 97, **97**, 127-128
Coates, Anne V, 174
Coburn, James, 11, **100**, 100-101, 174
Cody, Iron Eyes, 180-181
Collette, Toni, 24, 30
Collette, Yann, 24
Collins, Joan, 160
Columbia Comedy Shorts, The (book), 169
Columbus, Chris, 124
Combs, Jeffrey, 66
Come By Sunday (book), 169
Complete Prose of Woody Allen, The (book), 169
Con, The, 151
Condon, Bill, 53-54, 174
Connery, Sean, 17, 163
Connick Jr, Harry, 61
Connolly, Billy, 35, 65, 124-125

Conti, Tom, 39, **39**
Cook, Barry, 89-90
Cook, Rachael Leigh, 116-117, 156-157, **156**
Cookie's Fortune, 6, 166
Coppola, Francis Ford, 159
Coraci, Frank, 138-139
Cormack, Danielle, 130
Corruptor, The, 30-31
Costa-Gravras, 80
Costner, Kevin, 85
Cottafavi, Vittorio, 181
Countdown, 151
Cousin Bette, 31, 166
Cow, China, 21-22
Cox, Courteney, 160, 165
Craig, Daniel, 79
Cromwell, James, 18
Cronenberg, David, 45
Crosbie, Annette, 35
Croupier, 31
Crow, The: Stairway to Heaven, 151
Cruel Intentions, 31-32, **31**, 166
Cruise, Tom, 160, 161, 162, 164
Crush Proof, 32
Crystal, Billy, 91
Cube, 32, 172
Culkin, Kieran, 86
Culkin, Macaulay, 160
Culture, 174
Curry, Stephen, 27-28
Curtin, Jane, 13-14
Curtis, Jamie Lee, 56, **56**, 137
Curtis, Tony, 161
Cusack, Joan, 14-15
Cusack, John, 127-128, 164

Dafoe, William, 11, 136-137
Dahl, John, 112-113
Damme, Jean-Claude Van, 71, 165
Damon, Matt, 112-113, 114-115, 164
Dance of the Wind – Wara Mandel, 33
Dance With Me, 33-34, **33**, 166
Dancemaker, 174
Dancing at Lughnasa, 34
Dandry, Evelyne, 118
Dangerous Beauty see *The Honest Courtesan*
Daniels, Jeff, 90-91, 103-104
Dante, Joe, 120-121
Darnell, Eric, 13-14
Das, Nandita, 49
David and Lisa, 145
David Awards 1998, 165, 176
David di Donatello Awards 1998, 176
David Searching, 151
David, Larry, 122
Davidtz, Embeth, 52
Davis, Andrew, 102
Davis, Hope, 14-15, **34**, 35
Davis, Ossie, 40
Davison, Bruce, 14
Daytrippers, The, **34**, 35
Dead Husbands, 151
Dead Man on Campus, 145
Dead Man's Curve, 35
Dearden, James, 111
Dearly Devoted, 151
Death in the Shadows, 151
Deauville Festival of American Cinema 1998, 176
deBoer, Nicole, 32
Debt Collector, The, 35
Decleir, Jan, 29
Deep End of the Ocean, The, 36, **36**
Deep Impact, 9
Deep Rising, 36
Déjà Vu, 36-37, **37**
Delgado, Damian, 84
Demme, Jonathan, 19-20
Dench, Judi, 115-116, **116**, 126, 174
Denison, Michael, 181
Dennis Strikes Again, 151
Dentist 2, The, 151
Depardieu, Gerard, 159
Depp, Johnny, 47, 161, 162, 165
Deutch, Howard, 93
DeVito, Danny, 76
Diaz, Cameron, 9, **9**, 126-127, 135-136, **136**

DiCaprio, Leonardo, 159
Dickens, Kim, 143
Diem, Mike van, 29
Dien, Casper Van, 161
Digging to China, 145
Dignam, Erin, 79
Dillane, Stephen, 36-37, 49
Dillon, Matt, 126-127, **126**, 160, 161, 162
Dimension Films (website), 172
Dirty Little Secret, 151
Dirty Work, 145
Disappearance of Finbar, The, 37
Divorcing Jack, 38, **38**
Dobermann, 38-39, **39**
Domergue, Faith, 181
Don't Go Breaking My Heart, 39, **39**
Donner, Richard, 73-74
Donohoe, Amanda, 109
Donovan, Martin, **95**, 95-96
Doom Generation, The, 39-40
Dorff, Stephen, 23, **23**
Dotrice, Michele, 27
Double Jeopardy, 151
Double Tap, 151, **151**
Douglas, Michael, 102, **102**, 160, 163
Douglas, Shirley, 19
Downey, Robert Jr, 133
Dr Dolittle, 8, **8**, 40, 159, 172
Dream for an Insomniac, 145
Dream Life of Angels, The – La Vie Revée des Anges, 40, 177
Dreamworks skg (website), 172
Dreyfus, James, 94
Driller Killer, The, 146
Drive, 146
Driver, Minnie, 55, 63, 164
Duchovny, David, 103, 141, **141**
Duguay, Christian, 16
Dunne, Griffin, 105
Dunst, Kirsten, 120-121
Duris, Romain, 51, **51**
Dussollier, Andre, 95
Duval, James, 39-40
DuVall, Clea, 46
Duvall, Robert, 29-30, 174

East Side Story, 41
Eastwood, Clint, 131-132
Easy Riders, Raging Bulls (book), 169
Eccleston, Christopher, 42-43, 57-58, 105-106, **106**
Eckhart, Aaron, 129, 142, **142**
Eden, 151
Edwards and Hunt: The First American Road Trip see *Almost Heroes*
Edwards, Anthony, 39
Edwards, Blake, 162
Edwards, Meredith, 181
Edwards, Penny, 181
Eel, The – Unagi, 41-42, **41**
Ehle, Jennifer, 19, 128-129
8MM, 42, **42**
Election Night, 174
Elise, Kimberly, 19-20
Elizabeth, 42-43, **43**, 166, 174
Ellie Nesler Story, The: Judgement Day, 146
Ellin, Doug, 69-70
Embrace the Darkness, 151
Emmerich, Noah, 132-133
Emmerich, Roland, 54-55
Enemy of the State, 8, 43-44, **44**, 162
Ephron, Nora, 142-143
Esposito, Jennifer, 66, **66**
Eternity and a Day – Mia Eoniotita Ke Mia Mera, 44
European Film Awards 1998, 176
Evans, Lee, 126-127
Evans, Robert, 159, 161
Eve's Bayou, 45, **45**
Ever After, 44-45
Everett, Rupert, 63
Every Mother's Worst Fear, 151
Everything that Rises, 146
Evidence of Blood, 151
eXistenZ, 45
Exorcist, The: Out of the Shadows (book), 169

Faculty, The, 46, **46**
Fall, The, 146
Farm, The: Angola U S A, 174
Farrelly, Bobby, 126-127
Farrelly, Peter, 126-127
Fawcett, Farrah, 161
Fear and Loathing in Las Vegas, **46**, 47
Feast, Michael, 108
Felix Awards 1998, 176
Fell, Norman, 181
Ferrell, Will, 93
Festen – The Celebration, 47
Feuillere, Edwige, 181
Fiennes, Joseph, 8, 42-43, **43**, 115-116
Fiennes, Ralph, 17, **17**, 107-108, 162
54 (film title), 47-48
Film Follies: The Cinema Out of Order (book), 169
Film Music Good CD Guide (book), 169-170
Film Posters of the 70s (book), 170
Final Justice, 151
Finding North, 48
FIPRESCI Prizes, 175
Fire, 49
Firelight, 49, 166
Firestorm, 146
First 9½ weeks, The, 151
Firth, Colin, 115-116
Fishburne, Laurence, 82-83, **144**
Fisher, Carrie, 161
Flanagan, Fionnula, 138
Flemyng, Jason, 76-77, 109-110, **109**
Fletcher, Dexter, 76-77
Flockhart, Calista, 164
Foley, James, 30-31
Fonda, Bridget, 118, 130-131, 159
For Richer or Poorer, 50
For Which He Stands, 151
Forces of Nature, 48, 49-50, 163
Ford, Harrison, 9, 119, **119**
Forlani, Claire, 83-84
Forster, Robert, 12
Fortenberry, John, 93
Foster, Jodie, 161
Fox Searchlight (website), 172
Fox, Kerry, 140, **140**
Fox, Michael J, 161
Foyt, Victoria, 36-37
Frain, James, 60, 137
Frakes, Jonathan, 124, **124**
Frank, Scott, 174
Frankenheimer, John, 111-112
Fraser, Brendan, 9, 23, 53-54, **54**, 90, **90**
French Academy Awards 1999, 176-177
Fricker, Brenda, 98
Friel, Anna, 72, **72**, 111, 155, **155**
Frisch, Arno, 50, **50**
Frost, Sadie, 27
Funny Games, 50, **50**, 166
Furlong, Edward, 11-12, 101
Futuresport, 151

Gable, Christopher, 181
Gadjo Dilo, 51, **51**, 166, 166-167
Gallo, Vincent, 25
Gamble, David, 174
Gambon, Michael, 34, 104-105
Gang Related, 51-52
Ganz, Bruno, 44
Garcia, Andy, 68
Gatlif, Tony, 51
Gazzara, Ben, 25, 57, 123
Gellar, Sarah Michelle, 31-32
Genies Awards 1999, 175-176
Genius of the System, The: Hollywood Filmmaking in the Studio Era (book), 170
George Formby: A Troubled Genius (book), 170
Gerber, Tony, 117
Gere, Richard, 163
Get Real, 52, **53**
Gibson, Brian, 124-125
Gibson, Mel, 9, **9**, 73-74, **73**, 100
Gidwani, Kitu, 33
Gilbert, Andrew S, 70, **71**
Gilliam on Gilliam (book), 170

Gilliam, Terry, 47
Gillian, Marie, 24
Gingerbread Man, The, 52
Girard, Francois, 109-110
Girls Town, 52-53
Glatter, Lesli Linka, 108
Gloria, 53
Glover, Danny, 13-14, 19-20, 73-74, **73**
Gods and Monsters, 53-54, **54**, 167, 174
Godzilla, 8, 54-55, **55**, 172
Gold, Ernest, 181-182
Goldbacher, Sandra, 55
Goldberg, Whoopi, 36
Goldblum, Jeff, 60-61
Golden Globe Awards 1999, 177
Goldman, James, 182
Goldsmith, Jerry, 174
Golino, Valeria, 117
Gomer, Steve, 19
Good, Meagan, **45**
Goodall, Louise, 91
Gooding, Cuba Jr, 139
Goring, Marius, 182
Gorton, Brad, 52, **53**
Gosain, Bhaveen, 33
Governess, The, 55
Grade, Lew, 182
Graham, Heather, 133, 155
Grammer, Kelsey, 109
Grandfather, The, 174
Grant, Hugh, 8, 9, 9, 94, **94**
Gray, F Gary, 92
Grazioli, Irene, 109-110
Great Movie Scores, The: From the Films of Steven Spielberg, 167
Greatrex, Richard, 174
Grewal, Shani, 55
Griffin, Luke, 37
Griffiths, Rachel, 12, 38, **38**, 60, **60**, 130, 174
Grosbard, Ulu, 36
Gruffudd, Ioan, 122
Guadagni, Nicky, 32
Gullette, Sean, 102-103
Guru in 7, 55

Hackman, Gene, 13-14, 43-44, 133
Haines, Randa, 33-34
Half Baked, 151
Hall, Conrad L, 174
Hall, Huntz, 182
Halloween: H20, 56, **56**
Hamilton, Linda, 162
Hana-Bi, 56-57, **57**
Hancock, Sheila, 78-79
Haneke, Michael, 50
Hanks, Tom, 8, 9, 9, 114-115, **114**, 143, **143**, 163, 174
Hannah, John, 90, **90**
Happiness, 57
Hardie, Kate, 31, 57-58
Harison, Tony, 108
Hark, Tsui, 71, 133
Harrelson, Woody, 127-128, **128**
Harris, Ed, 124, 174
Harris, Richard, 165
Harrison, Noel, 36-37
Hart, Ian, 88, 128-129
Hartley, Hal, 58
Hartner, Rona, 51, **51**
Hassing, Louise, 64, **64**
Hatfield, Hurd, 182
Hav Plenty, 151
Hawke, Ethan, 159
Hawkins, Taylor, 164
Hawthorne, Nigel, 81, 162
Hayek, Salma, 46, **46**
Hayes, Patricia, 182
Haynes, Todd, 134-135
Haywood, Chris, 70, **71**
He Got Game, 58
Headey, Lena, 64-65
Healy, Darren, 32
Hearn, George, 19
Heart, 57-58
Heche, Anne, 110, **110**, 119, **119**
Heigl, Katherine, 24-25
Helgeland, Brian, 100-101

Henriques, Julian, 19
Henry Fool, 58
Henry, Gregg, 100
Henshall, Douglas, 96, 128-129
Henson, Elden, 86, **86**
Henstridge, Natasha, 123
Her Own Rules, 152
Hercules, 9
Herek, Stephen, 60-61
Herman, Mark, 74-76
Hershey, Barbara, 121-122
Herskovitz, Marshall, 61
Heston, Charlton, 14-15
Hewitt, Jennifer Love, 66, **66**
Hickey, John Benjamin, 48
Hickson, Joan, 182
Hidden Agenda, 152
Hideous Kinky, 58-59, **59**
High Art, 59-60
Hilary and Jackie, 60, **60**, 167, 174
Hillcoat, John, 130
Hinds, Ciaran, 129-130
Hirschfelder, David, 174
His Bodyguard, 152
Hit and Run, 152
Hobson, Valerie, 182-183
Hodges, Mike, 31
Hoffman, Dustin, 80
Hoffman, Philip Seymour, 99
Holiday Romance, 174
Hollander, Tom, 19
Hollow Man, The, 165
Hollywood Foreign Press Association
Awards 1999, 177
Hollywood Hex (book), 170
Holy Man, 60-61
Home Fries, 146
Honest Courtesan, The, 61
Hoodlum, 146
Hope, 147
Hope Floats, 61, 167
Hopkins, Anthony, 82, 83-84, 160
Hopkins, Stephen, 77
Horrocks, Jane, 74-76, **76**
Horse Whisperer, The, 62, 174
Hoskins, Bob, 27, 31, 99
How Stella Got Her Groove Back, 62
Huet, Fedja van, 29
Huffman, Felicity, 123
Hughes, Bronwen, 49-50
Hughes, Ian, 130
Hughes, Miko, 84, 85
Human Traffic, 62
Hunchback of Notre Dame, The, 152
Hung, Samo, 89
Hunt, Bonnie, 69-70
Hunted, The, 152
Hunter, Holly, 76
Huppert, Isabelle, 110
Hurt, John, 78-79, **79**
Hurt, William, 77, 79
Hush, 147, **147**
Huston, Anjelica, 44-45
Hutton, Timothy, 103
Hytner, Steve, **48**, 49-50

I am Jackie Chan: My Life in Action
(book), 170
I Got the Hook Up, 152
I Know What You Did Last Summer, 6
I Stand Alone see *Seul Contre Tous*
*I Still Know What You Did Last
Summer*, 66, **66**
I Think I Do, 66-67
I Want You, 67, **67**
Ice Cube (pseudonym), 103
Ideal Husband, An, 63, **63**
Idiots, The – Idioterne, 63-64, **64**, 172
If Only, 64-65
Ifans, Rhys, 57-58, 94, **94**, 155-156
Iglesia, Àlex de la, 101
Imamura, Shohei, 41-42
Imposters, The, 65, 167
In Dreams, 65
In God's Hands, 152
In the Doghouse, 152
Independent Spirit Awards 1999, 177
Inheritors, The – Die Siebtelbauern, 65-66
Insomnia, 66

International Film Critics' Association
Prizes, 175
Isaacs, Jason, 38
Iscover, Robert, 116-117
Ishii, Ogo, 13
It Came From the Sky, 152
Ivory, James, 121-122

Jack Frost, 68, 172
Jackie Chan's Who Am I? – Ngo Hai Sui, 68
Jackson, Samuel L, 45, 92, **92**
Jacob, Irene, 136-137
Jacobi, Derek, 79
Jaffrey, Saeed, 55
Jaglom, Henry, 36-37
James Cagney (book), 170
James Whale: A New World of Gods
and Monsters (book), 170
Jane Austen's Mafia! see *Mafia!*
Jane, Thomas, 129, **129**
Janssen, Famke, 36
Jarmusch, Jim, 142
Jean, Vadim, 109
Jenkins, Megs, 183
Jenkins, Tamara, 120
Jeter, Michael, 11
John Barry: A Life in Music (book), 170
John, Rosamund, 183
Johnson, Mark Steven, 117-118
Johnson, Tim, 13-14
Jolie, Angelina, 156, 163
Jolly Roger, 174
Jones, Gemma, 27
Jones, Hatty, 81, **81**
Jones, Henry, 183
Jones, Kirk, 138
Jones, Leslie, 11
Jordan, Neil, 65
Jorgensen, Bodil, 63-64
Jorgenson, Knud Romer, 64, **64**
Just the Ticket, 68

Kahn, Michael, 174
Kaminski, Janusz, 174
Kane, David, 128-129
Kanin, Garson, 183
Kapoor, Shashi, 117
Kapur, Shekhar, 42-43
Karyo, Tcheky, 38-39, **39**, 130
Kasdan, Jake, 143
Katic, Branka, 22
Kattan, Chris, 93
Kaye, Tony, 11-12, 161, 164
Kazan, Elia, 174
Keach, Stacy, 11-12
Keaton, Michael, 68
Keeslar, Matt, 72-73
Kelley, DeForest, 183
Kelly, David, 138
Kempson, Rachel, 36-37, **37**
Kendal, Felicity, 99
Kerrigan, Justin, 62
Khambata, Persis, 183
Khosa, Rajan, 33
Kidman, Nicole, 105, 161, 164
Kiley, Richard, 183
Kilmer, Val, 16-17, 107-108
King and I, The, 69, **69**, 172-173
Kingsley, Ben, 16, 99
Kingston, Alex, 162
Kinoshita, Keisuke, 183
Kinski, Natassja, 78
Kishimoto, Kayoko, 56-57
Kiss or Kill, 70, **71**
Kissing a Fool, 69-70, **70**
Kitano, Takeshi 'Beat', 56-57, **57**
Klein, Saar, 174
Knock Off, 71
Knowledge of Healing, The, 71
Kon, Satoshi, 101-102
Kouf, Jim, 51-52
Kounen, Jan, 38-39
Kovalyov, Igor, 113
Krabbe, Jeroen, 73
Kristofferson, Kris, 23, 33-34, 121-122
Kubrick, Stanley, 183-184, **183**
Kudrow, Lisa, 30, 95-96
Kumble, Roger, 31-32

Kurosawa, Akira, 184, **184**
Kurt and Courtney, 71
Kusturica, Emir, 22
Kwietniowski, Richard, 78-79

Laborit, Emmanuelle, 21
LaBute, Neil, 142
Ladd, Diane, 163
LaGravanese, Richard, 76
Lam, Ringo, 133
Land Girls, The, 72, **72**, 167
Landau, Martin, 141
Lange, Jessica, 31, **147**
Larsen, Thomas Bo, 47
Lasseter, John, 26
Last Days of Disco, The, 72-73
Last Days, The, 174
Last Rites, 152
Last Seduction 2, The, 152
Latifah, Queen, 76
Laurie, Hugh, 31
Laurie, Piper, 46, **46**
Law, Jude, 45, 140, **140**
Leary, Denis, **152**
Leave it to Beaver, 147
Lee, Spike, 58
Left Luggage, 73
Legion, 152
Lehmann, Michael, 91
Leigh, Jennifer Jason, 45
Leland, David, 72
Lemmon, Jack, 93
Lemmons, Kasi, 45
Lennox, Alyra, **33**
Lenny Bruce: Swear to Tell the Truth, 174
Lenoir, Blandine, 115
Leonard Maltin's 1999 Movie & Video
Guide (book), 170
Leong, Po Chih, 140
Lepage, Robert, 93
Lester, Adrian, 106-107
Lethal Weapon 4, 73-74, **73**, 159, 173
Leto, Jared, 134
Levin, Marc, 119
Lewis, Gary, 96
Lhermitte, Thierry, 81-82
Libolt, Alain, 17
Lien, Jennifer, 11-12
*Life is All You Get – Das Leben ist eine
Baustelle*, 74, **74**
Life is Beautiful – La Vita e Bella, 74,
75, 163, 164, 167, 173, 174
Lifebreath, 147
Lillard, Matthew, 35, 157, **157**
Lindsay, Robert, 38
Link, Caroline, 21
Linney, Laura, 132-133
Lion King II, The: Simba's Pride`, 147
Lion's Gate Entertainment (website), 172
Lipman, Maureen, 27
Lira, Soia, 28-29
Little Voice, 74-76, **76**, 167, 173, 174
Living Out Loud, 76
Lloyd, Christopher, 90-91
Loach, Ken, 91
Lock, Stock and Two Smoking Barrels, 8,
76-77, **77**, 167, 173
Loewi, Fiona, 78-79
Lohan, Lindsay, 98-99
Lollobrigida, Gina, 164
London Film Critics' Awards 1999, 177
Lopez, Jennifer, 13-14, 97, **97**
Los Angeles Film Critics' Association
Awards 1998, 177-178
Los Locos see *Posse II: Los Locos*
Lost in Space, 8, 77
Lost Son, The, 77-78, **78**
Lothar, Susanne, 50
Love and Death on Long Island, 78-79,
79
Love is Strange, 152
Love is the Devil, 79
Love, Murder and Deceit, 152
Loved, 79
Lovett, Lyle, **95**, 95-96
Lowensohn, Elina, 140
Luchini, Fabrice, 24

Lumet, Sydney, 53
Lumley, Joanna, 99
Luppi, Frederico, 84

Mac, Bernie, 103
MacKinnon, Gillies, 58-59
Mackintosh, Steven, 72, **72**
Macmillan International Film
Encyclopedia, The (book), 170
Macy, William H, 103-104, **104**
Mad City, 80, **80**
Madden, John, 115-116, 174
Madeline, 80-81, **81**
Madsen, Michael, 123
Maelen, Christian, 66-67
Mafia!, 147
Magic Sword, The: Quest for Camelot,
81, 174
Maguire, Tobey, **6**, 103-104
Maher, Joseph, 184
Maker, The, 147
Makhmalbaf, Samira, 14
Making Movies (book), 170
Makkena, Wendy, 48
Malick, Terrence, 127-128, 174
Malkovich, John, 112-113
Mamet, David, 123
Man on the Flying Trapeze: The Life
and Times of W.C. Fields (book), 170
Mandoki, Luis, 85
Mann, Gabriel, 59-60
Manners, David, 184
Manny and Lo, 148
Manojlovic, Miki, 16
Marais, Jean, 184-185
Marceau, Sophie, 49, 81-82
Margolis, Mark, 102-103
Marilyn for Beginners (book), 170
Marin, Cheech, **98**, 99-100
Marquise, 81-82
Mars, 152
Marshall, E.G., 185
Marshall, Tonie, 135
Marthouret, Francois, 118
Mashkov, Vladimir, 127
Mask of Zorro, The, 82, **82**, 174
Mason, Anthony, **28**
Massey, Anna, 27, 36-37
Masterminds, 147
Matrix, The, 6, 8, 82-83, **83**, 164, 173
Matthau, Walter, 93
May, Elaine, 174
May, Jacquetta, 52
Maybury, John, 79
Mayer, Daisy von Scherler, 80-81, 140
Mazello, Joseph, 117-118
McAnuff, Des, 31
McCole, Stephen, 10-11
McCormack, Catherine, 61, 72
McDormand, Frances, 81, **81**
McDougall, Charles, 57-58
McDowall, Roddy, 185, **185**
McGillis, Kelly, 16-17, 98
McGrath, Liam, 122-123
McGregor, Ewan, 111, **111**, 134-135,
160
McGuigan, Paul, 10-11
McInnerny, Tim, **8**
McKay, Jim, 52-53
McKee, Gina, **8**
McKellen, Ian, 14, 53-54, **54**, 174
McKidd, Kevin, 10-11, 19
McNamara, Pat, 35
McNamara, William, 25
Mead, Nick, 125
Mean Guns, 152
Meany, Colm, **152**
Meara, Anne, 35
Medak, Peter, 123
Meet Joe Black, 83-84, **84**
Meet the Deedles, 148
Mehta, Deepa, 49
Men With Guns, 84, 148
Menges, Chris, 77-78
Mercenary 2, 152
Mercury Rising, 84, **85**
Merlet, Agnes, 16
Mesonero, Luis, 64, **64**
Message in a Bottle, 85, 173
Meteorites!, 152

Metroland, 86
Meyers, Jonathan Rhys, 37, 55, 134-135, 161
Meyers, Nancy, 98-99
MGM (website), 172
Michell, Roger, 94, 129-130
Michie, John, 88-89
Mighty, The, 86, **86**
Mighty Joe, 86-87, **87**, 174
Millennium Movies – End of the World Cinema (book), 170
Miller, Claude, 30
Miller, George, 18
Miller, Jonny Lee, 104-105, **105**, 163
Miller, Sam, 12
Miller, Troy, 68
Minami, Suma Kaho, 13
Miner, Steve, 56
Minion, The, 152
Minority Report, 162
Miramax (website), 172
Misadventures of Margaret, The, 87
Misérables, Les, 87-88, **88**
Mitchell, Radha, 59-60
Mitevska, Labina, 67, **67**
Mojo, 88
Monk Dawson, 88-89
Montenegro, Fernanda, 28-29, 174
Moore, Demi, 164, 165
Moore, Julianne, 63, 108
Moran, Nick, 76-77, 161
More, 174
Moreau, Jeanne, 44-45
Moretti, Nanni, 14
Morrison, Paul, 122
Morse, David, 92
Moss, Carrie-Anne, 82-83
Mottola, Greg, 35
Movies: A Crash Course (book), 170
Mr Murder, 152
Mr Nice Guy – Yige Hao Ren, 89
Ms Scrooge, 152
Muhe, Ulrich, 50
Mulan, 8, 9, 89-90, **89**, 159, 167, 174
Mullan, Carrie, 58-59, **59**
Mullan, Peter, 91, **91**, 96
Mummy, The, 8, 90, **90**, 165, 167, 173
Murder at Devil's Glen, 148
Murphy, Eddie, **8**, 9, **9**, 40, 60-61
My Best Friend's Wedding, 9
My Favorite Martian, 90-91
My Giant, 91
My Husband's Secret Life, 152
My Name is Joe, 91, **91**, 167
Myers, Mike, 47-48, 163

Nahon, Philippe, 115
Nail, Jimmy, 124-125
Naked City, 152
Naked City 2, 152
Nalcakan, Lokman, 30
Natali, Vincenzo, 32
National Board of Review of Motion Picture Awards 1998, 178
National Society of Film Critics' Awards 1999, 178
Neeson, Liam, 87-88, 160
Negotiator, The, 92, **92**
Neil Simon's The Odd Couple II, 93
Neill, Sam, 62
Neilson, Anthony, 35
New Line Cinema (website), 172
New York Film Critics' Circle Awards 1998, 178
Newley, Anthony, 185, **185**
Newman, Paul, 85, 133
Newman, Randy, 174
Newton Boys, The, 174
Newton, Thandie, **18**, 19-20, 20, 20-21
Niccol, Andrew, 174
Nicholas' Gift, 148
Nichols, Mike, 106-107
Nicholson, Jack, 163
Nicholson, William, 49
Night at the Roxbury, A, 93
Nightwatch, 148
Nighy, Billy, 124-125, **125**
Niro, Robert De, 111-112
Nivola, Alessandro, 21, 67, 157-158, **158**

No, 93
No Laughing Matter, 152
Noe, Gaspar, 115
Noell, Anne, **33**
Noiret, Philippe, 7
Nolte, Nick, 11, 174
Noose, 152, **152**
Norman, Marc, 174
Norrington, Stephen, 23
Norris, Chuck, 161
Northam, Jeremy, 63, **63**, 87
Northern Lights, 148
Norton, Edward, **10**, 11-12, 112-113, 164, 174
Norton, Richard, 89
Not In This Town, 152
Notting Hill, 8, **8**, 9, 94, **94**, 165, 167-168, 173

O'Connor, Frances, 70
O'Connor, Pat, 34
O'Neal, Ryan, 143
O'Neill, Dick, 185
October Films (website), 172
Odd Couple II, The see *Neil Simon's The Odd Couple II*
Of Gods and Monsters (book), 170
Ogier, Bulle, 135
Oldman, Gary, 77
Olivewira, Vinicius de, 28-29
On Connait La Chanson – The Same Old Song, 95
One True Thing, 174
One-Seventh Farmers, The see *The Inheritors*
Opposite of Sex, The, 95-96, **95**
Orgazmo, 96
Orphans, 96
Orr, James, 161
Oscars 1998, 174
Other Voices Other Rooms, 96
Our Mother's Murder, 152-153
Ousdal, Sverre Anker, 66
Out of Sight, 97, **97**, 168, 173, 174
Out to Sea, 148
Outsider, The, 153
Overnight Delivery, 153
Owen, Clive, 31
Oxenberg, Catherine, 159, 161
Ozon, Francois, 118

Paggi, Simona, 174
Painted Angels, 98
Pakula, Alan J., 185-186
Palma, Brian De, 121
Paltrow, Gwynneth, 9, **8**, **9**, 102, **102**, 115-116, **147**, 160, 161, 162, 163, 174
Pandora Project, The, 153
Paradis, Vanessa, 161, 165
Paramount Classics (website), 172
Parent Trap, The, 98-99
Parker, Oliver, 63
Parker, Trey, 96
Parkes, Shaun, 62
Parting Shots, 99
Past Perfect, 153
Patch Adams, 99, 162, 174
Patric, Jason, 142, **142**
Patrick, Robert, 46, **46**
Patterson, Will, 39
Paul, Christiane, 74
Paulie, 98, 99-100
Paxton, Bill, 86-87, 118, **118**
Payback, 9, 100-101, **100**, 173
Peck, Bob, 186
Pecker, 101
Peckinpah – A Portrait in Montage (book), 170
Peeping Tom (book), 170
Pellington, Mark, 14-15
Penn, Leo, 186
Penn, Robin Wright, 79, 85
Penn, Sean, 127-128, 162
Pentagon Wars, The, 153
Peploe, Mark, 136-137
Pera, Marilla, 28-29
Perdita Durango, 101
Perez, Rosie, 101
Perez, Vincent, 24, **24**

Perfect Blue, 101-102, **101**, 173
Perfect Murder, A, 102, **102**
Personals, The: Improvisation on Romance in the Golden Years, 174
Petrie, Donald, 90-91
Pfeiffer, Michelle, 36, **36**, 107-108
Phantoms, 148-149
Phifer, Mekhi, 66
Philipchuk, Misha, 127, **127**
Phillippe, Ryan, 31-32, 47-48, 163, 165
Phillips, Lou Diamond, 21-22
Phoenix, Joaquin, 42, 110
Pi, 102-103
Pidgeon, Rebecca, 123, **123**
Pikser, Jeremy, 174
Pilkington, Lorraine, 62
Piovani, Nicola, 174
Pitt, Brad, 83-84, **84**
Pixar (website), 172
Place in the Land, A, 174
Platt, Oliver, 65
Players Club, The, 103
Playing by Heart, 168
Playing God, 103
Pleasantville, 6, **6**, 103-104, **104**, 174
Plowright, Joan, 33-34, 126
Plummer, Amanda, 12
Plunkett & Macleane, 104-105, **105**
Poe Cinema, The (book), 170
Police Story 4, 153
Poodle Springs, 149
Porizkova, Paulina, 129, **129**
Portal, Alexia, 17
Posey, Parker, 30, **34**, 35, 39-40, 58, 87, 142-143
Posse II; Los Locos, 153
Postlethwaite, Peter, 12
Potter, Monica, 99
Power of Glamour, The (book), 170
Practical Magic, 105
Price Above Rubies, A, 105-106, **106**
Priestley, Jason, 78-79, **79**, 163
Primary Colors, 106-107, 174
Prince of Egypt, The, 9, 107-108, **107**, 164, 168, 173, 174
Prince of Egypt, The: A New Vision in Animation (book), 170
Prinze, Freddie Jr, 66, 116-117
Progeny, 149
Project S, 153
Prometheus, 108
Promises and Lies, 153
Proposition, The, 108
Psycho, 108, 173
Pullman, Bill, 143
Pure Drivel (book), 170
Purgatory, 153

Quaid, Dennis, 98-99
Quest for Camelot: The Magic Sword see *The Magic Sword*
Quinlan's Film Directors (book), 170
Quinlan, Kathleen, 91
Quinn, Aidan, 16

Radziwilowicz, Jerzy, 115
Raimi, Sam, 118
Ranga, Dana, 41
Rat Pack Confidential (book), 170
Ratner, Brett, 113
Rea, Chris, 99
Rea, Stephen, 124-125, **151**
Real Howard Spitz, The, 109
Red Violin, The, 109-110, **109**, 168
Redford, Robert, 62
Redgrave, Lynn, 53-54, 163, 174
Redgrave, Vanessa, 36-37, **37**, 162
Rednikova, Ekaterina, 127
Reed, Oliver, 99, 162, 163, 186, **186**
Reeves, Keanu, 9, **9**, 82-83
Reeves, Saskia, 57-58
Regnier, Natacha, 40, **177**
Regret to Inform, 174
Reichle, Franz, 71
Reitman, Ivan, 119
Remsen, Bert, 186
Renauld, Isabelle, 44
Renfro, Brad, 14
Reno, Jean, 54-55, 111-112

Rescuers: Stories of Courage – Two Couples, 153
Rescuers: Stories of Courage – Two Families, 153
Resnais, Alain, 95
Return to Paradise, 110, **110**
Revenant, The, 153
Rhames, Ving, 97
Ricci, Christina, 25, 95-96
Rich, Richard, 69
Richie Rich's Christmas Wish, 153
Ride, 153
Rien Ne Va Plus, 110
Rigg, Diana, 99
Ringmaster, The, 149
Ripoll, Maria, 64-65
Ripper, The, 153
Ritchie, Guy, 76-77
Rivette, Jacques, 115
Riviere, Marie, 17
Riza, Bella, 58-59, **59**
Robbins, Tim, 14-15
Robert Siodmak (book), 170
Roberts, John, 99-100
Roberts, Julia, 9, **9**, 94, **94**, 124, 161
Roberts, Nia, 122
Robertson, Iain, 35
Rocks, Paddy, **38**
Rocksavage, David, 96
Rodat, Robert, 174
Rodriguez, Robert, 46
Rogers, Charles 'Buddy', 186
Rogers, Roy, 186-187
Rogue Trader, 111, **111**
Rohmer, Eric, 17
Rois, Sophie, 65-66
Rolle, Esther, 187
Romand, Beatrice, 17
Ronin, 111-112, **112**
Rooney, Mickey, 18
Roos, Don, 95-96
Rosen, Dan, 35
Ross, Gary, 103-104
Ross, Lee, 86
Rossellini, Isabella, 73
Rossington, Norman, 187
Rounders, 112-113
Rowlands, Gena, 86, 99-100
Ruben, Joseph, 110
Rugrats Movie, The, 8, 9, 113, 163, 173
Rush, Geoffrey, 42-43, 87-88, 115-116, 174
Rush Hour, 113, **113**, 161
Russo, Rene, 73-74
Ruzowitzky, Stefan, 65-66
Ryan, Meg, 142-143
Ryan, Terence, 25
Ryan, Thomas Jay, 58
Ryder, Winona, 163

Salles, Walter, 28-29
Sanders, Jon, 98
Sandler, Adam, 9, 138-139, **138**
Sandre, Didier, 17
Sant, Gus Van, 108
Santamaria, Claudio, 20-21
Sarandon, Susan, 124, 133, 164
Saville, Philip, 86
Saving Private Ryan, 8, **8**, 114-115, **114**, 160, 163, 168, 174
Sayle, Alexei, 125
Sayles on Sayles (book), 170
Sayles, John, 84
Scacchi, Greta, 109-110, **109**, 160
Schaech, Johnathon, 160
Schell, Maximilian, 73
Schneider, Rob, 71
Schrader, Paul, 11, 130
Schreiber, Liev, 34, 35
Schumacher, Joel, 42
Schwarz, Simon, 65-66
Schwimmer, David, 69-70, 119
Sciorra, Annabella, 139, **139**
Scorpion Spring, 153
Scott, Campbell, 65, 123, **123**
Scott, Dougray, 44-45
Scott, George C, 53
Scott, Jake, 104-105
Scott, Tony, 43-44

Screams and Nightmares (book), 170
Screencraft: Cinematography (book), 170
Seago, Howie, 21
Seagrove, Jenny, 39
Secombe, Harry, 163
Secret Defense, 115
Serrault, Michel, 16, 110
Seul Contre Tous – I Stand Alone, 115
Seven (book), 170
Seventy Light Years: A Life in the Movies (book), 170
Severdzan, Bajram, 22, **22**
Sevigny, Chloe, 72-73
Sewell, Rufus, 61, 163
Shadyac, Tom, 99
Shaiman, Marc, 174
Shakespeare in Love, 8, **8**, 9, 115-116, **116**, 168, 174
Shakur, Tupac, 51-52
Shalhoub, Tony, 99-100
She's All That, 116-117
She's So Lovely, 149
Sheedy, Ally, 59-60
Sheen, Charlie, 160, 161
Shields, Brooke, 164
Shimizu, Misa, **41**, 41-42
Shore, Simon, 52
Shostakovitch: The Film Album, 168
Shue, Elisabeth, 31, 165
Side Streets, 117
Siege, The, 117
Silverstone, Ben, 52, **53**
Simba's Pride see The Lion King II: Simba's Pride
Simm, John, 62
Simon Birch, 117-118
Simple Plan, A, 118, **118**, 174
Sinclair, Harry, 130
Singer, Bryan, 14
Sinise, Gary, 131
Sirtis, Marina, 124, **124**
Sitch, Rob, 27-28
Sitcom, 118
Six Days, Seven Nights, 119, **119**
Sizemore, Tom, 114-115, **114**
Skarsgard, Stellan, 66
Skeet, Brian, 87
Skjoldbjaerg, Erik, 66
Slam, 119
Slater, Christian, 135-136, 163
Sliding Doors, 8, 9
Sling Blade, 119-120, **120**
Sloan, Brian, 66-67
Slums of Beverly Hills, 120
Small Soldiers, 120-121
Smith, Anjela Lauren, 19
Smith, Charles Martin, 11
Smith, Ian Michael, 117-118
Smith, Jada Pinkett, 140, 159
Smith, Maggie, 126
Smith, Scott B, 174
Smith, Will, 9, **9**, 43-44, **44**, 159
Smollett, Jake, **45**
Smollett, Jurnee, **45**
Snake Eyes, 121, **121**
Snipes, Wesley, 23, **23**
Snitch see Noose
Soderbergh, Steven, 97
Sohn, Sonja, 119
Soldier Boyz, 153
Soldier's Daughter Never Cries, A, 121-122, 168
Solomon & Gaenor, 122
Solondz, Todd, 57
Sometimes... They Come Back for More, 153
Sommers, Stephen, 36, 90
Sony Pictures Entertainment (website), 172
Sorvino, Mira, 16-17
Sour Grapes, 122
Southpaw, 122-123
Spacek, Sissy, 11, 23
Spacey, Kevin, 92
Spall, Timothy, 124-125
Spanish Prisoner, The, 123, **123**
Sparrow, Walter, 108
Special Report: Journey to Mars, 153
Species II, 123

Speck, David, 96
Speer, Hugo, 125
Spicer, Bryan, 50
Spiceworld The Movie, 9
Spielberg, Steven, 114-115, 162, 174
Sprecher, Jill, 30
Spree, The, 153
Stallone, Sylvester, 13-14, 162
Stand Off, 153
Stansfield, Lisa, 125
Stanton, Andrew, 26
Stanton, Harry Dean, 86
Star Trek: Insurrection, 124, **124**
Star Wars, 6
Star Wars Encyclopedia (book), 171
Star Wars Episode I The Phantom Menace, 164, 165, 168
Star Wars: The Action Figure Archive (book), 171
Starship Troopers, 6
Statham, Jason, 76-77
Stepmom, 9, 124
Stewart, Patrick, 124
Still Crazy, 124-125, **125**
Stiller, Ben, 126-127, 142, **142**, 143
Stillman, Whit, 72-73
Stoler, Shirley, 187
Stoltz, Eric, 159
Stone, Sharon, 13-14, 53, 86, **86**
Stoppard, Tom, 174
Story (book), 171
Stott, Ken, 35, 104-105
Stowe, Madeleine, 108
Strasberg, Susan, 187
Streep, Meryl, 34, 124
Streisand, Barbra, 159
Strickland, David, 163
Substitute 2, The, 153
Suicide Kings, 149
Sulejmani, Sabri, 22, **22**
Sullivan, Kevin Rodney, 62
Sundance Film Festival Awards 1999, 178
Sunrise over Tiananmen Square, 174
Sunset Heights, 153
Superman: The Complete History (book), 171
Sutherland, Donald, 16, 137
Sweeney, Steve, 76-77, **77**
Sweet Smell of Success (book), 171
Swing, 125
Swinton, Tilda, 79
Switchback, 149-150, **149**
Szubanski, Magda, 18

Taghmaoui, Said, 58-59
Talos the Mummy, 153
Tango, 174
Taylor, Elizabeth, 162
Taylor, Lili, 52-53
Tea With Mussolini, 126
Temple, Julien, 137
10 Things I Hate About You, 168
Tennant, Andy, 44-45
Tenney, Anne, 27-28
Testud, Sylvie, 21
There's Something About Mary, 8, 126-127, **126**, 160, 168, 173
Theron, Charlize, 28, **28**, 86-87
Thewlis, David, 20-21, 38
Thief, The – Vor, 127, **127**
Thin Red Line, The, 127-128, **128**, 166, 168, 174
Thin Red Line, The: Melanesian Choirs: The Blessed Islands, 168
This Year's Love, 128-129
Thomas, Betty, 40
Thomas, Kristin Scott, 62
Thompson, Emma, 106-107
Thompson, Kay, 187
Thomsen, Ulrich, 47
Thomson, Anna, 96
Thornton, Billy Bob, 15-16, 106-107, 118, **118**, 119-120, 120, 174
Thornton, James, 12
Three Colours Trilogy, The (book), 171
Thurman, Uma, 17, **17**, 87-88, **88**, 159
Thursday, 129, **129**

Tickell, Paul, 32
Tilly, Jennifer, 24-25
Time Out Film Guide (book), 171
Titanic, 9, 160, 166
Titanic Town, 129-130
To Have and To Hold, 130
Todorovic, Srdan, 22
Toll, John, 174
Tomlinson, Ricky, 74
Topless Women Talk About Their Lives, 130
Toro, Benicio Del, 47
Toshack, James, 133
Touch, 130
Town Has Turned to Dust, A, 153
Travolta, John, **29**, 29-30, 80, **80**, 106-107
Trieb, Tatjana, 21
Trier, Lars von, 63-64
Troche, Rose, 19
Trucks, 153
True Crime, 131-132, **131**
Truman Show, The, 8, 132-133, **132**, 163, 173, 174
Truth or Consequences N.M., 150
Tucci, Stanley, 65
Tucker, Anand, 60
Tucker, Chris, 113, **113**
TV Times Film & Video Guide (book), 171
20th Century Fox (website), 172
Twilight, 133
Twin Dragons – Shuanglong Hui, 133
Two Girls and a Guy, 133
Tyler, Liv, 15-16, 104-105

Ulee's Gold, 168
Ulrich, Skeet, 130-131
Underwood, Ron, 86-87
Unexpected Life, An, 153
United International Pictures (website), 172
Universal Pictures (website), 172
Urban Legend, 134, **134**
Urbaniak, James, 58

Van, Marina De, 118
Vartan, Michael, 35
Vaughn, Vince, 108, 110
Velvet Goldmine, 134-135, 174
Venice International Film Festival Awards 1998, 178
Venora, Diane, 131-132
Venus Beuty – Venus, Beaute (Institut), 135, **135**
Versace Murder, The, 150
Vertigo: The Making of a Hitchcock Classic (book), 171
Verveen, Viviana, 32
Very Bad Things, 135-136, **136**
Victor, 174
Victory, 136-137
VideoHound's Golden Movie Retriever 1999 (book), 171
VideoHound's World Cinema (book), 171
Vigo – Passion for Life, 137
Vinterberg, Thomas, 47
Viper, 153
Virgien, Norton, 113
Virgin Encyclopedia of Stage & Film Musicals, The (book), 171
Virus, 137
Visions of Armageddon (book), 171
Vogel, Jurgen, 74, **74**
Voight, Jon, 43-44

Wachowski, Andy, 82-83
Wachowski, Larry, 82-83
Wagner, Natasha Gregson, 133, 134, **134**
Wahlberg, Mark, 21-22
Wakamatsu, Takeshi, 13
Waking Ned, 138, 166, 168
Walken, Christopher, 23, 130-131
Waller, Tom, 88-89
Walsh, J.T., 92, 103-104, 119-120
Walt Disney Pictures (website), 172
Walters, Julie, 129-130
Warbeck, Stephen, 174

Ward, Vincent, 139
Warner Bros (website), 172
Warner Bros Animation Art (book), 171
Washington, Denzel, 58, 117
Washington, Isaiah, 131-132
Waterboy, The, 138-139, **138**, 161
Waters, John, 101
Watson, Emily, 60, **60**, 86, 174
Weaving, Hugo, 82-83
Weber, Billy, 174
Weber, Steven, 122
Wedding Singer, The, 8
Weir, Peter, 132-133, 174
Weisz, Rachel, 67, 72, 90, **90**, 162
Wenham, David, 24
Wenk, Richard, 68
Wexler, Tanya, 48
What Dreams May Come, 139, **139**, 173, 174
When Danger Follows You Home, 153
When Life Departs, 174
When the Bough Breaks 2: Perfect Prey, 153
When the Trumpets Fade, 150
Whitaker, Forest, 61
White Lies, 153
Whitfield, Lynn, 45, **45**
Whitman, Mae, 61
Who Am I? see Jackie Chan's Who Am I?
Wild America, 150
Wilkinson, Tom, 55
William Shakespeare's A Midsummer Night's Dream, 166
Williams, John, 174
Williams, Robin, 99, 139, **139**
Williams, Saul, 119
Williams, Treat, 36, **36**
Williams, Vanessa L, 33-34, **33**, 160
Willis, Bruce, 9, **9**, 15-16, 84, **85**, 117, 165
Wilson, Andy, 103
Wilson, Hugh, 23
Winfrey, Oprah, 19-20
Winkler, Irwin, 16-17
Winner, Michael, 99
Winslet, Kate, 58-59, **59**, 161, 163
Winterbottom, Michael, 67
Wisdom of Crocodiles, The, 140, **140**
Wise, Ernie, 187
Witherspoon, Reese, **6**, 21, 163, 165
Witness: The Making of Schindler's List (book), 171
Women in Horror Films, 1930s (book), 171
Wong, Che-Kirk, 21-22
Woo, 140
Woods, James, 131-132, **131**
Woods, Rowan, 24
Woods, Skip, 129
Woody Allen: A Biography (book), 171
Woolf, John, 187
Writer's Journey, The (book), 171
Wu, Ronny, 24-25

X-Files, The, 8, 141, **141**, 173

Yakin, Boaz, 105-106
Yakusho, Koji, **41**, 41-42
Year of the Horse, 142
Yoakam, Dwight, 119-120
You've Got M@il, 9, 142-143, **143**, 162, 173
Young, Frederick A., 187
Young, Robert, 27, 187
Your Friends & Neighbours, 142, **142**, 166
Yun-Fat, Chow, 30-31

Z-4195, **13**
Zallian, Steven, 29-30
Zeffirelli, Franco, 126
Zegers, Kevin, 11
Zellweger, Renee, 105-106
Zero Effect, 143
Zeta-Jones, Catherine, 82, 158, **158**, 163, 164
Zimmer, Hans, 174
Zonca, Erick, 40
Zwick, Edward, 117